ENVIRONMENTAL ISSUES & OBLIGATIONS

CONTINUING EDUCATION IN REAL ESTATE

Anthony Schools®

Environmental Issues & Obligations

Continuing Education in Real Estate

Acknowledgments

The publisher gratefully wishes to thank the following individuals and organizations for their assistance in the preparing this book: Stanley S. Reyburn, Christopher Ferré (CALC24), Robert Fontana, Martin W. Lawson, James Ragan, Charles H. Smith, Jack Wilkinson, Advisory Commission on Regulatory Barriers to Affordable Housing, Brende & Shapiro Tree & Shrub Care, California Association of REALTORS®, California Department of Health Services, California Department of Real Estate, California Seismic Safety Commission, East Bay Municipal Utility District, Environmental Assessment Association, Pacific Bell, Pacific Gas & Electric Company, and World Resources Institute.

Cover: Roy Okano & Associates

Editorial and Executive Offices
Anthony Schools Corporation
15942 Foothill Blvd., Suite 100
San Leandro, CA 94578

© 1993 by Anthony Schools® Corporation

Parts of this book were previously published as *Agency Relationships in Real Estate* © 1989 and *Ethics of Real Estate: Code of Professional Conduct* © 1990 by Anthony Schools® Corporation

All rights reserved. No part of this book may be reproduced in any way or by any means without permission in writing from the publisher.

ISBN 0-941833-43-7

DISCLAIMER
This material is for educational purposes only. In no way should any statements or summaries be used as a substitute for legal or tax advice.

10 9 8 7 6 5 4 3 2

Printed in Hong Kong

CONTENTS

List of Exhibits iv

Overview v

1. **Federal Environmental Legislation** 1
2. **State & Local Environmental Legislation** 25
3. **LULUs & NIMBYs** 49
4. **Architectural Elements of Energy Conservation** 75
5. **Title 24: California's Energy Code** 95
6. **Landscaping & the Environment** 115
7. **Earthquake Safety** 135
8. **Hazardous Material in the Home** 157
9. **Environmental Inspections: Regulatory Concerns** 177
10. **Phase I Environmental Inspections** 199
11. **Phase II & III Environmental Inspections** 219
12. **Environmental Disclosure Requirements** 241
13. **Taxes, Real Estate & the Environment** 265
14. **Agency in Real Estate** 285
15. **Ethics of Real Estate** 307

Appendix 329

Index 337

Exhibits

The National Environmental Policy Act of 1969 2
RCRA Findings 8
Finding and Purpose, Endangered Species Act 10
Definitions: Key Terms in the Endangered Species Act 11
Endangered and Threatened Species Consultation Procedures 12
The Secretary of the Interior's Standards for Rehabilitation 16
The Public Resources Code 25
Initiative Proposition 65 30
Residential Energy Conservation Ordinance (RECO) 76
Building Orientation and the Sun 81
Historic Architectural Styles 86
Construction Elements 87
California Climate Zones 96
Prescriptive Packages for Climate Zone 3 90
Point System Summary 101
Certificate of Compliance: Residential 102
Mandatory Measures Checklist: Residential 104
Energy Sources 106
PG&E Energy Use Leaflet 108
Sample Energy Audit 112
Plants for Erosion Control 121
Fire-Retardant Plants 123
Fire-Prone Plants 123
Water-Conserving Plants 124
Residential Earthquake Hazards Report 137
Earthquake Maps 151
Glossary of Terms: Hazardous Materials 173
EAA Phase I Inspection Report 203
Risk Categories, Phase I Report 193
RTC Suggested Phase I Report Format 216
RTC Suggested Phase II Report Format 228
RTC Suggested Phase III Report Format 234
Glossary of Terms: Phase II and III Inspections 236
Geologic, Seismic and Flood Hazard Disclosure Form 246
Real Estate Transfer Disclosure Statement Form 254
Smoke Detector Statement of Compliance 260
Disclosure Form, Real Estate Agency Relationships 304
California Real Estate Law Disclosure Chart 329

Overview

COURSE 1
FEDERAL ENVIRONMENTAL LEGISLATION

This course gives an overview of major federal environmental laws in two broad areas of concern: pollution and conservation. It covers the philosophy and legislative intent behind NEPA, RCRA, and the Endangered Species Act, and the provisions of these and other important laws affecting use and value of real estate: Clean Water and Air Acts, CERCLA, National Historic Preservation Act, etc.

Introduction
   Early Legislation

National Environmental Policy Act
   Purpose
   Philosophy
   Procedures
   Environmental Impact Statement

Air, Water, Land Use
   Water Quality
   Air Quality
   Land Use

Toxics and Waste Disposal
   RCRA
   Hazardous Waste Sites
   CERCLA (Superfund)
   Other Laws on Toxics

Endangered Species Act, 1973
   Definitions
   Procedures

National Historic Preservation Act of 1966
   The National Register
   Provisions of the Act
   Tax Credits
   Section 106 Review

Overview: HUD Statutory Worksheets
   Historic Properties
   Floodplain and Wetland Protection
   Coastal Zone Management
   Sole Source Aquifers
   Wildlife
   Endangered Species
   Wild and Scenic Rivers
   Water Quality
   Solid Waste Management
   Farmlands Protection
   HUD Environmental Standards

   Applicability and Exclusions

The Americans with Disabilities Act, 1990
   Employment
   Public Facilities
   Public Entities
   Enforcement
   Tax Credits

Issues Raised by Federal Environmental Legislation
   Economic Issues
   Government Role
   Scientific Issues

COURSE 2
STATE & LOCAL ENVIRONMENTAL LEGISLATION

This course outlines major California environmental laws, including CEQA, the California Environmental Quality Act), Proposition 65 (the Safe Water and Toxic Enforcement Act), and the Public Resources Code. Both content and philosophy of these laws are presented. Land use regulations are examined at both state and local levels—subdivision controls, zoning, general plans, building codes, and historical resources—and their effects on the use and development of real estate are considered.

Introduction

The Public Resources Code
   Administration, Geology and Mines, Oil and
      Gas, Forestry, Parks, Public Lands,
      Highways, Surveying, Conservation,
      Resorts, CCC, CEQA, License Plate Fund,
      L.A. Commission, Energy, Coastal Zones

California Environmental Quality Act
   Purposes
   Environmental Impact Report

Proposition 65: Safe Drinking Water and Toxic Enforcement Act of 1986
   Summary
   Warnings
   Other Toxics Legislation: California
      Environmental Superfund Act

Building Standards
   Part One: Building Standards Commission
   Part Two: State Building Code

Overview **V**

Part Three: State Electrical Code
Part Four: State Mechanical Code
Part Five: State Plumbing Code
Part Six: Building Requirements
Part Seven: Elevator Safety Regulations
Part Eight: State Historical Building Code
Local Building Ordinances

Historical Resources
State Office of Historic Preservation
Historical Resources Commission
State Landmarks Program
Incentives
Regulations

Subdivision Controls: State Laws
The Subdivided Lands Act
The Subdivision Map Act

Local Land Use Regulations
General Plans
Zoning
Other Mechanisms
Example: Carmel's Zoning Code
Example: Project Review, City of Palm Desert
Redevelopment
Trends in Land Use

COURSE 3
LULUS & NIMBYS

This course looks at clashes between environmental and development concerns, and other situations where citizens protest "Not In My Back Yard." It examines various categories of "locally unwanted land uses"—waste disposal, prisons, highways, institutional housing—and the motives and strategies of proponents and opponents. Special attention is given to the recent HUD commission report on regulatory barriers to affordable housing, and to questions of property value and discrimination.

Introduction
LULU, NIMBY, BANANA, NIMTOO
Perspectives and Processes
Affordable Housing: the Kemp Report
Property Values: Appraisal and Discrimination

Locational Conflict Issues
Proponent Perspectives
Opponent Perspectives

Processes and Strategies for Issue Resolution
Legislative Background
Administrative: The EIR
Political
Proponent Strategies
Opponent Strategies

Bringing Proponents and Opponents Together

Affordable Housing: The Kemp Report
Regulatory Inhibitions
NIMBY Influence
Environmental Concerns
Recommendations

"Not In My Back Yard": Excerpts
Affected Populations
Government's Role
Regulatory Barriers in the Suburbs
Regulatory Barriers in Cities
Environmental Protection and Affordable Housing
Competing Objectives
NIMBYism
Growth Controls: The California Example
Zoning
Lending Practices
Commission Recommendations
Success Stories

LULUs, Property Values, and the Real Estate Professional
Appraisal Considerations
FNMA Appraisal Guidelines
FNMA Underwriting Guidelines
Demographics: HUD Guidelines
Disclosure
Discrimination

COURSE 4
ARCHITECTURAL ELEMENTS OF ENERGY CONSERVATION

This course discusses residential design location, construction, and appliances as they affect energy use. The licensee will learn to advise buyers and sellers on conservation features which are present or can be added to a home, and on possible local energy conservation retrofit or disclosure requirements.

Introduction

Disclosure and Retrofit Requirements
Residential Energy Conservation Ordinances (RECO)
Berkeley
San Francisco

Architectural Features that Conserve Energy
Orientation
Siting
Location and Size of Windows
Type of Window
Roof Overhang

Shape of the Home
Type of Construction
Historic Architectural Styles
    Construction Elements
Wall and Ceiling Insulation
Mass of the Building Materials
Color of Roof and Walls
Shading: Awnings, Trellises, and Trees

Additional Energy Conservation Measures
New Appliances
Lighting
Heating Systems
Fireplaces
Solar Water Heaters
Cooling
Water Conservation Devices

COURSE 5
TITLE 24: CALIFORNIA'S ENERGY CODE

This course explains California's energy conservation code, Title 24, and how utility savings through energy conservation can be an important consideration in buying or selling a home. The course explains how the standards in Title 24 are related to California's 16 climate zones. Compliance procedures and calculations are explained. Other topics are PG&E's energy conservation incentives for construction, retrofitting, and appliances; the California Home Energy Efficiency Rating System (CHEERS); and the "energy efficient mortgage."

Introduction
Legislation
Results
Benefits
Title 24 in the Real Estate Market

Title 24 Standards—A Closer Look
Climate Zones
Building Types
Building Components
Building Envelope
HVAC and Plumbing
Lighting

Compliance Procedures
Compliance Options
Documentation

PG&E's Energy Conservation Incentives
Goals
Energy Sources
Financial Incentives
Energy Efficiency Facts

CHEERS: California Home Energy Rating System
Purpose
CHEERS—How It Works
Energy Efficient Mortgages (EEM)
CHEERS and the Real Estate Professional

COURSE 6
LANDSCAPING & THE ENVIRONMENT

This course discusses the role of landscaping in a property's value, comfort, safety, and water and energy savings. Topics include site preparation (drainage, fill, stabilizing areas with potential for slides or flooding, what hazards to look for), remedial sitework, fire hazards in urban-wildland interface zones, fire- and drought-resistant planting, water conservation (soil preparation and plant selection), hardscaping (decks, trellises, pools, paths), and aesthetic and functional principles of landscape design.

Introduction
Disclosure
Property Value
Cost Savings

Site and Soil Problems: Flooding, Landslides, Drainage
Site Preparation
Flooding
Landslides and Slippage
Site Preparation
Landscaping to Reduce Flood and Slide Hazards

Fire Hazards and Landscaping
Urban-Wildland Interface
Vegetation Management

Landscaping to Conserve Water and Energy
Benefits
Drought Tolerant Planting
Plant Selection
Soil Preparation
Watering Efficiently
Low Maintenance Landscaping
Trees
Hardscaping

Landscape Design Principles
Energy Conserving Design
Orientation to the Sun
Functional Landscape Design Issues
Design Principles

Overview

COURSE 7
EARTHQUAKE SAFETY

This course is based on the Seismic Safety Commission's *Homeowner's Guide to Earthquake Safety*, which must now be given to all buyers of pre-1960 homes. This course will enable the licensee to understand the new seismic disclosure requirements and explain them to sellers and buyers. Topics covered are legal disclosure requirements, common seismic weaknesses in homes, procedures for correcting them, and earthquake preparedness.

Introduction

Legal Requirements for Selling Your Home
    How to Comply
    Laws on Earthquake Hazard Disclosure

Weaknesses in Residential Buildings
    Unbraced Water Heater
    Foundation Not Anchored
    Weak Cripple Walls
    Pier-and-Post Foundations
    Houses on Tall Walls or Posts
    Unreinforced Masonry Foundation
    No Foundation
    Old Concrete Foundations
    Room Over Garage
    Unreinforced Masonry Walls
    Unreinforced Masonry Chimneys
    Home Design
    Home Contents

Getting the Work Done
    Do It Yourself
    Professional Help
    Costs: Strengthen or Repair?
    Earthquake Insurance
    Property Tax Exemption

Geologic Hazards
    Information Sources
    Ground Shaking
    Ground Failure
    Tsunami
    Dam Failure
    Fault Rupture

Be Prepared for Earthquakes
    Plan Ahead
    During an Earthquake
    After an Earthquake

COURSE 8
HAZARDOUS MATERIAL IN THE HOME

This course is based on the DRE / Department of Health Services booklet *Environmental Hazards: A Guide for Homeowners and Buyers*. The licensee will learn about the hazardous characteristics, occurrence, and methods of testing and mitigation of asbestos, formaldehyde, lead (in paint and pipes), radon, and hazardous wastes, and will be better able to explain these to clients. Sources of additional information and a glossary of terms are included.

Introduction
    Disclosure Requirements

Asbestos
    Asbestos In the Home
    Dangers of Asbestos
    Determining Asbestos Content
    Asbestos Removal

Formaldehyde
    Levels in the Home
    Pressed-Wood Products
    Urea Formaldehyde Foam
    Dangers of Formaldehyde
    Formaldehyde Detection
    Hazard Reduction

Lead
    Dangers of Lead
    Lead Paint in Older Homes
    Determining Lead Content
    Removal of Lead Paint
    How Much Lead in Drinking Water
    Lead in Drinking Water
    Hazard Reduction

Radon
    Occurrence
    Dangers of Radon
    Radon In The Home
    Radon Measurement
    Reducing Indoor Radon Levels
    Radon in Water

Hazardous Wastes
    Disposal and Spills
    Efforts to Locate and Clean Up
    Effect of a Hazardous Waste Site
    Disclosure
    Information Sources

Household Hazardous Waste
    What Products Are Hazardous
    Storing Hazardous Products

Environmental Issues & Obligations

Disposal of Hazardous Waste
Information

Ground Water Contamination
Dangers
Testing
EPA Actions

Glossary of Terms

COURSE 9
ENVIRONMENTAL INSPECTIONS: REGULATORY CONCERNS

This course explains the legal and regulatory background to the recent proliferation of environmental inspection requirements. It explains the role of CERCLA and FIRREA in lenders' and secondary market agencies' growing concern over potential liability for hazards on properties they finance or acquire through foreclosure. The Innocent Landowner Defense is explained, and Phase I, II, and III inspections are introduced.

Introduction
Liability for Cleanup
Inspection Requirements
Regulators' Guidelines

FNMA Hazards Management Procedures
Liability Issues
Lenders' Duties
Phase I Assessment
Phase II Assessment
Consultants' Qualifications
Unacceptable Environmental Conditions
Remedial Actions
Ongoing Operations and Maintenance
Environmental Superlien States
Responsibilities after Loan Commitment
Nonperforming Loans (Defaults)
Liquidation: Documents to Close the File

Resolution Trust Corporation Environmental Guidelines
Scope of Environmental Issues
Environmental Issues and Property Values
RTC Environmental Policies
RTC Actions on Hazards

Innocent Landowner Defense (CERLA)
Innocent Landowner Defined
Information Required
Excerpts from Proposed Amendment
Phase I Audit Defined

Federal Home Loan Bank System—Office of Thrift Supervision

Introduction
Risks to Institutions
Environmental Risk Policy
Policy Components
Types of Reports

COURSE 10
PHASE I ENVIRONMENTAL INSPECTIONS

This course explains the Phase I environmental inspection, a diagnostic screening for possible environmental problems on a property needing further investigation. Both documentary research (existing toxics databases and site history) and site inspection (how to recognize "red flags" suggesting asbestos, PCBs, lead, tanks, etc.) are covered in detail. The student is taken step by step through two Phase I report formats, those of the Environmental Assessment Association and the RTC.

Introduction
Consumer Protection

What is a Phase I?
Documentary Research
Field Inspection
Relation to Phase II
Inspector Qualifications
California Registered Environmental Assessor

Research: Government Databases
Federal Government Record Systems
State Record Systems

Site Inspection
EAA Residential Phase I Report
Major Hazardous Substances: Field Guide
Asbestos
Radon
Lead-based Paint
Tanks
Polychlorinated Biphenyls (PCBs)

RTC: Phase I Outline
Introduction
Historic Site Conditions
Potential Environmental Threats
Site Reconnaissance
Environmental Setting
Conclusions and Recommendations

Overview **ix**

COURSE 11
PHASE II & III ENVIRONMENTAL INSPECTIONS

This course explains the Phase II and III environmental site assessments (ESAs) that can be triggered if the Phase I suggests hazards on a property. The RTC procedures and report form are outlined. The student will learn what to look for as a client or reader of these advanced inspections, which involve laboratory testing and technical proposals for site remediation.

Introduction
- Value of Inspections
- Nonresidential Properties

Phase II and III Overview
- Phase II: Technical Analysis
- Initial Phase II
- Expanded Phase II
- Phase II Report Format
- Phase III: Remediation

Phase II Guidelines
- Phase I Results
- Recommendation for a Phase II ESA
- Types of Phase II ESAs
- Selection Rationale
- Initial Phase II ESA Components
- Development of the Sampling Plan
- Extent and Locations of Sampling
- Plan Format and Content
- Preparing for Sampling
- Conducting the Sampling Visit
- Sample Shipping and Analysis
- Recommendations
- Expanded Phase II
- Report Format

Phase III ESA: RTC Guidelines
- General Approach
- Part 1: Preliminary Screening
- Part 2: Detailed Evaluation of Selected Alternatives
- Feasibility Study Report

Costs Associated with Phase II and III
- Field and Laboratory Work
- Corrective Action

Glossary of Terms

COURSE 12
ENVIRONMENTAL DISCLOSURE REQUIREMENTS

This course explains major new and continuing real estate disclosure requirements, with an environmental emphasis. It covers the reasons for disclosure, the concept of material facts, the basic Real Estate Transfer Disclosure Statement, and specific disclosures related to natural hazards (earthquake, flood, fire), toxics (asbestos, waste sites), and land use (codes and other restrictions). Responsibilities of seller, licensee, and buyer are explained.

Introduction
- Material Facts: Structural Defects
- Environmental Concerns
- Legal Restrictions
- History of the Property

Evolving Disclosure Requirements
- Necessity of Written Disclosures
- Affirmative Duty
- Legal Principles
- Professionalism

Natural Hazard Disclosures
- Earthquakes
- Flood Hazard Area
- Fire Hazard

Environmental Hazards
- Practitioner Issues
- Toxic Disclosures Act
- Asbestos Hazard Disclosure Act
- Restricted Use of Hazardous Waste Sites
- Hazards to Renters
- Airport Noise Disclosure

Seller's Disclosure Responsibilities—California Law
- Seller's Written Disclosure Form
- Inspection and Disclosures by Seller's Agent to Buyer
- Pest Control Disclosures

Public and Private Restrictions
- Zoning and Building Codes
- Assessments
- Private Restrictions

COURSE 13
TAXES, REAL ESTATE & THE ENVIRONMENT

This course presents current federal and state income tax laws that affect the real estate industry, including changes created by and since the Tax Reform Act of 1986. Topics include tax rates and brackets, capital gains, passive vs. active income, depreciation, interest deductibility, 1099-S and FIRPTA reporting, exchanges, and tax credits. The course also discusses the World Resources Institute proposal for "green fees," user fees on environmentally harmful activities. The examples discussed include carbon taxes, solid waste charges, and congestion tolls on highways.

Introduction
    TRA '86
    Green Fees

Continuing Effects of TRA '86
    Continuing Revisions
    Major Tax Changes

Income and Deductions
    Active Activity
    Portfolio Activity
    Passive Activity
    Passive with Active Participation
    Depreciation
    Interest Deductions

Reporting and Taxation
    Alternative Minimum Tax
    Real Estate Reporting
    Tax Deferred Exchanges
    Elimination of Tax Credits

Green Fees: Shifting The Tax Burden To Support The Environment
    Current Tax System
    Possible Alternatives

Proposals for Environmental Charges
    Solid Waste Charges
    Congestion Tolls on Urban Highways
    Carbon Taxes
    Other "Green Fees"
    Green Fees: Arguments For
    Opposing Arguments

COURSE 14
AGENCY IN REAL ESTATE

This course presents the fundamentals of agency law—the basic law that governs the relationship between a broker and buyer or seller in a real estate transaction. Special focus is given to AB 1034.

Introduction
    Statutory Basis

Principal-Agent Relationship
    Legal Effect of Agency Relationship
    Types of Agency
    Creation of the Agency
    Judicial Interpretation
    Termination of Agency
    Authority of the Agent
    Delegation of Duties
    Employee or Independent Contractor

Whose Agent Are You?
    General Rules
    Listing Brokers
    Seller's Agent
    Selling and Cooperating Brokers
    Buyer's Broker

Licensee's Duties to Principal
    General Fiduciary Duties
    Duties under Real Estate Law
    Specific Duties in Real Estate Transactions
    Care, Skill, and Diligence
    Licensee's Duty to Investigate

Duties to Parties Other than Principal
    Caveat Emptor is Dead
    Traditional Rule
    Expanded Rule
    Secret Profits

Dual Agency Relationships
    Example: Escrow
    Changing Roles
    "No Listing" Transactions

Authority of Agent and Liability of Principal
    Notice
    Torts of the Agent
    Scope of the Agency

Breach of Duties
    Intentional Breach
    Negligent Breach
    Innocent Breach
    Tortious Acts of Subagents

Delegation of Duties
    "Subagent"
    Tortious Acts of Subagents

Agency Relationships in Modern Brokerage Practice

COURSE 15
ETHICS OF REAL ESTATE

This course discusses ethical behavior in real estate practice. It begins with an introduction to the concept of ethics, and details Commissioner's Regulation 2785 (Revised 1990), the Code of Professional Conduct. Each section of the Code is illustrated with either a case study or an example.

Introduction
    The Department of Real Estate
    Professional Organizations
    Law and Ethics
    DRE's Major Concerns

Unlawful Conduct in Sale, Lease, and Exchange Transactions
    Misrepresenting Market Value
    Existence of Offers
    Commissions Negotiable
    Broker Affiliation
    Closing Costs
    Deposits
    Buyer's Qualifications
    Unauthorized Changes
    Misrepresenting Security Value
    "Puffing"
    Misrepresenting Size and Boundaries
    Concealing Use Restrictions
    Nondisclosure of Material Facts
    Failing to Present Offers
    Bias in Presenting Competing Offers
    Nondisclosure of Agent's Interest (Seller's Agent)
    Nondisclosure of Agent's Interest (Buyer's Agent)
    Interest in Referrals
    Refunding Deposits

Unlawful Conduct in Loan Transactions
    Misrepresenting Loan Availability
    Misrepresenting Borrower's Qualifications
    Underestimating Costs
    Misrepresenting Priority of a Lien
    "Free" Services
    False Information on Loan Payments
    Not Accounting for Advance Fees

Suggestions for Professional Conduct: Sale, Lease, and Exchange Transactions
    Service
    Communication
    Enforcement
    Advertising
    Offers
    Knowledge
    Cooperation
    Arbitration
    Expertise
    Discrimination Prohibited
    Value Opinions
    Codes of Ethics

Suggestions for Professional Conduct: Loan Brokerage
    Service
    Communication
    Knowledge
    Expertise
    Discrimination Prohibited
    Value Opinions
    Status Reports
    Net Proceeds
    Codes of Ethics

COURSE 1
Federal Environmental Legislation

INTRODUCTION

For owners, buyers, and sellers of real estate, environmental protection legislation imposes regulations and obligations that would not exist without it, so there can be a temptation to think of it as a nuisance, as government interference, even as "bad law." But in real estate terms it is also an important means of consumer protection. A prime objective of the real estate profession is to protect the integrity of value in real property. Environmental inspection and disclosure requirements clarify the situation of the buyer, seller, and lender vis à vis possible hazards on the property. Furthermore, it can usually be argued that efforts to protect the environment—whether clean rivers, plant and animal species, or historic structures—ultimately convert to stabilization and enhancement of property values.

Early Legislation Most of the major federal environmental laws—the National Environmental Policy Act, the Resource Conservation and Recovery Act, the Endangered Species Act, the National Historic Preservation Act—date from the mid-1960s and after. However, there were forerunners to many of these acts; environmental problems have been recognized for many years, and have generally fallen into two broad concerns, pollution and conservation. Among the early laws:

Rivers and Harbors Act of 1899 (33 USC §407). As part of this legislation on navigable waterways, a permit is required from the Army Corps of Engineers in order to dump any "refuse" in navigable waters.

Antiquities Act of 1906 (16 USC §§431-433). Primarily to protect Native American remains on federal property, this law empowered the President to designate federally owned landmarks, and directed the Army, Interior, and Agriculture departments to survey archaeological sites. Even earlier in the field of conservation, the first National Park (Yellowstone) was established in 1872, followed by Yosemite and Sequoia in 1890.

NEPA

The National Environmental Policy Act (42 USC §§4321-4347), 1969, known as NEPA, is the most wide-ranging federal environmental law, and will be described here in some detail. It defines environmental concerns broadly, establishes the Environmental Protection Agency and Council on Environmental Quality, and creates the now familiar Environmental Impact Statement.

Purpose The following excerpts set forth the Act's purposes, which are shared by most other environmental laws.

Philosophy "NEPA's purpose is not to generate paperwork—even excellent paperwork—but to foster excellent action. The NEPA process is intended to help public officials make decisions that are based on understanding of environmental consequences and take actions that protect, restore, and enhance the environment." (§1500.1)

The National Environmental Policy Act of 1969, as Amended[*]

An Act to establish a national policy for the environment, to provide for the establishment of a Council on Environmental Quality, and for other purposes.

Purpose.

Section 2. The purposes of this Act are: To declare a national policy which will encourage productive and enjoyable harmony between man and his environment; to promote efforts which will prevent or eliminate damage to the environment and biosphere and stimulate the health and welfare of man; to enrich the understanding of the ecological systems and natural resources important to the Nation; and to establish a Council on Environmental Quality.

Title I

Declaration of National Environmental Policy

Section 101.

(a) The Congress, recognizing the profound impact of man's activity on the interrelations of all components of the natural environment, particularly the profound influences of population growth, high-density urbanization, industrial expansion, resource exploitation, and new and expanding technological advances and recognizing further the critical importance of restoring and maintaining environmental quality to the overall welfare and development of man, declares that it is the continuing policy of the Federal Government, in cooperation with State and local governments, and other concerned public and private organizations, to use all practicable means and measures, including financial and technical assistance, in a manner calculated to foster and promote the general welfare, to create and maintain conditions under which man and nature can exist in productive harmony, and fulfill the social, economic, and other requirements of present and future generations of Americans.

(b) In order to carry out the policy set forth in this Act, it is the continuing responsibility of the Federal Government to use all practicable means, consistent with other essential considerations of national policy, to improve and coordinate Federal plans, functions, programs, and resources to the end that the Nation may—

(1) fulfill the responsibilities of each generation as trustee of the environment for succeeding generations;

(2) assure for all Americans safe, healthful, productive, and esthetically and culturally pleasing surroundings;

(3) attain the widest range of beneficial uses of the environment without degradation, risk to health or safety, or other undesirable and unintended consequences;

(4) preserve important historic, cultural, and natural aspects of our national heritage, and maintain, wherever possible, an environment which supports diversity, and variety of individual choice;

(5) achieve a balance between population and resource use which will permit high standards of living and a wide sharing of life's amenities;

(6) enhance the quality of renewable resources and approach the maximum attainable recycling of depletable resources.

(c) The Congress recognizes that each person should enjoy a healthful environment and that each person has a responsibility to contribute to the preservation and enhancement of the environment.

Section 102. The Congress authorizes and directs that, to the fullest extent possible: (1) the policies, regulations, and public laws of the United States shall be interpreted and administered in accordance with the policies set forth in this Act, and (2) all agencies of the Federal Government shall—

(A) Utilize a systematic, interdisciplinary approach which will insure the integrated use of the natural and social sciences and the environmental design arts in planning and in decision making which may have an impact on man's environment;

(B) Identify and develop methods and procedures, in consultation with the Council on Environmental Quality established by Title II of this Act, which will insure that presently unquantified environmental amenities and values may be given appropriate consideration in decision making along with economic and technical considerations;

(C) Include in every recommendation or report on proposals for legislation and other major Federal actions significantly affecting the quality of the human environment, a detailed statement by the responsible official on—

(i) The environmental impact of the proposed action,

(ii) Any adverse environmental effects which cannot be avoided should the proposal be implemented,

(iii) Alternatives to the proposed action,

(iv) The relationship between local short-term uses of man's environment and the maintenance and enhancement of long-term productivity, and

(v) Any irreversible and irretrievable commitments of resources which would be involved in the proposed action should it be implemented.

* Public Law 91-190, 42 USC 4321-4347, January 1, 1970, as amended by Public Law 94-52, July 3, 1975, and Public Law 94-83, August 9, 1975.

Procedures The Regulations for Implementing the Procedural Provisions of the National Environmental Policy Act lay out the procedures for carrying out "'action-forcing' provisions to make sure that federal agencies act according to the letter and spirit of the Act."

Environmental Impact Statement Under NEPA, an environmental impact statement (EIS) is required in every recommendation or report on:

- Proposals, for
  - Legislation and
    - Other major federal actions
      - Significantly
        - Affecting
          - The quality of the human environment.

Each of these terms is defined, and the regulations discuss form, content, and timing of the EIS.

Form. The text of final environmental impact statements shall normally be less than 150 pages and for proposals of unusual scope or complexity shall normally be less than 300 pages. Environmental impact statements shall be written in plain language and may use appropriate graphics so that decision makers and the public can readily understand them.

Discussion of Alternatives. This section is the heart of the environmental impact statement. It should present the environmental impacts of the proposal and the alternatives in comparative form, thus sharply defining the issues and providing a clear basis for choice among options by the decision maker and the public. In this section agencies shall:

- Rigorously explore and objectively evaluate all reasonable alternatives, and for alternatives which were eliminated from detailed study, briefly discuss the reasons for their having been eliminated.

- Devote substantial treatment to each alternative considered in detail, including the proposed action, so that reviewers may evaluate their comparative merits.

- Include reasonable alternatives not within the jurisdiction of the lead agency.

- Include the alternative of no action.

- Identify the agency's preferred alternative or alternatives, if one or more exists, in the draft statement and identify such alternative in the final statement unless another law prohibits the expression of such a preference.

- Include appropriate mitigation measures not already included in the proposed action or alternatives.

Applicability. NEPA applies to "federal actions." This term includes not only "projects directly undertaken by Federal agencies"—such as highway construction—but the federal "action" of approving other projects that require federal permits or review—for example, private construction in wetland or flood plain areas.

EIS Process. The federal agency must first determine whether an EIS needs to be prepared. This decision is based on experience ("whether the proposal is one which normally requires an EIS"), consultation (with "state and local agencies, Indian tribes, and interested private persons and organizations"), and, in cases of uncertainty, a preliminary environmental assessment.

No Impact. If the agency determines not to prepare an EIS, it issues a finding of no significant impact (FONSI), which in certain circumstances is subject to review by other agencies and the public before the decision to bypass the EIS becomes final.

Impact Expected. If significant impact may result, an EIS must be prepared, and the following steps occur.

- *Lead Agency.* If more than one federal agency is involved, one is designated the *lead agency* to supervise preparation of the EIS.

- *Scoping.* This is a term coined for "determining the scope of issues to be addressed and identifying the significant issues related to a proposed action," and eliminating insignificant issues from unnecessary study. This is done with input from other agencies, affected Indian tribes, and "other interested persons (including those who might not be in accord with the action on environmental grounds)."

- *Draft EIS.* A draft is prepared in accordance with the scope decided upon. It must satisfy as far as possible the requirements for a final EIS, so that recipients can make informed and meaningful comments.

- *Commenting.* Comments by other agencies and the public are an essential part of the EIS process. The lead agency is required to "affirmatively solicit" comments, and respond to them in the final EIS.

- *Final EIS.* The degree of revision depends largely on comments received. Possible responses to comments include:

  - Modifying alternatives including the proposed action

  - Developing and evaluating alternatives not seriously considered in the draft

  - Supplementing analyses and making factual corrections

  - Explaining why comments do not warrant further response.

Environmental Referrals. If a proposed federal action is determined by the Administrator of the Environmental Protection Agency to be "unsatisfactory from the standpoint of public health or welfare or environmental quality," it may be referred to the Council on Environmental Quality. The Council (appointed by the President) also has jurisdiction in emergencies when there is no time for full review of an action. A subsequent law created an Office of Environmental Quality, to provide professional and administrative staff to the Council.

AIR, WATER, LAND USE

NEPA serves as a charter and umbrella for other, more specific federal environmental laws, both older and newer. Some of the most important of these are the following:

Water Quality **Clean Water Act.** (Water Pollution Control Act, Water Quality Improvement Act, 1948, amended 1966, 1970, 1972, 1987, etc.; 33 USC §1251 et seq.). This legislation has forerunners in the Rivers and Harbors Act of 1899, mentioned above, in the Oil Pollution Act of 1924, and others. It addresses the results of centuries of dumping into rivers, wells, lakes, canals, and reservoirs by individuals and businesses. The Act provides standards for the control of introduction of pollutants into surface and underground waters, establishes a permit process, and makes polluters liable for cleanup costs. It also encourages research on alternative methods of disposal and provides grants for sewage treatment plants. Amendments made in 1987 require certain industries to pretreat their wastes before discharging them.

Safe Drinking Water Act. Passed in 1974 and amended in 1986, this act expands upon previous legislation, authorizing the Environmental Protection Agency to limit the amounts of various contaminants in drinking water. It bans lead pipe and lead solder in public water systems, and expands protection of ground water sources. Where water quality legislation up to the 1970s concentrated on sewage and industrial waste, attention is now turning to less obvious sources of toxic chemicals, and what is referred to as "non point-source pollution," such as urban runoff and the flow of pesticides, fertilizers, and animal wastes from farmland.

Water Quality Management Plans. Section 208 of the Safe Drinking Water Act requires states and localities to develop areawide comprehensive plans for improving water quality. States have the primary role in water quality management—they establish water quality standards, determine sewage treatment construction priorities, issue National Pollutant Discharge Elimination System (NPDES) permits, and prepare Water Quality Management Plans or "208 Plans."

Air Quality **Clean Air Act.** Originally passed in 1955 (42 USC §7401 et seq.), this legislation addresses both fixed sources of air pollution (primarily factories) and vehicular emissions (motor vehicles and airplanes). Like the water quality laws, it establishes quantitative standards for various specified pollutants, sets goals for reaching and penalties for violating the standards, and promotes research and development. It provides technical and financial assistance to state and local governments, and authorizes the establishment of regional air pollution control programs.

Land Use **Coastal Zone Management Act of 1972 (CZMA).** This is considered the first national legislation to require land development controls as part of a federally-funded state planning process. By encouraging coastal states (including those on the Great Lakes) to develop coastal zone management plans, the act provides a mechanism for balancing the interests of recreational use, environmental control, and development. Projects that "directly affect" lands or water in the coastal zone must be carried out in a manner consistent with the approved state coastal zone management program.

Farmland Protection Policy Act of 1981. This is Subtitle I of the Agricultural and Food Act of 1981. It requires federal agencies to minimize the extent to which their programs contribute to the unnecessary and irreversible commitment of farmland to nonagricultural uses, and requires that where practical, federal programs be compatible with state, local and private programs and policies to protect farmland. Federal agencies must conduct a farmland conversion impact rating when a proposed project may convert farmlands to nonagricultural uses, and must consider requiring mitigation measures.

Other Conservation Laws. Other federal conservation laws and regulations address flood plains, wetlands, wilderness, and wild and scenic rivers generally; designate specific protected areas; and deal with management of natural resources of many types—forests, oil, minerals, fish and wildlife.

TOXICS AND WASTE DISPOSAL

This is the area of environmental legislation that has had the greatest impact on the real estate industry in recent years, through buyers' and especially lenders' concerns about property value and liability.

RCRA **Resource Conservation and Recovery Act (RCRA).** The Solid Waste Disposal Act, 1965, was expanded in 1970 and 1976 to create the present RCRA (42 USC §6901 et seq.). This act gives the federal Environmental Protection Agency (EPA, USEPA) authority to make and enforce regulations on owners and operators of hazardous waste facilities, and to enact means of defraying the cleanup costs. Included in the act are provisions for state environmental protection agencies and state or regional solid waste plans, federal assistance in planning and cleanup, and guidelines for handling recycled oil, sanitary landfills, and the upgrading of open dumps.

Administration. The act establishes an Office of Solid Waste at the federal level and spells out the duties and responsibilities of its administrator. Among other things, the office issues permits for the treatment, storage, or disposal of hazardous materials, and assists in developing state guidelines for hazardous waste programs.

Research and Information. Included in the act is a substantial research, development, demonstration, and information component (§6981 et seq.), mandating studies on hazardous wastes and recycling opportunities for materials ranging from glass to tires. This section provides funding for informational literature for agencies and the general public, and grants for resource recovery systems and demonstration projects.

Philosophy. The reasons for this legislation are set forth in the "Findings" that begin the text of the act (§6901). Important issues addressed in these findings include growth, progress, and standard of living; local vs. federal responsibility; the increasing scarcity of land; health hazards; and dependence on foreign and nonrenewable energy sources.

RCRA Findings

(a) Solid Waste. The Congress finds with respect to solid waste—

(1) that the continuing technological progress and improvement in methods of manufacture, packaging, and marketing of consumer products has resulted in an ever-mounting increase . . . of the mass of material discarded . . . .

(2) that the economic and population growth of our Nation, and the improvements in the standard of living enjoyed by our population, have required increased industrial production . . ., demolition of old buildings, the construction of new buildings, and industrial, commercial, and agricultural operations, [which] have resulted in a rising tide of scrap, discarded, and waste materials;

(3) that the continuing concentration of our population in expanding metropolitan and other urban areas has presented . . . problems in the disposal of solid wastes . . . .

(4) that . . . the problems of waste disposal . . . have become . . . national in scope . . . and necessitate federal action through financial and technical assistance and leadership . . . .

(b) Environment and Health. The Congress finds with respect to the environment and health, that—

(1) although land is too valuable a national resource to be needlessly polluted by discarded materials, most solid waste is disposed of on land in open dumps and sanitary landfills;

(2) disposal of solid waste and hazardous waste in or on the land without careful planning and management can present a danger to human health and the environment;

(3) as a result of the Clean Air Act, [and] the Water Pollution Control Act, . . . greater amounts of solid waste (in the form of sludge and other pollution treatment residues) have been created.

(4) open dumping is particularly harmful;

(5) hazardous waste presents, in addition to the problems associated with non-hazardous solid waste, special dangers to health and requires a greater degree of regulation . . . .

(6) . . . many of the cities in the United States will be running out of suitable solid waste disposal sites . . . .

(c) Materials. The Congress finds with respect to materials that—

(1) millions of tons of recoverable material which could be used are needlessly buried each year;

(2) methods are available to separate usable materials from solid waste; and

(3) the recovery and conservation of such materials can reduce the dependence of the United States on foreign resources and reduce the deficit in its balance of payments.

(d) Energy. The Congress finds with respect to energy, that—

(1) solid waste represents a potential source of solid fuel, oil, or gas that can be converted into energy;

(2) the need exists to develop alternative energy sources . . . to reduce our dependence on . . . petroleum products, natural gas, nuclear and hydroelectric generation; and

(3) technology exists to produce usable energy from solid waste.

Hazardous Waste Sites The provisions of the Act most relevant to real estate buyers, sellers, and lenders are contained in Resource Conservation and Recovery Act §§6921 through 6934, headed "Hazardous Waste Management." The Administrator is authorized to identify and list types of hazardous wastes; establish standards for labeling, record-keeping, storage, and tracking of wastes that are generated, transported, stored, or disposed of; issue permits for storage, treatment, or disposal of hazardous waste; and assist the states in developing hazardous waste programs.

Enforcement. Inspection and enforcement powers are extensive, and fines for one who "knowingly generates, stores, treats, transports, disposes of, or otherwise handles any hazardous waste" in violation of the permit and procedural requirements are up to $50,000 per day, or $250,000 for an act of "knowing endangerment."

Additional Listed Substances. When the state or federal government adds a substance to its list of hazardous wastes, operators who generate, store, treat, or dispose of that substance must notify the authorities of the activity and its location.

Site Inventory. States are directed to "as expeditiously as practicable, undertake a continuing program to compile, publish, and submit to the Administrator an inventory describing the location of each site within such State at which hazardous waste has at any time been stored or disposed of," stating:

- Locations where storage or disposal took place before permits were required
- Amount, nature, and toxicity of the hazardous waste at each site
- Name and address or corporate headquarters of the owner
- Types or techniques of treatment or disposal used
- Current status of the site.

EPA Inventory. If the state program is not adequate, the EPA Administrator shall carry out the inventory in that state.

Grants. The Administrator may make grants to the states for purposes of carrying out the inventory and may make grants to reimburse any state which conducted an inventory before the enactment of the Solid Waste Disposal Act Amendments of 1980.

Monitoring, Analysis, and Testing. If the Administrator determines that hazardous waste at any facility or site may present a substantial hazard to human health or the environment, he or she may order the owner or operator to conduct monitoring, testing, analysis, and reporting to ascertain the nature and extent of the hazard.

Previous Owners and Operators. If the site is no longer in operation, and the Administrator finds that the current owner could not reasonably be expected to have actual knowledge of the hazardous waste, the testing and reporting may be required of the most recent previous owner or operator who could reasonably be expected to have such actual knowledge.

Public Records. As a product of these inventories, the EPA maintains lists of "notifiers" (regulated hazardous waste generation, transportation, treatment, storage, and disposal sites) and "open dumps." These databases are accessible at EPA regional offices, and should be consulted when an industrial site or other potentially hazardous property is being purchased.

CERCLA (Superfund)	**Comprehensive Environmental Response, Compensation and Liability Act of 1980 (CERCLA).** (42 USC §9601 et seq.) This is the Superfund law. It provides authority and funding for cleaning up hazardous materials. A database of toxic sites, CERCLIS, is maintained under this law. The Superfund Amendments and Reauthorization Act of 1986 (SARA) further defines who is liable to pay for cleanup of contamination caused by past activities, and establishes an "innocent purchaser defense." (This is discussed in more detail in Courses 9 through 11, on environmental inspections and cleanup.)
	Property Values. In some cases, the cost of cleaning up a hazardous waste site can far exceed the value of the property. Buyers, sellers, and lenders need to be aware of liability provisions under CERCLA/SARA and take steps to establish an innocent purchaser defense or, where contamination is found, to obtain data for factoring the costs associated with cleanup into the transaction.
Other Laws on Toxics	**Federal Insecticide, Fungicide and Rodenticide Act (FIFRA), 1947.** (7 USC §135) This early law regulates pesticides and similar "economic poisons." Among other things, it prohibits the sale of pesticides which have not been registered with the Secretary of Agriculture.
	Toxic Substance Control Act. (15 USC §2601 et seq.) This act addresses the introduction of toxic materials—mercury, lead, hydrocarbons, other chemicals, pesticides, medical waste, and poisonous substances—into the environment. It places restrictions on their disposal and use.

ENDANGERED SPECIES ACT, 1973 (16 USC §1531 ET SEQ.)

One of the most widely publicized federal conservation laws is the Endangered Species Act, which lends itself to dramatic portrayals of spotted owls and tiny butterflies standing in the way of jobs, and bureaucrats operating as the "God Squad." The philosophy behind this law is set forth in its opening section. The finding about "esthetic, ecological, educational, historical, recreational, and scientific value" is one which is paralleled in many other conservation laws.

Findings and Purpose, Engangered Species Act

The Congress finds and declares that—

(1) various species of fish, wildlife, and plants in the United States have been rendered extinct as a consequence of economic growth and development untempered by adequate concern and conservation;

(2) other species of fish, wildlife, and plants have been so depleted in numbers that they are in danger of or threatened with extinction;

(3) these species of fish, wildlife, and plants are of esthetic, ecological, educational, historical, recreational, and scientific value to the Nation and its people;

(4) the United States has pledged itself as a sovereign state in the international community to conserve to the extent practicable the various species of fish or wildlife and plants facing extinction . . .;

(5) encouraging the States and other interested parties, through Federal financial assistance and . . . incentives, to develop and maintain conservation programs . . . is a key to meeting the Nation's international commitments and to better safeguarding, for the benefit of all citizens, the Nation's heritage in fish, wildlife, and plants.

Environmental Issues & Obligations

Definitions

Key terms in the Endangered Species Act include the following:

Action means all activities or programs of any kind authorized, funded, or carried out, in whole or in part, by Federal agencies in the United States or upon the high seas. Examples include promulgation of regulations and the granting of licenses, contracts, leases, easements, rights-of-way, permits, or grants-in-aid, as well as actions directly or indirectly causing modifications to the land, water, or air.

Action area means all areas to be affected directly or indirectly by the Federal action and not merely the immediate area involved in the action.

Applicant refers to any person or entity that requires formal approval or authorization from a Federal agency as a prerequisite to conducting an action.

Biological assessment refers to information prepared by or under the direction of the Federal agency concerning species and habitat present in the action area, and the evaluation of potential effects of the action on such species and habitat.

Biological opinion is the document that states the opinion of the Service [defined below] as to whether or not the Federal action is likely to jeopardize the continued existence of listed species or result in the destruction or adverse modification of critical habitat.

Conserve means to use all methods necessary to bring any species to the point at which the protections of this Act are no longer necessary, e.g., scientific resources management, law enforcement, habitat acquisition and maintenance, and propagation.

Critical habitat means specific areas occupied by the species on which are found those physical or biological features essential to the conservation of the species. Except in special circumstances determined by the Secretary, critical habitat shall not include the entire geographical area which can be occupied by the threatened or endangered species.

Endangered species means any species which is in danger of extinction throughout all or a significant portion of its range other than a species of the Class Insecta determined by the Secretary to constitute a pest whose protection would present an overwhelming and overriding risk to man.

Listed species means any species of fish, wildlife, or plant determined to be endangered or threatened. Listed species are found in 50 CFR 17.11-17.12.

Major construction activity is a construction project (or other undertaking having similar physical impacts) which is a major Federal action significantly affecting the quality of the human environment as referred to in the National Environment Policy Act.

Reasonable and prudent alternatives refers to alternative actions identified during formal consultation that can be implemented in a manner consistent with the intended purpose of the action, that are economically and technologically feasible, and that would avoid the likelihood of jeopardizing the continued existence of listed species or destruction of critical habitat.

Service means the U.S. Fish and Wildlife Service or the National Marine Fisheries Service, as appropriate.

Species includes any subspecies of fish or wildlife or plants, and any distinct population segment of any species of vertebrate fish or wildlife which interbreeds when mature.

Threatened species means any species which is likely to become an endangered species within the foreseeable future throughout all or a significant portion of its range.

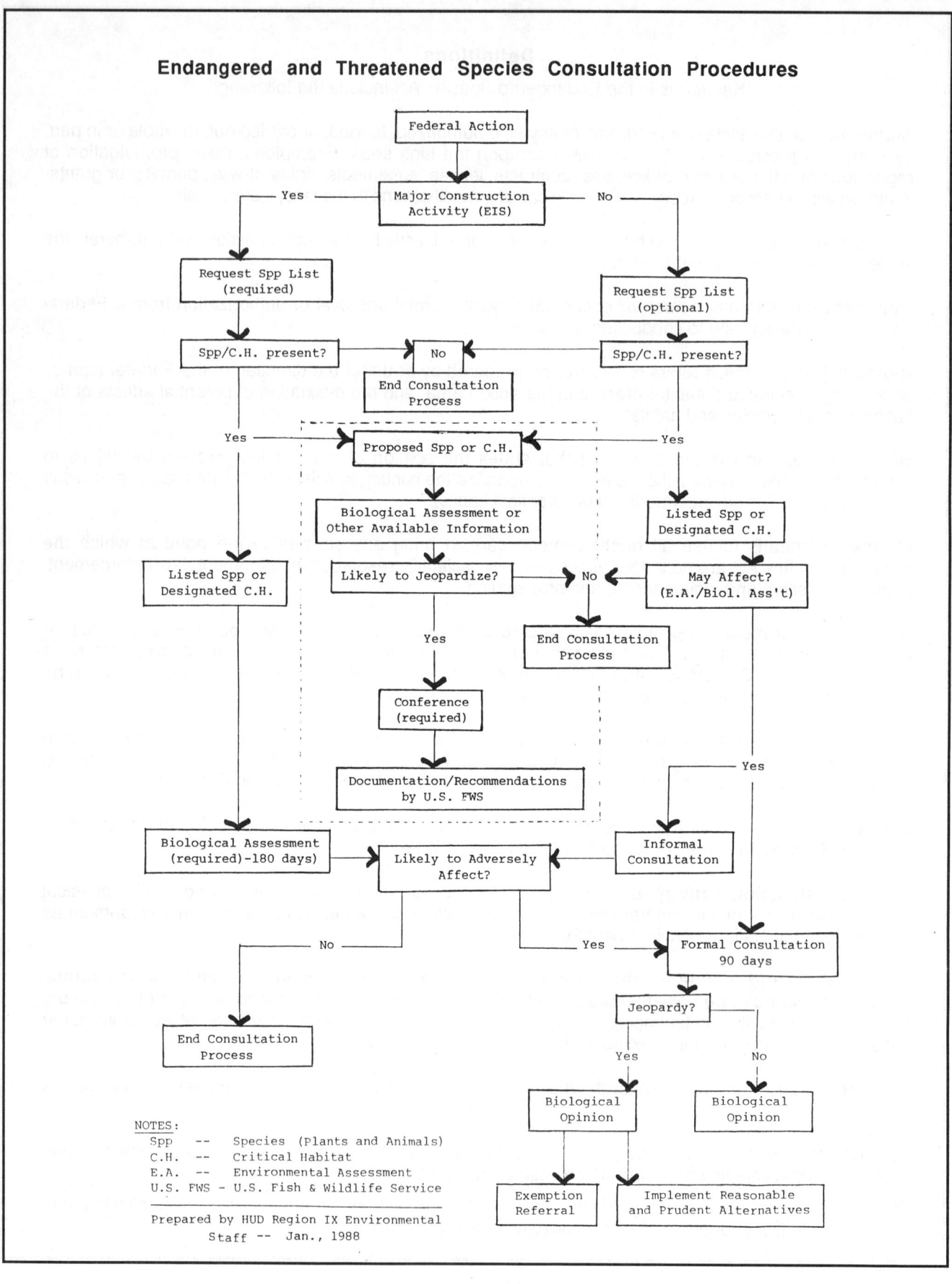

Applicability. The Endangered Species Act is designed to insure that government does not authorize, fund, or carry out any activity that is likely to jeopardize continued existence of endangered species. It is through government funding and authorization (permits of various kinds) that the act affects the private real estate sector.

Balancing Priorities. The act acknowledges potential conflicts with other priorities—even environmental ones—and provides that federal agencies shall cooperate with state and local agencies to resolve water resource issues in a manner consistent with the conservation of endangered species.

Constitutionality. Soon after its passage, courts determined that the Endangered Species Act does not violate the due process clause of the Fifth Amendment because its provisions have a rational basis (*Delbay Pharmaceuticals, Inc. vs. Department of Commerce,* 1976, DC Dist. Col., 409 F. Supp. 637), and that it is a constitutional exercise of police power since protection of endangered species is a matter of general concern and in the public interest (*People vs. K. Sakai Co.,* 1976, 1st Dist., 56 Cal. App. 3d 531, 128 Cal. Rptr. 536).

Affirmative Duty. Other cases have held that the act gives the Fish and Wildlife Service an affirmative duty to increase populations of protected species. Regulations permitting hunting from half an hour before sunrise until sunset were held inconsistent with this duty since endangered species might be misidentified during twilight hours (*Defenders of Wildlife vs. Andrus,* 1977, DC Dist. Col.; 428 F. Supp. 167).

Procedures The act and subsequent regulations (50 CFR Part 402) set up detailed procedures for assembling factual information, balancing economic and environmental considerations, and proposing alternatives. Time limits are built into the process, to reduce excessive or unpredictable delays. The government is charged to take affirmative steps to protect, conserve, and restore endangered species to levels that would permit removal from the endangered species list.

Determination of Endangered Species. The Secretary of the Interior determines whether any species is endangered or threatened because of any of the following:

- Destruction of its habitat or range

- Overutilization for commercial, recreational, or other purposes

- Disease or predation

- Inadequacy of existing regulations

- Other natural or manmade factors.

The Secretary is required to make these determinations solely on the basis of the best scientific and commercial data available.

Designation of Critical Habitat. The Secretary designates *critical habitat* for each listed species, on the basis of the best scientific data available and after taking into consideration the economic impact and any other relevant impact. The Secretary may exclude any area from critical habitat if the benefits of exclusion outweigh the benefits of designation, unless failure to designate the area as critical habitat will result in extinction of the species.

Consultation. When an "action" is proposed—either a federal project or one requiring a federal permit or license—consultation begins. If a prospective applicant has reason to believe that the action may affect listed species or critical habitat, it may request "early consultation." In that case a *biological assessment* evaluates the potential effects of the action on listed and proposed species and habitat and determines whether formal consultation is necessary. The Fish and Wildlife Service provides a species list.

Completion Time. If a permit or license application is involved, the biological assessment may not take longer than 180 days unless the agency provides the applicant with a written explanation. Depending on findings, the consultation process may end at any of several points. For example:

- If the biological assessment indicates that there are no listed species or critical habitat present that are likely to be adversely affected, then formal consultation is not required.

- If during informal consultation it is determined that the action is not likely to adversely affect listed species or critical habitat, the consultation process is terminated, and no further action is necessary.

- If any action may affect listed species or critical habitat, formal consultation is required.

- Formal consultation between the federal agency and the Service normally concludes within 90 days. Within 45 days after concluding formal consultation, the Service delivers a *biological opinion* to the federal agency and any applicant.

Biological Opinions. The biological opinion includes detailed discussion of the effects of the action on listed species or critical habitat, and the Service's opinion on whether action is likely to jeopardize the continued existence of a listed species or critical habitat (a "jeopardy biological opinion"), or is not likely to jeopardize (a "no jeopardy biological opinion").

Alternatives. A "jeopardy" biological opinion must discuss reasonable and prudent alternatives, if any. If the Service is unable to develop such alternatives, it will indicate that to the best of its knowledge there are none. The Service may also provide discretionary conservation recommendations.

Exemption. Following the issuance of a biological opinion, if the federal agency determines that it cannot comply, it may apply for an exemption. Procedures for exemption applications by federal agencies and others are found in the Code of Federal Regulations, 50 CFR Part 451.

NATIONAL HISTORIC PRESERVATION ACT OF 1966 (16 USC §470 ET SEQ.)

Successor to the 1906 Antiquities Act and the Historic Sites Act of 1935 (16 USC §§461-467), the National Historic Preservation Act of 1966 (NHPA) addresses conservation of the human-made environment. The 1935 act created the National Historic Landmark program to preserve sites of national significance like Independence Hall in Philadelphia. The 1966 act creates a much more inclusive National Register of Historic Places, which lists districts, sites, buildings, structures, and objects not only with national significance, but also with local, regional, or state significance.

The National Register This is the nation's official inventory of districts, sites, and buildings with local, state, and national significance in history, architecture, or archaeology. There are four criteria for eligibility. A property only needs to qualify under one of the four.

- Criterion A. Association with significant events and patterns of history
- Criterion B. Association with significant persons
- Criterion C. Embodiment of a distinctive type or period of architecture, or high artistic values
- Criterion D. Potential for yielding information (usually archaeological).

Generally religious properties, properties less than 50 years old, properties significant for association with living people, and moved or significantly altered buildings are not eligible, but there are exceptions.

Nomination Process. Anyone may nominate a property for the National Register, but if the owner objects, the application can only be submitted for determination of National Register eligibility. Applications are received by the State Office of Historic Preservation and must be accepted by both the State Historical Resources Commission and the Secretary of the Interior through the Keeper of the National Register.

Provisions of the Act National Register properties receive protection from adverse impacts of federal actions through Section 106 of the act, requiring review prior to alteration or destruction. The act also establishes a requirement for states to conduct historic surveys, a matching grant-in-aid program for the National Trust for Historic Preservation, and an Advisory Council on Historic Preservation. Amendments in 1980 made the Advisory Council an independent federal agency and required owner consent on National Register listings.

Relation to NEPA. Historic properties are among the resources that must be assessed in environmental impact statements on federally funded or licensed projects under the National Environmental Policy Act. At a minimum, "historic" means properties on or determined eligible for the National Register.

Tax Credits In 1976, Congress enacted tax incentives to encourage rehabilitation of historic buildings, through accelerated depreciation for income-producing property listed on the National Register. As amended by the Tax Reform Act of 1986, there are currently (1993) two rehabilitation tax credits:

- A 10 percent credit for work on commercially-used buildings constructed before 1936

Federal Environmental Legislation

The Secretary of the Interior's Standards for Rehabilitation

The Standards that follow were originally published in 1977 and revised in 1990 as part of Department of the Interior regulations (36 CFR Part 67, Historic Preservation Certifications). They pertain to historic buildings of all materials, construction types, sizes, and occupancy and encompass the exterior and the interior of historic buildings. The Standards also encompass related landscape features and the building's site and environment as well as attached, adjacent, or related new construction.

Rehabilitation is defined as the process of returning a property to a state of utility, through repair or alteration, which makes possible an efficient contemporary use while preserving those portions and features of the property that are significant to its historic, architectural, and cultural values.

The Standards are to be applied to specific rehabilitation projects in a reasonable manner, taking into consideration economic and technical feasibility.

1. A property shall be used for its historic purpose or be placed in a new use that requires minimal change to the defining characteristics of the building and its site and environment.

2. The historic character of a property shall be retained and preserved. The removal of historic materials or alteration of features and spaces that characterize a property shall be avoided.

3. Each property shall be recognized as a physical record of its time, place, and use. Changes that create a false sense of historical development, such as adding conjectural features or architectural elements from other buildings, shall not be undertaken.

4. Most properties change over time; those changes that have acquired historic significance in their own right shall be retained and preserved.

5. Distinctive features, finishes, and construction techniques or examples of craftsmanship that characterize a property shall be preserved.

6. Deteriorated historic features shall be repaired rather than replaced. Where the severity of deterioration requires replacement of a distinctive feature, the new feature shall match the old in design, color, texture, and other visual qualities and, where possible, materials. Replacement of missing features shall be substantiated by documentary, physical, or pictorial evidence.

7. Chemical or physical treatments, such as sand-blasting, that cause damage to historic materials shall not be used. The surface cleaning of structures, if appropriate, shall be undertaken using the gentlest means possible.

8. Significant archeological resources affected by a project shall be protected and preserved. If such resources must be disturbed, mitigation measures shall be undertaken.

9. New additions, exterior alterations, or related new construction shall not destroy historic materials that characterize the property and its environment. The new work shall be differentiated from the old to protect the historic integrity of the property and shall be compatible with the massing, size, scale, and architectural details to protect the historic integrity of the property and its environment.

10. New additions and adjacent or related new construction shall be undertaken in such a manner that if removed in the future, the essential form and integrity of the historic property and its environment would be unimpaired.

Note: To be eligible for Federal tax incentives, a rehabilitation project must meet all ten Standards.

Certain treatments, if improperly applied, or certain materials by their physical properties, may cause or accelerate physical deterioration of historic buildings. Inappropriate physical treatments include, but are not limited to: improper repointing techniques; improper exterior masonry cleaning methods; or improper introduction of insulation where damage to historic fabric would result. In almost all situations, use of these materials and treatments will result in denial of certification. In addition, every effort should be made to ensure that the new materials and workmanship are compatible with the materials and workmanship of the historic property.

Guidelines to help property owners, developers, and Federal managers apply the Secretary of the Interior's Standards for Rehabilitation are available from the National Park Service, State Historic Preservation Offices, or from the Government Printing Office. For more information write: National Park Service, Preservation Assistance Division-424, P.O. Box 37127, Washington, D.C. 20013-7127.

- A 20 percent credit for "Certified Historic Structures," buildings listed on the National Register, if work is done in conformity with the Secretary of the Interior's Standards (see below). The building's use must be depreciable, that is, held for investment or used in the taxpayer's trade or business.

Secretary of the Interior's Standards for Rehabilitation. This document, with accompanying interpretive guidelines, is used in determining if a rehabilitation project qualifies as a "certified rehabilitation" eligible for tax credits. The standards are aimed at retaining and preserving those architectural features and materials that are important in defining a building's historic character. Many cities have adopted the Secretary's Standards for local review of work on historic buildings.

Section 106 Review Section 106 of National Historic Preservation Act requires that every federal agency "take into account" how each of its "undertakings" could affect historic properties and afford the Advisory Council a reasonable opportunity to comment on the agency's project.

Applicability. Federal "undertaking" includes a broad range of federal activities: construction, rehabilitation and repair projects, demolition, licenses, permits, loans, loan guarantees, grants, federal property transfers, and many other types of involvement. For purposes of Section 106, any property listed in *or eligible for* the National Register of Historic Places is considered "historic."

Procedure. The Section 106 process is outlined in the Code of Federal Regulations at 36 CFR Part 800. It broadly parallels the review processes under the Endangered Species Act and under NEPA.

- ***Determine if Federal Undertaking.*** If so, define area of potential effect.

- ***Identify and Evaluate Historic Properties.*** The federal agency responsible for an undertaking must identify historic properties that the undertaking may affect, both those already on the National Register and others that may be eligible.

- ***Assess Effects.*** If historic properties are found, the agency then assesses what effect its undertaking will have on them.
  - No effect: the undertaking will not affect historic properties
  - No adverse effect: the undertaking will affect one or more historic properties, but the effect will not be harmful
  - Adverse effect: the undertaking will harm one or more historic properties.

- ***Consult.*** If an adverse effect will occur, the agency consults with the state preservation office and others to find ways to make the undertaking less harmful. A Memorandum of Agreement (MOA) outlines measures the agency will take to avoid or mitigate the adverse effect. In some cases the decision is that the adverse effects must be accepted in the public interest. The Advisory Council may comment during the consultation process or on the completed Memorandum of Agreement.

Federal Environmental Legislation

OVERVIEW: HUD STATUTORY WORKSHEETS

In 24 CFR Part 50 (1982) the Department of Housing and Urban Development (HUD) set out procedures for complying with NEPA "and the other provisions of law which further the purposes of NEPA." This document forms a convenient summary and checklist of environmental laws, since "HUD and/or applicants must comply, where applicable, with all environmental requirements, guidelines, and statutory obligations under the following authorities and HUD standards." The laws and regulations, grouped by topic, are listed below:

Historic Properties (1) The National Historic Preservation Act of 1966 as amended (16 USC §470 et seq.).

(2) Executive Order 11593, Protection and Enhancement of the Cultural Environment, May 13, 1971 (36 FR 8921 et seq.).

(3) The Archeological and Historic Preservation Act of 1974, which amends the Reservoir Salvage Act of 1960 (16 USC §469 et seq.).

(4) Procedures for the Protection of Historic and Cultural Properties (Advisory Council on Historic Preservation—36 CFR Part 800).

Floodplain Management and Wetland Protection (1) Flood Disaster Protection Act of 1973 (42 USC §4001, et seq.), as amended.

(2) Executive Order 11988, Floodplain Management, May 24, 1977 (42 FR 26951 et seq.) and Executive Order 11990, Protection of Wetlands, May 24, 1977 (42 FR 26961 et seq.) in accordance with the procedures set forth in Part II–Decision-Making Process, Floodplain Management Guidelines, U.S. Water Resources Council (43 FR 6030, February 10, 1978).

(3) HUD General Statement of Policy: Implementation of Executive Orders 11988 and 11990 (44 FR 47623, August 14, 1979).

Coastal Zone Management The Coastal Zone Management Act of 1972 (16 USC §1451 et seq.), as amended.

Sole Source Aquifers The Safe Drinking Water Act of 1974 (42 USC §201, 300 et seq., and 21 USC §349), as amended.

Wildlife The Fish and Wildlife Coordination Act of 1958 (16 USC §661 et seq.), as amended.

Endangered Species The Endangered Species Act of 1973 (16 USC §1531 et seq.), as amended.

Wild and Scenic Rivers The Wild and Scenic Rivers Act (16 USC §1271 et seq.), as amended.

Water Quality The Federal Water Pollution Control Act as amended by the Federal Water Pollution Control Act Amendments of 1972 (33 USC §1251 et seq.), and later enactments.

Air Quality	The Clean Air Act (42 USC §7401, et seq.), as amended.
Solid Waste Management	The Solid Waste Disposal Act as amended by the Resource Conservation and Recovery Act of 1976 (42 USC §6901, et seq.), and later enactments.
Farmlands Protection	Farmland Protection Policy Act of 1981 (7 USC §4201 et seq.).
HUD Environmental Standards	(1) Noise Abatement and Control (24 CFR 51B)
	(2) Explosive and Flammable Operations (24 CFR 51C)
	(3) Toxic Chemicals/Radioactive Materials (HUD Notice 79-33)
	(4) Airport Clear Zones and Accident Potential Zones (24 CFR 51D)
Applicability and Exclusions	A full environmental assessment and FONSI or EIS is required under NEPA for major projects including new construction and urban renewal projects. Certain actions, activities, and programs are categorically excluded from the NEPA requirements but not from the environmental statutes, executive orders, and HUD standards listed above. For these cases, HUD does not consider an EIS but still has the worksheets cited above for screening for environmental effect. This screening represents a *minimum* level of environmental review for federally related actions today. Projects in this category include:

- An individual action on a one-to-four family dwelling or five or more units on scattered sites

- Training grants and technical assistance

- Certain low-impact acquisition, property disposition, rehabilitation and/or modernization projects

- The Existing Housing Program under Section 8 of the U.S. Housing Act

- Interstate Land Sales Registration actions

- Mortgage purchase commitments and mortgage purchases by the Government National Mortgage Association pursuant to the Emergency Home Purchase Assistance Act of 1974

- Demonstration projects costing less than $1 million that do not result in physical change

- Interest reduction assistance and rent supplement payments on existing construction

- Acquisition of an existing structure retained in the same use

- Certain purchased or refinanced housing and medical facilities

- Various administrative and financial procedures.

THE AMERICANS WITH DISABILITIES ACT, 1990

Not primarily an environmental law, the Americans with Disabilities Act (ADA), 42 USC §12101, can have direct environmental effects when a building, natural feature, or part of the infrastructure is modified to improve access. More generally, it is included in this course because it is a new law with far-reaching effects on employers, owners and users of real estate, and real estate businesses. Its provisions cover two broad areas—accessibility and employment—where people with disabilities have faced obstacles. Its broad language is in effect a bill of rights for disabled people.

Employment There are an estimated 16 million persons who have been unable to find work due to discrimination because of a physical or mental disability. Title I of the ADA prohibits discrimination in employment.

Prohibited Acts. When an employer limits, segregates or classifies an applicant or employee in a way that affects opportunities or status because of disability, it constitutes discrimination, whether intentional or not. Examples include:

- Exclusion from jobs on the basis of disability unless the ability in question is an "essential function" of the job.
- Failure to make "reasonable accommodations" for disabled workers, such as modifying building access, equipment, schedules, etc., unless the business can show that it would experience "undue hardship."
- Using testing or assessment procedures geared to the exclusion of those with physical, sensory, or mental handicaps, unless the ability the test is measuring is an essential job function.
- Asking about a job applicant's disability or requiring pre-employment medical examinations.
- Discriminating against a person because he or she is related to or associates with a disabled person.

Applicability. Implementation of Title I is required as of July 26, 1992, for employers with twenty-five or more employees and July 26, 1994, for employers with fifteen to twenty-four employees. For real estate offices, "employees" includes salespeople classified as independent contractors. "Employers" includes all businesses except Indian tribes and certain nonprofit organizations. Government employers are covered separately in Title II.

Definition of Disability. Disabilities covered by the act range from those obvious to outsiders, such as impairment of sight, hearing, or mobility, to HIV infection, dyslexia, epilepsy, alcoholism, and various mental and emotional conditions. This list may be expected to change as the law evolves. A condition is a "disability" if it "substantially limits one or more of an individual's major life activities."

Qualified Individual. A "qualified individual with a disability" is defined as a person with a disability who, with or without reasonable accommodation, can perform the essential functions of the job in question.

Public Facilities Title III applies to "public accommodations and services," which covers almost all business establishments, including professional offices, transit depots, libraries, etc. A business may not deny an individual or class of individuals the opportunity to participate in or benefit from the business's goods, services, or facilities on the basis of a disability.

Accommodations. Workplace accommodations can mean such items as braille markings in elevators, voice activated computers, desks, and partitions placed with adequate room for wheelchair users, and so on. Structural modifications to allow access are required effective January 26th, 1992 (January 26th, 1993, for new construction designed for occupancy in 1993). Both landlord and tenant are responsible for access to a building.

Exemptions. Failure to make reasonable modifications in policies, facilities, or services is considered discrimination, unless the entity can demonstrate that modifications would fundamentally alter the nature of the business. Removal of architectural, communication, and other barriers is required where it is "readily achievable."

Public Entities | The employment and access requirements placed on private businesses in Titles I and III have parallels for government programs, activities, services (including transportation), and employment. Rules are basically the same as for private businesses (equal and integrated access to programs, services, and employment), and the exceptions are similar—accommodations are not required that would impose an undue financial burden, fundamentally alter the nature of a service, or destroy the significance of a historic landmark.

Enforcement | Legal remedies provided in the act are pursued by private civil action, and include attorney's fees, hiring, reinstatement, back pay, court orders to stop discrimination, modification of facilities, and damages. If there is a pattern of discrimination the Attorney General may prosecute, and civil penalties may be imposed, up to $50,000 for a first violation and up to $100,000 for each subsequent violation. The administrative agencies for enforcement are the Equal Employment Opportunity Commission for Title I, and the Department of Justice for Titles II and III. The law encourages "alternative means of dispute resolution" instead of litigation.

Tax Credits | There is a Disabled Access Tax Credit for small businesses, for 50 percent of "eligible access expenditures" up to $10,000 (with a $250 deductible), and a deduction up to $15,000 per year for removal of architectural and transportation barriers. There are also credits for part of the first-year wages of a new employee with a disability who is referred by specific rehabilitation agencies.

ISSUES RAISED BY FEDERAL ENVIRONMENTAL LEGISLATION

Environmental legislation is not the least controversial of the many areas in which the federal government operates. The issues cross party, class, and regional lines, and range from economics to local self-determination to theology to questions of scientific fact. Among many other points for consideration are the following:

Economic Issues | How does the cost of complying with environmental laws balance against the benefits—and benefits to whom?

- Value of protecting wildlife and old-growth forests versus potential loss of jobs and higher cost of lumber.

- Value of preserving the snail darter versus the TVA's water project and its benefits to humans.

- Probability that costs of reducing emissions or cleaning up spills will be passed on to the consumer, who is already struggling to make ends meet.

- Lack of solid evidence whether historic designation or location in a coastal conservation area enhances a property's value, or makes it a white elephant.
- The possibility that private enterprise, following its economic self-interest, would self-regulate more cost-effectively than under compulsion, and would devise ways to make recycling and alternative energy profitable.

Government Role Is the federal government interfering in matters far too local—or too cosmic?

- Species have originated and passed into extinction over the ages due to predation, climate, and population changes: is endangered species legislation a futile attempt to play God and stay the course of nature?
- Given variations in climate, topography, population density, and intangible economic and aesthetic values, can the federal government define "environmental quality" in terms appropriate for the whole nation?
- Does administration from Washington impose more red tape, expense, and delay than if environmental matters were left to local jurisdiction?
- Are federal agencies as well equipped to regulate local polluters—or protect local natural or historic resources—as local government and local public opinion, who know the parties, the history, and the issues?

Scientific Issues Is the federal government informed enough to legislate on scientific matters, or flexible enough to adjust to technological advances?

- Have certain technologies, such as sea water conversion and nuclear fusion, been dismissed out of hand by conservative federal regulators?
- What assurance is there that regulators are not overestimating the dangers of some toxics, and overlooking others, as they did DDT for decades?

Example: Air Quality Legislation

Regional Variation. In the United States, major metropolitan areas such as Pittsburgh and Los Angeles have been grappling with air pollution for a long time. Industrial and vehicular emissions, along with temperature inversions and other local geographical characteristics, have resulted in air quality below the level considered safe for human health and well being. Air pollution control districts have been established in such key areas to monitor the particulates in the air and enlist industry to reduce the level of air pollution. Not all areas have problems of air pollution, however. Many of these standards have questionable application in rural America. Yet in most areas of the country open burning of waste is no longer allowed, even where it might be a more appropriate approach than landfill.

Worldwide Scope. On the other hand, no area's air is truly isolated. Since the atmosphere can carry pollutants great distances from their source, it can be argued that there is need for not only federal but even international controls. The release of hazardous emissions from the nuclear reactor at Chernobyl made the world aware of the dangers from aerial transmission of hazardous materials.

Cost-Benefit Questions. Conversion of industrial facilities and vehicles to meet higher air pollution standards can be very expensive. Commuting by public transit can take much longer than driving alone. Legislation can attempt to weight the balance in tradeoffs like these. Implementation will vary with local and national changes in the political and economic climate.

HIGHLIGHTS TO REMEMBER

FEDERAL ENVIRONMENTAL LEGISLATION

Background and Purpose

Environmental protection is consumer protection: stabilizes and enhances property values

Major federal laws date from 1960s and after

Two broad types of concern, pollution and conservation

Origins: National Parks 1872, Rivers and Harbors Act 1899 (restricted dumping), Antiquities Act 1906 (archaeological sites)

NEPA: National Environmental Policy Act, 1969 and Amendments

Widest-ranging federal environmental law, umbrella and charter for more specific regulations

Establishes Environmental Protection Agency and creates environmental impact statement

Extensive statement of purpose, shared by other environmental laws

To make sure federal agencies act responsibly, without excessive paperwork

Environmental Impact Statement (EIS)

Required by NEPA for federal actions significantly affecting the environment

No EIS needed if agency makes a "finding of no significant impact" (FONSI)

NEPA says EIS must be concise and in plain language, for public and decision makers

Prescribed review process including public comment and analysis of alternatives

Agency must evaluate all reasonable alternatives (including "no action") and mitigations

Air, Water, Land Use

Clean Water and Safe Drinking Water Acts regulate waterways and water supply respectively: industrial wastes, lead in water supplies, non point source pollution (runoff)

Clean Air Act (1955) sets goals for decreasing industrial and vehicular emissions through penalties and research and development

Coastal Zone Management Act and Farmland Protection Policy Act regulate use of sensitive lands

Toxic Waste Disposal

Area of greatest concern among real estate buyers and lenders, especially over liability

Resource Conservation and Recovery Act (RCRA) mandates cleanups and solid waste plans

> Purpose and findings: economic and population growth produce waste; land is too valuable to pollute and fill; solid waste is a source of recoverable material and energy
>
> Federal and state inventories of hazardous waste sites include open dumps and "notifiers"
>
> System of permits, tracking, monitoring, testing, and record keeping for regulated hazardous waste sites; heavy fines for violations

Comprehensive Environmental Response, Compensation and Liability Act of 1980 (CERCLA)

> Establishes Superfund for cleanup of targeted sites and CERCLIS database of toxic sites
>
> Innocent landowner (purchaser) defense in SARA clarifies who is liable to pay for cleanup

Endangered Species Act, 1973

- Prevents federal government from carrying out, funding, or authorizing any actions that jeopardize endangered species
- Species become endangered through disease or predation, hunting or harvesting, destruction of habitat
- Does not apply to "species of the Class Insecta determined to constitute . . . an overriding risk to man"
- Balances environmental and economic priorities; upheld by courts
- Affirmative duty to increase populations of protected species, not just refrain from harm
- Affects private parties through federal permits or funding
- Consultation and review process through Fish and Wildlife Service
- Key terms: endangered species, critical habitat, biological assessment and opinion, jeopardy opinion, reasonable and prudent alternatives

National Historic Preservation Act of 1966

- Establishes National Register of Historic Places
- Buildings, districts, and sites of national, state, and local significance
- Significance may relate to persons, patterns of history, architecture, or archaeology
- National Register properties are eligible for rehab tax credits, and impact on listed or eligible properties must be assessed under NEPA
- Secretary of the Interior's Standards for Rehabilitation for review of tax act projects
- Section 106 of NHPA requires review of impact of federal "undertakings" (includes funding and loan guarantees) on historic resources

HUD Statutory Worksheets for Projects Exempt from NEPA's EIS Requirement

- Checklist of environmental statutes, guidelines, executive orders, etc. representing *minimum* level of environmental review
- Exempt "projects" are only financing and administrative procedures and certain low-impact rehab work
- Topics include historic properties, floodplains and wetlands, coastal zones, aquifers, wildlife and endangered species, wild and scenic rivers, water quality, air quality, solid waste, farmlands

Americans with Disabilities Act (ADA), 1990

- Direct effect on environment through access modifications to buildings and other facilities
- Broad effect on employers and providers of services, through prohibitions on discrimination and requirement for "reasonable accommodation"
- Disability defined as a condition that "substantially limits one or more major life activities"
- Enforcement by civil action; Attorney General may prosecute if pattern of discrimination

Issues Raised by Federal Environmental Legislation

- Economic: balancing costs and benefits .
- Role of government: federal vs. local; attempt to legislate the course of nature
- Scientific issues: is government informed enough to legislate, when even scientists disagree?

COURSE 2
State & Local Environmental Legislation

INTRODUCTION

Many uses compete for land: housing, business, agriculture, recreation. Government regulations attempt to balance these needs. A constant concern of both politicians and their constituents is the delicate balance between existing and proposed projects. This is the purpose of environmental impact reports, zoning laws, planning commissions, and privately imposed use restrictions. Most states have environmental laws of their own, paralleling federal laws on the state level, or addressing distinctive local concerns, or enacting more vigorous controls than the federal government does. So do cities and counties.

Important California laws with federal counterparts are the California Environmental Quality Act, CEQA, which parallels the National Environmental Policy Act (NEPA), and the California Environmental Superfund Act. Our building code (Title 24 of the California Code of Regulations) shares with those of other states a common descent from the FHA minimum property standards and the model codes issued by various professional organizations. On the other hand, California's distinctive Safe Drinking Water and Toxic Enforcement Act of 1986 is an initiative passed by the state's voters. Other laws unique to California deal with water allocation, seismic hazards, coastal protection, and other issues arising out of the California environment.

THE PUBLIC RESOURCES CODE

An entire code of California law deals with environmental matters. The Public Resources Code addresses public lands and parks, fish and wildlife, mining, energy conservation, and much more. This is the body of law that establishes CEQA, the State Historic Landmarks program, the Coastal Zone Conservation Commission, and the California Conservation Corps. A summary of the contents of this code will indicate the range of environmental legislation in California.

Administration Division 1, Administration. Establishes the Department of Parks and Recreation, Department of Conservation, Division of Forestry, and Mining and Geology Board.

Geology and Mines Division 2, Geology, Mines and Mining. Addresses mining claims, reclamation of mined lands, placer mining water pollution, plus seismic issues—special studies zones and strong-motion instrumentation program.

Oil and Gas Division 3, Oil and Gas. Covers wells, leases, and other aspects of production; also geothermal resources.

Forestry Division 4, Forests, Forestry and Range and Forage Lands. Topics include fire fighting and fire prevention, lumbering and reforestation, and preservation of big trees.

Parks Division 5, Parks and Monuments. State park system, historical resources, wilderness preservation, wild and scenic rivers, watersheds and wetlands, county parks and museums, bonds and other funding for parks and recreation facilities.

Public Lands	Division 6, Public Lands. Administration, leasing, and sale of state owned lands, with special provisions for extractive (oil, gas, mineral) activities, school lands, and swamp lands; grazing on federal lands.
Highways	Division 7, Fish, wildlife, and recreation in relation to state highway projects.
Surveying	Division 8, Surveying and Mapping. Establishes California Coordinate System.
Conservation	Division 9, Resource Conservation. Establishment and operation of resource conservation districts (such as the Tahoe Resource Conservation District); creates a Division of Resource Conservation and State Resource Conservation Commission.
Resorts	Division 11, Resort Improvement Districts. Provides for bond and tax funding.
CCC	Division 12, California Conservation Corps.
CEQA	Division 13, Environmental Quality. This division is CEQA, the California Environmental Quality Act.
License Plate Fund	Division 13.5, The California Environmental Protection Program. Establishes the environmental license plate fund and specifies uses for money from sale of personalized plates: air pollution control, environmental education, park acquisition, protection of fish and wildlife and endangered species, etc.
L.A. Commission	Division 14, The Ventura-Los Angeles Mountain Coastal Study Commission.
Energy	Division 15, Energy Conservation and Development. Establishes a State Energy Resources Conservation and Development Commission to conduct studies of energy needs and sources, promote use of energy efficient appliances, develop energy conservation standards for new buildings, etc. Building standards are enforced by local governments; the state provides technical assistance.
Coastal Zones	Division 18, California Coastal Zone Conservation Commission. Powers, planning procedure, permits, and enforcement. Under the California Coastal Act of 1976, special regulations apply to the approximately 1,000 miles of coastline on the state's western border. The coastal zone is generally defined as seaward to the outer limit of the state's jurisdiction and inland to the highest elevation of the nearest coastal mountain range. Development projects in this area must be approved by the Coastal Commission.

CEQA

The California Environmental Quality Act, California's counterpart of NEPA, is found in Division 13 of the Public Resources Code. It was enacted in 1970, one year after NEPA. Like NEPA, it applies to public agencies, requiring them to document, consider, and if possible reduce the environmental impacts of their actions. It applies to state, local, county, and regional agencies, and because local agencies' actions include issuing building permits, it often affects private owners and developers. CEQA is the law that establishes the Environmental Impact Report.

Purposes The opening sections of CEQA set forth the assumptions and purposes underlying the law. Among CEQA's stated aims are:

- To maintain a quality environment for the people of California
- To provide an environment that is healthful and pleasing to the senses
- To demonstrate that every citizen has a responsibility to contribute to the preservation of the environment
- To encourage concerted efforts between the private and public sectors for management of natural resources and waste disposal
- To require all agencies that regulate activities to give major consideration to preventing environmental damage while providing a decent home and satisfying living environment for every Californian
- To provide the people of the state with clean air and water, enjoyment of aesthetic, natural, scenic, and historic environmental qualities, and freedom from excessive noise
- To prevent the elimination of fish and wildlife species due to man's activities, and preserve for future generations representations of all plant and animal communities and examples of the major periods of California history
- To require government agencies at all levels to consider qualitative factors as well as economic and technical factors, and long-term benefits and costs, in addition to short-term benefits and costs, and to consider alternatives to proposed actions affecting the environment.

Environmental Impact Report The EIR under CEQA parallels the environmental impact statement (EIS) under NEPA, and is more familiar to most Californians since most construction and development projects are regulated on the local or state level. The steps in defining, preparing, reviewing, and acting upon an EIR are similar to those in NEPA: initial study, possible negative declaration, scoping, public review and response to comments on the draft EIR, finding, and mitigations.

Purpose of EIR. CEQA states that the purpose of an environmental impact report is "to provide public agencies and the public in general with detailed information about the effect which a proposed project is likely to have on the environment; to list ways in which the significant effects of such a project might be minimized; and to indicate alternatives to such a project."

Applicability. CEQA applies to all California "governmental agencies," to all "discretionary" "projects" that those agencies "carry out, approve, or finance" that have "potential for resulting in physical change in the environment." Key terms are defined as follows:

- *Project*. Like an "undertaking" in NEPA, this may be government action as direct and tangible as freeway construction, as intangible as adopting an ordinance, or as indirect as granting a "permit, lease, or other entitlement."

- *Discretionary*. This describes projects that require the public agency to exercise judgment in deciding whether or not to approve the activity. The opposite—not subject to CEQA—is a *ministerial* project, where the agency's approval is only a matter of applying the law (for example, issuing a building permit where the only requirements are complying with zoning and building codes and paying the fee).

State & Local Environmental Legislation

☐ *Significant Effect on the Environment.* According to CEQA guidelines, a project will normally have a significant effect on the environment if it will:

- Conflict with adopted environmental plans and goals of the community where it is located;
- Have a substantial, demonstrable negative aesthetic effect;
- Substantially affect a rare or endangered species of animal or plant or the habitat of the species;
- Interfere substantially with the movement of any resident or migratory fish or wildlife species;
- Breach published national, state, or local standards relating to solid waste or litter control;
- Substantially degrade water quality;
- Contaminate a public water supply;
- Substantially degrade or deplete ground water resources;
- Interfere substantially with ground water recharge;
- Disrupt or adversely affect a prehistoric or historic archaeological site or a property of historic or cultural significance to a community or ethnic or social group; or a paleontological site except as a part of a scientific study;
- Induce substantial growth or concentration of population;
- Cause an increase in traffic which is substantial in relation to the existing traffic load and capacity of the street system;
- Displace a large number of people;
- Encourage activities which result in the use of large amounts of fuel, water, or energy;
- Use fuel, water, or energy in a wasteful manner;
- Increase substantially the ambient noise levels for adjoining areas;
- Cause substantial flooding, erosion, or siltation;
- Expose people or structures to major geologic hazards;
- Extend a sewer trunk line with capacity to serve new development;
- Substantially diminish habitat for fish, wildlife, or plants;
- Disrupt or divide the physical arrangement of an established community;
- Create a potential public health hazard or involve the use, production, or disposal of materials which pose a hazard to people or animal or plant populations in the area affected;
- Conflict with established recreational, educational, religious, or scientific uses of the area;
- Violate any ambient air quality standard, contribute substantially to an existing or projected air quality violation, or expose sensitive receptors to substantial pollutant concentrations;
- Convert prime agricultural land to non-agricultural use or impair the agricultural productivity of prime agricultural land;
- Interfere with emergency response plans or emergency evacuation plans.

Stronger Than NEPA. Compared to the federal law, CEQA places a higher value on environmental protection when it conflicts with economic growth. NEPA requires federal agencies to "consider" adverse environmental impacts, while CEQA requires agencies to *implement* feasible mitigation measures or alternatives for projects that will otherwise cause significant adverse impacts. Project modification is not required where it is infeasible, however.

Unavoidable Adverse Effects. Sometimes a project has significant impacts that cannot be or are not mitigated. The agency may nevertheless approve the project by making a "statement of overriding considerations" setting forth specific reasons why the project's benefits outweigh its "unavoidable adverse environmental effects." The most important overriding consideration is usually housing. CEQA itself refers to "protection of the environment, *consistent with* the provision of a decent home and suitable living environment for every Californian"—the official state housing policy.

PROPOSITION 65: SAFE DRINKING WATER AND TOXIC ENFORCEMENT ACT, 1986

The Safe Drinking Water and Toxic Enforcement Act of 1986 is contained in the Health and Safety Code, Chapter 6.6, §25249. It is commonly known as Proposition 65, the number under which it was carried as a ballot initiative in November 1986. The Department of Health Services of the State of California is the principal agency enforcing this act.

Summary — This law is intended to assure that the business community does not expose individuals to harmful chemicals without first giving clear and reasonable warning, nor discharge such chemicals into drinking water. There are certain allowable exceptions to these provisions. The Governor is to publish lists of the chemicals designated. The bill further requires government employees who obtain information about illegal discharges of hazardous waste materials to disclose this information to the local Board of Supervisors and health officer.

Warnings — Health hazards to the general public (invitees) are posted in places of business warning of microwave use, gasoline fumes, smoking on the premises, etc. Warnings are also published in newspapers of general circulation of the existence of hazardous materials at business locations such as aircraft factories and chemical manufacturers, and mailed with utility bills.

Cancer Producing Chemicals. The law applies specifically to chemicals that are "known to the state to cause cancer or reproductive toxicity," "in the opinion of the state's qualified experts" or by virtue of an agency of the state or federal government formally requiring the chemical to be labeled or identified as causing cancer or reproductive toxicity.

Exemptions. There is a grace period subsequent to a chemical's being identified as hazardous: twenty months for discharge into drinking water, and twelve months for issuing warnings. Other exemptions depend on proof that the discharged chemical will not enter any source of drinking water and that even 1000 times the actual exposure to the substance will not harm reproductive capacity or cause cancer. Burden of proof is on the discharger.

INITIATIVE PROPOSITION 65

The people of California find that hazardous chemicals pose a serious potential threat to their health and well-being, that state government agencies have failed to provide them with adequate protection, and that these failures have been serious enough to lead to investigations by federal agencies of the administration of California's toxic protection programs. The people therefore declare their rights:

(a) To protect themselves and the water they drink against chemicals that cause cancer, birth defects, or other reproductive harm.

(b) To be informed about exposures to chemicals that cause cancer, birth defects, or other reproductive harm.

(c) To secure strict enforcement of the laws controlling hazardous chemicals and deter actions that threaten public health and safety.

(d) To shift the cost of hazardous waste cleanups more onto offenders and less onto law-abiding taxpayers.

The people hereby enact the provisions of this initiative in furtherance of these rights.

CHAPTER 6.6
SAFE DRINKING WATER AND TOXIC ENFORCEMENT ACT OF 1986

25249.5. Prohibition on Contaminating Drinking Water. No person in the course of doing business shall knowingly discharge or release a chemical known to the state to cause cancer or reproductive toxicity into water or onto or into land where such chemical passes or probably will pass into any source of drinking water.

25249.6. Required Warning. No persons in the course of doing business shall knowingly and intentionally expose any individual to a chemical known to the state to cause cancer or reproductive toxicity without first giving clear and reasonable warning.

25249.7. Enforcement.

(a) Any person violating or threatening to violate Section 25249.5 or Section 25249.6 may be enjoined in any court of competent jurisdiction.

(b) Any person who has violated Section 25249.5 or Section 25249.6 shall be liable for a civil penalty not to exceed $2500 per day for each such violation in addition to any other penalty established by law.

(c) Actions pursuant to this section may be brought by the Attorney General in the name of the people of the State of California or by any district attorney or by any city attorney of a city having a population in excess of 750,000, prosecutor in any city or city and county having a full-time city prosecutor, or as provided in subdivision (d).

(d) Actions pursuant to this section may be brought by any person in the public interest if . . . neither the Attorney General nor any district attorney nor any city attorney or prosecutor has commenced and is diligently prosecuting an action against such violation.

25249.8 List of Chemicals Known to Cause Cancer or Reproductive Toxicity.

(a) On or before March 1, 1987, the Governor shall cause to be published a list of those chemicals known to the state to cause cancer or reproductive toxicity within the meaning of this chapter, and he shall cause such list to be revised and republished in light of additional knowledge at least once per year thereafter.

(b) A chemical is known to the state to cause cancer or reproductive toxicity within the meaning of this chapter if in the opinion of the state's qualified experts it has been clearly shown through scientifically valid testing according to generally accepted principles to cause cancer or reproductive toxicity, or if a body considered to be authoritative by such experts has formally identified it as causing cancer or reproductive toxicity, or if an agency of the state or federal government has formally required it to be labeled or identified as causing cancer or reproductive toxicity.

(c) On or before January 1, 1989, and at least once per year thereafter, the Governor shall cause to be published a separate list of those chemicals that at the time of publication are required by state or federal law to have been tested for potential to cause cancer or reproductive toxicity but that the state's qualified experts have not found to have been adequately tested as required.

(f) **"Warning"** within the meaning of Section 25249.6 need not be provided separately to each exposed individual and may be provided by general methods such as labels on consumer products, inclusion of notices in mailings to water customers, posting of notices, placing notices in public news media, and the like, provided that the warning accomplished is clear and reasonable. In order to minimize the burden on retail sellers of consumer products including foods, regulations implementing Section 25249.6 shall to the extent practicable place the obligation to provide any warning materials such as labels on the producer or packager rather than on the retail seller, except where the retail seller itself is responsible for introducing a chemical known to the state to cause cancer or reproductive toxicity into the consumer product in question.

(d) **Penalties**. The court shall also impose upon a person convicted of violating subdivision (b) or (c) a fine of not less than $5,000 or more than $100,000 for each day of violation. If the act which violated subdivision (b) or (c) caused great bodily injury or caused a substantial probability that death could result, the person convicted of violating subdivision (b) or (c) may be punished by imprisonment in the state prison for up to 36 months, in addition to the term specified in subdivision (b) or (c), and may be fined up to $250,000 for each day of violation.

Section 4. . . . (b) Any designated government employee who obtains information in the course of his official duties revealing the illegal discharge or threatened illegal discharge of a hazardous waste within the geographical area of his jurisdiction and who knows that such discharge or threatened discharge is likely to cause substantial injury to the public health or safety must, within seventy-two hours, disclose such information to the local Board of Supervisors and to the local health officer.

(c) . . . The felony conviction for violation of this section shall require forfeiture of government employment within thirty days of conviction.

(d) Any local health officer who receives information pursuant to subdivision (b) shall take appropriate action to notify local news media and shall make such information available to the public without delay.

Section 5. (a) All civil and criminal penalties collected pursuant to this chapter shall be apportioned in the following manner:

(1) Fifty percent shall be deposited in the Hazardous Substance Account in the General Fund.

(2) Twenty-five percent shall be paid to the office of the city attorney, city prosecutor, district attorney, or Attorney General, whichever office brought the action, or in the case of an action brought by person, to such person.

(3) Twenty-five percent shall be paid to the department and used to fund the activity of the local health officer to enforce the provisions of this chapter.

Other Toxics Legislation: California Superfund The California Environmental Superfund Act of 1981 is found in Chapter 7 of the California Health and Safety Code, §§25370-25382. It is California's equivalent to the federal government's Resource Conservation and Recovery Act (RCRA), and establishes an environmental superfund for cleaning up polluted sites within the state. The principal agent of enforcement is the California Environmental Protection Agency with assistance from other state and local agencies. Enforcement may be initiated in various ways, including citizen complaints that hazardous materials or pollutants are being handled in an unsafe manner. Violators may be subject to fines or imprisonment.

BUILDING STANDARDS

Minimum building standards for structures in California are found in Title 24 of the Code of Regulations. Regulation of building practices became widely accepted with the Minimum Property Standards established by the Federal Housing Administration in the mid-1930s. Most states and municipalities have based their local building codes upon FHA's minimum property standards, with modifications to meet the particular needs of the locale. In California, major changes to the building codes were made after the Long Beach earthquake of 1933, and modifications are regularly made as more is learned from subsequent quakes and other disasters. Codes are also updated to reflect changes in national model codes, such as the Uniform Building Code of the International Conference of Building Officials, and progress in technology. Los Angeles had a thirteen story height limit for many years due to concern for earthquake damage. It was not until the rocker form of foundation was perfected that building officials felt safe in approving structures above that height. Title 24 deals with structural integrity for all classifications of structures erected throughout the state. (Popular use of the term "Title 24" refers to its energy conservation provisions: see Course 5.) Title 24 is organized as follows:

Part One: Building Standards Commission This commission includes the Secretary of State and Consumer Services Agency, and ten appointed members representing the public, design professions, the building and construction industry, local government, building officials, fire and safety officials, and labor. All changes to building codes are reviewed by this commission. Criteria for adoption include finding that the proposed standard is in the public interest, is not unreasonable or capricious, and is cost effective based on overall benefits. The commission publishes bound editions of the code in its entirety every three years, and annual supplements and emergency supplements in between.

Part Two: State Building Code This section of Title 24 is the model building code that municipalities and counties can adopt and modify to meet their needs. The definition of an environmentally safe, secure, and habitable structure is set out through detailed description of structural components and design features. Ninety-three chapters deal with specific construction techniques as well as administrative matters.

 ☐ *Chapter 1*. This chapter sets out administrative procedures as well as the purpose of the code, promoting public health and safety. It also deals with OSHA (Occupational Safety and Health Administration) matters.

 ☐ *Chapter 5*. This chapter deals with maximum floor areas, building heights, health and safety apparatus (toilets, fire alarms, etc.), handicapped access, building components and structural systems (outlined in detail in the remaining chapters), and turning radii for everything from wheelchairs in halls to automobiles in parking areas. Underlying each regulation is the concern that the structure is not only suitable for the purpose intended, but safe and secure for human habitation.

- *Chapters 6 through 93.* Each chapter covers a specific occupancy—agricultural, residential, retail, office, industrial, or special purpose, public as well as private. Health and safety matters such as explosives, radiation, fire protection, exiting, energy conservation, protective signaling systems, ventilation, and the like are addressed.

Part Three: State Electrical Code — Improper wiring is one of the main causes of costly and deadly fires. This segment establishes standards for both rough electrical in the construction phase and finished electrical systems qualified for a certificate of occupancy from local building authorities. Most local authorities have adopted the National Electrical Code of the National Fire Protection Association.

Part Four: State Mechanical Code — This section covers heating, ventilating, and cooling equipment used in any structure. Standards are established for refrigeration equipment, incinerators, and heat producing appliances, with special attention to mechanical systems for hospitals and other health care facilities. Increasing attention is being given to how these systems affect air quality. The uniform code in this area is the Uniform Mechanical Code of the International Conference of Building Officials and the International Association of Plumbing and Mechanical Officials.

Part Five: State Plumbing Code — In many instances the same subcontractor provides the mechanical system and the plumbing system. The plumbing code covers materials standards, drainage systems, vents and venting, indirect waste piping, wet vented systems and special wastes, traps and interceptors, joints and connections, plumbing fixtures, water distribution, building sewers, fuel gas piping, water heaters and vents, requirements for the physically handicapped, unfired pressure vessels (storage tanks and the like), service piping for welding and cutting, and rain water systems. Potential for toxics entering sewage and waste disposal systems is high, either through human misuse or design malfunction. The integrity of plumbing systems is essential for health and safety.

Part Six: Special Building Requirements — This portion covers structures that have special requirements due to the intensity of occupancy. The following types of structures are considered, usually with special attention to ventilation and life safety.

- Agricultural buildings
- Educational buildings
- Places of employment
- Local detention facilities
- Schools of cosmetology
- Health facilities
- Public safety
- Public works (public school buildings and access to public buildings by the physically handicapped)
- Housing.

State & Local Environmental Legislation

Part Seven: Elevator Safety Regulations

Equipment safety rules and inspection procedures are established not only for building elevators, but for escalators, hoistways (like the Palm Springs Tramway), freight elevators, hand elevators, moving walks, freight platform hoists, hand powered platforms, manlifts, and other similar devices.

Part Eight: State Historical Building Code

Designated historical buildings are eligible for special treatment under the State Historical Building Code (SHBC). In making repairs, alterations, and additions necessary for the preservation, restoration, rehabilitation, moving, or continued use of a historical building or structure, certain departures from current codes are allowed.

Purpose. The principle is that the intent of a building code—protecting the health and safety of the occupants—may be met on the historic building's own terms. There must be a good historical reason for any departures. As an extreme example, adobe is not an acceptable building material today, but adobe structures that are still standing can be maintained in kind, and need not be replaced in modern materials. (Actually the thickness of adobe walls created a very comfortable and energy-efficient interior environment.)

Use. Currently the greatest interest in the SHBC is likely to be for seismic work on unreinforced masonry (URM) buildings. The SHBC is interpreted and applied by the local building official and a State Historical Building Safety Board. The ability to use the SHBC can be an economic advantage.

Local Building Ordinances

Any local authority may establish building standards stricter than the underlying state law. Throughout the state, local authorities have expanded their building codes to areas of local concern.

Examples. In the City of Los Angeles a variety of requirements apply prior to the transfer of residential property. A 9A report is required showing the approved permitted use for the property and subsequent permits for alterations or additions. Water saving devices are required on toilets and showers. These items must be retrofitted prior to close of escrow, as must a hard wire smoke detector. (Most counties now require smoke detectors in all structures, but some allow battery operated models.) All sliding glass doors to the outside must have shatterproof glass. Each county and municipality throughout the state has similar but individual retrofit ordinances.

Environmental Concerns. Requirements continue to evolve on the basis of experience, particularly with regard to earthquake and fire, and energy and water conservation. One requirement being considered in some jurisdictions is fire sprinklers in single family residences. Cities including Los Angeles have passed ordinances requiring owners of unreinforced masonry buildings to retrofit those buildings to withstand a 5.0 magnitude earthquake.

Responsibility to Investigate. The real estate licensee should be aware of local retrofit ordinances and verify that the existing improvements are in compliance with local building codes. With older buildings, it is important to find out whether structural modifications will trigger requirements for updating the plumbing, electrical, and mechanical systems of the structure.

HISTORICAL RESOURCES

In addition to the National Register of Historic Places and the State Historical Building Code, various state and local laws and programs exist to recognize and protect historical resources.

State Office of Historic Preservation The State Office of Historic Preservation (OHP), headed by the State Historic Preservation Officer (SHPO), is the state agency most directly responsible for formulating and implementing preservation policies. Appointed by the Governor, the SHPO administers the state's historic preservation program, defined under the National Historic Preservation Act of 1966. The State Office is a division within the Department of Parks and Recreation.

Historical Resources Commission The State Historical Resources Commission, with seven members appointed by the Governor, is responsible for evaluating applications and recommending resources for listing on the National Register, the State Historic Landmarks program, and State Points of Historical Interest. Under the Public Resources Code it is charged with conducting a statewide inventory of historic resources, establishing criteria for evaluating historic resources, and developing a statewide historic resources plan.

State Landmark Programs The State Historical Landmarks program was created in 1931 to designate California Registered Historical Landmarks. These are structures and sites with regional and statewide significance to the history of California. Other designations are State Point of Historical Interest (of local rather than statewide significance), and the newly created State Register of Historic Resources, which will bring together properties identified under various state, federal, and local designation programs, and give them consistent treatment under CEQA.

Incentives Since the mid-1970s various state and federal tax incentives have been enacted to encourage the preservation, and rehabilitation of significant buildings and neighborhoods. Most current federal and state incentive programs are designed for commercial properties. They have been successfully used in the renovation of older office buildings and reuse of abandoned warehouses and factories. In contrast, there are few financial incentives to restore or preserve historically or architecturally significant homes.

Mills Act. The Mills Act (California Government Code §50280 et seq.) a property tax reduction in exchange for a twenty-year contract with the local government requiring restoration of the property, maintenance of its historic characteristics, and a certain amount of public access. It has been little used. The Mills Act is the only state tax incentive, except for income tax deductions from donations of easements, which applies to historic single family homes.

Marks Historical Rehabilitation Act of 1976. The Marks Act authorizes general law cities to issue tax exempt revenue bonds for rehabilitation of historic buildings. They must designate a rehabilitation area and adopt criteria for the selection of eligible properties. The cities can create below market financing rates by selling tax exempt securities (secured by specific project revenues) for the purpose of assisting historic rehabilitation.

State Historical Building Code. Use of this alternative code can often save money by making it unnecessary to bring the building into conformity with current code, as long as it meets life safety requirements on its own terms.

Regulations **State.** The SHPO has major responsibility for reviewing California projects under CEQA and Section 106 of the National Historic Preservation Act. The State Historical Resources Commission determines National Register eligibility, the usual trigger for CEQA and Section 106 review.

Local. Most of the actual regulations on what an owner (or government) can do with a historic property are enacted at the local level, in a variety of landmarks or preservation ordinances and design review ordinances which are as diverse as the communities in California.

- *Similarities.* Most ordinances generally parallel state and federal legislation, with some means of identifying resources the community believes to have historic value, and some means of recognizing and, usually, protecting them. (Typical protection is design review of major alterations, and a few months' to a year's delay of demolition in order to seek alternative uses for the structure.) Most ordinances are administered by a board or commission of interested citizens (often political appointees), with support from the local planning or building department.

- *Differences.* Ordinances vary considerably with the communities' size, age, values, and political and economic climate. Criteria for landmark designation may follow the National Register exactly, or they may be different in order to recognize particular local values. The effects of designation may be purely honorific and commemorative (plaques on sites of past events or vanished structures), or they may extend to a virtual prohibition on demolition, as for certain structures in San Francisco. Developers who work in more than one city often find the variety of ordinances baffling.

- *Efforts Toward Consistency.* The State Office of Historic Preservation has issued a "Model Cultural Resources Management Ordinance for California Cities and Counties," with recommended language from statement of purpose to appeals and penalties. The State Office also operates a Certified Local Government program, for communities whose ordinances meet the State Office's standards and whose commissioners are professionally qualified in history, architecture, and related fields.

SUBDIVISION CONTROLS: STATE LAWS

Subdivision means, generally, division of a large tract of land into lots or parcels for sale to the public. Extensive land use and consumer protection regulations govern subdivisions in California, as a result of frauds and abuses during the early development and expansion of cities in this state.

The Subdivided Lands Act The Subdivided Lands Act is contained in the Business and Professions Code, §§11000-11202, and was enacted in 1933. Administered by the Real Estate Department, it is designed to prevent fraud and to protect buyers. The Real Estate Commissioner inquires not only into fundamental physical characteristics of subdivisions, but also into matters of title, financing, handling of purchasers' deposit money, and methods of conveying the interests contracted for.

Subdivision Defined. Subdivisions are defined in this law as improved or unimproved land or lands divided, or proposed to be divided, for sale, lease, or financing, immediate or future, into five or more lots or parcels of less than 160 acres each (unless sold or leased for oil or gas rights), or five or more undivided interests in a parcel or parcels of any size. Special provisions apply to condominium projects and other types of cooperative ownership.

Standard Subdivisions. Standard subdivisions are the most common type. Unimproved lots are offered with utilities installed. Lots are bought by individuals building their own homes and by building contractors who may purchase a number of lots. Many subdividers construct the dwellings themselves, offering house and lot packages complete with financing.

Other Types. The act also defines and regulates planned developments, community apartment projects, condominiums, stock cooperative projects, out-of-state subdivisions, and land projects. (A land project is a subdivision of fifty or more unimproved parcels, located in a sparsely populated area, offered for sale, lease, or financing for residential purposes.)

Requirements. Before any lots are offered for sale or lease, the owner, subdivider, or agent must file with the Real Estate Commissioner a Notice of Intention to Subdivide, a questionnaire with additional information, and a title report, copy of any trust deed or mortgage on the land, copies of papers to be used in the sale of the land, copy of recorded maps, and copies of any conditions and restrictions affecting the lots.

Public Report. The Commissioner makes an investigation and inspection of the proposed subdivision, and publishes a *public report* of the findings. The Commissioner must find that the land is suitable for the use represented by the subdivider. No subdivider may legally offer any lots for sale until the public report has been issued, and the subdivider must furnish an accurate copy of it to each prospective buyer. A *preliminary public report* may be issued if the subdivider has not met all the requirements of local and state agencies but appears certain to do so.

The Subdivision Map Act

The Subdivision Map Act is contained in Government Code §66410 et seq. It is the successor to the Map Filing Act of 1929. It regulates the physical layout of subdivisions and the filing of subdivision maps with the county recorder. While the Subdivided Lands Act looks mainly at title and financing, the Subdivision Map Act's purview includes environmental matters.

Maps. There are two types of map requirements under the act, "tentative and final" maps for the more complex subdivisions creating five or more parcels or units, and less detailed "parcel maps" for subdivisions containing only two, three, or four parcels, or the following situations:

☐ Where the whole parcel before division contains less than five acres, each parcel created by the division abuts upon a public street or highway, and no dedications or improvements are required by the governing body.

☐ Any parcel or parcels divided into lots or parcels, each of a gross area of twenty acres or more, and each of which has an approved access to a maintained public street or highway.

☐ Any parcel or parcels having approved access to a public street or highway which comprises a part of a tract zoned for industrial or commercial development, and which has the approval of the governing body as to street alignments and widths.

☐ Any parcel divided into lots or parcels, each of a gross area of forty acres or more or a quarter-quarter section or larger, as specified by local ordinances.

Areas Regulated: Environmental Concerns. Under the Subdivision Map Act, local authorities have control over the general layout, streets, lot sizes, and improvements including road surfacing, gutters, sidewalks, drainage, water mains, and sewage disposal facilities. They will usually look at the following aspects of the development:

- Property location and physical boundaries
- Topographical features
- Public utility access
- Natural surroundings of the area
- Means of ingress and egress
- Composition of the neighborhood
- Drainage
- Location in FEMA flood zone
- Soil stability disclosed by geological report
- Proximity to known earthquake faults
- Availability of water—in some areas subdividers have to wait in line for subdivision approval because of water rationing procedures
- Dedications of public easements, parks, recreational facilities, or school sites.

Enforcement. Implementation of the Subdivision Map Act is vested in the governing body of each county and city. Enforcement of the act in many instances is delegated to the planning commission of the city or county.

Commissioner's Role. The physical improvement of subdivisions is regulated by the local authorities, and the Real Estate Commissioner does not enforce the Map Act. The Commissioner's responsibility under the Subdivided Lands Act, of informing prospective buyers of true conditions in the subdivision, does include physical aspects, however.

Procedure. The basic procedure for processing a subdivision, as set forth in the Subdivision Map Act, is as follows:

- *Tentative Map*. The subdivider prepares a tentative map and files it with the city or county.
- *Final Map*. After investigation, study, and recommendations by the local governing unit, a final map is prepared, incorporating all changes required by the city or county on the tentative map.
- *Recording*. Certificates consenting to recordation of the final map and offering public areas for dedication are obtained from all persons having recorded interests in the property; the subdivider enters into an agreement with the city or county for the improvement of streets and easements, supported by a performance bond; and then the final map is recorded.
- *Possible Annexation*. If the land is outside the city limits, but annexation is planned, the map may be submitted to the city for approval, conditional upon annexation.

Relation to Local Ordinances. By the express terms of the Map Act, cities and counties are required to have supplemental local subdivision ordinances. Local ordinances have no statewide uniformity and the regulations of each local governing agency must be examined. Most local ordinances are quite comprehensive, and should be studied carefully before initiating any land development program.

LOCAL LAND USE REGULATIONS

Local authorities throughout the state have ordinances designed to protect the public health and safety, and increasingly also the environment. Many ordinances, especially in the areas of planning, building codes, and subdivision controls, reflect powers delegated or mandated by the state. Others are purely local, or distinctive local versions of statewide laws. Examples include water and energy conservation ordinances, shatterproof glass required on exterior sliding doors by the City of Los Angeles, smoke detector requirements, and landmarks ordinances. These ordinances vary from one jurisdiction to another, and are usually administered by the planning departments or offices of building and safety. The prudent buyer, seller, developer, or user of real estate will inquire into local regulations on a case by case basis. It is on the local level that environmental regulations most affect the real estate market.

General Plans   By law every city and county in California must adopt a comprehensive, long-term general plan of development. Each general plan must include at least seven *elements* (areas of concern): land use, circulation, housing, open space, conservation, safety, and noise. Depending on the community's location, its general plan may also need policies for coastal development, protection of mineral and forestry resources, and development within seismic zones. The general plan may also include optional elements such as recreation, historic preservation, and public services. All elements and parts of a general plan must constitute an integrated, internally consistent, and compatible statement of policies for the city or county.

Authority. The general plan is the local constitution upon which all other local land use regulations and programs are based. State law now specifically provides that zoning and subdivision approvals must be consistent with the general plan. A court decision in 1980 established the requirement that city and county public works projects must also be consistent with the general plan, and in 1982 the legislature enacted a law requiring counties to prepare solid waste management plans consistent with the county's general plan.

Format. The format of general plans varies with local conditions, needs, and philosophy. Typically general plans address each of the required elements as follows: (1) background information on the local economy, population characteristics, existing land use, environmental constraints, and public facility capacities; (2) goals and policy statements to guide community development; (3) maps showing the distribution of various types of land uses, population density, and land use intensity; and (4) measures to implement general plan policy.

Preparation and Adoption. A general plan is adopted by resolution of the local legislative body, but state law gives the planning commission major responsibility for preparing the plan and making recommendations for its adoption, amendment, and implementation.

State & Local Environmental Legislation

Specific Plans. Specific plans are a mechanism to implement local general plans. Specific plans combine zoning regulations, capital improvement programs, detailed site development standards, and other regulatory schemes into one document tailored to the needs of a particular area. Specific plans can reduce the uncertainty faced by developers in the review process, since they give details on location of improvements, streets and roads, standards for population density, conservation plans, flood plain or unstable terrain information, permissible types of construction, and transportation facilities.

Zoning

Zoning is the main legal tool for carrying out local general plans. As an exercise of the police power, zoning must be used to promote the public health, safety, and general welfare. The power to zone is delegated to local governments by the state constitution, and state law sets standards for exercise of the zoning power.

Limits on Power. The governing authority of a city or county has the power to adopt ordinances establishing zones within which structures must conform to specified standards as to character, location, and use. Zoning restrictions, to be valid, should be substantially related to the protection of public health, safety, morals, and general welfare. They must be uniform, not discriminatory nor created for the benefit of any particular group. Public authorities may enjoin or abate improvements or alterations which are in violation of a zoning ordinance.

Relation to General Plan. State law specifically requires that zoning be consistent with the objectives, policies, general land uses, and programs specified in the general plan, and sets out procedures for citizens to seek legal remedies for local government non-compliance.

Content of Ordinances. State law specifies in very general terms the types of zoning ordinances that may be enacted. Most ordinances specify the following for each zone: permitted uses, uses allowed with a conditional use permit, minimum parcel size, height limits, lot coverage limitation, setback standards, and density standards. Zoning laws typically prohibit the use of residentially zoned land for stores, commercial land for manufacturing, etc. Innovative zoning techniques include planned unit development zones, floating zones, inclusionary zoning, and special purpose overlay or combining zones.

Zoning Symbols and Descriptions. There is little consistency in the zoning symbols and descriptions used by local governments in California. The letters R, C, and M or I are commonly—but not universally—used for residential, commercial, and manufacturing or industrial, often in combination with a number indicating density.

Examples. A setback requirement prohibits the erection of a building or structure within a certain number of feet from the curb or street line. This may be for aesthetic reasons, or so that when a city or country widens a street there is no need of condemning buildings. Recently zoning has been used as a tool for promoting affordable housing by requiring developers to devote a certain percentage of a project to housing for low to moderate income purchasers. Other examples of zoning regulations are height limits, landmark designations, and the requirement of a minimum size (such as 5,000 square feet) for each lot on which a single-family residence is constructed.

Rezoning and Variances. The zoning of land may be changed or waived. Cities often undertake rezoning after revisions to their general plans, to maintain consistency with the plan. Citizens can also ask for rezoning. If an owner of real estate zoned for residential use feels that the property would be more beneficial in commercial use, the owner can petition the planning commission for a change or an exception to the zoning law to allow commercial use.

- *Rezoning.* If a change is desired for a number of parcels, there would probably be a petition for rezoning.

- *Variance.* If only a single lot is involved, the owner would probably ask for an exception, commonly called a variance, or a conditional use permit. This is a one-time adjustment, not a change of zoning. State law provides that a variance may be granted where "strict application of the zoning ordinance deprives such property of privileges enjoyed by other property in the vicinity and under identical zoning classification."

- *Appeals.* If the petition for a change or variance is refused by the planning commission, an appeal may be made to the local legislative body. If they refuse, recourse may be made to a court of law if the appellant feels the law is unfairly discriminatory.

- *Downzoning.* A highly sensitive area is downzoning, which can reduce the market value of property. This practice has been taken to court throughout the country, and planning commissions have been rebuked in certain cases. However, unless zoning controls can be proven to be arbitrary, unreasonable, or capricious, or to deprive property of virtually all reasonable use, they are generally upheld on the basis of the government's police power to regulate in the interest of public health, safety, and general welfare.

The Planning Commission. Zoning ordinances are enacted by local legislative bodies (usually the board of supervisors for a county and the city council for a city). Recommendations for zoning ordinances are usually given by the local planning commission. Every county is required by law to have a planning commission and every city is permitted to have one. Commissioners are appointed by the chief executive of the city or county (the chair of the board of supervisors or the mayor), with the approval of the local legislative body.

Speeding Up Routine Matters. To reduce the workload of the planning commission and legislative body, many communities have zoning administrators, zoning boards, or boards of zoning adjustment to handle routine permits and appeals. These systems leave the city council, board of supervisors, and planning commission more time for policy issues.

Other Mechanisms
Among other tools available to implement the general plan are regulation of subdivisions, creation of enterprise zones and redevelopment agencies, adoption of tax incentives, construction of roads, water, and sewer facilities, acquisition of land for parks, and park and school dedication requirements.

Land Use Restrictions. Developers do not have carte blanche to convert any parcel to any use in most areas of the country. In addition to restrictions imposed publicly through the planning process, there are private restrictions established by prior owners or developers. In highly restricted areas, such as Rancho Palos Verdes in Southern California and the Blackhawk development in Northern California, plans for any contemplated improvement must be reviewed and approved by an architectural committee.

Example: Carmel's Zoning Code

The self-image a community promotes through zoning regulations might be an urban financial center, an industrial giant, or a residential village. The following excerpts from the distinctive land use code of Carmel, California, illustrate how one community legislates its scenic and artistic character.

Home Occupations. The use of not more than two (2) rooms in a single-family residence by a person residing therein as the studio of an artist, writer, or musician, or by a teacher of the arts having not more than two (2) pupils under instruction at any one time. For the purpose of interpreting this section the arts shall include only the following: painting and related graphics, music, dance, drama, sculpture, writing, photography, weaving, ceramics, needlecraft, jewelry, glass and metal crafts.

Use of houses in the R-1 district for seminars, retreats, business meetings or occupancy or use by persons for a purpose other than providing a place to reside as a permanent resident eligible to register to vote in Carmel-by-the-Sea Municipal Elections is illegal except as otherwise provided in this Code . . . .

Limitations on the maximum allowable height of structures are established for the following purposes:

> *To protect the value and enjoyment of neighboring properties by avoiding excessively massive buildings or buildings which dominate over neighboring structures.*
>
> *To preserve reasonable access to light, air and privacy for all properties.*
>
> *To prevent the inequitable loss of private views or the unreasonable interference with significant public views resulting from excessively tall or poorly planned structures.*
>
> *No building shall have more than two stories.*
>
> *No building or portion thereof shall exceed twenty-four feet in height above existing or finished grade . . .*
>
> *The allowable square footage of floor area for all R-1 building sites shall not exceed forty-five percent (45%) of the total square footage area of the building site . . .*
>
> *No further subdivision of land shall be permitted between the first public road and the Pacific Ocean due to the extraordinary terrain and scenic characteristics of this area and lot line adjustments shall only be allowed where no new building site is created and the minimum lot size is not decreased below 6,000 square feet in area.*

Example: Project Review, City of Palm Desert

The following examples summarize review requirements for development under the City of Palm Desert zoning ordinance. Other localities' procedures and standards will vary. In totally planned communities, such as Mission Viejo, Valencia, Irvine Ranch, Penasquitos, Foster City, or Stanford University's properties at Palo Alto, the rules are laid out in advance. But even in unplanned communities, developers must deal with elaborate regulations and powerful forces of public opinion.

Zoning. Rezoning issues, if the project deviates from the general plan

Building Design. Review of the design for the proposed improvements (new or remodeling) may be perfunctory if the project does not:

Violate the local zoning ordinance.

Vary the lot area requirement by more than 10%.

Involve a reduction of more than 10% of the area reserved for landscaping. (Landscaping and trees are receiving increasing attention in the planning process, due to environmental concerns for clean air, water conservation, and fire safety.)

Increase or decrease floor areas by more than 10%.

Increase the ground area covered by structures by more than 5%.

Environmental Assessment. Depending upon the scope of the project, an environmental impact report may be required, in accordance with the California Environmental Quality Act.

Topographical Information and Maps.

Natural topographic features with an overlay of the proposed contours of the land after completion of the proposed grading. (This is for the purpose of assuring proper drainage and erosion control)

Slope analysis with at least five-foot contour intervals and a slope analysis showing the following slope categories:

10-15%   16-20%   21-25%   26-30%   31-35%   36% and over

Elevation of existing topographic features and elevations of any proposed building pads, street centerline, and property corners.

Locations and dimensions of all proposed cut and fill operations.

Locations and details of existing and proposed drainage patterns, structures, and retaining walls.

Locations of disposal sites for excess or excavated material.

Locations of existing trees, other significant vegetation and biological features. (Certain cities and counties have ordinances regulating removal of certain trees, such as oaks in Thousand Oaks and San Luis Obispo County, and may require that improvements be placed to preserve the existing trees.)

Locations of all significant geological features, including bluffs, ridgelines, cliffs, canyons, rock outcroppings, fault lines, and waterfalls. (Structural integrity may be affected by these geological factors.)

Locations and sizes of proposed building areas and lot patterns, in relation to the topography.

Site Plans and Architectural Drawings.

Architectural characteristics of the proposed buildings.

Vehicular and pedestrian circulation patterns including street widths and grades and other easements and public rights of way. (The project may require easement dedications by the developer to provide access and utilities. The traffic circulation study looks at potential congestion that may be created by the project, and its impact on air quality.)

Utility lines and other service facilities, including water, gas, electricity and sewage lines.

Landscaping, irrigation and exterior lighting plans.

Locations and designs of proposed fences, screens, enclosures, and structures.

Drainage facilities. (Proper drainage is essential not only for the runoff of storm waters, but to assure health and safety.)

Geological Studies. *Reports and surveys with recommendations from foundation engineers or geologists based upon surface and subsurface exploration, stating land capabilities, soil types, soil openings, hydrologic groups, slopes, runoff potential, percolating data, soil depth, erosion potential and natural drainage patterns. Where septic tanks are required, percolating and leaching abilities of the soil are important. Where water has to be obtained from the site, it is important to determine if adequate non-toxic water resources are available from the water table.*

Archeological Studies. *If existing evidence seems to indicate that significant artifacts or historical sites may be encountered, studies should be undertaken in advance, to avoid unexpected and costly delays.*

Other. *Additional information on the project might include:*

Average natural slope of the land (for drainage purposes)

Area of impermeable surfaces (to show areas where drainage into the soil is not possible)

Acreage and square footage calculations (to assure compliance with zoning regulations concerning front, rear, and side line setbacks and minimum lot square footage requirements)

Ratio of open space to total land area (to determine that the improvements comply with site coverage requirements)

Ratio of parking area to total land area (to assure compliance with minimum parking requirements)

Description of maintenance program for proposed development involving joint or common ownership (in the case of condominiums, planned unit developments and the like, common area maintenance as a means of value preservation is a vital issue to planners)

Any other specific information relevant to the applicant's proposal. The unique nature of a project may mean that the authorities require additional information in order to evaluate it.

Regional Programs: Air Quality Management Districts. These are districts established in urban areas throughout the country where pollutants discharged into the air have posed the greatest danger for human health. The duties of these districts are to monitor air quality and advise the general public when particulates in the atmosphere reach critical levels. In Southern California, there is a smog alert system. In addition, AQMDs have required industry to install equipment to reduce the release of pollutants. In Southern California monitoring vehicles patrol the roads and freeways to detect vehicles that emit excessive pollutants into the air.

Redevelopment   Redevelopment is an activity carried out by city and county governments to attract new development, or to encourage rehabilitation of blighted urban areas. By declaration of the Legislature, fundamental purposes of redevelopment include increasing employment opportunities for low-income persons and expanding the supply of low and moderate-income housing.

Structure. Community Redevelopment Agencies (CRAs) are authorized under the Community Redevelopment Law (Health and Safety Code §33000 et seq.) to carry out redevelopment programs at the local level. A CRA is established by local ordinance, subject to a referendum, declaring the need for such an agency in the community. The governing board of a CRA is appointed by the local legislative body and may be either a separate body or the same as the local legislative body.

Powers. The agency can sue and be sued, acquire property by eminent domain, assemble and dispose of property, construct public improvements, borrow money from any public or private source, and engage in a wide range of development activities mandated by redevelopment law. Special financing provisions apply (bonds and tax increment funding), and there are requirements for replacement for all housing units destroyed or removed from the low and moderate income market as a result of redevelopment activities.

Eminent Domain. Eminent domain is the right vested in government to take private property for a public use by paying just compensation. "Government" as used here includes states, counties, and cities, as well as the federal government. *Condemnation* is the court procedure to implement the power of eminent domain. Eminent domain is used for the development of freeways, parks, public buildings, airport extensions, and so forth, as well as for redevelopment.

Compensation. When property is taken for public use the owner is entitled to compensation for its fair value. If the price offered by the government is not acceptable to the owner, the government is obliged to file condemnation proceedings in court. After hearing testimony of the owner's and government's appraisers, the court will determine a fair value and render a money judgment to the owner and award title to the government.

Trends In Land Use   Laws evolve as the economic, social, and political climate changes. In California one can anticipate the following economic and political directions for the future, and can also anticipate that they will have repercussions in state and local regulations.

Redevelopment. Recycling of older urban areas, whether through replacement or rehabilitation of existing structures, is a trend that will continue, as less and less land is available for first-generation development.

Planned Communities. In some areas the trend will be more and larger master planned communities. There the issue of adequate infrastructure is addressed completely and in advance, since transportation arteries, utility availability, and supportive services all fall within the initial planning process.

Intercommunity Planning. Organizations such as the Southern California Association of Governments (SCAG) and Association of Bay Area Governments (ABAG), in which communities combine to coordinate planning, may become more prevalent as a means of survival. Communities such as the Inland Empire and the Antelope Valley depend on connections with other parts of the region in order to exist.

Long Range Planning. Planning and zoning are often based on master plans that are outmoded for their communities. Thousands of acres around the Palmdale Airport in northern Los Angeles County are zoned for industry, with little prospect of such development. When the laws on the books are not relevant to actual conditions, regulators fall back on interim "finger in the dike" methods and the development process becomes unpredictable. The solution is long range planning and regular updating of master plans.

Infrastructure. Roads, water delivery systems, and police and fire services are normally funded by taxation. Since reallocation of the taxpayer's dollars is politically sensitive, infrastructure funding does not always coincide with the actual development of an area. The burgeoning Antelope Valley residential area of Southern California, for example, depends for access to employment centers on the Antelope Valley Freeway—but this freeway is not designed to accommodate rush hour traffic.

Utilities. Water is always a problem for Californians, particularly in recurring drought periods. At such times planning authorities may refuse to issue building permits or allow new sewer connections. Certain areas have waiting lists for water service. Utilities, particularly electricity, have escalated in cost to the consumer due to increased fuel costs and operating expenses. Atomic power plants, such as Southern California Edison's in the San Clemente area, are not likely to provide much relief until concerns over safety are overcome. Since utilities are part of the costs of developing and maintaining real estate, overall affordability is affected accordingly.

Housing Affordability. The most basic economic constraint on any project today is that the intended consumers are having great difficulty getting the funds necessary to acquire or lease real estate. Businesses are attempting to streamline operations by using more part time and temporary workers with no benefits. These practices have reduced the overall average effective wage and driven many who were formerly job holders to strike out on their own. These new entrepreneurs usually begin with a lower level of earnings, and are not favored by increasingly conservative lenders. Median priced homes in many areas of California are only within the reach of 15 to 20 percent of the population. At the same time, government regulations at all levels—including environmental regulations—are often cited as one of the factors driving up housing costs. Course 3 looks at some aspects of this interplay.

HIGHLIGHTS TO REMEMBER

State & Local Environmental Legislation
- Regulations attempt to balance competing demands for land and other resources
- State and local laws may parallel federal laws, or address distinctive local conditions

Public Resources Code
- Divisions on mines and geology, public lands, parks, coastal zones, fish and wildlife, etc.
- Establishes CEQA, State Historic Landmarks, California Conservation Corps, environmental license plate fund

CEQA: The California Environmental Quality Act
- Parallel to NEPA, requires public agencies to study effects of their actions
- Actions include granting permits, so CEQA affects private developers
- Purposes: healthful and pleasing environment, species protection, public-private cooperation, preventing environmental damage by public agencies
- Environmental Impact Report (EIR): presents probable effects of proposed project, ways they might be mitigated, and alternatives to the project
- Applies to all "discretionary" "projects" that agencies "carry out, approve, or finance" with potential for "significant effect" on the environment
- Includes effects on water supply, air quality, energy use, waste, plants or animals, historic resources, population and traffic patterns, noise, etc.
- CEQA requires mitigations, NEPA only requires agencies to "consider" effects
- "Statement of overriding considerations" may find that benefits outweigh adverse effects

Proposition 65: Safe Drinking Water and Toxic Enforcement Act of 1986
- Passed by initiative; preamble saying state has failed to protect citizens
- Covers "chemicals known to cause cancer or reproductive toxicity"; two parts:
    - Warnings of health hazards to public and workers, posted and published
    - Restrictions on discharge of chemicals into water supply
- Civil and criminal penalties; actions brought by prosecutors or citizens

California Environmental Superfund: toxic cleanup, enforced by state EPA

Building Standards: Title 24 of Code of Regulations
- Updated by Building Standards Commission: underlying concern is health and safety
- Sections dealing with electrical, mechanical, plumbing, special occupancies (schools, workplaces, health facilities), elevators
- State Historical Building Code allows certain departures from current code
- Local building codes may be stricter than state code; typical requirements include fire sprinklers and water and energy saving devices
- Local variation means owner or developer must investigate regulations case by case

Historical Resources
- State Office of Historic Preservation (State Historic Preservation Officer) reviews California projects under CEQA and Section 106 of National Historic Preservation Act (public and quasi-public projects)

State Historical Resources Commission recommends listing on the National Register, State Historic Landmarks, and other designations

Benefits: cost savings under Historical Building Code; possible tax reduction under Mills Act contract; Marks Act allows city revenue bonds for rehabilitation

Most regulation is at the local level, through landmark designation and design review

Ordinances vary greatly, depending on community's values, age, politics, etc.

Subdivision Controls

Originated as consumer protection in 1929-1933

Subdivided Lands Act: administered by Department of Real Estate

- Especially concerned with title, financing, deposit money, sales terms, ownership
- Required for divisions into five or more parcels: standard subdivisions, planned developments, condominiums, cooperatives, etc.
- Commissioner investigates and issues preliminary and final Public Report to prospective buyers

Subdivision Map Act: administered by local governing body

- Concerned with physical layout of subdivisions and recording of map
- Tentative and final map required for most subdivisions, less detailed parcel map for under five parcels and certain other exceptions
- Environmental concerns: topography, drainage, flood or seismic zone, soil stability

Cities and counties also have their own subdivision ordinances, usually complex

Local Land Use Regulations

General plans: required by state law, for every city and county

Long-term development plan, with prescribed topics (elements):

- Mandatory: land use, circulation, housing, open space, conservation, safety, noise
- Optional: recreation, preservation, public services
- Depend on location: coastal development, forest and mineral resources, seismic

Local constitution: zoning and other regulations must be consistent with general plan

Practical applications are elaborated in "specific plans"

Zoning: use of police power to promote public health, safety, and general welfare

- Permitted uses, lot sizes, density, setbacks, site coverage, height limits, etc.
- Residential, commercial, and industrial zones; no statewide consistency
- Flexibility through variances, rezoning, downzoning, appeals; administered by planning commission or administrator

Redevelopment

Authorized by state law, to attract new development or improve "blighted" areas

Redevelopment agency (local legislative body or appointees) has special powers including eminent domain and bond and tax increment financing

Special protections for low and moderate income housing supply

- Eminent domain requires just compensation: amount may be determined in court

COURSE 3
LULUs & NIMBYs

INTRODUCTION

Over the past fifteen years or so, people living near prospective public works projects and institutions have opposed them—in many cases successfully—because of their perceived threat to a community's quality of life. Concerns can be environmental (pollution, conservation, preservation) or social and political (crime, public image, moral hazards). This conflict has become familiar under the nicknames NIMBY, LULU, and BANANA. Cries of NIMBY can often disrupt real estate markets. Real estate professionals must understand the issues, processes, and strategies, before they can decide on the most effective guidance to give their clients and customers.

LULU LULU is an acronym for "Locally Unwanted Land Use." It is a land use that a community's inhabitants perceive as a threat to their quality of life. The threat can be environmental, social, or political. Examples include new or expanded transportation, industrial, penal, solid and hazardous waste, power, water resources, and water treatment facilities, and housing for specific populations (low income, homeless, mentally ill). Some communities extend LULU to large residential developments in general, or to any increase in population or activity.

NIMBY NIMBY—the best known of these terms—is the acronym for "Not In My Back Yard," the rallying cry attributed to community residents when they try to stop a LULU or at least lessen its adverse impacts. NIMBY can be an unjustly derogatory term: opponents are often sincerely concerned about not only their own but anyone's back yard, especially when the issue is environment versus development.

BANANA BANANA is a relatively new acronym coined by frustrated and cynical developers to recognize that opposition to certain types of LULUs becomes so severe that proponents cannot build their projects at all. BANANA means "Build Absolutely Nothing Anywhere Near Anything."

NIMTOO In the words of the Kemp report (see below), "Only at their peril will politicians interested in keeping constituents happy discount neighborhood group concerns about preserving the character of the community. The Not In My Term Of Office—NIMTOO—phenomenon is an inevitable offshoot of NIMBY sentiment."

Perspectives and Processes The first part of this course will examine locational conflict issues from the perspectives of facility proponents and opponents, and the processes and strategies for resolving such issues.

Affordable Housing: the Kemp Report The second section presents a recent study, titled *"Not In My Back Yard": Removing Barriers to Affordable Housing,* prepared in 1991 for President Bush and Secretary of Housing and Urban Development Jack Kemp by a national commission appointed "to study government regulations that drive up housing costs for American families" (cited here as the Kemp report). The commission identified federal, state, and local regulations that, intentionally or otherwise, have an exclusionary effect on affordable housing and the people who would occupy it.

Property Values: Appraisal and Discrimination The third section looks at some issues affecting property values, a classic NIMBY concern. In appraisal and market analysis in particular, the real estate professional must confront NIMBY questions, and must present a realistic picture of market attitudes without taking political or discriminatory positions. FNMA and HUD have guidelines for evaluating a property's neighborhood, to help the licensee walk this fine line.

LOCATIONAL CONFLICT ISSUES

This section looks at LULUs as large-scale and quasi-public projects—highways, jails, power plants, public housing projects, and the like—where the developer and the government are either one and the same or operating in concert. On a smaller scale, local governments constantly mediate between neighbors and businesses over such zoning type NIMBY issues as home offices, in-law units, fast-food restaurants, and "adult businesses." A later section will illustrate that governments at all levels can also engage in direct or indirect NIMBYism. When a government, developer, or agency proposes a facility that turns out to be a LULU because it might cause significant adverse impact, both proponents and opponents usually have compelling arguments.

Proponent Perspectives Government agencies and developers argue for the right to flexibility in siting projects with respect to *need, equity, feasibility, burden,* and *acceptability*.

Need. The "need" argument is that communities cannot survive without freeways, rapid transit, industries, jails, waste disposal facilities, power plants, reservoirs, water treatment plants, and housing for everyone. The more we cluster in urban areas, the more we need what some people are going to consider LULUs.

Equity. This argument is that LULUs should be distributed equally among jurisdictions. No community should have them all. There are two problems with this principle. First, some LULUs are less objectionable than others. Is a community more burdened by a water treatment plant or a jail? Second, some communities can better absorb the impacts of a LULU than others. They might even see benefits, if the project brings needed jobs and revenue. This is one reason that some rural communities in California have pursued prisons, and Indian reservations have made land available for atomic waste disposal.

Feasibility. Some types of LULUs cannot be put just anywhere. For example, State of California and Los Angeles County officials have long pursued an extension of the Long Beach Freeway through the city of South Pasadena to the Foothill Freeway. Despite strong opposition, there are few alternatives other than realigning the route in the same general area, or not building the extension at all. A flood control dam can only go on a few reaches of a river. A solid waste landfill cannot go over a ground water basin. If it is placed far out in the desert (as is now being planned in Southern California to avoid opposition in urban areas), transportation costs will increase the amount that every resident pays for disposal services. There are technical, economic, and environmental reasons for siting LULUs in some places and not others.

Burden. This argument is that communities that cause the need for LULUs should accommodate them. Yet economies of scale require large facilities to serve many communities—even a whole region. It makes no economic sense to place a state prison in every community that has produced convicted felons, and few communities can afford their own power plants or waste treatment facilities.

Acceptability. Some projects should probably not be perceived as LULUs at all. One can make a case that "affordable housing" (housing for low-income families, often but not always publicly assisted), for example, can actually benefit a community by contributing to its diversity and ensuring that the people who work in the community can also live there. Halfway houses, homeless shelters, and similar social service programs are often small operations, with little physical impact on their neighborhoods and great social value. Proponents of landfills and prisons argue that technology may now be so sophisticated as to eliminate any public health or safety problems.

Opponent Perspectives

NIMBY opposition arises for reasons of *fear, unfairness, distrust, community image, property values, nuisance,* and *self-determination.*

Fear. Perceptions, correct or not, produce fear for health and safety. Industries, solid and hazardous waste facilities, and power plants can pollute the water and air, prisoners might break out of jail, nuclear plants might leak, and dams might fail—as indeed they have. Housing for low-income, homeless, and mentally ill individuals is opposed with claims that it leads to crime, dirt, noise, and bad influences on children. These are all classic NIMBY positions. Risk assessments can help analyze whether these fears are justified. Developers can apply strict design and operational standards make the risks less significant—less, perhaps, than other hazards that people face and accept. But residents who are afraid and distrustful of government and industry may not accept findings that the threat is insignificant or can be mitigated.

Unfairness or Inequity. "Why me?" This question is the other side to project proponents' desires for equity and communities' assuming their own burden. For facility proponents, "equity" means that LULUs should be distributed equally *among* jurisdictions. Some opponents might accept this principle if they didn't live near the proposed LULU. (No one would seek a LULU for his or her own back yard.) For others, the "inequity" exists wherever the brunt of the LULU is felt. Most LULUs benefit the targeted community a little and a much larger area significantly more: a county, a region, a whole state, or even many states. The targeted community alone bears the burden in increased noise, pollution, danger, or traffic congestion.

Nuisance. People frequently cite noise, dust, odors, and traffic caused by a facility as a reason to oppose it. In many cases these effects can be mitigated or overcome through technology or careful planning: emission controls, soundwalls, limited hours of operation, security devices, and the like, may reduce a project's effects to what federal and state standards define as "insignificant." If it is not possible to reduce nuisances sufficiently, the question becomes whether public benefit outweighs harm to specific neighborhoods.

Distrust. Many citizens are reluctant to believe promises from government and industry. We have long authorized our governments to regulate industry's excesses. But Vietnam, Three Mile Island, Watergate, and the savings and loan scandals have shaken trust in government too. Many communities can recall incidents in which local officials, wrapping themselves in the cloak of the public interest, broke the public trust. So when government and industry say that a proposed facility is safe, will not pollute, and will not lower property values, the neighbors may not believe them.

Community Image. Residents do not want to live in a "prison" or "dump" city. Their community's image is important to them. When most Californians think of Folsom, the image is probably not of a pleasant old town on the American River, but of a state prison. But not all perceived LULUs tarnish a community's image. Water and waste treatment facilities are clean, modern industrial plants. Oil companies have been creative with landscaping and other camouflaging to hide derricks in urban areas. Affordable housing can project a community image of openness and diversity. The image issue is usually most potent in small towns where the facility would be large enough to "define" the community, or in exclusive areas where image is highly valued. It is highly unlikely that residents of the Bel Air section of Los Angeles would accept any LULU, because of Bel Air's prestigious image. Carmel's distinctive zoning code protects its collective back yards against many activities that other communities accept without question.

Property Values. Since most people's homes are their most valuable investments, they fear any LULU that might depress the home's value. It is extremely difficult through market analysis to isolate and quantify the effect of a LULU. Even if homes in areas *with* the facility have different values from homes in seemingly comparable areas *without* it, the quality of a community's schools, transportation, parks, and public services all may affect property values more than the LULU. Comparisons of communities with and without prisons and other types of LULUs tend to indicate that the LULUs have no long-term effect on property values, although there may be a short-term effect when a LULU is proposed or new, because of widespread publicity and the departure of a certain number of households who individually decide not to live with the LULU. This suggests that it is mainly the fear of a LULU, rather than the LULU itself, that depresses property values.

Example

People tend to believe that community residences for special populations (including the elderly, mentally ill, substance abusers, and ex-offenders) will lower property values in the surrounding neighborhoods. A study of eight communities across the country by the Louisiana Center for the Public Interest disputed the belief. Such residences did not affect property values regardless of whether they were in upper middle class, single family, multiple family, low income, white, black, aged, or mixed neighborhoods. (John E. Seley, *The Politics of Public-Facility Planning*, 1983)

Self-Determination. Our community is ours, chosen because of the quality of life that the community offers. Decisions to change that quality of life should be ours, not those of some faraway federal, state, or regional official. But permitting every local NIMBY movement to turn away all LULUs results in a BANANA situation. This stalemate has caused federal and state governments to enact "anti-NIMBY" legislation. California now has laws preventing local governments from arbitrarily turning down affordable housing projects and requiring counties to have state prisons and plans for disposing of hazardous waste. In most other cases, self-determination prevails. Courts accept zoning as a valid local function, and the state legislature is reluctant to interfere.

Processes and Strategies for Issue Resolution

Federal, state, and local legislation establishes the background and ground rules for most NIMBY battles. Within this framework, the processes and strategies for resolving locational conflict issues fall into either the *administrative* or the *political* arena.

Legislative Background Two types of legislation affect NIMBY issues: one type regulating the *siting, construction,* and *operation* of certain types of LULUs, and the other requiring *environmental evaluations* of alternatives.

Siting, Construction, and Operation. For virtually every proposed LULU, there is some applicable federal, state, or local regulation. It is important for people deciding whether to support or oppose a proposed facility to understand what the regulations are. Here are just a few:

- *Housing.* California requires that every jurisdiction (county and city) provide for affordable housing in its general plan. As mentioned above, California law now prevents local governments from arbitrarily turning down affordable housing projects.

- *Hazardous Waste.* Federal laws establish controls on the generation, handling, and disposal of hazardous wastes. Federal and state laws prohibit the disposal of hazardous materials in sanitary landfills.

- *Water Supply.* Federal laws intended to prevent the degradation of ground water aquifers used as drinking water supplies can also prevent locating some types of facilities over aquifers.

- *Zoning.* Almost all local jurisdictions have zoning codes that allocate certain areas to certain uses. It will be more difficult to oppose a factory or power plant in an area already zoned for industry than in one currently zoned residential or recreational.

Environmental Evaluations. Almost every large-scale or government-sponsored project requires some degree of environmental evaluation of it and its alternatives. If the governing body with jurisdiction determines that the project will not have significant effects it may issue a negative declaration, and an EIS or EIR will not be required. There are two basic laws, federal and state, that may require an environmental evaluation.

- *NEPA.* The National Environmental Policy Act (NEPA) requires preparation of an environmental impact statement (EIS) for major federal actions that may have a significant effect on the quality of the human environment. In California, an EIS would be required for a project involving federal funding or jurisdiction. A hazardous waste disposal facility, a dam on a navigable river, a prison, and a water treatment plant are examples of projects that would almost certainly have some federal connection.

- *CEQA.* The California Environmental Quality Act (CEQA) may require preparation of an environmental impact report (EIR). This state requirement applies to all government and private projects that may have a significant effect on the quality of the human environment. The minimum level of environmental review is the governing jurisdiction's determination that an EIR is or is not required.

Definitions. In both laws, NEPA and CEQA, "significant effect" means that:

- A proposed project has the potential to degrade the quality of the environment, curtail the range of the environment, or achieve short-term, to the disadvantage of long-term, environmental goals;

- The possible effects of a project are individually limited but cumulatively considerable; or

- The environmental effects of a project will cause substantial adverse effects on human beings, either directly or indirectly.

Information Value. A LULU's EIS or EIR, if it has one, is the main source of information that people have to determine whether to support or oppose a project. A typical EIS or EIR contains:

- A description of the project's purpose and need;

- A description of the affected environment in terms of physical setting, air and water quality, biological and cultural resources, traffic, noise, public health and safety, aesthetics, and land use;

- A full description of the proposed project and its alternatives (including "no action" as an alternative);

- An evaluation of the environmental consequences and mitigation measures of the proposed project and its alternatives; and

- An analysis of the project's growth-inducing and cumulative impacts.

Reading the EIS or EIR, then is a must. Unfortunately, the typical document for a large project is hundreds or even thousands of pages long. Since Californians most frequently deal with the state process (the EIR) rather than the federal one (the EIS), the term EIR is used in the rest of this course, though the comments apply equally to both.

Administrative: the EIR

A government body (state agency, county board of supervisors, city council, or special district board of directors) ultimately decides whether a LULU will be built and, if so, where. Every government-developed facility requires the appropriation of public funds. Every privately developed facility requires some type of government permit, though not necessarily an EIR. Occasionally, voters will authorize or kill a project through the ballot box. This means that every LULU decision is ultimately political. The first LULU battleground, however, is *administrative*. For the quasi-public projects discussed here, the administrative process is public review and comment on the EIR.

EIR Preparation. In most cases, the governing body with jurisdiction (the "lead agency") prepares the EIR, usually by hiring and overseeing a consultant firm specializing in such work. If the proposed facility is private, the developer will fund the EIR's preparation.

Public Input to EIR. Generally, the public has two opportunities—one early and one late—to participate in the EIR process: scoping and draft document review. After receiving input, the preparer develops the final EIR to present to the governing body for certification (approval).

Scoping. This is a bureaucratic term for the process by which the agency preparing the EIR determines the "scope" of the EIR—the potentially significant impacts to be studied. The initial document may present project alternatives with no preference indicated, or it may include a preferred project plus alternatives. The public has the opportunity, always in writing and usually in public meetings, to suggest potential impacts to be studied.

Effect of Public Input. Theoretically, after scoping the organization studies the suggested impacts and presents the results in the draft EIR. We say "theoretically" because most EIRs are not required to address most of the reasons that people cry NIMBY. Opponents are, therefore, likely to become frustrated and angry when they see the draft EIR months or even years later.

Draft EIR Review. California law requires a 45-day public review period for a draft EIR, although it is not uncommon to extend the review period to 60 days or longer. Normally, drafts go to other public agencies, to selected organizations potentially affected by the project, and to libraries for public review. The preparing agency occasionally distributes a summary of the draft EIR to a broader audience. The public has the opportunity to comment in writing and in public meetings recorded verbatim by a court stenographer. The final EIR (which goes to the appropriate governing body) must contain all public comments and the agency's responses (how it changed the EIR to incorporate each comment or why it did not do so).

NIMBY Issues and the EIR. As stated above, opponents are likely to become frustrated when they find that the draft EIR does not address most of their concerns. Remember the most common reasons for opposing a project: *fear, unfairness or inequity, distrust, community image, property values, nuisance,* and *self-determination.* Usually an EIR addresses only two of them: fear and nuisance.

- *Fear and Nuisance.* Fears normally deal with health and safety concerns, topics the EIR is equipped to handle. Analysts can estimate the extent to which LULUs might increase illness, injury, or crime rates, and propose measures to mitigate the risks. They study nuisances such as increased noise, traffic, and air pollution, and propose ways to reduce them.

- *Inequity.* Occasionally, an EIR will address *inequity* by proposing some type of compensation ("mitigation") for a community housing a LULU that benefits a much wider area. California requires a hazardous waste facility to give 10 percent of its gross receipts as tax payments to the affected community. Other forms of compensation have included building housing, schools, and other community facilities, making cash grants, giving price concessions on utility rates, training and hiring local workers, awarding a significant share of contracts to local firms, and creating very large buffer zones.

- *Other Subjective Issues.* What about opponents' other concerns? The draft EIR ignores *community image* and *self-determination,* which are political rather than environmental issues. In many situations, the draft EIR probably increases the public's distrust of government and industry.
    - It may not deal with most of the issues raised during the scoping process, leading people to call the whole process a sham.

- If the scoping document presented a "preferred" project alternative, the draft EIR still calls it the preferred one, giving the impression that the EIR studies were manipulated to ensure the most favorable designation for the project that the agency "wanted all along."

- It does not describe the *no action* alternative fully, which can lead opponents to exchange their cry of NIMBY for one that the LULU is unneeded, and does not satisfy those who contended all along that the LULU belonged in no one's back yard.

- It calls potential impacts insignificant when residents of the community find them very significant. This difference between the technical and the ordinary definition of "significant" can be particularly troubling, and converts the issue into a political one.

☐ *Property Values*. The NIMBY concern about property values is a complicated question. Since published data are scarce and almost never translatable to the LULU in question, EIR preparers would have to develop figures on a case-by-case basis. Their budgets rarely allow for it. CEQA requires them to examine property values only in relation to potential changes in land use that a LULU might cause in the nearby community. Most EIRs find that land uses would not change, so effects on property values are rarely studied. This too throws the issue into the political arena.

Example

One Orange County EIR looked at this issue. The LULU in question was a jail, and opponents said it would lower the value of nearby homes. The draft EIR concluded that the issue was not an environmental impact as defined by CEQA, but an appendix to the document discussed it. The preparers used published data on jails and prisons in other parts of the country and concluded that this jail would not depreciate property values in the community. Opponents called the data biased and inapplicable. While the opponents lost administratively on this issue, they won politically; the jail project was eventually dropped.

Final EIR Development and Certification. When a land use is seriously unwanted, opponents are rarely happy with the final EIR. Even if it makes needed changes with respect to nuisances, "The project is still a LULU. Don't put it in my back yard!" The governing body then has four choices. It can:

☐ Refuse to certify the EIR, thereby terminating the project and starting over somewhere else;

☐ Certify the EIR but select a studied alternative other than the currently preferred one, causing another group of opponents to cry NIMBY;

☐ Refuse to act on the EIR and send it back to the preparing agency for more study and for negotiation with the project's opponents to see if they can reach agreement; or

☐ Certify the EIR as presented and enter the political process of trying to get the LULU built.

Political Most governing bodies, especially elected ones, want to approve projects that their constituents will support. With highly controversial LULUs, however, there is often not enough room to satisfy all constituents, so decisions are delayed or projects are abandoned. While local officials may publicly resist state or federal "anti-NIMBY" legislation because it erodes local determination, they may secretly support it because it relieves them of responsibility. It is possible that term limits for elected officials will help alleviate this gridlock. On the other hand, there will always be new candidates campaigning on "no LULUs for my district." This situation has produced the acronym NIMTOO: "Not In My Term Of Office."

Balance of Power. While opponents of LULUs often start out with considerable power, they may not be able to sustain it over an unlimited period of time. The effects of doing without the LULU—landfill, prison, housing, etc.—may reach a crisis stage that requires a local governing body to take action regardless of the political consequences, or the state to enact anti-NIMBY legislation. Elected officials and the broader population may begin to see opponents simply as obstructionists, and they may lose their credibility and power.

Proponent Strategies The proponents of a LULU—whether government or private developers—usually employ one or more of the following political strategies:

- Mount a public-relations campaign to increase the size of the proponent base

- Reduce the scope of the LULU to a size acceptable to both sides

- Provide special benefits to the LULU-designated community

- Place the LULU in a sparsely populated or politically underrepresented area

- Sue the opponents

- Seek broad public approval through the ballot box.

Publicity. Astute developers do everything they can to address public concerns and try to remove or accommodate them so that the elected bodies can approve a LULU with general public acceptance or acquiescence, if not enthusiastic support. Many proponents open with a public-relations campaign. The plan is to win over the communities potentially benefiting from the LULU, so they emerge to demand the LULU as long as it is not in their own back yard. This can be a powerful "divide and conquer" strategy.

- *Examples*. Government proponents advertise in the print and electronic media, distribute brochures, speak to community groups, and try to obtain supportive newspaper editorials. Industry proponents add political contributions, charitable donations, and sponsorship of local events.

- *Results*. Success is far from guaranteed. The public is not going to demand a prison or a freeway, even in someone else's back yard, until its need is felt as a crisis, and public relations campaigns cannot simulate such crises, especially with widespread public distrust of government and industry.

Compromise. Reducing the scope of the LULU can be effective with facilities that people do not perceive as threatening their safety, health, or property values. It has been used most effectively with proposals to develop large "communities within communities." Playa Vista, for example, is a proposed massive residential, commercial, and recreational community on the Southern California coast south of Marina del Rey. Public opposition successfully blocked the project proposed by the Hughes Aircraft Company. A subsequent developer, Maguire-Thomas, has achieved greater public support by involving citizens in the planning and reducing the development's size. New community leaders have emerged to demand that Maguire-Thomas reduce the size even further. Reducing the scope of a sanitary landfill, a hazardous waste disposal facility, a prison, or a freeway, is less likely to satisfy opponents. In those cases, a LULU is still a LULU.

Special Benefits. Benefits may be offered as mitigations to the LULU-designated community to offset its burden: tax payments, community facilities, local hiring, and buffer zones have been mentioned above. Other possibilities include insurance programs and land-value guarantees. The latter concept is intriguing, since if proponents believe that a LULU does not significantly affect property values, the cost of a guarantee should be negligible. In practice, proponents seldom offer benefits as a political strategy, but governments and courts may impose them.

Examples

Incentives have been most common in hazardous-waste facility siting. Incentive packages which have been used for other types of facilities include:

- Price concessions on electricity to nearby residents, local worker training and hiring, and awarding contracts to local firms: Electricité de France in France

- Housing, schools, other community facilities, cash grants, and a state severance tax: Black Thunder Mine in Wright, Wyoming

- Payments for community assistance, pursuit of federal grants, and public participation in planning: Trident West Coast Submarine Base in Ktisam County, Washington. (S.A. Carnes et al., "Incentives and Nuclear Waste Siting," R.W. Lake, *Resolving Locational Conflict,* 1987.)

Relocation. For some types of LULUs, moving them into sparsely populated or politically underrepresented areas may be a solution. In the past "politically underrepresented" was likely to mean poor or minority communities, but today these neighborhoods are as politically astute as any others, and "relocation" of a LULU may be to quite distant places.

☐ *Examples.* Faced with overwhelming public opposition to siting needed jail facilities anywhere in urbanized Orange County, agencies proposed a large jail in a rural portion of Riverside County to serve both counties. Since no urbanized community in Southern California wants another sanitary landfill in its back yard, Southern California may be siting massive landfills in its vast eastern desert and transporting the waste by rail. The upscale community of Indian Wells, California, attempted to meet its affordable housing quota by annexing land in an existing lower-income community.

☐ *Practical Limits*. This strategy has not, so far, been successful with hazardous waste disposal sites, since they are unacceptable anywhere (BANANAs). Some surveys have indicated that people are comfortable with such sites only if they are at least 100 miles away. And most other LULUs must be close to the communities that need them. The Long Beach Freeway extension would be of no use in the Mojave Desert.

Litigation. Over the past few years, developers and even governments have taken their frustration at their opponents into court, using the Strategic Lawsuit Against Public Participation—the SLAPP. Most often, SLAPPs are libel or slander suits against individuals and groups; they may also sue for lost profits, cost of delays, and the like. Activist groups have countered with the SLAPP-back—countersuits that, more often than not, allege malicious prosecution. While the courts have yet to resolve several SLAPPs and SLAPP-backs, the trend in recent cases—especially at the appellate level—is not pro-developer. It can be difficult to prove libel or slander against residents who fear for their safety or health. Litigation can be used strategically to delay a project, perhaps until a change in political climate or until the other party gives up. But lawsuits lead to tension, mistrust, and hostility that are difficult to overcome.

Electoral Process. Occasionally governments seek public approval for a LULU through the ballot box, most often because they need citizen agreement to fund the project. One example is the Orange County Board of Supervisors' decision to ask voters to support a bond issue funding new jails in still controversial locations. The voters said no. NIMBY was probably not the issue; more taxes was. At least in the near future, unless there is a LULU crisis affecting a majority of voters, the ballot box does not appear to be a viable strategy for project proponents. However, at the state level, voters regularly pass school and prison and highway bonds, though they may not later welcome the resulting projects in their communities.

Opponent Strategies Opponents usually use one or more of the following political strategies, paralleling those available to proponents.

- Mount a public-relations campaign to enlist others and pressure decision makers

- Challenge the need for the LULU at all

- Lobby decision makers directly

- Sue on the adequacy of the EIR

- Try to change who makes the final decision

- Pursue special legislation.

Publicity. LULU opponents are generally more effective than proponents in public relations since the media often seem to share the public's distrust of government and industry. A public meeting on a controversial issue is usually reported from the skeptical public's point of view. Given this distrust, public relations campaigns mounted by LULU opponents can be highly effective political strategies. This is probably the opponents' strongest weapon, against the proponents' wealth and position.

Questioning the Need. Faced with a probable government decision to build a LULU, opponents may decide to challenge the need for it at all: for example, "we don't need new jails because there are alternatives to incarceration," "we don't need new landfills because we could recycle more of our waste," or "we don't need more freeways because we could use public transit." In the most publicized form, opponents challenging the need for LULUs stage sit-ins to obstruct construction. EIRs are in fact required to consider "no project" as one alternative.

Lobbying. Both sides have been active and successful over the years in lobbying decision makers. In the 1950s through the 1970s the public and its elected representatives usually supported any and all development, because it meant jobs, income, and progress. Today's political environment is drastically different. Now, no one wants a LULU in his or her back yard, and many think beyond their own back yards to their neighbors' and the world's. A whole body of environmental law backs up the NIMBY position. Today, decision makers have to decide whether LULUs solve more problems than they cause or cause more problems than they solve, and both sides are ready to offer advice.

Examples

Lobbying can move decision makers to reject or at least delay LULUs. Environmental disasters such as at Love Canal and Three Mile Island, more stringent environmental laws, more sophisticated data on adverse environmental impacts, and distrust of government and industry have combined to give LULU opponents the tools they need to lobby decision makers successfully.

This is not to say that construction of major facilities perceived as LULUs has ceased. A major new rapid transit system is under construction in Southern California. Los Angeles's new Century Freeway will soon be open for traffic. A dam is being built in San Bernardino County, and construction will start on another in Riverside County in 1995. You can undoubtedly add to this list.

On the other side of the ledger is the fact that opponents have been successful enough in lobbying to delay many projects. No one is building hazardous waste disposal facilities. Orange County does not have new jails after more than five years of planning. A jail in the City of Los Angeles was rejected in favor of a remote site in the Antelope Valley—with much planning still to be done. The Ventura County Board of Supervisors has not acted on a new private sanitary landfill after more than five years of planning and the developer's expenditure of at least $10 million. Maguire-Thomas thought it had an approved plan for its Playa Vista development in Los Angeles, but opponents have garnered political support that could lead to further downsizing.

At times, a developer walks away from a project because continuing to fight for it is just too costly. One classic case in 1977 involved Dow Chemical Company withdrawing its proposal to develop a $500 million petrochemical plant employing 1,000 people northeast of San Francisco, in the face of opposition from environmental groups and regulatory agencies. Dow spent $4.5 million unsuccessfully trying to obtain 65 government approvals necessary for the project.

Litigation. Since the early 1970s, one of the most effective strategies has been to sue the governing body certifying the EIR on the adequacy of the final document, charging that it fails to meet CEQA requirements. This strategy delays development of the LULU at least until the court rules. If the court rules in the opponents' favor, then the EIR process must be reopened to correct the deficiencies. In some cases the delay alone—which costs the developer money—has been enough to kill the project. Opponents are less likely to win in court today than earlier because over the past twenty years the courts have fairly well defined what makes an EIR adequate, and EIR preparers have learned from the court decisions. While they still expect to be sued on LULUs, one of their objectives is to prepare an EIR that will withstand all legal challenges.

Example

This example illustrates what seems to be a trend in how California courts are dealing with NIMBY lawsuits. In *Citizens of Goleta Valley vs. Board of Supervisors* (SO13629), the California Supreme Court ruled that Santa Barbara County did not have to include in its EIR on a proposed hotel an evaluation of alternative sites not owned by the hotel developer.

While the court did not make its rule absolute for all future developments, it did serve notice that LULU opponents could no longer count on the courts supporting them in delaying or stopping a project because its EIR did not discuss all conceivable alternatives.

Electoral Process. Opponents can also try to change who makes the decision. Many a politician has been elected, recalled, or not reelected because of NIMBY issues. Another method is to convince or force the governing body to put the LULU to a vote of the people. The initiative process has become a powerful electoral tool. The 1972 statewide Coastal Zone initiative has successfully controlled development along 1,264 miles of California's coastal shoreline. Initiatives have also been used at the local level. Several years ago Walnut Creek citizens adopted a growth-control initiative. However, the California Supreme Court invalidated this initiative by calling it a zoning ordinance in violation of Walnut Creek's pro-growth general plan (*Lesher vs. Walnut Creek*).

Special Legislation. A creative approach is to seek state or local legislation that seemingly bans all projects of a given type, but actually is directed against a specific project because it is the only one with the stated characteristics. A number of years ago the California Legislature considered a bill that would have prohibited construction of any jail within a specified distance of a major amusement park and a sports complex. Curiously, only one proposed jail in the entire state met the criteria: one near Disneyland and Anaheim Stadium. The legislation died, but the jail was never built. On a smaller scale at the local level, parking requirements are a common indirect way to restrict businesses and accessory housing units.

Bringing Proponents and Opponents Together

LULU, NIMBY, BANANA, and NIMTOO situations have created such a crisis in siting certain types of facilities that a new "conflict resolution" strategy has emerged. Conflict resolution employs negotiation techniques to ensure that all parties are satisfied ("win-win") rather than having one party win and the other lose ("win-lose"). In about a thousand cases a year across the country, proponents and opponents are employing independent mediators to help them reach consensus. In many more situations, the parties themselves are successfully employing conflict resolution strategies to reach "win-win" agreements. There is substantial literature that provides detailed guidance on how to pursue "win-win" solutions in LULU cases. The key ingredients to successful conflict resolution, with or without a mediator, are the following:

- Involvement of representatives of all parties who have the power to affect the ultimate agreement

- Agreement of all parties on the negotiation process

- Agreement of all parties on the problem

- Agreement of all parties to subordinate their individual powers to reaching agreement in the broader public interest

- A focus on interests to be promoted and protected rather than on positions and solutions to be defended

- Openness and full exchange of information

- Each party trusting the others

- Commitment of all parties to abide by the agreements reached and sell the agreements to their constituencies.

AFFORDABLE HOUSING: THE KEMP REPORT

One important use that often runs up against NIMBY-NIMTOO attitudes is affordable housing. A blue ribbon commission of twenty-two experts was appointed by the Bush Administration under HUD Secretary Jack Kemp to study this problem. The committee's findings were outlined in a report titled *"Not In My Back Yard": Removing Barriers to Affordable Housing* in 1991. This section presents highlights of that report.

Regulatory Inhibitions

In brief, the Commission found that "exclusionary, discriminatory, and unnecessary regulations constitute formidable barriers to affordable housing, raising costs by 20 to 35 percent. . . . The cost of housing is being driven up by an increasingly expensive and time-consuming permit-approval process, by exclusionary zoning, and by well-intentioned laws aimed at protecting the environment . . . ." Building codes, taxation, lending practices, wage regulations, and rent control all come in for their share of criticism. In other words, government (at all levels) is here cast in the NIMBY role.

NIMBY Influence   The report finds that local officials, responding to the NIMBY sentiments of their constituents, enact growth controls by limiting the number of building permits issued or imposing moratoria on sewer hookups, or regulate density by imposing minimum lot sizes or zoning only for single-family residences. The commission concluded that the citizens and public officials who exhibit NIMBYism through their support of restrictive regulations ". . . often push aside the compelling need for affordable housing. Instead of dealing with the negative side effects of growth and with infrastructure financing problems, they take the expedient course of declaring their communities off limits to most development . . . [and] invite those households seeking affordable housing to search in neighboring jurisdictions."

Environmental Concerns   The report also makes clear the delicate balance between environmental concerns and other types of public good. It has been criticized as providing ammunition for those who would weaken the Endangered Species Act and other environmental regulations, and for pitting environmental protection and affordable housing against each other with language like "widespread use of environmental protection as a stalking-horse for NIMBY groups."

Recommendations   The report examines the complex interplay of federal, state, and local regulations and grassroots public opinion, and in the large view, sees the solution in "working together: efforts to educate the public, build coalitions, and convince local policy makers to dismantle regulatory barriers." Thirty-one specific recommendations are made for federal, state, and local action. Excerpts from the report follow (edited for continuity).

"NOT IN MY BACK YARD": EXCERPTS

What does it mean if there is not enough "affordable housing"? Most urgently, it means that a low- or moderate-income family cannot afford to rent or buy a decent-quality dwelling without spending more than 30 percent of its income on shelter.

Affected Populations   Middle-income workers, such as police officers, firefighters, teachers, and other vital workers, often live many miles from the communities they serve, because they cannot find affordable housing there. Elderly people cannot find small apartments to live near their children; young married couples cannot find housing in the community where they grew up. Low-income and minority persons have an especially hard time finding suitable housing. Workers who are forced to live far from their jobs commute long distances by car, which clogs roads and highways, contributes to air pollution, and results in significant losses in productivity.

Government's Role   Government action is essential to any strategy to assist low- and moderate-income families in meeting their housing needs. But government action is also a major contributing factor in denying housing opportunities, raising costs, and restricting supply. In community after community across the county, local governments employ zoning and subdivision ordinances, building codes, and permitting procedures to prevent development of affordable housing. They fear that affordable housing will result in lower land value, more congested streets, and a rising need for new infrastructure such as schools.

Regulatory Barriers in the Suburbs

Some suburban areas, intent on preserving their aesthetic and socioeconomic exclusivity, erect impediments such as zoning for very large lots to discourage all but the few privileged households who can afford them. Some exclude multifamily housing. Many communities in suburban Chicago zone out manufactured housing and make use of estate zoning with five-acre lots as a minimum. Homesharing, which would allow elderly homeowners to use part of their home as rental units, is often prohibited by local zoning codes.

Impositions on Developers. Many of these communities are requiring that developers provide offsite amenities such as parks, libraries, or recreational facilities that can add substantially to the housing costs of new homeowners.

Regulatory Barriers in Cities

Any government regulation that adds to the cost of urban housing is especially significant because of the concentration of low-income households in central cities. Regulatory barriers in cities affect both the rehabilitation of older properties and new infill construction. Central-city reinvestment is further complicated by restrictive and racially discriminatory lending practices.

Codes Inhibiting Rehabilitation. Building codes are geared to new construction rather than to the rehabilitation of existing buildings. The codes often require state-of-the-art materials and methods in rehabilitation that are inconsistent with those originally used, for example, wholesale replacement of plumbing and electrical systems that are still quite serviceable.

New Construction. New infill units in some urban jurisdictions are more than 25 percent more expensive than identical units constructed in adjacent suburban localities that allow less costly material and methods. City building codes seldom provide for the construction of "no-frills" affordable housing such as the new single-room-occupancy (SRO) hotels that have recently proved so successful in San Diego. Waivers on code requirements in that city cut the cost of some SRO living units by as much as 60 percent.

Manufactured Housing. Manufactured housing is still frequently relegated to rural areas by local zoning ordinances. Local building codes sometimes mandate modifications to modular units that offset the savings these prefabricated units can provide for infill construction.

Accessory Units. Local zoning regulations often prohibit accessory apartments, which could be a significant source of affordable housing: as many as 3.8 million units could be added to the nation's rental housing supply through this means alone.

Rent Control. Where income from already decaying property is tightly controlled but costs are rising, landlords are not inclined to maintain or repair rental units.

Environmental Protection

Land Supply. Otherwise valuable environmental protection regulations seriously restrict the amount of land that is available for development. This raises the cost of what land remains open for homebuilding.

Delays. Regulations that mandate environmental impact studies increase developers' costs by prolonging the permitting process.

Mitigation Costs. In some instances, developers are required to set aside land for preserves, pay mitigation fees, or undertake mitigation projects (such as creating a new wetland). Recently, in Riverside County, California, the initial phases of creating a thirty-square-mile system of preserves for the Stevens kangaroo rat cost some $100 million. A special impact fee of $1,950 is now levied on each acre of Riverside County that is developed, with new homebuyers bearing the cost.

Bureaucratic Uncertainty. Considerable duplication exists between federal and state regulations, rendering the permitting process for wetlands development unnecessarily lengthy and complicated and therefore expensive. At the federal level, the jurisdictions of the Environmental Protection Agency (EPA) and the Army Corps of Engineers overlap considerably, at times introducing conflicting expectations and requirements into the permit process.

Competing Objectives Part of the problem involves a classic conflict among competing public policy objectives. Numerous federal, state, and local regulations that are intended to achieve specific, admirable goals turn out to have negative consequences for affordable housing.

NIMBYism NIMBY sentiment is so powerful because it is easily translatable into government action. It can variously reflect concern about property values, service levels, fiscal impacts, community ambience, the environment, or public health and safety. Its more perverse manifestations reflect racial or ethnic prejudice. Current residents and organized neighborhood groups can exert great influence over local electoral and land-development processes, to the exclusion of nonresidents, prospective residents, or, for that matter, all outsiders.

Local Autonomy. A long and fundamentally sensible tradition in the United States holds that regulations affecting land use should be promulgated at the local level because that is where their effects are most directly felt. But zealously guarded local control facilitates the translation of NIMBY sentiment into barriers to affordable housing.

Preserving Community Characteristics. In some instances, NIMBY sentiment involves opposition to development projects even though the projects would raise property values. Those who live in historic districts or in scenic, rural areas have often gravitated to such places precisely because of their unique characteristics, and they fear changes brought about by development, even if the proposed development involves very expensive homes.

Maintaining Service Levels. In California the number of lane-miles of congested freeways and highways has been rising 15 percent each year as the road system has used up the excess capacity built into it several decades ago. Daily trips take two or three times as long as they did a few years ago. Many areas are at or beyond the capacity of their water and sewer systems. Schools operate on double and triple sessions. A common response is to reduce the pressure on infrastructure and services by slowing development.

Reducing Fiscal Impacts. Residents' unwillingness to pay for infrastructure associated with growth has been a major issue in many communities. Property taxes have traditionally been the largest revenue source for local governments, but taxpayer revolts in the 1970s and early 1980s resulted in the passage of state laws restricting local governments' ability to raise revenue from property taxes. As of 1985, thirty-one states had imposed property tax rate limits.

Political Influence. Local officials have an interest in satisfying existing homeowners, who vote and pay taxes. Thus the Not-In-My-Term-Of-Office—NIMTOO—phenomenon is an inevitable offshoot of NIMBY sentiment. NIMBY groups regularly participate in the regulatory process at public forums and hearings on development issues, while formidable hurdles discourage nonresidents' participation.

Growth Controls: The California Example

Residents of California are naturally concerned about the effects of population and economic growth. One-quarter of all growth in the United States during the 1980s occurred in California. Foreign and domestic immigrants seek economic opportunity and a better standard of living. The state's $700 billion economy makes it one of the ten largest in the world, and its location on the Pacific rim guarantees its position in the fastest growing trade zone in the world.

Strain on Infrastructure. In many real respects, the quality of life may suffer in communities experiencing rapid growth, through road congestion, overburdened sewer and water systems, unhealthy air quality, and overcrowded school systems. Under these circumstances, the tendency to resort to the quick fix of placing restrictive regulations on development is not uncommon. By the end of 1988, 907 local growth-control or management measures had been enacted in California to slow development.

Loss of Revenue. The Proposition 13 cap on property taxes is not the only reason for local policies to restrict growth; many California communities had adopted restrictive ordinances and regulations before 1978. But limitations on revenue to pay for infrastructure have forced policymakers either to find new sources of financing or to limit growth.

Devices Used. Growth-limiting devices include downzoning to increase lot size and allow fewer housing units to be built; zoning land for agricultural use, removing it from the residential development inventory; placing caps on building permits; and tying growth to the infrastructure needed to support it.

Example

The California courts specifically addressed the question of a city restricting extension of utility service outside its boundaries to achieve growth control when the City of Santa Rosa was challenged by a developer. The trial court upheld the city position that it was not a public utility and, therefore, not required to extend service to noncontiguous development. The court determined that the city's urban development strategy was a valid exercise of police powers.

Zoning

Zoning is intended to ensure that contiguous land uses are compatible by requiring that they conform to a master plan or accepted set of public purposes.

NIMBY Bias. To some extent, the bias against affordable dwelling units was already apparent in the 1926 *Euclid vs. Ambler* case, in which the U.S. Supreme Court established zoning as an appropriate use of the police powers that states could delegate to cities. In justifying the exclusion of apartments from areas where single-family housing dominated, the court in *Euclid* likened their proximity to "a pig in the parlor instead of the barnyard." One amicus curiae brief equated the promotion of public welfare with the enhancement of community property values. Multifamily housing was simply assumed to have a negative effect on single-family property values.

Inclusionary Zoning. Local governments sometimes counteract the exclusionary effects of their own zoning ordinances with "inclusionary" measures. A locality agrees to relax its restrictions on density in return for a developer agreeing to provide some moderately priced units. Inclusionary zoning used as a remedy to exclusionary practices raises issues including equal protection and uncompensated takings. Where it occurs as a variance to a more restrictive zoning ordinance, its use is subject to the inclinations of whoever may be interpreting the ordinance and granting exceptions.

Lending Practices Fannie Mae's and Freddie Mac's underwriting standards are oriented towards suburban, growing, homogeneous, and higher income areas. These standards work against more diverse building types and mixed-use neighborhoods, which are more difficult to assess and to underwrite.

Inner-City Programs. Fannie Mae and Freddie Mac have anti-discrimination and anti-redlining guidelines, but have not consistently followed them. Their charters require that a reasonable portion of their mortgage purchases support the national goal of providing adequate housing for low- and moderate-income families. They have developed pilot programs to purchase mortgages in inner-city, minority neighborhoods, but Fannie Mae, Freddie Mac, and lenders still view these as "special programs" and have not incorporated them into standard underwriting processes.

Community Reinvestment Act. To force lenders to meet their responsibilities, Congress enacted the Community Reinvestment Act (CRA). CRA required that each time an institution applied for a new branch, merger, or other structural change, it had to demonstrate it was meeting the depository and credit needs of its local communities. CRA permitted community organizations to challenge these applications. As a result of these challenges, lenders have agreed to commit additional funds to mortgages in urban neighborhoods.

Results. Through 1990, there have been at least 195 CRA agreements in 63 cities and metropolitan areas and in ten states that have at least one statewide agreement. These activities have produced more than $8 billion in private investment. These agreements have been obtained only through the tenacity of community groups that bring the challenges. The regulatory agencies still remain passive players, too often waiting for community group action.

Commission Recommendations The Commission proposed thirty-one recommendations for federal, state, and local government and private action, directed at reducing regulatory impediments to affordable housing. Highlights include the following.

Federal. The Commission envisions the federal government as a vehicle for stimulating state (as well as local) regulatory reform efforts. The federal government must also set an example by reviewing its own regulatory system to remove or reform those regulations that impede housing affordability.

States. Because states delegate authority to local governments to regulate land use and development, states should take the lead in removing regulatory barriers to affordable housing.

Local. Concerted educational and group actions are needed at the local level to expose the negative consequences of certain regulations, build coalitions for regulatory reform, and stimulate local barrier-removal efforts.

Specifics **Integrate Barrier Removal into Federal Housing Programs.** The 1990 National Affordable Housing Act prohibits HUD from conditioning assistance upon any local policies, no matter how restrictive or burdensome they may be. The Commission strongly recommends removal of this prohibition. It is wrong to provide housing assistance to governments that choose to maintain policies that limit housing affordability.

Make Affordable Housing a Federal Priority. Establish an effective balance between protecting other societal goals and achieving housing affordability.

- A housing impact analysis should be required of every federal agency before it promulgates any major rule or rule revision

- Remove barriers to central city investment and end all discrimination by federal financial regulatory agencies and the secondary mortgage market

- Amend the Davis-Bacon Act, which regulates wage rates in the building industry, wetlands regulations, and the Endangered Species Act, to ensure an adequate balance among social goals.

Protect the Right to Affordable Housing. The federal government should become an active participant in seeking judicial review of excessive or discriminatory development controls and regulations.

- Promote legal review of regulatory barriers through active legal intervention, technical assistance, and participation as a friend of the court

- Encourage development of model codes and ordinances, specifically a new model state zoning enabling act with a fair-share component, model impact fee standards, and model land-development and subdivision ordinance

- Establish a regulatory reform clearinghouse to collect information on state and local regulatory developments, and a HUD Office of Regulatory Reform to assist states and localities

- Build support for regulatory reform in cooperation with public interest organizations, industry groups, and state and local governments.

State Responsibility and Leadership. Housing affordability must be a state goal. States should simplify the maze of state and local regulations, and ensure that regulations meet state goals, with minimum overlap and duplication.

- State zoning reform, with a requirement that each locality have a housing element subject to state review and approval; state authority to override local barriers; and requirements for a variety of housing types and densities

- State subdivision ordinances and standards, which could either be mandatory or serve as a model ordinance for use by localities

- Building code reform to promote uniformity and eliminate obsolete or unnecessary prescriptive requirements

- Policy and funding plans to provide and maintain adequate infrastructure to support affordable housing and growth

- Removal of barriers to certain types of affordable housing options, notably manufactured housing, accessory apartments, and single-room-occupancy.

Success Stories Two California examples, from San Francisco and San Diego, are cited in the report to demonstrate that "just as NIMBY issues can unite a community's residents against affordable housing, so too can common interests unite concerned citizens, public interest groups, private developers, and business people in support of reforming regulatory barriers to affordable housing."

Working Together: Examples

BRIDGE Housing Corporation. BRIDGE is a nonprofit California corporation specializing in building affordable housing. The cornerstone of BRIDGE operations is its development trust fund that generates eight to ten times its face amount in value added to property. The fund operates as a revolving source of working capital. In addition, BRIDGE secures Low Income Housing Tax Credits for corporate investors in its projects; arranges long- and short-term tax-exempt debt financing from state, county, and local governments; and cooperates with private and nonprofit sponsors to obtain community approvals for affordable housing projects.

Between 1983 and mid-1990, BRIDGE projects yielded construction of 2,241 units (1,283 offered at below-market prices or rents), 700 units under construction (484 to be offered at below-market prices or rents), and 1,408 units in various stages of project approval. The combined value of all BRIDGE projects is more than $350 million, with about 60 percent of all completed and planned units affordable to low- and very low-income families. One BRIDGE project combined development by BRIDGE and a private-sector builder with tax credits purchased by a large oil company, which allowed very low rent levels. The project also benefitted from voter-approved exemption from the local growth-control ordinance (including overwhelming voter approval by those in the immediate neighborhood of the project). Other projects include land donations, density bonuses, tax-exempt bond financing, and local rental assistance programs coordinated and implemented by BRIDGE.

SROs in San Diego. Single-room occupancy (SRO) hotels have generally been thought of as run-down, seedy places that are best done away with through urban redevelopment. Prior to 1986, building a new downtown SRO for the homeless and the working poor was unthinkable in San Diego, where tourism was important to the local economy and where downtown revitalization was a top priority for local officials. Between 1975 and 1985, many large cities lost a substantial portion of their SROs to demolition or conversion to other uses. In San Diego, this loss amounted to approximately one-third of all SROs.

Faced with a decreasing ability to provide this type of housing, the city in 1986 created an SRO Task Force composed of representatives from both the public and private sectors, including nonprofit organizations and those representing households who would occupy affordable housing. It set out to accomplish several objectives simultaneously: passage of an SRO-preservation ordinance, adoption by the city of an SRO program, and creation of a constituency for SRO housing so that it would become politically acceptable for the City Council to issue necessary waivers and approvals.

The Task Force worked with a private developer who proposed to build the Baltic Inn because he believed that it was profitable to construct a new SRO hotel. The plan had to be sold to both the business community and public officials, from whom cost-cutting waivers of building, plumbing, and electrical codes would be needed if the project were to be profitable. NIMBY opposition was mollified somewhat by Task Force efforts to inform neighbors that the likely occupants of the Baltic were largely people who could pay their way if given the opportunity to live in safe, affordable housing. Furthermore, low-wage workers could live within walking distance of downtown businesses, which would bolster the dwindling supply of these workers.

The Baltic Inn was completed in early 1987. In July of that year, San Diego adopted an SRO Program, which promoted the construction of more SROs and, in November, passed an SRO Preservation Ordinance. The latter contained a "supply-threshold" formula that prevents further demolitions when the supply of SRO units drops below the threshold. The city provided builders with financial incentives, including reduced water and sewer connection and capacity charges, and low-interest rate loans to underwrite rents for very low-income occupants. San Diego has become an active advocate for new SRO construction. From April 1987 through the end of 1990, San Diego builders added a total of nearly 2,000 SRO rooms to downtown San Diego.

LULUs, Property Values, and the Real Estate Professional

As noted earlier, studies have found little tangible evidence that LULUs, in themselves, disrupt real estate markets. Theoretically almost any use can be designed and operated to avoid or minimize the impacts that people find most threatening. An engineer once said that the technology exists to design and build a dam on top of the San Andreas Fault that would withstand the largest possible earthquake. The main problem, aside from cost, would be public disbelief.

NIMBY cries and subsequent effects, therefore, result mostly from residents' *perceptions* about how a LULU will alter their lives. If people believe that a LULU will lower their property values, then it probably will—at least in the short run. If enough people decide to sell, they will create an oversupply resulting in sales below the earlier market. Speculators may buy the properties at bargain rates and make substantial profits if the LULU turns out to be a good neighbor and property values rise again. If people believe that a LULU will tarnish their community's image, then it probably will—at least in the short run. The greatest difficulty for the appraiser or other real estate professional is in dealing with new or proposed LULUs: later on, the local market will have adjusted to them on its own.

Appraisal Considerations Real estate values are widely held to depend on "location, location, and location." Introduction of a LULU can change the actual or perceived character of a location. Whether in a formal appraisal or in a market analysis, the real estate professional is faced with putting a dollar value on such changes, and guidelines and precedents are sketchy at best, beyond the obvious prohibition that "race and the racial composition of a neighborhood are not considered reliable appraisal factors" (Uniform Residential Appraisal Report form).

Neighborhood Appraisal Factors. The following list of factors generally considered in neighborhood analysis contains many that have direct or indirect LULU/NIMBY potential.

Physical or Environmental		Social	Economic	Governmental
Location within the community	Street patterns	Population characteristics	Relation to community growth	Taxation and special assessments
Barriers and boundaries	Pattern of land use	Community and neighborhood associations	Economic profile of residents	Public and private restrictions
Topography	Conformity of structure	Crime level	New construction and vacant land	Schools
Soil, drainage, and climate	Appearance		Turnover and vacancy	Planning and subdivision regulations
Services and utilities	Special amenities			
Proximity to supporting facilities	Nuisances and hazards			
	Age and condition of residences and other improvements			

FNMA Appraisal Guidelines The FNMA Uniform Residential Appraisal Report requires the appraiser to "provide a narrative description of the factors, favorable or unfavorable, that affect marketability (including, but not limited to, neighborhood stability, appeal, property conditions, vacancy, and rent control)." The appraiser is to summarize all forms of depreciation and acknowledge any environmental conditions that he or she observed or knew about: "Environmental conditions [hazards] relate to any natural or man-made characteristics that are present in, or affect, the subject neighborhood. . . . The appraiser must comment on a hazard's influence on the property's value and marketability and make appropriate adjustments in the overall analysis of the property's value. Since the appraiser is neither expected nor required to be an expert in the field of environmental hazards, . . . information provided by the real estate broker can help the appraiser's determination of the property's fair market value."

Underwriting Guidelines

FNMA offers the following guidelines on neighborhood ratings. Note that LULUs might be relevant to these criteria.

"Our appraisal report forms provide neighborhood ratings that are designed to summarize principal items in a neighborhood that generally are considered important by purchasers when they select a home. . . . The appraiser should explain any changes, either favorable or unfavorable, that have occurred (or are currently underway) if they will affect the marketability of the properties within the neighborhood.

"Appeal to Market. Essentially, this is a summary rating of the extent to which all aspects of the neighborhood will appeal to the typical purchaser in the market. An individual property, by itself, cannot overcome a generally prevailing reluctance of the market to invest in a neighborhood. On the other hand, a relatively weak property in a strong, viable neighborhood is likely to sustain its value, although it still must be carefully analyzed."

FNMA Form 1025. The instructions for FNMA's Small Residential Income Property Appraisal Report contain further comments on neighborhood analysis: "A neighborhood analysis should consider the *influence of social, economic, government, and environmental forces on property values in the subject neighborhood* . . . . The appraiser should collect pertinent data, make a visual inspection of the neighborhood to observe its physical characteristics and boundaries, identify *land uses and any signs that they are changing,* and rate the relative quality of the neighborhood. The results of the analysis will enable the appraiser to understand *market preferences* and price patterns, . . . to determine the *influence of nearby land uses,* and to identify any other value influences affecting the neighborhood. Appraisers should extend their search of the subject market area as far as necessary to assure that *all significant influences affecting the value* of the property are reflected in the appraisal report."

Demographics: HUD Guidelines

In preparing environmental assessments for housing projects, HUD instructs its staff to look at a wide variety of factors, including not only land uses but also the demography and "character" of existing neighborhoods.

Definition. "The physical characteristics of a neighborhood include the quality and type of housing units, commercial, public and social services, its size, location and boundaries. The social dimension or demographic character of a neighborhood is determined by household and population size, density, age, ethnic and minority composition, as well as income, education, and employment profiles. Finally, there is the psychological and social interaction. This refers to the residents' sense of neighborhood, their perceived relationship with their surroundings and others within the neighborhood boundaries, and the strength of their various organizational ties and support systems (formal and informal)."

Assessment Questions. "When considering the project's impact on demography and neighborhood character, the focus of inquiry is on the following questions:

☐ "What are the identifiable neighborhoods within the sphere of likely impact of the proposed project? What are the factors which contribute to the character of the neighborhoods?

- "Will the proposed project significantly alter the demographic characteristics of the neighborhood?"

- "Will the proposed project result in physical barriers or reduced access which will isolate a particular neighborhood or population group, making access to local services, facilities and institutions or other parts of the city more difficult or extremely inconvenient?"

- "Will the proposed project substantially alter residential, commercial or industrial land uses?"

Disclosure In California real estate law, disclosure means an affirmative obligation to inform the buyer of real property about all "material facts" known to the seller or seller's agent, even if the buyer does not ask about them, and even if they are damaging to the seller. Material facts are those which might affect a buyer's decision. Beyond the physical items like geological and structural defects checked off on the Real Estate Transfer Disclosure Statement (see Course 12), there are many gray areas involving information that may or may not be considered material facts; some of these involve NIMBY issues.

Livability. With respect to the neighborhood, "material facts" are not always clear cut. For example, high volumes of traffic at certain times of the day, proposed street or transit programs that could affect traffic, proposals that could increase noise levels in the neighborhood, proposals that could increase property taxes, or a rising local crime rate may or may not need to be disclosed.

LULUs. The presence of, or a proposal for, a perceived LULU similarly may or may not be considered a material fact. Current public attitudes suggest that at least the following facilities, whether existing or proposed, require disclosure as a matter of prudence if not law: new transportation systems, major industrial plants, penal institutions, solid and hazardous waste disposal facilities, power plants, water resources facilities such as dams and flood control channels, water treatment plants, and mental health and drug rehabilitation facilities. The responsibility to disclose proposed nearby housing developments would seem to depend on their anticipated effects on neighborhood conditions such as traffic, noise, and crime. Disclosure is more of a problem with proposals than with existing LULUs, since buyers can see the latter for themselves.

Discrimination Labeling opposition to a project NIMBYism often carries an implied charge of discrimination, an accusation that the opponent is directly or indirectly (through housing, jobs, etc.) opposing not a project but a class or group of people—the poor, minorities, the disabled, etc. When this is indeed the case, a considerable body of state and federal law sets limits to what will be tolerated, and imposes severe penalties for violation.

HIGHLIGHTS TO REMEMBER

LULUs & NIMBYs

LULU: Locally Unwanted Land Use, may be unwanted for reasons of fear, inequity, distrust, community image, etc.

NIMBY: Not In My Back Yard, the bottom-line reason for opposing a LULU

BANANA: Build Absolutely Nothing Anywhere Near Anything, developers' characterization of NIMBY opposition that has reached the point of total obstruction

NIMTOO: Not In My Term Of Office, the easiest way out for politicians reluctant to antagonize NIMBY constituents

Locational conflict issues

With large-scale, quasi-civic projects (highways, jails, housing projects), conflict is usually government/developer vs. neighbors

Proponent arguments

Need: communities cannot survive without utilities and services
Equity: areas benefiting from utilities and services should provide sites
Feasibility: some uses can only operate in certain locations
Burden: economies of scale mean one community will house centralized services for many
Acceptability: objections to some uses are based solely on irrational fears and prejudices

Opponent arguments

Fear: for health and safety, either environmental (pollution) or social (crime)
Unfairness and inequity: one community forced to bear the burden for many
Nuisance: noise, traffic, and odors; can often be mitigated to some extent
Distrust: of government and industry
Community image, property values, self-determination

Processes and strategies for resolution

Laws form the background and ground rules
    Siting, construction, operation:
        Federal laws govern areas like hazardous waste disposal and clean water
        State laws require every local jurisdiction to provide for affordable housing

    Environmental evaluations: CEQA or NEPA may require EIR or EIS (major projects)
        Looks for "significant effect" on human environment
        Provides extensive information on all aspects of proposed project

Administrative processes: public review and comment on EIR-EIS

Public participates in "scoping" and "draft document review" stages of EIR-EIS
EIR usually does not address political and social NIMBY concerns, only tangible nuisances and dangers

Political strategies

Proponents:

Public relations campaign
Compromise on the size of the project
Mitigations: special benefits to the affected community
Relocation: put the project in a remote or apolitical area
Litigation: SLAPP, Strategic Lawsuit Against Public Participation
Electoral process: seek voter approval, especially for funding

Opponents:

Public relations (opponents usually have advantage with the media)
Questioning the need for the project anywhere ("no project" must be considered in EIR)

Lobbying decision makers
Litigation, most commonly on adequacy (or nonexistence) of an EIR
Electoral process: put the issue to a vote, or elect new policy-makers
Special legislation: may obstruct a specific use under guise of a general regulation

Conflict Resolution:
With or without a mediator, to achieve win-win outcomes

KEMP REPORT: BARRIERS TO AFFORDABLE HOUSING
Commission report prepared under HUD Secretary Jack Kemp in 1991

Finds that "exclusionary, discriminatory, and unnecessary regulations" exclude affordable housing projects and drive up cost of all housing

Specific criticism of endangered species and wetland protection, building codes, and NIMBY attitudes

Suburban barriers: large lot zoning, excessive demands on subdividers

Urban: restrictive building codes, rent control, prohibitions on manufactured housing and accessory units

Environmental protection: reduced land supply, delays and bureaucratic uncertainty, cost of mitigations

NIMBY arguments: preserving community characteristics and homogeneity, maintaining service levels and reducing fiscal impacts

Local political processes are biased in favor of residents, against "outsiders"

Growth controls: powerful movement in California, using zoning and subdivision controls

Lending practices:
FNMA/FHLMC standards favor upper-income, suburban type properties
Anti-redlining and anti-discrimination guidelines lack enforcement
Community Reinvestment Act designed to force lenders to support affordable housing

Recommendations:
Federal: stimulate reform at state and local levels
State: review zoning and land use processes to promote housing affordability
Local educational efforts and coalitions for regulatory reform

Successful examples:
BRIDGE Housing Corporation in San Francisco: revolving capital fund, plus advocacy to obtain community approval for housing projects
SROs in San Diego: task force won code waivers to rehabilitate and build new single room occupancy housing

LULUS, PROPERTY VALUES, AND THE REAL ESTATE PROFESSIONAL

Property value is a major concern, but it is difficult to document the effect of a LULU

Fine line between acceptable appraisal factors and discrimination or irrational NIMBY fears

Appraiser must explain changes "affecting marketability of properties within the neighborhood," including "influences of nearby land uses"

HUD guidelines for environmental assessment of housing projects include "demographic/neighborhood character"

Disclosure: Required for "material facts," those that might affect buyer's decision

May include NIMBY issues like traffic, crime rate, institutions

Environmental Issues & Obligations

COURSE 4
Architectural Elements of Energy Conservation

INTRODUCTION

The energy efficiency of a home directly affects the comfort of its owners and the utility costs they pay every month. These factors in turn affect the desirability and value of the home. There are no universal energy conservation disclosure requirements in real estate in California, though there may be local requirements. The primary impact of energy conservation is in marketing properties and advising clients. Licensees who are knowledgeable about energy conservation have these advantages:

- They can recognize existing conservation features that add value and comfort to the home, which are positive points to stress when listing and marketing.

- They can advise clients on which conservation improvements will add value to the home.

- They can point out inefficiencies in a home that affect the operating costs or underlying value of the home, when representing buyers or advising sellers.

- They can inform clients about existing energy conservation codes, and trends that may affect the value of the property in the near future.

This course covers not only common energy conservation measures such as insulation, but the lesser-known architectural features that can dramatically affect energy conservation.

DISCLOSURE AND RETROFIT REQUIREMENTS

There are no state-mandated disclosures regarding energy conservation. Items such as the presence and condition of visible insulation might be included in the disclosure of all "material facts" known to the seller, but they are not specifically asked about on the Real Estate Transfer Disclosure Statement form. There is, however, a trend at the city level to require either that the sellers complete basic conservation measures before escrow closes or that the buyers accept responsibility for completing work within a specified time after closing. The ordinances are typically enforced by the title companies during escrow and by the local building departments after the sale. Licensees should check with city officials and local title companies regarding local energy conservation ordinances.

Residential Energy Conservation Ordinances (RECO) Some cities in California have already passed ordinances that require buyers or sellers to complete basic energy conservation measures. Berkeley's and San Francisco's ordinances are discussed here. Given the political pressure for conserving energy rather than building more power plants, and the growth of transfer disclosures and "point of sale" repairs, more cities will almost certainly be passing similar ordinances in the near future.

Berkeley Berkeley's RECO is one of the first such ordinances, and a model for future ordinances around the state. It is not only instructive as an example of what licensees elsewhere can expect in the future, but also serves as a primer on the "Top Ten" energy conservation items to look for in residential properties. The ordinance includes short descriptions of each conservation project and notes state codes where applicable. (Exhibit 1)

Escrow Closing Date _____ Address of Property _____

Title Company _____ Escrow # _____

Number of Residential Structures _____ Number of Units per Structure: A____ B____ C____
D____ E____ F____ G____ H____ I____

CITY OF BERKELEY
ORDINANCE 6099 (RECO)

FORM C

RESIDENTIAL ENERGY CONSERVATION ORDINANCE
TRANSFER OF RESPONSIBILITY FROM SELLER TO BUYER

This form transfers responsibility for compliance with RECO (Ordinance 6099) provisions checked below from seller to buyer. Unchecked measures remain the responsibility of seller. Buyer has one year to complete the items checked below, arrange a RECO inspection, and file a Certificate of Compliance (Form A) with the City of Berkeley, City Planning Department, Codes and Inspections Division, 2180 Milvia Street, Berkeley, CA 94704. Buyers cannot transfer responsibility for any of the items to future buyers <u>unless</u> they have met the maximum required expenditure for this sale to comply with RECO, and have filed a Form A, Certificate of Compliance with itemized receipts attached with the City of Berkeley.

Responsibility for the following are transferred to the buyer:

1. Insulate ceiling to R-30. [ ]
2. Seal and insulate furnace ducts to R-3. [ ]
3. Insulate storage water heaters to R-6. [ ]
4. Install low-flow shower and faucet devices or fixtures. [ ]
5. Insulate hot water pipes to R-3 in pumped recirculating water heating systems. [ ]
6. Insulate water heater pipes to R-3. [ ]
7. Replace incandescent lights with lamps of at least 25 lumens per watt. [ ]
8. Weatherstrip exterior doors. [ ]
9. Block air-flow and heat loss through chimney. [ ]
10. Replace or modify toilets to reduce amount of water used. [ ]

Seller/Owner _____ Buyer _____
(Printed Name) (Printed Name)

Seller/Owner _____ Buyer _____
(Signature) (Signature)

Address _____ Address _____

Phone Number ( ) _____ Phone Number ( ) _____

I have notified both buyer and seller of the requirements of Ordinance 6099, [ ]
but I do not know of my own knowledge that the property is in compliance.

I have notified both buyer and seller of the requirements of Ordinance 6099. [ ]
I know that the property is in compliance and have so represented it to the buyer.

Agent _____ Address _____

Subsequent to this sale, the property will be:

1. Owner occupied [ ]
2. Rental property [ ]

Selling Price: _____

Maximum Required Expenditure Amount: _____

<u>A $15 FILING FEE IS REQUIRED FOR EACH STRUCTURE/UNIT</u>

Exhibit 1.1 Berkeley Residential Energy Conservation Ordinance (RECO)

BERKELEY'S RESIDENTIAL ENERGY CONSERVATION ORDINANCE

Under the Residential Energy Conservation Ordinance (Ordinance No. 6099), the following steps must be taken in residential units prior to their sale or major renovation:

1. Install ceiling insulation to bring the thermal resistance value of the ceiling insulation to R-30 in buildings where existing ceiling insulation value is R-11 or less, except in those buildings having no attic or inaccessible attic space between the roof and ceiling below. Inaccessible is defined such that the roof slope is less than two and one half inches in 12 inches and the vertical clear height from the top of the bottom chord of the truss or ceiling joist to the underside of the roof structural members or rafters at the roof ridge is less than twenty-four inches (24").

2. Seal leaks in furnace ducts at all joints in the ducting system and at the plenum with pressure sensitive tape or mastic, and insulate all furnace ducts to at least a thermal resistance value of R-3 except where ducts are inside heated space, between floors, inside interior walls or partitions, are asbestos coated, or otherwise inaccessible without alteration.

3. Insulate all domestic storage water heaters with an external insulation blanket rated at a minimum thermal resistance value of R-6, except where a minimum clearance of two inches from a wall or other permanent fixture does not exist, or where the thermal resistance of the total water heater insulation jacket is in excess of R-12. For purposes of safety, water heaters that are having insulation blankets installed must also meet all legal requirements including the requirement of a pressure-temperature (PT) Safety Release Valve.

4. Install low-flow devices with a maximum rated flow rate of no more than three (3) gallons per minute in all shower fixtures, two and three quarters (2.75) gallons per minute for sink and lavatory faucets, and four (4) gallons per minute for all other faucets; or replace with fixtures designed to meet the same limits.

5. Insulate to at least a thermal resistance value of R-3 hot water pipes in pumped, recirculating domestic water heating systems. Exemptions shall be granted where hot water pipes are between floors, inside interior walls, or otherwise inaccessible without alteration.

6. Insulate to at least a thermal resistance of R-3 exposed hot water pipes and cold water pipes within twenty-four inches (24") of water heater.

7. Replace incandescent light bulbs located in common areas of multiple unit structures with lamps that have an efficiency of at least 25 lumens per watt, such as fluorescent lamps.

8. Install approved weatherstripping on all exterior doors.

9. Install approved dampers, doors or other devices to obstruct or block air-flow to reduce heat-loss through chimneys.

10. Replace existing tank or flushometer-type toilets with fixtures designed to use no more than one and six tenths (1.6) gallons per flush, or modify existing fixtures to use the minimum volume necessary for correct operation (e.g. water dams, water filled bottles or water bags in tank). Whenever a toilet is replaced in a renovation it must be with an "ultra-low-flow" model.

If after taking title to a residential structure or a unit in Berkeley (as defined in the code), you find that it does not meet the above requirements, you may:

Bring the property into compliance, and recover your costs and damages – including higher utility bills paid due to lack of compliance with the requirements, inspection fees, and attorney's fees – from the seller and/or agent(s).

Berkeley Residential Energy Conservation Ordinance (RECO)   **Exhibit 1.2**

Basic Residential Energy Conservation Checklist (Berkeley Ordinance). These items yield the most conservation for the least cost, and are therefore important assets to identify for your clients.

- ☐ Insulation in ceilings
- ☐ Insulation on furnace and heating ducts
- ☐ Insulation on water heaters
- ☐ Low-flow showerheads and faucets
- ☐ Insulation on hot water pipes in recirculating water heating systems
- ☐ Insulation on hot and cold water pipes of water heater
- ☐ Low-wattage fluorescent lighting
- ☐ Weatherstripping on exterior doors
- ☐ Devices that reduce heat loss through chimneys
- ☐ Low-flow toilets

San Francisco San Francisco enacted a Residential Energy Conservation Ordinance effective September 20, 1982, and amended in 1983 and 1991. It requires residential property owners to provide certain energy and water conservation measures to lessen the impact of rising energy costs and water usage on renters and homeowners alike. Property owners are encouraged to comply with the requirements even if they do not intend to sell in the near future, and compliance is required upon sale of single and two family dwellings, apartment buildings (including each condominium unit sold), and residential hotels, as well as upon application for metering conversion or major improvements.

Exemptions. No inspection is required if proof of compliance has already been properly recorded, or for tourist hotels, mobile homes, live/work occupancies, or buildings constructed after July 1, 1978.

Title Transfer Exemptions. Transfers of title that result from an operation of law rather than by purchase are exempt. Examples include transfers pursuant to court order, default, conservatorship, etc., and transfers between co-owners or certain relatives.

Requirements. Effective September 20, 1982, owners of residential property who wish to sell their property, must obtain a valid energy inspection, install certain energy and (since 1991) water conservation devices or materials, and then obtain a certificate of compliance. All of this must occur prior to transfer of title, and the seller must provide a copy of the compliance certificate to the buyer prior to title transfer. The items listed below apply to one and two family dwellings; for apartment buildings there are additional requirements for central heating systems.

- ☐ Insulate accessible attic space to a minimum value of R-19. Existing R-11 insulation is deemed acceptable as meeting ordinance requirements. Cellulose, fiberglass, or certain other insulation materials may be blown directly over all types of wiring. Electrical junction boxes, flues, and light fixtures must be kept clear or protected from all insulation materials. Prior to insulation in areas with knob and tube wiring, the wiring must be inspected and approved.

- ☐ Weatherstrip all doors leading from heated to unheated areas. Combination rigid metal and vinyl bead type strip is the most durable and effective. All sides of the door must be weatherstripped, including the threshold. Foam and felt type strip is not acceptable, and all stripping must be permanently secured.

- ☐ Insulate hot water heaters. A jacket of R-6 insulation value or greater must be provided. Pressure relief valves must be present in order to prevent any explosion hazards. Additionally, the first 4 feet of hot water line must be insulated to a minimum R-4 value. Fiberglass pipe wrap or precut closed cell foams with a wall thickness of 3/4 inch or greater are most commonly used for this job.

- ☐ Installation of low-flow showerhead. The maximum flow permitted through a showerhead is 2.5 gallons per minute (previously 3 gpm and amended in July, 1991). Showerheads need not be replaced when it is necessary to remove the supply piping to remove the showerhead.

- ☐ Caulk and seal openings in building exterior. Reduce air infiltration by closing any openings or cracks greater than 1/4 inch wide, such as pipes to plumbing fixtures, mail-slots without flaps, and open pantry vents.

- ☐ Insulate accessible heating and cooling ducts. Insulation with a R-3 value or greater must be provided for all heating and cooling ducts, and secured with nails or baling wire, not duct tape.

- ☐ Faucet aerators. An aerator with a flow restrictor is to be installed on all sink faucets that are designed to accept aerators. Faucets not designed to accept aerators are exempt.

- ☐ Toilets. All toilets must be either low-flush (3.5 gallons or less) or be retrofitted with a permanently installed device such as a quick-closing flapper device or dual-option flushing mechanism. Water displacement devices such as toilet dams are not acceptable. Toilets that cannot be modified without impeding functioning or flushing are exempt.

Compliance Procedure. Compliance is accomplished by obtaining an energy inspection from the city's Bureau of Building Inspection (BBI) /Housing Inspection Division (HID) or a certified private energy inspector. After the inspection the owner or owner's agent files a copy with the Bureau, completes any required work, and obtains a final certification of compliance inspection. After approval a copy of the completed certificate of compliance is recorded with the county recorder's office. Proof of compliance must be recorded prior to or concurrent with transfer of title.

Escrow Account. The seller or seller's authorized agent may transfer responsibility for compliance to the buyer provided the buyer agrees to comply within 180 days of transfer of title, and seller agrees that funds equal to one percent of the purchase price (for a single or two family dwelling, not to exceed $1,000) shall be placed in an escrow account and disbursed according to the terms of the ordinance.

Maximum Costs. For one or two family dwellings and individual condominiums and co-op units, the maximum required expenditure is $1,000. For multi-unit buildings, the maximum is one percent of the assessed value or purchase price.

ARCHITECTURAL FEATURES THAT CONSERVE ENERGY

Think of a house that has been designed for "energy conservation." Do you imagine a nontraditional design loaded with exotic technology? Actually, some of the most effective conservation measures require no new technology; they can be found in many well-planned traditional homes. We all know that insulation in the attic conserves energy, but there are other important conservation features in a house that we may not associate with saving energy. These are "hidden" in the siting, design, and materials of a house. Basic architectural features that can have a major effect on heating, air conditioning, and other energy use are: orientation, siting, location and size of windows, type of window, roof overhang, shape of the home, type of construction, mass of the building materials, color of roof and walls, and shading by means of awnings, trellises and trees.

Orientation The most basic energy conservation consideratioon is the orientation of the home—how the house sits in relation to the cardinal points of north, south, east, and west. The sun shines more on the south wall and less on the north; consequently, houses with large southern exposures are warmer than those with large surfaces facing north. The morning sun hits the east wall and the afternoon sun the west, so homes with protected western exposures are cooler in summer.

What To Do. The first step toward saving energy is to make use of the home's orientation. Shading the walls and windows facing south will keep the house cooler in summer; large windows facing north will make the house harder to heat in winter.

- ☐ *South side.* Gets the most sun; the warmest side. Large windows help warm the house in winter but may need to be shaded in summer.

- ☐ *North side.* Receives the least amount of direct sunlight; the coolest side. Minimize window openings that leak heat in winter.

- ☐ *West side.* Shade in summer to minimize heat gain.

- ☐ *East side.* Morning sun helps warm the house in winter.

Siting Each house is sited in a neighborhood and a geographic location. These factors also affect energy gain and loss. Nearby buildings and hills can shade a home, causing it to be cooler in both summer and winter. Houses with large glass doors or windows oriented to a view usually pay a price in heat gain and loss: to the north, heat loss; to the south, heat gain.

What To Do. Most homes are oriented and sited not to the sun or even to the topography but to the grid created by street and lot lines. There is not much you can do to change the orientation or siting of a house, but there are ways to improve energy conservation once the effects of siting and orientation are recognized.

Location and Size of Windows After orientation and siting, window size and location are the most significant elements to assess when looking at propertiesn with an eye to energy conservation. Windows are usually the single most important architectural factor affecting energy use.

Heat. Large sliding glass doors and windows facing the north will lose large quantities of heat through this glass in winter. Houses with lots of windows in walls facing south will gain heat in summer. Heat gain may or may not be undesirable, depending on the climate.

Environmental Issues & Obligations

Building Orientation and the Sun

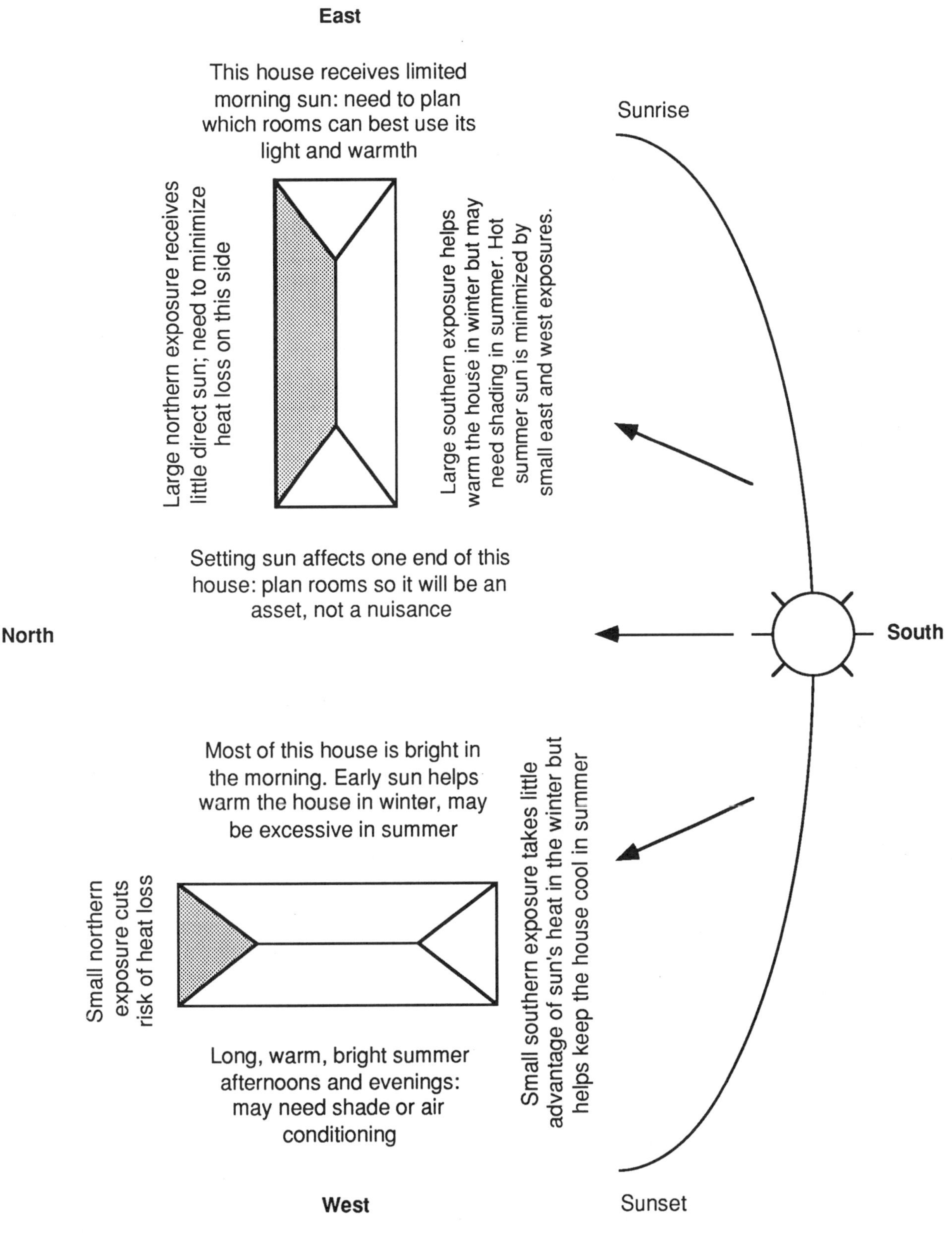

East

This house receives limited morning sun: need to plan which rooms can best use its light and warmth

Large northern exposure receives little direct sun; need to minimize heat loss on this side

Large southern exposure helps warm the house in winter but may need shading in summer. Hot summer sun is minimized by small east and west exposures.

Sunrise

Setting sun affects one end of this house: plan rooms so it will be an asset, not a nuisance

North

South

Most of this house is bright in the morning. Early sun helps warm the house in winter, may be excessive in summer

Small northern exposure cuts risk of heat loss

Small southern exposure takes little advantage of sun's heat in the winter but helps keep the house cool in summer

Long, warm, bright summer afternoons and evenings: may need shade or air conditioning

West

Sunset

Architectural Elements of Energy Conservation

Light. Windows affect the electrical bill by reducing the need for artificial light. Rooms with plenty of natural light are usually more inviting.

Comfort. Kitchens and breakfast rooms with windows facing east receive the morning sun and are warmer and more cheerful in the early hours.

Ventilation. In summer, homes with natural cross-ventilation and plenty of opening windows will be easier to keep cool than homes with small, poorly placed windows. The higher the window opening is placed in the wall, the more heat it will allow to escape in summer, as heat rises to the top of the room. Opening skylights are a real boon in summer as well.

Aesthetics. Well-designed homes have their largest windows where they will do the most good: opening up views and picking up light and warmth from southern exposures. Homes built with little regard for siting and orientation may suffer from poor window placement and unexploited views.

Trade-Offs. In general, there is a trade-off between heat loss and comfort in the placement of windows: homes with lots of windows are brighter and more pleasant than houses with few openings, but they also lose more heat through the large expanses of glass.

Code Requirements. Title 24, the state building code, recognizes and quantifies this trade-off in its energy conservation requirements (see Course 5). Builders and remodelers must increase the amount of insulation they use or use triple-pane windows if they install large expanses of glass in a new home or addition.

Type of Window The type of window heavily influences the cost of heating and cooling a home. The most important factor is the number of panes—layers of glass—used in the window. A single pane (also called single glazed) window has only one thin sheet of glass separating the outside from the inside. We all know intuitively there is very little insulating value in a sheet of glass 1/16 of an inch thick.

Single or Double Pane. Modern homes generally have double pane windows. It is not the extra sheet of glass that provides the insulation, but the air or gas trapped between the sheets. Some brands are filled with argon gas, which is a better insulator than air. Triple pane windows provide the most insulation, but they are also the most expensive.

Ratings. Windows are rated by their "U-value," which measures the heat flow through the glass. The smaller the U-value, the better a window insulates against heat and cold.

Sash Material. Another factor that affects the energy conservation value of windows is the sash or frame. Wood sash makes the best insulator, but is the most expensive type of window. Vinyl and aluminum are other common sash materials, with aluminum providing the least insulation.

Style of Window. Another consideration is the style of window: double-hung, sliding, casement, and awning are the common varieties. Older double-hung windows and inexpensive aluminum sliding windows tend to suffer most from air filtration—they leak air where the window fits into the jamb. Warm air leaks out of the house and cool air leaks in during cold weather, making it more expensive to heat the house. This can often be minimized by installing weatherstripping.

- ☐ Casement and awning windows are hinged at either the side or the top. Modern ones generally fit tightly against a gasket or rubber seal inside the frame, so they are less prone to air filtration.

- ☐ Jalousie or louver windows were popular in certain eras of California home construction but are now rarely installed because of the tremendous air filtration allowed by the slats of glass. (They are also easy for burglars to open).

- ☐ Many ranch-style homes have "picture windows" in the living room which are fixed glass, one sheet of glass secured in a frame. Since there are no opening parts, these windows should not have air filtration problems until the frame begins to deteriorate.

New Technologies. There are several new technologies that can lower heat transfer through windows.

- ☐ "Low-E" windows are coated with a substance that cuts heat transfer from the outside to the inside of the home.

- ☐ Reflective glass acts as a mirror, turning back much of the sunlight and heat. This is used in consistently hot climates where heat gain in winter is not wanted.

- ☐ Heat-absorbing glass is available for very cold climates.

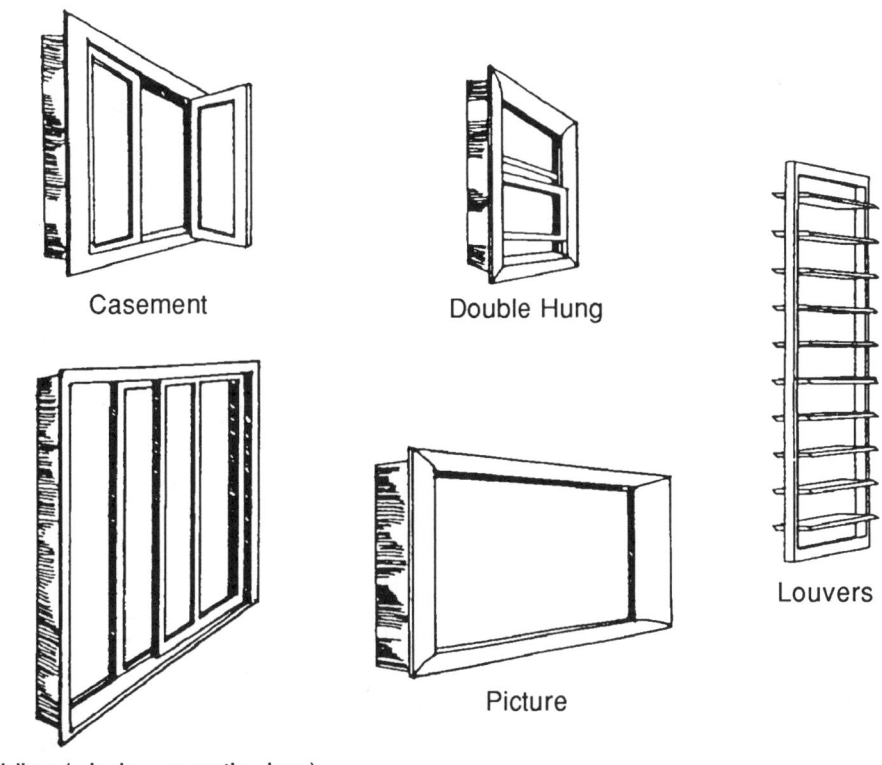

Casement

Double Hung

Louvers

Sliding (window or patio door)

Picture

Quality of Installation. Like any other energy conservation measure, the success of window insulation depends on proper installation. The best quality window can still leak due to sloppy construction. Although licensees are not expected to be construction experts, they will be helping their clients by looking for signs of quality work, such as beads of caulking around the outside of the frame and tight fit when the window is closed.

Roof Overhang Another architectural feature with a major impact on energy gain and loss is the roof overhang. Homes with large, eaveless walls facing south may need to be shaded to avoid getting too much sun and heat in the summer. Houses built with deep overhangs will gain less summer heat yet still pick up light and warmth in the winter when the sun is low.

Regional Styles. Architectural styles from elsewhere in the country, such as eaveless Cape Cod salt box houses, are poor choices in those parts of California that receive long hours of hot summer sun. A Cape Cod style home in a hot climate will be expensive to cool in summer unless the south windows and walls are shaded by awnings, trellises, or deciduous trees and shrubs.

California Architecture. The indigenous architectural types—Spanish-influenced stucco homes with tile roofing, bungalows with deep eaves and porches, and single-story ranch style houses—are better suited to California's weather in part because energy-efficient eaves and patios are inherent elements of their design.

Cost. Eaveless designs are often used by developers because they are cheaper to build. In the long run, however, the savings to the builder may be paid for many times over by the buyer, in higher utility bills.

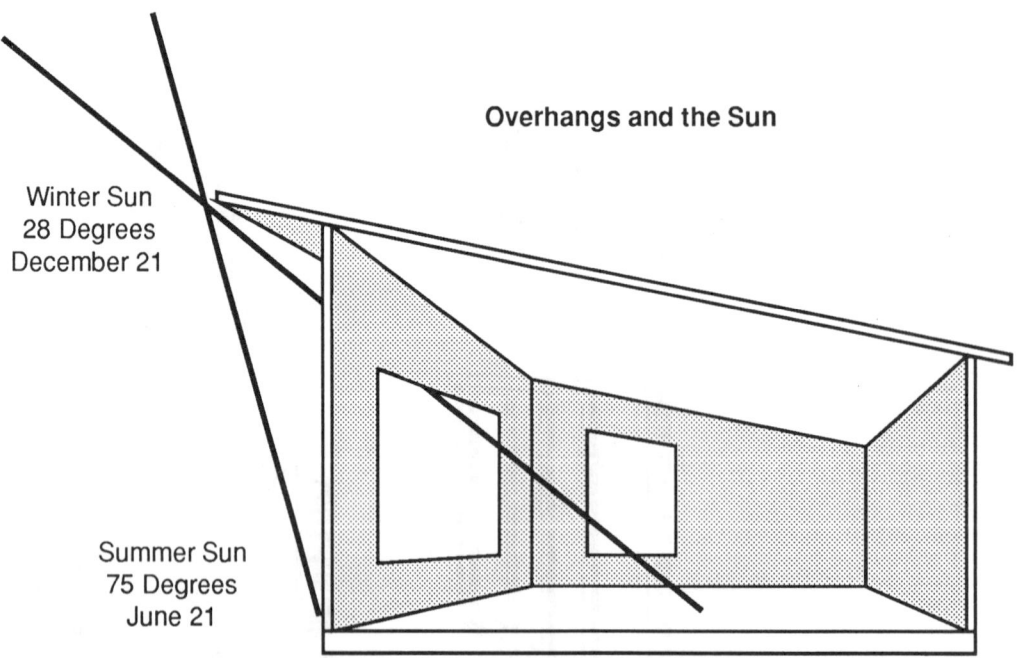

Overhangs and the Sun

Winter Sun 28 Degrees December 21

Summer Sun 75 Degrees June 21

Shape of the Home Square-shaped houses are easier to keep warm than houses with long and narrow or irregular plans, because corners and wall surfaces lose heat. This is more of a concern in very cold climates than in California.

Type of Construction The vast majority of California homes are of double-wall wood frame construction. While one sees masonry (brick or concrete block) and adobe homes from time to time, seismic and cost considerations have limited their popularity.

Foundation. Wood frame houses in California are typically built on one of three types of foundation:

- ☐ Concrete slab on grade
- ☐ Raised wood floor and perimeter foundation
- ☐ Basement.

Although heat rises, a significant amount of heat can be lost through uninsulated wood floors that sit on piers or perimeter foundations. Concrete slabs not only lose less heat in winter, they also add mass which tends to retain heat and keep a house warmer. Basements, less common in California than in other areas of the country, lose heat in winter if the floor has not been insulated.

Siding. The type of siding is less critical to energy conservation than the amount of insulation in the walls and the quality of the seal around doors, windows, and other joints in the exterior walls. Air filtering through cracks in the walls is a primary cause of heat loss. Common types of siding on California houses include:

- ☐ Wood plank
- ☐ Plywood (often called T1-11 or textured plywood siding)
- ☐ Stucco
- ☐ Aluminum or vinyl.

Vapor Barrier. An important element in wall construction is the vapor barrier and sheathing. Hidden inside the wall between the studs and the siding, the vapor barrier (either tar paper or a modern sheet product like DuPont's Tyvek) helps keep moisture out of the walls and adds a measure of protection against air filtration.

Old Houses. In very old homes, the siding (usually wood plank) was sometimes nailed directly over the studs. With no sheathing (generally plywood in modern homes) and no vapor barrier installed under the siding, these older buildings tend to "leak like sieves."

Masonry Construction. Adobe walls and hollow concrete block walls that have been filled with insulation and adequate grout both have excellent insulation value. If the walls have been properly reinforced, masonry and adobe can withstand earthquakes; if they have not been well engineered and lack steel reinforcing bars, however, they are poor risks in a quake.

Types of Roofing. Common roof types in California are composition shingle, wood shingle, tile, and metal (steel or aluminum). As with siding, the amount of insulation in the attic is more critical than the type of roofing in assessing energy conservation value. In general, roofing with more mass, such as tile, provides more insulation and heat retention than thin, lightweight roofing such as wood or metal. (Fire resistance is also a concern with wood shingle roofs.)

Historic Architectural Styles

Through successive styles, America's history can be traced in its housing stock. Many of the architectural features that affect energy use are inherent in the style of the house, among them wall and roof materials, type of foundation, size and type of windows, roof overhang, ceiling height, and building shape. It is important to understand a house's style in order to recognize built-in energy efficiencies and inefficiencies, and to correct the inefficiencies without compromising the house's character.

Greek Revival, 1820-1860. A drive through the towns and countryside of the South or Midwest will show the powerful influence of classicism on 19th century American houses and public buildings. Everywhere there is evidence of the Greek influence—flat or low-pitched roofs, columns at the entrance or along the entire front. Fine plantation homes displayed the style; so did rude whitewashed farmhouses. Some of the earliest pioneer houses surviving in California—four walls and a low gable roof—are a minimal, vernacular form of Greek Revival.

Octagon Houses, 1850-1860. A book published in 1848 argued that the octagon enclosed 20% more floor space than a square with the same total length of wall, and claimed that living in such a house induced an amiable spirit and conferred benefits on yet-unborn children. The style was never widely popular, but it reflects the experimental spirit of its times. San Francisco and Santa Cruz have octagon houses used as museums.

Italianate, 1860s-1880s. With its tall, narrow, arched windows, classical features, and bracketed cornice, this style was thought at the time to show force of character. Miniature Italian Renaissance palazzos, these houses sometimes have wooden "quoins" simulating stonework at the corners. The conservationist John Muir owned a 17-room Italianate in Martinez, California, built in 1882.

Stick, 1880s. Similar in general form and construction to the earlier Italianate and later Queen Anne (all three are generically called "Victorians"), the Stick is distinguished by square bays, straight vertical or horizontal boards used as ornament, and sometimes ("Stick-Eastlake") stylized floral millwork. These houses emphasize the vertical, with high ceilings and tall windows.

Queen Anne, 1880-1900. This is the style often popularly called "Victorian." It is an ornate, asymmetrical design with turrets and towers, curved railings, verandas, surface sculpture, and textured exterior walls—definitely not a shrinking violet. The Carson house in Eureka is probably California's most famous Queen Anne.

Craftsman, 1890-1920. Characteristic of this style are the prominent rafters and other structural timbers. The roof is often gently pitched and deeply overhanging. Wood siding and shingles are earth colored. This style expresses a back-to-nature movement in such features as sleeping porches and big rustic stone or clinker brick fireplaces.

Mission Style, 1890-1920. Based on the architecture of early Spanish missions, this style originated in California. Characteristics include a curved gable, red tile roof, wide overhanging eaves, arcade, stucco wall surfaces, and sometimes a bell tower.

Colonial Revival, 1895-1910. The Colonial is a boxy house with clapboard siding, broad windows, hip roof, and classical detailing such as columns or a temple-like pediment on porch or dormer. These were built in great numbers in turn-of-the-century "streetcar suburbs."

Bungalow, 1900-1940. A small (1000-1200 square feet), one-story house with a gently pitched roof, the bungalow first became fashionable on the West Coast. It was well suited to narrow urban lots; Chicago has tens of thousands. For a time the style was so popular that it warranted its own publication—*The Bungalow Magazine.*

Prairie School, 1900-1920. Frank Lloyd Wright and other Chicago architects made this horizontal, ground-hugging style fashionable. The roof is flat or low-pitched and extends far beyond the brick or stucco walls. Windows are large, and ornament geometrical. There is sometimes a raised section in the center of the house, with ground-floor wings extending beyond it.

Period Revivals, 1920s-1930s. These include Spanish, Tudor, French Provincial, Cape Cod, etc. According to the costume chosen, exterior features will include tile or slate roofs, half-timbering, round turrets, wrought iron, leaded glass, clapboard siding, or shutters. Period revival houses come in all sizes, from mansions to tiny tract homes. Period styles have become fashionable again in new construction in the 1980s and 1990s, particularly for "executive" homes.

California Ranch, 1940s-1960s. As a one-story, usually modest-sized house, the ranch style evolved from the bungalow. During the housing boom of the 1950s and 1960s, ranch designs increasingly supported an indoor/outdoor lifestyle, especially in California. A cousin to the ranch is the split level. This term came into the language in 1946, reflecting one of the variations in stock styles offered by developers during the post World War II years.

Construction Elements

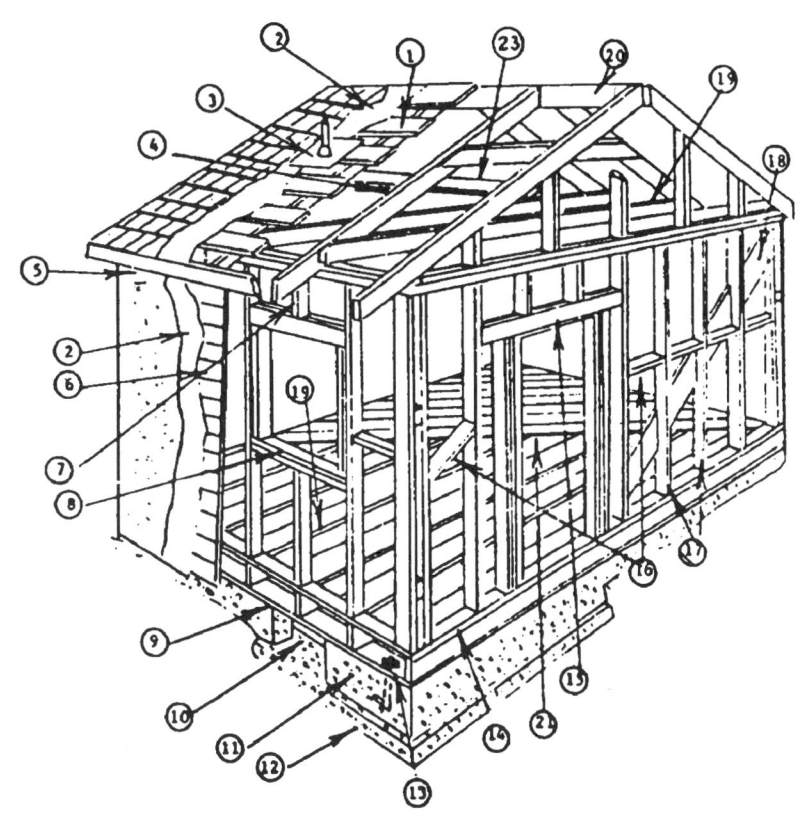
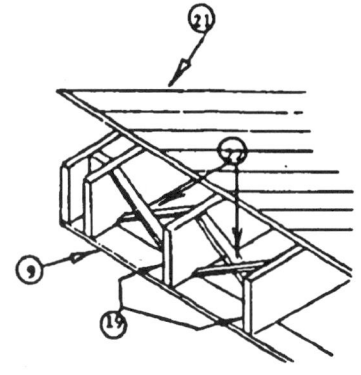
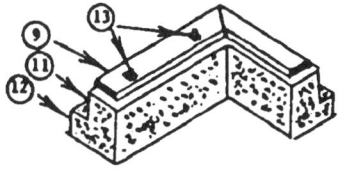

1. *Spaced (or Open) Sheathing*—boards nailed to rafters as base for roof.
2. *Building Paper*—used between sheathing and roof or siding (vapor barrier).
3. *Flashing*—metal used to protect against water seepage.
4. *Rafters*—sloping members of roof to support sheathing.
5. *Eave*—protruding underpart of roof overhanging the wall.
6. *Solid Sheathing*—boards nailed to studs as base for wall.
7. *Cripple*—stud above or below a window or door opening.
8. *Sill*—bottom of a door or window frame.
9. *Mud Sill*—treated member bolted to foundation.
10. *Crawl Space*—unexcavated area under house. FHA: 18" minimum.
11. *Foundation*—concrete base of house.
12. *Footing*—expanded portion of concrete foundation.
13. *Anchor Bolt*—used for fastening mud sill to the foundation.
14. *Sole Plate*—support on which the studs rest.
15. *Header*—beam over door or window; also called a lintel.
16. *Fire Stop*—used to block flames from spreading to the attic.
17. *Studs*—vertical 2" x 4" framework of walls—spaced 16" on center.
18. *Bracing*—diagonal boards on wall to prevent sway.
19. *Joists*—members supporting floor or ceiling loads.
20. *Ridge Board*—top beam for support of rafters.
21. *Subflooring*—rough boards laid on joists to support flooring.
22. *Bridging*—wooden pieces between joists to stiffen and hold them.
23. *Purlin*—a horizontal member which braces and stabilizes the rafters.

Architectural Elements of Energy Conservation

Wall and Ceiling Insulation Insulation is measured in "R-value," which is the resistance of the material to conducting heat. A single pane of regular glass has an R-value of 1. Most insulation has R-values of between 11 and 30.

Date of Construction. Most pre-1960 homes did not have insulation installed during construction; homes built in the 1970s and 1980s should be insulated.

Inspection. The most cost-effective conservation item, and the easiest to identify, is insulation in the ceiling. Inspection requires only a ladder and a flashlight. Find the ceiling access (usually a square lid in a large closet or in a hallway) and look around the attic. The spaces in between the ceiling joists (the boards that the ceiling is nailed to) should be filled with one of these types of insulation:

- *Fiberglass Batt.* The most common variety and the easiest to install, this is also called "blanket insulation" or "batt insulation." It comes in rolls that are just the right width to fit between the joists. This insulation is generally pink or off-white in color and looks a bit like cotton candy on the top. There may be an aluminum or plastic vapor barrier on the side facing down on the ceiling. This is also the most common variety used in walls and floors.

- *Loose Fill Insulation.* This gray fiber material is poured out of bags into the spaces between the joists. In some cases it has to cover the joists completely to reach the proper insulation thickness. It should be spread evenly and not compacted.

- *Air-Blown Cellulose Fiber.* This gray-colored material is perhaps the best insulation from an environmental point of view, because it is made of recycled and treated newsprint. It requires a special blower and hose to install.

Walls. It is rarely practical to remove wallboard to see if the walls have been insulated, but one can often peek into the wall by removing an electrical outlet plate. The insulation should be visible by shining a flashlight in the crack between the box and the wallboard.

Floors. It is usually possible to see if the floor has been insulated by crawling under the house or going into the basement. Heat loss through a floor can add up to one-third of a home's heating bill.

Pipes and Ducts. A significant amount of expensive heat is lost through exposed hot water pipes, water heaters, and furnace heating ducts. Check for:

- Insulation-wrapped water heaters and hot water pipes leading out of the heater

- Insulation wrapped around heating ducts, which are usually in the attic or basement ceiling.

Weatherstripping. Another key insulation material to look for is weatherstripping, the thin pieces of metal and rubber that keep warm air from escaping through cracks around doors and windows.

Mass of the Building Materials   As noted in the discussion of roof and foundation, building materials with great mass such as concrete, clay tiles, and bricks retain heat longer than thin, light materials such as plywood or sheet metal. One of the principles of passive solar design (designing to save energy without using any "active" systems with pumps or fans) is to add some mass to the interior of the building.

Mass As Heat Collector. Concrete slabs (especially those covered with a dark colored ceramic tile flooring) and masonry fireplaces are common features which add mass to conventional wood frame homes. Mass is especially helpful in gathering and retaining heat if it is located on or near the southern exposure of the home, where most of the sun's heat reaches the home in winter.

Color of Roof and Walls   No one wants to drive a black car through the desert in the summer, and the same applies to a dark roof and walls in a hot climate. But in cooler climates, a dark colored roof and walls are desirable because they gain much more heat in winter than lighter colored materials.

Shade: Awnings, Trellises, Trees   **Construction.** Architectural features that shade the south and west, such as awnings above windows or trellises, are valuable energy conservation items as well as potentially attractive additions to a home.

Landscaping. The same is true of deciduous trees and shrubs on the south and west exposures. The trees provide significant cooling in summer by shading windows and walls from direct sunlight and by cooling air around the house. In winter, the leaves drop off and the winter sun is allowed to warm the south and west windows and walls.

Cost Saving. According to Pacific Gas and Electric Company (PG&E), deciduous trees on the south, east, and west sides of a home can cut air conditioning costs by 30 percent during summer, and vines on trellises protecting the west wall can reduce the wall's surface temperature by as much as 40 degrees.

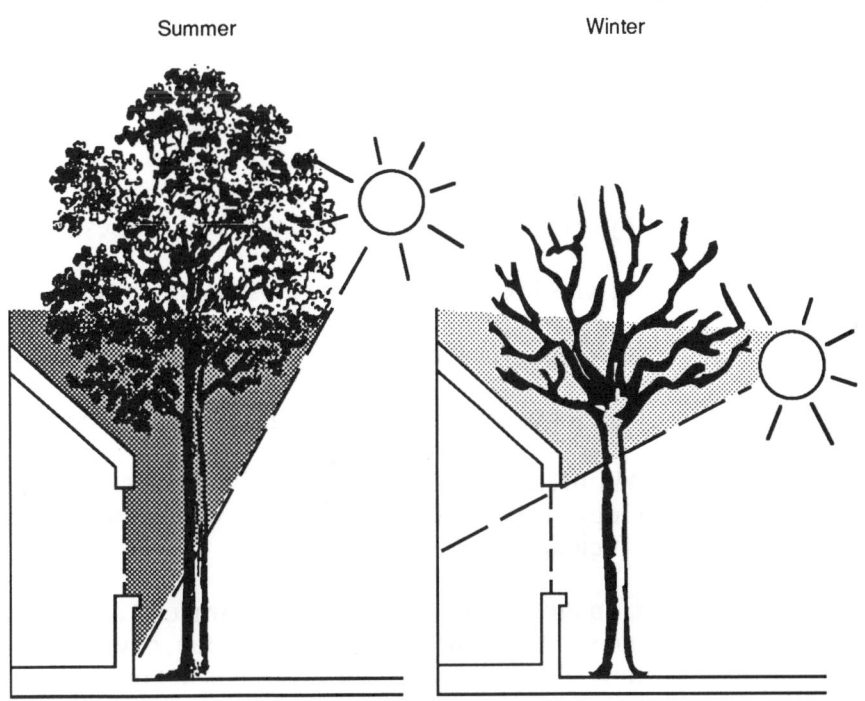

Summer   Winter

Architectural Elements of Energy Conservation **89**

ADDITIONAL ENERGY CONSERVATION MEASURES

After identifying architectural features that affect energy conservation, the licensee and homebuyer should inspect appliances and look for possible retrofit measures that will directly conserve energy.

New Appliances One of the great conservation successes of the past twenty years is the vastly improved efficiency of American made home appliances. A new refrigerator uses only half as much energy as one made in 1973. Government regulations are requiring manufacturers to design even more efficiency into appliances in the near future.

- Refrigeration accounts for 25 percent of a typical urban family's electricity bill, or up to $200 in annual utility bills, so a new refrigerator is a definite asset in a home.

- New electronic-ignition gas ranges and cooktops save as much as 40 or 50 percent compared to older pilot light variety.

All new appliances are labeled by law with a yellow "Energy Guide" sticker which indicates the estimated annual cost of operating the appliance.

Lighting **Incandescent or Fluorescent.** Huge savings can be gained by switching from incandescent to compact fluorescent light bulbs. Not only does a compact fluorescent light use 75 percent less electricity than the regular bulb, it lasts about ten times longer. It screws into the socket just like a regular bulb. The compact fluorescent costs a lot more—$12 to $15 each—but this is recovered within two years by lower electricity bills.

Outdoor Lighting On Demand. Another item to consider is outside lighting operated by a motion detector. The security lights come on only when needed, rather than being left on all night.

Heating Systems **Furnaces.** Up to 40 percent of energy use is for heating, and modern furnaces are more efficient than older models. Furnaces are rated with an Annual Fuel Utilization Efficiency (AFUE) number. The higher the AFUE number, the more efficient the furnace. PG&E recommends buying units with an AFUE of 78 percent or higher. The higher efficiency furnaces cost more initially, but as with other energy conserving devices, the extra investment is quickly paid back by energy savings.

Types. There are three basic type of furnaces:

- Gas fired forced air (the most common type)

- Electric heating

- Hot water or steam heating (radiators in rooms)

Maintenance. A furnace is only as efficient as all its parts. Dirty air filters, clogged gas jets, and leaking or uninsulated ducts all drastically lower the efficiency of a furnace.

Conservation Devices. Gas furnaces are more efficient if they have an automatic damper or induced draft fan, devices which keep heat from rising out through the flue when the furnace is not on.

Heat Pumps. Heat pumps are devices that gain or lose heat from the outside air and use that energy to replace heating and air conditioning. They are recommended for homes with electrical heating systems. Although expensive to install (about $2,000), they can save up to 40 percent of the home's annual heating and cooling costs.

Fireplaces A fireplace traditionally adds value to a home, but in energy terms there is a big difference between one that helps heat a home and one that actually siphons heat out of the house. An inefficient fireplace can actually drain more warm air out of the house than it adds.

Efficient Use. There are both devices and operating methods that can cut this heat loss. The methods are:

- Close the doors to the living room when using the fireplace so heated air from other rooms is not drawn in to fuel the fire. Open a window near the fireplace a crack to allow fresh air in to feed the fire, or open the outside air intake if there is one.

- Lower the thermostat in the living room when using the fireplace.

- Keep the flue damper closed when the fireplace is not in use.

Conservation Devices. These devices help disperse the heat into the room instead of letting it go up the chimney.

- Glass screen

- Convective grate

- Radiant grate. The radiant and convective grates collect heat and radiate it into the room more efficiently than standard grates or the brick lining of the fireplace.

- Blower/fan unit

- Fireplace insert. A metal fireplace insert fits inside a conventional masonry brick fireplace. These inserts are often equipped with a small electric fan that forces the heat collected by the metal sides of the unit out into the room.

- Damper. The fireplace should have an easily operable flue damper, which closes off the chimney when the fireplace is not being used.

- Unit construction. Many modern fireplaces are metal units faced with brick or stone to resemble masonry fireplaces. These modern fireplaces are generally equipped with the energy efficient devices listed above.

Solar Water Heaters It is easy to spot roof-mounted solar water heating panels. Most solar water heater systems were put in during the 1970s and 1980s when a federal tax credit was given to homeowners who installed them. If the systems are in good working order, they can cut water heating bills by up to 50 percent.

Cooling Fans, both ceiling fans and "whole house" fans that vent to the outside, are an old technology that still works well in pulling hot air up and out of the house. Fans are an efficient way of cooling without using air conditioning.

Air Conditioning. Central air conditioning units are rated by SEER (Seasonal Energy Efficiency Ratio), and room units are given a similar EER (Energy Efficiency Ratio) number. The higher the number, the more efficient the unit. Ratings generally range from 9 to 14, but only those rated 10 or higher are recommended.

Water Conservation Devices

Water conserving devices save energy too. They do so not only by reducing the amount of gas or electricity needed to heat hot water, but also because a tremendous amount of electricity is used to pump water from the Sierra to millions of homes throughout the state. Given the many recent years of drought and the continued population growth in California, conserving water is a task that all Californians must share.

Low-Flow Shower Heads and Faucets. Many shower heads are clearly marked with the water flow they allow per minute. Low-flow shower heads cut the gallons per minute from about five to eight to about three or four. Very low-flow heads reduce this to less than 2 gallons per minute. This can cut hot water use by 50 percent. Low-flow faucet aerators in the kitchen and bathroom sinks can also cut hot water use in half.

Inspection. A simple way to test the flow rate of a shower head is to turn the shower full on and time how long it takes to fill an empty half-gallon milk carton. If the carton is filled in less than ten seconds, it is not a low-flow shower head.

Low-Flow Toilets. Low-flow toilets are standard in new homes. These fixtures save up to half the water needed to flush old-fashioned toilets.

Landscaping. Water-conserving landscaping replaces thirsty lawns with drought-resistant plants. In hot climates any kind of landscaping can help reduce energy use for air conditioning because it cools the air surrounding the house.

HIGHLIGHTS TO REMEMBER

ARCHITECTURAL ELEMENTS OF ENERGY CONSERVATION

Energy efficiency affects desirability and value of a house, through comfort and cost of operation

Disclosure and Retrofit Requirements

No statewide energy conservation disclosures, but significant "material facts" should be disclosed

Local regulations: check for city or county retrofit or disclosure requirements

- Berkeley Residential Energy Conservation Ordinance (RECO) requires retrofit on sale: insulation, low-flow plumbing, low-wattage lighting, weatherstripping, fireplace dampers
- San Francisco ordinance requires inspection and recorded certificate of compliance on sale: insulation and water-conserving appliances

Architectural Features That Conserve Energy

Energy efficiency or inefficiency is inherent in many aspects of the house itself: siting, shape, building materials, etc.

Orientation. South and west walls receive most heat from the sun: take advantage in winter, shade in summer

Siting. Consider shade from nearby buildings or hills, effect of windows oriented to a view

Windows. Major factors in heat gain and loss, light, ventilation, comfort, and aesthetics

- Double or triple pane windows provide insulation by air or gas between the layers
- Sash material affects heat transfer: wood provides most insulation, aluminum least
- Style affects tightness of fit: double-hung allow most air filtration, casement the least of movable sash types, if installation has been well done
- High-tech glass treatments: heat-absorbing glass, Low-E, reflective glass

Roof overhang. Suitably sized eaves can block excess summer heat but let in low winter sun

Shape of house. Square is most efficient to heat, since corners and long wall surfaces lose heat

Type of construction. Most California houses are double-wall wood frame

- Foundation: slab on grade retains heat better than house raised above basement, piers, or perimeter foundation
- Wall material: siding (wood, stucco, etc.) is less critical than quality of construction and presence of vapor barrier and sheathing within the walls
- Masonry (brick or concrete block) is energy-efficient, but expensive to build and poor earthquake risk
- Roofing: attic insulation is most important to energy conservation, heavier roofing (tile) insulates and retains heat better than light material (wood, metal)

Insulation. Measured in R-value, where R-1 is the insulation value of a single pane of glass

- Ceilings: easy to inspect in attic; typically fiberglass batt, loose fill, or air-blown cellulose (recycled from newspaper)
- Walls: inspect through electrical outlet plate

Floor: heat loss through floor can represent 1/3 of heating bill

Pipes and ducts should be wrapped: water heater, hot water pipes, heating ducts

Weatherstripping around doors and windows

Mass of building materials. Concrete, tile, and bricks retain heat (and cold) longer than less massive materials

Can be used as heat collectors in passive solar design

Color of roof and walls can be used to absorb or reflect heat as needed

Shade. Awnings and trellises, trees and shrubs can help regulate heat according to the season

Additional Energy Conservation Measures

To improve upon the house's inherent energy profile. Initial cost is repaid in energy savings

Appliances have vastly improved in efficiency in past 20 years

Labeled by law with estimated annual cost of operation

Lighting. Fluorescent bulbs cost more to buy but much less to operate than incandescent

Heating. New furnaces have Annual Fuel Utilization Efficiency (AFUE) rating: 78 or higher is desirable

Fireplaces can lose more heat than they add unless used wisely and fitted with heat-conserving devices

Solar water heating: installed mainly in 1970s-80s using tax credits; can cut water heating costs 50%

Air conditioning. Rated by Seasonal Energy Efficiency Ratio (SEER, EER): 10 or higher is desirable

Water conservation. Saves energy in water heating, and pumping water to urban areas

Low flow plumbing: standard for showers is 3 to 4 gallons per minute

Landscaping cools the air around the house, saves cooling costs in hot climates

COURSE 5
Title 24
California's Energy Code

INTRODUCTION

The energy crisis of the 1970s was a wake-up call for energy conservation. The oil embargo produced near-panic in the United States and other industrial countries. It was clear that the future of the industrial world's economy was directly connected to the availability of energy supplies and the sensible use of these resources. As a result, cars, appliances, and buildings have all changed radically in the past 20 years in the interest of energy conservation.

Legislation California reacted more vigorously than most states, creating the California Energy Commission in 1977. The California Energy Commission developed an energy code that included Title 24, a set of regulations that establishes standards of energy conservation for new homes, remodeled homes, and nonresidential buildings. Title 24 is designed to reduce energy consumption and encourage energy conservation.

Results Title 24 has been a tremendous success. A new house built since 1977 consumes 40 percent less energy than a similar home built before Title 24 was enacted. The California Energy Commission estimates that Title 24 and other energy conservation programs have saved California consumers $1.9 billion in electricity costs and $1.1 billion in natural gas costs since 1977. Overall energy use per household in California has dropped since 1980.

Benefits Improved energy efficiency makes California less affected by imported oil and natural gas prices and reduces environmental pollution. It also reduces the need for new power plants, the high costs of which are passed on to consumers. While California at large benefits, individual consumers benefit, too. Homeowners and tenants enjoy quieter, cleaner, more comfortable buildings, lower monthly energy bills, and long-term cost savings.

Title 24 in the Real Estate Market Homebuyers are more cost conscious than ever. The dramatic utility savings available through energy conservation can be a real selling point for a home. The real estate professional should be able to discuss the basics of Title 24 with clients so that they understand the value of energy conservation, both for the utility savings and for the enhanced resale value of a home if it can be presented as energy efficient.

Consumer Education. If clients are buying a new home, the seller or agent can inform them that it has met Title 24 standards and show in what areas it may even exceed the mandatory measures. If they are buying a preowned home, clients will want to know how energy efficient it is; that knowledge may make the difference to the sale. An energy audit prepared in advance by a certified energy consultant can be a valuable sales and negotiating tool.

Benefits. Title 24 is a valuable planning tool for energy conservation in construction and remodeling. The consumer will appreciate it as soon as the utility bills arrive—energy costs will be a lot less than in older homes.

TITLE 24 STANDARDS—A CLOSER LOOK

Title 24 standards are based on energy efficiency rather than rationing, austerity, or cutbacks. They utilize built-in conservation features that combine energy savings with a high level of comfort for the home's occupants.

Climate Zones The standards are designed for the many climates of California. The California Energy Commission has designated sixteen individual climate zones in the state and created standards for each one. A homeowner in Eureka will have to meet standards appropriate for a cool, wet area while a homeowner in Palm Springs must build to meet energy standards appropriate for a dry desert climate. The map of California's climate zones show the care taken to create a realistic set of regulations.

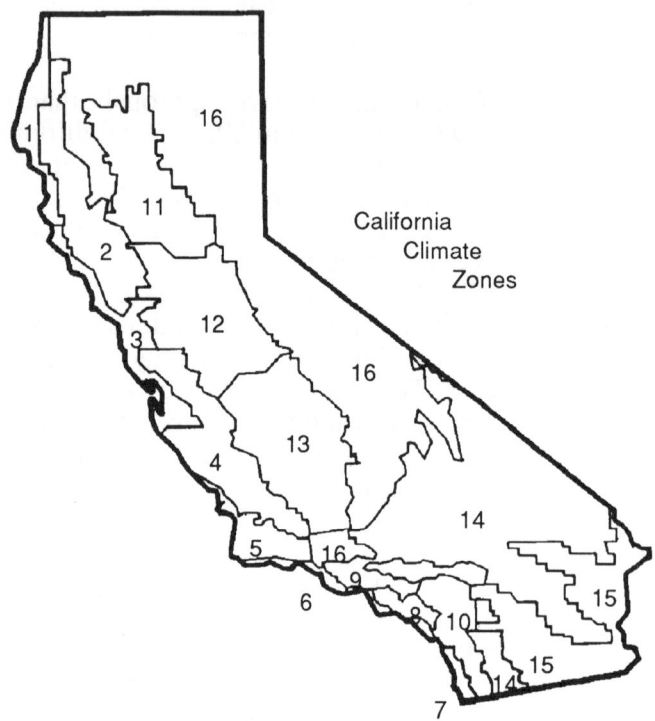

California Climate Zones

Building Types Different sets of standards apply to different types of California building construction. The regulations include residential and nonresidential standards.

Building Components Basically, the Title 24 standards establish requirements (measures) for three major building components:

☐ Building envelope

☐ HVAC (heating, ventilation, and air conditioning) and plumbing system

☐ Lighting system.

Building Envelope Envelope measures apply to wall, ceiling, and floor insulation levels, doors, and windows. An efficient envelope minimizes the need for artificial heating or cooling to maintain a comfortable indoor climate.

Walls, Floors, and Ceilings. Typical insulation R-values for the opaque envelope components are R-13 for 2x4 stud walls, R-19 for 2x6 stud walls as well as raised floors, and R-30 for ceilings.

Windows. The windows, referenced as "fenestration units" in Title 24, are seen in two thermodynamic ways. The first deals with heat loss through the overall unit, and the second with heat gain.

- ☐ *Heat Loss.* Heat loss is measured in "U-value." The lower the U-value (0.75 BTU per hour per degree Fahrenheit per square foot), which is the mathematical reciprocal of the R-value (1 divided by the R value), the slower the heat transfer through the glass.

    - *Window Construction.* Window components that affect the U-value are the frame materials (metal, vinyl, wood, etc.), the number of panes of glass, and the airspace between the panes (if any). For example, typical double-paned windows have a half-inch air space between panes.

    - *Type of Glass.* The type of glass also affects heat loss. There is a significant difference between standard clear glass and glass with an energy-efficient low-E coating. A good example of an energy conserving fenestration product is Andersen's "High Performance" unit—these windows have wood frames, two panes of glass with a 3/8 inch airspace, and low-E coated glass.

- ☐ *Heat Gain.* The second measure is the fenestration unit's heat gain, which takes into account year-round solar gain. In summer California's inland climate zones such as the Central Valley and southern deserts experience excessive heat in window areas facing west and south, especially if they are not shaded by overhanging roofs, vegetation, low-E glass or blinds. In winter, south-facing windows are beneficial in all climate zones. They bring available solar heat into structures at a time when it is needed.

HVAC and Plumbing If the residence requires heating or cooling—and most do—Title 24 address the HVAC (heating, ventilation, and air conditioning) system. HVAC systems have a great effect on the structure's overall energy consumption. Title 24 includes standards for space conditioning equipment, efficiency and controls (such as thermostats), duct construction, ventilation requirements, and economizers. Title 24 also addresses water-related installations—heating, plumbing, swimming pool and spa heaters—that must meet efficiency requirements.

Lighting Lighting system measures include standards for efficient general purpose lighting in residential kitchens and bathrooms. Fluorescent lighting is recommended. There are also standards for nonresidential lighting based on energy use per square foot of floor area.

COMPLIANCE PROCEDURES

Who enforces Title 24 standards? When applying for a building permit through the local building department, the applicant must also submit Title 24 energy documentation. The building department checks this documentation to make sure the project complies with the energy code.

Compliance Options What does the Title 24 compliance and documentation entail? The designer or builder has two options for demonstrating that a building meets the Title 24 energy standards: *prescriptive* and *performance*.

Prescriptive. The prescriptive method is the simplest way to comply with the standards. Taking the prescriptive approach, the designer chooses one of several alternative component packages set forth in the regulations (Exhibit 1), and shows compliance with Title 24 by specifying and installing the minimum requirements.

- *Method*. Tables are established for each climate zone, setting out several ways of meeting conservation goals in that climate. The alternatives incorporate tradeoffs—more wall insulation in exchange for larger window areas, for example. The designer does not have to re-do the energy calculations, since the packages are pre-approved.

- *Lack of Flexibility*. This method has one major drawback. By choosing a given package, the designer gives up flexibility in the choice of design elements that relate to energy use. For example, Package E allows 20 percent glass area to floor area ratio. If a home has a 21 percent glass to floor ratio it does not comply with Title 24 under the prescriptive method.

Performance. To allow more flexibility, most designers and builders take the other method of compliance—the performance approach. This approach allows negative energy-use features (such as excessive west-facing glass) to be offset by positive features (for instance, high-efficiency HVAC equipment) on a case-by-case basis. There are two compliance methods with the performance approach—the point system and computer simulation.

- *Point System*. The point system (Exhibit 2) assigns positive points ("+") to energy features that exceed levels used to develop the standard energy budget. It assigns negative points ("–") to features below these levels. Title 24 compliance is achieved as long as the overall score is zero or positive.

- *Computer Simulation*. The computer method simulates the overall energy use of a building through the entire year. It is the most flexible and detailed of the Title 24 compliance methods. The goal is to arrive at a figure equal to or less than the allowed energy budget (measured in Kbtu per square foot per year). This is derived from the building's needs for heating, cooling, and water heating.

Documentation Whether the prescriptive or performance approach to Title 24 compliance is used, the Energy Commission requires that two forms be submitted documenting compliance.

Certificate of Compliance. The Certificate of Compliance form (Exhibit 3) is required with the plans so that the energy specifications become a permanent part of the approved set of building blueprints.

Mandatory Measures Checklist. A second form, the Mandatory Measures Checklist (Exhibit 4), represents minimum energy conservation levels for the envelope, HVAC and plumbing, and lighting that must be met or exceeded.

Professional Assistance. As of July 1, 1992, an updated Title 24 energy code is in effect. Because of its complexity and the possibility of delays, the builder, real estate licensee, or client may want to employ an energy consultant. The consultation fee is usually nominal compared to the project cost, and may save significant time and money.

Prescriptive Packages for Climate Zone 3

Table 3-Z3:

Component	Package A	Package B	Package C[11]	Package D	Package E
BUILDING ENVELOPE					
Insulation Minimums:					
Ceiling	R-30	R-30	R-38	R-30	R-30
Wall[1]	R-13	R-19	R-25	R-13	R-13
"Heavy" Wall	(R-4.5)	(R-3.5)	N/A	(R-2.44)	(R-2.44)
"Light Mass" Wall	[R-5.0]	[R-5.0]	N/A	N/A	N/A
Slab Floor Perimeter	R-7	R-7	R-7	NR	NR[2]
Raised Floor	R-13	R-19	R-30	R-19[3]	R-19
FENESTRATION					
Maximum U-Value[12]	1.10	0.65	0.40	0.75	0.75
Maximum Total Area	NR	16%	14%	20%	20%
Maximum Total Nonsouth Facing Area	9.6%	NR	NR	NR	NR
Minimum South Facing Area	6.4%	NR	NR	NR	NR
SHADING COEFFICIENT[4]					
South Facing Glazing	NR	NR	0.66	0.66	0.66
West Facing Glazing	NR	NR	0.66	0.66	0.66
East Facing Glazing	NR	NR	0.66	0.66	0.66
North Facing Glazing	NR	NR	0.66	0.66	0.66
THERMAL MASS[5]	REQ	NR	REQ	20%	5%
INFILTRATION CONTROL					
Continuous Barrier	NR	NR	NR	NR	NR
Air-to-Air Heat Exchanger	NR	NR	NR	NR	NR
SPACE HEATING SYSTEM[6]					
Electric Resistance Allowed	NO	NO	YES[7]	NO	NO
If Gas, AFUE=	78%	78%	78%	78%	78%
If Heat Pump,					
Split System HSPF[8] =	6.8	6.8	6.8	6.8	6.8
Single Package System HSPF =	6.6	6.6	6.6	6.6	6.6
SPACE COOLING SYSTEM					
If Split System A/C, SEER =	10.0	10.0	10.0	10.0	10.0
If Single Package A/C, SEER[9] =	9.7	9.7	9.7	9.7	9.7
DOMESTIC WATER HEATING TYPE					
System must meet budget, see §151(b) and 151(f)(8)	Meets Budget	Meets Budget	Meets[10] Budget	Meets Budget	Meets Budget

LEGEND: NR = Not Required; N/A = Not Applicable; REQ = Required

See notes following Table 3-Z16.

California Energy Commission; revised January 1992   Exhibit 1.1

Prescriptive Packages for Climate Zone 3

Notes To The Prescriptive Packages In Tables 3-Z1 Through 3-Z16

1. The value in parentheses is the minimum R-value for the entire wall assembly excluding interior and exterior air films if the wall weight exceeds 40 pounds per square foot. The value in brackets is the minimum R-value for the entire assembly if the heat capacity of the wall meets or exceeds the result of multiplying the bracketed minimum R-value by 0.65. The insulation must be integral with or installed on the outside of the exterior mass. The inside surface of the thermal mass, including plaster or gypsum board in direct contract with the masonry wall, shall be exposed to the room air. The exterior wall used to meet the R-value in parentheses can not also be used to meet the above thermal mass requirement.

2. Use Package E if the proposed building is based on a raised floor. If Package E requires slab insulation (Climate Zone 16), the insulation must be installed along any slab portions of the raised floor building, except for portions to which the exceptions in Section 151(f)1.B apply.

3. Use Package D if the proposed building is based on a slab floor. Package D requires raised floor insulation to be installed under any raised floor portion of the slab floor building.

4. A combined shading coefficient (SC) of 0.66 corresponds to clear dual glazing fenestration products with standard exterior and interior shading devices, such as insect screens and light drapes. If the package specifies a shading coefficient of 0.66, the building official shall assume that standard exterior and interior shading will be installed by the builder or occupant. If the package specifies a shading coefficient of 0.40 or lower, the builder shall meet the requirements of Section 151(f)3.

5. If the package requires thermal mass, meet the requirements of §151(f)4. When using the performance approach, the mass requirement for Package D is based on having 20% of the ground floor slab area exposed to conditioned space with no thermal resistance material on the surface. The remaining 80% of the ground floor slab area has a surface R-value of 2.0. The slab is composed of concrete at least 3.5" thick with a volumetric heat capacity of 28, a conductivity of 0.98 and a surface conductance of 1.3.

   The mass requirement for Package E is based on having mass equivalent in performance to 5% of the ground floor area of an exposed 2" thick concrete slab with a volumetric heat capacity of 28, a conductivity of 0.98, a surface conductance of 1.3 and no thermal resistance on the surface.

6. Automatic setback thermostats must be installed in conjunction with all space heating systems, in accordance with §151(f)9 of the Standards (see Chapter 2 for exceptions).

7. Ducts in Package C shall be insulated to an installed value of at least R-8.

8. HSPF means "Heating Seasonal Performance Factor."

9. Until January 1, 1993, the minimum SEER for single package air conditioner systems is 8.9.

10. Electric resistance water heating is allowed as the main heat source in Package C only if the water heater is located within the building envelope and a minimum of 25% of the energy for water heating is provided by a passive or active solar system or a wood stove boiler. The wood stove boiler credit is not allowed in climate zones 8, 10 and 15, nor in localities that do not allow wood stoves.

11. Package C is the only package that allows electric space heating. Package C may be used only if the building is in an area (1) where natural gas is not currently available, and (2) where extension of natural gas service is impractical, as determined by the natural gas utility.

12. The fenestration U-value rating procedures and labeling requirements of Section 116(a)2 go into effect on July 1, 1992 for all fenestration products except dual-pane, aluminum-frame fenestration products, for which the procedures and requirements are optional until July 1, 1993. During this one-year period: (1) if prescriptive package D or E is used, dual-pane, alumunium-frame glazing may be assumed to meet the U-value specified in the package used; (2) if a performance method is used, dual-pane, aluminum-frame glazing may be assumed to have the U-value specified in the package (D or E) on which the performance budget is based.

Exhibit 1.2 California Energy Commission; revised January 1992

Point System Summary

```
POINT SYSTEM SUMMARY                                      P-2R    page 5 of 14
-----------------------------------------------------------------------------
Project Name: Gallanter Residence             |Date: 1/7/1993
                                              |
Documentation: CALC 24                        |COMPLY 24 User 1159
-----------------------------------------------------------------------------

BUILDING DATA
-------------
  Conditioned Floor Area    2383 sqft    Number of Stories    2
  Occupancy Type            Single Fam Det

SCORE CARD                            Measure                     Points
------------------------              -------                     ------
1.  Roof Insulation                   0.0305   (U-Value)             0

2.  Wall Insulation                   0.0729   (U-Value)             2

3.  Raised Floor Insulation           0.0422   (U-Value)     ⎤
                                                             |
3a. Controlled Vent Crawlspace        0.0      (R-Value)     |->   0
                                                             |
4.  Slab Edge Insulation              0.9000   (f2 factor)   ⎦

5.  Infiltration                   Standard                          0

6.  Glass Heat Loss                   0.75       21.9%              -1
                                                            Sum 1-6   1

7.  Fenestration Heat Gain                SC
       Orientation    Area    % Glass    Open      Eff %     SER
       -----------    -----   -------    ----      -----     -----
       North           0.0     0.0   x   0.00   =   0.0      0.00    -1
       East          182.3     7.7   x   0.60   =   4.6      0.95     0
       South         195.6     8.2   x   0.61   =   5.0      0.95     0
       West          144.0     6.0   x   0.66   =   4.0      0.93     0
       Skylight        0.0     0.0   x   0.00   =   0.0      0.00     0

8.  Interior Thermal Mass             0.10                           0

9.  Exterior Wall Mass                0.00                           0
                                                            Sum 7-9  -1
10. Heating System                                                   0
       Zonal Control: No
11. Cooling System                                                   0

12. Water Heating (see DHW Worksheet)                       =        0
                                                                    ---
                                                    Point Total:     0
```

CALC 24, Berkeley, CA

Exhibit 2

Certificate of Compliance: Residential

```
CERTIFICATE OF COMPLIANCE: Residential (part 1 of 2)      CF-1R    page 1 of 14
-------------------------------------------------------------------------------
Project Name: Gallanter Residence                       | Date: 1/7/1993
      Address: 4199 Garden Lane                         |------------------------
               El Sobrante, CA                          | Building Permit No
                                                        |------------------------
Designer: Homevisions Consulting Group                  | Checked by / Date
                                                        |------------------------
Documentation: CALC 24                                  | COMPLY 24 User 1159
-------------------------------------------------------------------------------
GENERAL INFORMATION
   Compliance Method:              COMPLY 24 version 4.05
   Climate Zone:                   3
   Conditioned Floor Area:         2383 sqft
   Building Type:                  Single Fam Det
   Building Front Orientation:     90 deg (E)
   Number of Dwelling Units:       1
   Floor Construction Type:        Raised Floor

BUILDING SHELL INSULATION
Component                          U-Value   Location/Comments
---------------------------        -------   -------------------------------
R-15 Wall (W.15.2x4.16)            0.0729    FIRST FLOOR
R-15 Wall (W.15.2x4.16)            0.0729    SECOND FLOOR
R-30 Roof(R.30.2x4.24)             0.0305    FIRST FLOOR
R-30 Roof(R.30.2x4.24)             0.0305    SECOND FLOOR
R-19 Floor(F.19.2x.16)             0.0554    SECOND FLOOR/Over Open
R-19 Floor(F.19.2x.16)             0.0416    FIRST FLOOR/R-6 Crawlspace
Slab Perimeter w/R-0.0             0.9000    FIRST FLOOR

FENESTRATION                                Shading Devices                    Frame
Orient.     Area   U-Val  Type    Interior           Exterior       OH SF     Type
--------    -----  -----  ------  ----------------   ----------     -- --    -----
Front (E)   54.0   0.75   Double  Std Drape          none           N  N     Metal
Front (E)   95.0   0.75   Double  Std Drape          none           N  N     Metal
Front (SE)  33.3   0.60   Double  Std Drape          none           N  N     Wood
Left  (S)   66.6   0.75   Double  Std Drape          none           N  N     Metal
Left  (S)   89.0   0.75   Double  Std Drape          none           N  N     Metal
Left  (S)   20.0   0.60   Double  Std Drape          none           N  N     Wood
Left  (SW)  20.0   0.75   Double  Std Drape          none           N  N     Metal
Back  (W)   88.0   0.75   Double  Std Drape          none           N  N     Metal
Back  (W)   14.0   0.75   Double  Std Drape          none           N  N     Metal
Back  (W)   14.0   1.40   Double  Std Drape          none           N  N     Metal
Back  (NW)  28.0   0.75   Double  Std Drape          none           N  N     Metal

THERMAL MASS                         Area   Thick
Type                      Covering   (sf)   (in)   Location/Description
----------------------    --------   -----  -----  --------------------
Concrete, Heavyweight     Exposed      54   3.50   Slab on Grade
```

Exhibit 3.1   CALC 24, Berkeley, CA

Certificate of Compliance: Residential

```
CERTIFICATE OF COMPLIANCE: Residential (part 2 of 2)   CF-1R   page 2 of 14
---------------------------------------------------------------------------
Project Name: Gallanter Residence               | Date: 1/7/1993
                                                |
Documentation: CALC 24                          | COMPLY 24 User 1159
---------------------------------------------------------------------------
```

HVAC SYSTEMS System Type	Minimum Efficiency	Distrib Type and Location	Duct RVal	TStat Type	Location/Comments
Furnace	0.800 AFUE	Ducts in Crawl	4.3	SetBck	RESIDENCE ✲
No Cooling	10.000 SEER	Ducts in Crawl	4.3	SetBck	

WATER HEATING SYSTEMS System Name	Distribution Type	Water Heater Type	No. in Sys	Energy Factor	Tank Size (gal)	Ext. Insul R-Val
RHEEMGLAS 44V40 (SG)	Standard	StorGas	2	0.62	39.0	12.0

SPECIAL FEATURES/REMARKS
✲ = The Residence will use 2 Gas Furnaces (Min. = 80% AFUE).

COMPLIANCE STATEMENT
This Certificate of Compliance lists the building features and performance specifications needed to comply with Title 24, Parts 1 & 6 of the California Code of Regulations, and the administrative regulations to implement them. This certificate has been signed by the individual with overall design responsibility. When this certificate of compliance is submitted for a single building plan to be built in multiple orientations, any shading feature that is varied is indicated in the Special Features/Remarks section

DESIGNER or OWNER
(Per Business & Professions Code)
Homevisions Consulting Group
3817 San Pablo Dam Rd.
El Sobrante, CA
(800)773-2834   Lic #:_____

_____
(signature)   (date)

DOCUMENTATION AUTHOR
Chris Ferre'
CALC 24
1250 Addison Street, #1074
Berkeley, CA 94702
(510) 548-0382

Christopher Ferré   1/7/93
(signature)   (date)

ENFORCEMENT AGENCY
Name:_____
Title:_____
Agency:_____
Telephone:_____

_____
(signature/stamp)   (date)

Mandatory Measures Checklist: Residential   MF-1R

NOTE: Lowrise residential buildings subject to the Standards must contain these measures regardless of the compliance approach used. Items marked with an asterisk (*) may be superseded by more stringent compliance requirements listed on the Certificate of Compliance. When this checklist is incorporated into the permit documents, the features noted shall be considered by all parties as binding minimum component performance specifications for the mandatory measures whether they are shown elsewhere in the documents or on this checklist only.

DESCRIPTION	DESIGNER	ENFORCEMENT
Building Envelope Measures	✓	
* §150(a): Minimum R-19 ceiling insulation.	✓	
§150(b): Loose fill insulation manufacturer's labeled R-Value.	N/A	
* §150(c): Minimum R-13 wall insulation in framed walls (does not apply to exterior mass walls).	✓	
* §150(d): Minimum R-13 raised floor insulation in framed floors; minimum R-8 in concrete raised floors.	✓	
§150(l): Slab edge insulation - water absorption rate no greater than 0.3%, water vapor transmission rate no greater than 2.0 perm/inch.	N/A	
§118: Insulation specified or installed meets California Energy Commission quality standards. Indicate type and form.	✓	

§116-17: Fenestration Products, Exterior Doors and Infiltration/Exfiltration Controls
  a. Doors and windows between conditioned and unconditioned spaces designed to limit air leakage.
  b. Manufactured fenestration products have label with certified U-value, and infiltration certification.
  c. Exterior doors and windows weatherstripped; all joints and penetrations caulked and sealed.
	✓	

§150(g): Vapor barriers mandatory in Climate Zones 14 and 16 only.	N/A	
§150(f): Special infiltration barrier installed to comply with §151 meets Commission quality standards.	✓	

§150(e): Installation of Fireplaces, Decorative Gas Appliances and Gas Logs
  1. Masonry and factory-built fireplaces have:
    a. Closeable metal or glass door
    b. Outside air intake with damper and control
    c. Flue damper and control
  2. No continuous burning gas pilots allowed.
	N/A	

Space Conditioning, Water Heating and Plumbing System Measures		
§110-13: HVAC equipment, water heaters, showerheads and faucets certified by the Commission.	✓	
§150(i): Setback thermostat on all applicable heating systems.	✓	

§150(j): Pipe and Tank Insulation
  1. Indirect hot water tanks (e.g., unfired storage tanks or backup solar hot water tanks) have insulation blanket (R-12 or greater) or combined interior/exterior insulation (R-16 or greater).
  2. First 5 feet of pipes closest to water heater tank, non-recirculating systems, insulated (R-4 or greater).
  3. All buried or exposed piping insulated in recirculating sections of hot water system.
  4. Cooling system piping below 55°F insulated.
  5. Piping insulated between heating source and indirect hot water tank.
	N/A	

* §150(m): Ducts and Fans
  1. Ducts constructed, installed and sealed to comply with UMC Sections 1002 and 1004; ducts insulated to a minimum installed value of R-4.2 or ducts enclosed entirely within conditioned space.
  2. Exhaust fan systems have backdraft or automatic dampers
  3. Gravity ventilating systems serving conditioned space have either automatic or readily accessible, manually operated dampers..
	✓	

§114: Pool and Spa Heating Systems and Equipment 1. System is certified with 78% thermal efficiency, on-off switch, weatherproof operating instructions, no electric resistance heating and no pilot light.	N/A	

2. System is installed with:
    a. At least 36" pipe between filter and heater for future solar heating.
    b. Cover for outdoor pools or outdoor spa.
  3. Pool system has directional inlets and a circulation pump time switch.
	N/A	

§115: Gas-fired central furnace, pool heater, spa heater or household cooking appliance have no continuously burning pilot light. (Exception: Non-electrical cooking appliance with pilot < 150 Btu/hr.)	✓	
Lighting Measures		
§150(k): 40 lumens/watt or greater for general lighting in kitchens and rooms with water closets: and recessed ceiling fixtures IC (insulation cover) approved.	✓	

Revised January 1992

Exhibit 4   California Energy Commission; revised January 1992

PG&E's Energy Conservation Incentives

In 1989, PG&E joined with fourteen other major stakeholders in California's energy and environmental future to come to a consensus on how to meet the state's growing energy needs. This group of utilities, government regulators, consumer advocates, and environmentalists—which came to be known as the California Collaborative—decided that the state's energy policy should shift away from increased production and toward energy efficiency.

Goals PG&E's goal is to motivate California homebuyers into exceeding Title 24 standards and achieving an even higher level of energy efficiency. This will benefit everyone—the consumer, PG&E, the environment, and the state's overall economy.

Business Decision. PG&E had more than the environment in mind. As a shareholder-owned corporation, it found that its profitability was hurt by the high construction costs of new energy-producing plants. A policy of energy efficiency would reduce PG&E's overhead, allowing the company to enjoy higher profitability by maximizing the use of existing power plants rather than having to build expensive new facilities.

New Construction. One type of motivation is created by PG&E's New Construction Incentive Program, which offers cash and other incentives to builders who agree to incorporate energy efficiency improvements suggested by PG&E into the homes they build. In addition, PG&E also provides rebates and coupons for energy-related improvements to existing homes.

Appliances. Even small savings add up. Many new appliances have tags indicating their energy use per year and comparing them to similar models with the lowest and highest energy cost. By shopping for energy conservation as well as quality, a consumer can save hundreds of dollars of energy costs over the appliance's life span. New refrigerators, stoves, washers, and dryers carry these "Energy Guide" tags. In some cases PG&E offers rebates of $50 and more to purchasers of energy-efficient appliances.

Financial Incentives **Existing Structures.** PG&E has created an effective program of rebates designed to encourage consumers to create an energy-efficient home. Specifics vary from year to year, but include a wide range of promotions.

- *Appliances and Improvements.* The 1992 rebate program included rebates on refrigerators, ceiling insulation, central air conditioners, and multiple refrigerators (in apartment buildings). A $100 rebate was the incentive to reduce heating and cooling cost with ceiling insulation. Purchase of a new high-efficiency central air conditioner resulted in a rebate of $120 to $1,000 or more. By exceeding federal energy standards by 20 percent or more while purchasing at least five new refrigerators, apartment owners could receive a $50 to $100 rebate for each refrigerator.

- *Smaller Items.* The 1992 PG&E coupon program included less ambitious conservation measures as well: shade trees, water heater blankets, shower heads, and furnace and air conditioner filters. Shade trees can cut costs on air conditioning, so PG&E offered up to two $5 rebates for their purchase. It also offered a $5 discount coupon for water heater blankets. Other coupons offered as much as 50 percent ($4 maximum) on a low-flow shower head, and a $1 discount on two furnace or air conditioner filters.

Title 24: California's Energy Code

Energy Sources

Primary Energy Sources. Energy is either *primary* or *derived*. Primary forms can be used directly (oil, gas) or converted to electricity.

Fossil Fuels. Petroleum and natural gas are the most important primary sources of energy in California.

- In the mid-1980s, oil provided 56 percent of all the energy supplied.
- California uses somewhat more natural gas (29 percent of total energy supplied) than the US as a whole (25 percent).
- Coal is much less used in California than in the US generally. While most electrical generation in the country is coal-based, California generates more than 50 percent of its electricity from natural gas.

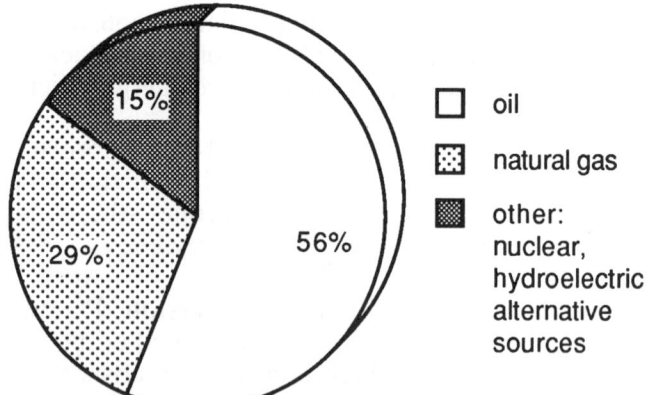

Sources of Primary Energy in California

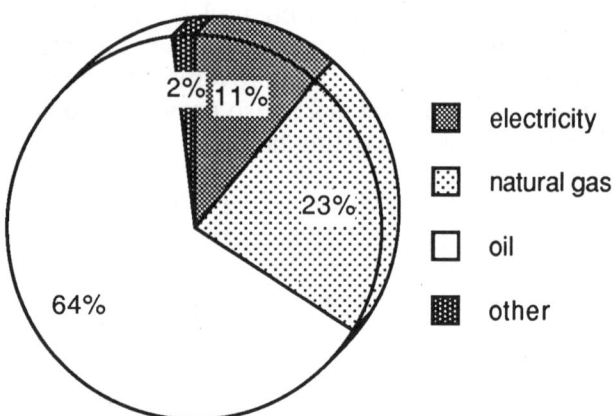

Energy Reaching the End User in California

Oil. Since California is a major oil-producing state (Kern County alone pumps 8 percent of US production), 70 percent of oil used in California comes from in-state wells. Most of the imported oil comes from Alaska.

Electricity. This is a derived form of energy, which must be produced from one of the primary sources. Despite its importance in the household market, electricity makes up only about 11 percent of the total energy delivered to end users.

Alternative Sources. One way of conserving our finite supply of fossil fuels is to develop other ways of producing electricity. Although not yet a major factor, alternative energy sources (also called *renewables*) have produced about 5 percent of the electricity delivered in recent years. The relative contribution of various renewables to that 5 percent is shown below. California leads the world in the use of geothermal energy to produce electricity. One estimate is that in the future geothermal energy will contribute 7.4 percent of the electricity used in the state.

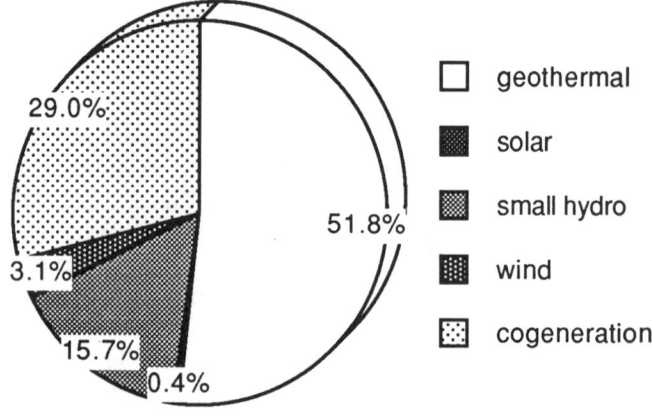

Alternative Sources of Electricity

Environmental Issues & Obligations

New Construction. PG&E is providing both financial motivation and education to help homebuilders exceed Title 24 standards.

- *Home Cooling Systems.* The California Comfort Homes program provides cash incentives to builders and individuals who build homes cooled more efficiently than the state requires. These incentives are designed to cover a major portion of the added building costs. According to PG&E, high-performance air conditioners, windows, wall and ceiling insulation, and other measures will improve energy efficiency and occupant comfort, and save thousands of dollars in energy bills over the life of the home.

- *Commercial Buildings.* New commercial construction is also addressed. PG&E offers incentives of up to fifty cents a square foot to commercial developers whose buildings are at least 15 percent more energy efficient than required by the state. Energy-efficient lighting, ventilation, and air conditioning are especially encouraged, with no predetermined limits on the total incentive amount. In small commercial projects, the entire added cost of energy conservation may be picked up by PG&E.

- *Demonstration Homes.* PG&E has model Showcase Homes in many new subdivisions. Open to the public, the homes are designed to demonstrate how energy efficient appliances and building design can achieve a 50 percent reduction in energy use, and to encourage consumers to make energy efficiency a priority in their own homes. The company provides technical and financial assistance for design and construction to participating builders. Even advertising support is provided.

- *Builder Education.* PG&E has built the $7.5 million Pacific Energy Center in San Francisco to provide a firsthand look at energy efficient technologies and design techniques. The 25,000-square-foot center will offer demonstrations, seminars, and data resources. It is primarily aimed at helping building owners, facility managers, architects, engineers, designers, and builders create more energy efficient commercial and residential buildings.

Energy Efficiency Facts PG&E has compiled the following energy efficiency facts and suggestions to underscore the potential savings from energy conservation.

- A new, energy-efficient refrigerator uses up to 50 percent less energy than a refrigerator manufactured in 1973.

- Compact fluorescent light bulbs use up to 75 percent less energy than standard incandescent bulbs.

- Compact fluorescent light bulbs last up to 10 times longer than standard incandescent light bulbs.

- Gas clothes dryers cost 75 percent less to operate than electric clothes dryers.

- Poorly maintained air conditioners use 10 to 30 percent more energy than properly maintained units.

SPOT THE BIG SPENDERS
Residential Energy Consumption

		ESTIMATED ENERGY USE *	ESTIMATED ENERGY COST **
HEATING	**Space Heating, Gas:**		
	Small Furnace (60,000 Btu)	.6 therms per hour	36¢/hour
	Large Furnace (100,000 Btu)	1 therm per hour	60¢/hour
	Space Heating, Electric:		
	Portable Heater (1500 watt)	1.5 kwh per hour	18¢/hour
	Baseboard Heater (6 ft. unit)	3 kwh per hour	36¢/hour
	Furnace (10 kw)	10 kwh per hour	$1.20/hour
	Heat Pump (2.5 ton)	3-5 kwh per hour	36¢-60¢/hour
AIR CONDITIONER	Window/wall (110 volt)	1.5 kwh per hour	18¢/hour
	Window/wall (220 volt)	2.6 kwh per hour	31¢/hour
	Central (3 ton)	4.5 kwh per hour	54¢/hour
	Portable Fan	.2 kwh per hour	2.4¢/hour
WATER HEATING (includes all uses)	Electric	300-400 kwh per month	$36.00 - $48.00/month
	Gas	20-30 therms per month	$12.00 - $18.00/month
	Heat pump water heater	175-225 kwh per month	$21.00 - $27.00/month
REFRIGERATOR/ FREEZER	Refrigerator-frost-free, 16 cu. ft.	100-150 kwh per month	$12.00 - $18.00/month
	Refrigerator-frost-free, 20 cu. ft.	115-180 kwh per month	$13.80 - $21.60/month
	Refrigerator-partial auto., 12cu. ft.	50-90 kwh per month	$6.00 - $10.80/month
	Refrigerator-manual defrost, 10 cu. ft.	35-60 kwh per month	$4.20 - $7.20/month
	Freezer-frost-free, 15 cu. ft.	70-150 kwh per month	$8.40 - $18.00/month
		40-90 kwh per month	$5.00 - $10.80/month
LIGHTING	General household	50-200 kwh per month	$6.00-$24.00/month
SWIMMING POOL	Sweep Pump (3/4 HP)	1 kwh per hour	12¢/hour
	Filter Pump (1-1/2 HP)	1.5 kwh per hour	18¢/hour
	Filter Pump (2 HP)	2 kwh per hour	24¢/hour
	Gas Heater (400,000 Btu)	4 therms per hour	$2.40/hour
SPA	Electric Heater (1,500 watt)	1.5 kwh per hour	18¢/hour
	Electric Heater (5,500 watt)	5.5 kwh per hour	.66¢/hour
	Electric Heater (11,000 watt)	11 kwh per hour	$1.32/hour
	Gas Heater (75,000 Btu)	.75 therms per hour	45¢/hour

* Estimated energy use is based on average operation conditions. Your particular use can vary.
** Estimated costs based on 12¢ per kwh and 60¢ per therm.

Market Research Department
1/2/91

Reprinted with permission, PG&E

		ESTIMATED ENERGY USE	ESTIMATED ENERGY COST
LAUNDRY	Clothes Dryer, Electric	5 kwh per load	55¢/load
	Clothes Dryer, Gas	.22 therms,.5 kwh per load	19¢/load
	Steam iron (hand)	1 kwh per hour	11¢/hour
	Washing Machine***		
	Cold water only, 50 gallons	.25 kwh per load	3¢/load
	Warm wash, cold rinse	.11 therms, .25 kwh per load	10¢/load
	Hot wash, warm rinse	.33 therms, .25 kwh per load	23¢/load
WATER BED		75-175 kwh per month	$9.00-$21.00/month
ENTERTAINMENT	Radio-phonograph	.03 kwh per hour	1¢/3hours
	TV:		
	Black and white, solid state	.07 kwh per hour	1¢/hour
	Color	.23 kwh per hour	3¢/hour
HOUSEHOLD GOODS	Clock	2 kwh per month	24¢/month
	Electric Blanket:		
	Twin	.5 kwh per night	6¢/night
	Double/queen	.75 kwh per night	9¢/night
	King	1 kwh per night	12¢/night
	Night light, 4-watt (on 24 hours)	3 kwh per month	36¢/month
	Vaccum cleaner	.75 kwh per hour	9¢/hour
	Hair dryer (1,200 watt)	1.2 kwh per hour	14¢/hour
	Fireplace, gas	.2 therms per hour	12¢/hour
KITCHEN	Broiler, portable electric	1.5 kwh per hour	18¢/hour
	Coffeemaker (per brew)	.12 kwh per brew	1¢/brew
	Coffeemaker (warm setting)	.4 kwh per hour	5¢/hour
	Deep fryer, electric	1 kwh per hour	12¢/hour
	Dishwasher: ***		
	Normal cycle	1 kwh,.2 therms per load	23¢/load
	Energy saver cycle	.5 kwh,.12 therms per load	13¢/load
	Frying pan, electric	1 kwh per hour	12¢/hour
	Grill, gas barbecue	.25 therm per hour	15¢/hour
	Microwave oven, 5 minutes	.1 kwh per 5 minutes	1¢/5minutes
	Range, electric:		
	Oven	1.33 kwh per hour	16¢/hour
	Surface	1.25 kwh per hour	15¢/hour
	Self-cleaning feature	6 kwh per cleaning	72¢/cleaning
	Range, gas (pilotless):		
	Oven	.09 therm per hour	5¢/hour
	Surface	.07 therm per hour	4¢/hour
	Self-cleaning feature	.50 therm per cleaning	30¢/cleaning
	Pilot light usage	.20 therm per day	12¢/day
	Toaster	.08 kwh per use	1¢/use
	Toaster oven, electric portable	.50 kwh per hour	6¢/hour
	Waffle iron (3-4 servings)	.33 kwh per use	4¢/use

*** Estimates are based on gas water heating. Add 20¢-50¢ per load for electric water heat.
Now that you know where your energy dollar goes, you can better control your PG&E bill.

Reprinted with permission, PG&E

Title 24: California's Energy Code

- Raising the air conditioner thermostat setting by six degrees can save 20 percent or more on cooling costs.

- A deciduous shade tree that protects the home from the summer sun can cut cooling costs up to 20 percent.

- Using light-colored paint on building exteriors can reduce cooling costs by 10 to 15 percent.

- Up to 25 percent of heating and cooling can be lost through leaky ductwork.

- Ceiling insulation can save up to 33 percent in annual heating and cooling costs.

- Insulating the water heater and the first three feet of pipe coming from the tank can reduce water heating costs by 10 percent.

CHEERS: CALIFORNIA HOME ENERGY EFFICIENCY RATING SYSTEM

CHEERS (California Home Energy Efficiency Rating System, Inc.) is a nonprofit partnership of public and private enterprises founded in 1990. Information on the organization and its programs can be obtained from Greg French, Executive Director, 1700 Adams Avenue, Suite 102, Costa Mesa, CA 92626, (714) 540-0501.

Purpose CHEERS's wide-ranging list of members includes California's investor-owned utilities, municipal utilities, real estate brokers, building industry officials, financial institutions, environmentalists, consumer advocates, and the California Energy Commission. What could all of these diverse interests agree on?

- That a uniform statewide home energy rating system (CHEERS) was needed for new and existing housing in California.

- That public education and communication were needed for such a program.

- That means to facilitate the financing of energy efficiency measures were needed.

The result, they felt, would be a much higher standard of residential energy efficiency for California residents.

Potential Value. There is a tremendous potential for energy savings in the United States. More than 107 million existing homes are currently consuming $100 billion annually in energy costs. No less than 90 million of these homes are classified as energy inefficient. Thus CHEERS has the potential to save hundreds of millions of dollars for consumers by conserving energy in the pre-Title 24 housing sector.

Implementation. The CHEERS concept is based on a nationwide home energy rating program. CHEERS is scheduled to start in 1993 with pilot programs in Northern and Southern California. These initial programs will test the premises of the program, database, marketing, training, and rating activities. Statewide implementation will come after the pilot program is completed.

CHEERS—How It Works

Basically, CHEERS is designed to rate homes on energy efficiency, and provide homeowners with estimates of utility costs for the home and a list of suggested energy efficiency improvements. This list gives homeowners the option of deciding which improvements can best help them reduce energy bills.

Rating System. The rating system ranges from 1 to 100 points. A home rated 100 would use no energy at all. Homes that meet Title 24 standards would usually receive ratings of 75 to 80 points. A less efficient home would rate lower.

Report Format. The sample energy report (Exhibit 5) shows the potential for substantial savings in a typical home. Based on local utility rates, the numeric rating (1 to 100 points) will be used to inform homeowners of estimated utilities costs. Homeowners will receive a list of suggested energy improvements, to use at their discretion to reduce their energy bills.

Inspection Service. The CHEERS ratings will be done by private companies, such as certified energy consultants, and utilities whose employees have been trained to administer the CHEERS program. As with most consumer services, market demand will help set the price of the rating service. It is forecast that demand will be high, as consumers will appreciate the value of the program. So CHEERS inspections are likely to be priced reasonably.

Example. As an illustration of how CHEERS will work, picture a home after a CHEERS inspection has been made. The inspector uses the CHEERS database to assess the information and comes back with a rating of 48. This means the homeowner has some distance to go to make the house as energy efficient as a new Title 24-compliant structure. With the rating, the homeowner also gets a cost estimate of gas and electric energy bills using baseline estimates of various appliance uses. Perhaps most important, the owner receives recommendations of measures to reduce your home's utility costs. These might range from adding more insulation to replacing old windows. Then it is up to the homeowner to decide what steps to take.

Energy Efficient Mortgages (EEM)

One key to making the CHEERS concept a reality is financing. Homeowners wishing to implement energy conservation recommendations such as a new furnace, windows, appliances, or insulation often need capital to make these improvements. Accordingly an integral proposal in the CHEERS program is the "energy efficient mortgage."

Special Financing. The energy efficient mortgage (EEM) will allow lenders to stretch debt-to-income ratios in lending by documenting the current and future energy efficiency of the home through the CHEERS program. It also provides financing at the time of purchase to make needed energy efficiency improvements.

Example. The following example illustrates how these two concepts—CHEERS and EEM—will be linked for the homeowner's benefit:

You've fallen in love with a spacious old home. While deciding what sort of offer to make, you remember that energy conservation can save you money. So you pay a small fee for a CHEERS energy audit, knowing that you can probably finance recommended upgrades with your lender.

Sample Energy Audit Report

Prepared for: Name **Richard Pearlman**
Address **1544 Channing Way, Berkeley**
Auditor Signature **Christopher Tous**
Date **1/22/93**   Audit # **701100**

HOME NOW

Heating Efficiency Score

0   10   20   30   40   (50)   60   70   80   90   100

Worst — (No energy features)   Best — (No heating bill)

$ approx. **$1450**
Estimated Annual Heating Cost

IMPROVED HOME

Heating Efficiency Score

0   10   20   30   40   50   60   (70)   80   90   100

Worst — (No energy features)   Best — (No heating bill)

$ approx. **$1050**
Estimated Annual Heating Cost

Rated Features now in the home:					ENERGY FEATURES	Add these Features for improved Rating:
very leaky	leaky	(moderately tight)	tight	very tight	N.A.	INFILTRATION LEVEL	Improve to "moderately tight" (add caulking & weatherstripping)
R-0	R-11	(R-19)	R-30	R-38	N.A.	CEILING INSULATION	Add: (R-11), R-19, R-30, R-38 To get a total of (R-30), R-38
R-0	R-7	(R-11)	R-19	R-19+	N.A.	WALL INSULATION	Add R-11
(R-0)	R-7	R-11	R-19	R-19+	N.A.	FLOOR INSULATION	(Add R-19)
single pane	single with drapes	double pane	(double with drapes)	triple	N.A.	WINDOW TREATMENT	Add storm windows or replace sash to get a double layer on each window
	absent		installed		(N.A.)	NEW HEATING SYSTEM	Install
	(absent)		installed		N.A.	FLAME RETENTION BURNER	(Install)
	(absent)		installed		N.A.	PIPE INSULATION	(Install)
	absent		installed		(N.A.)	DUCT INSULATION	Install

Estimated Improvement Costs: $ **1525**

Features in the home, but not rated:				ENERGY FEATURES	Add these important Features too. (Not rated)
absent	installed	(N.A.)		WINDOW INSULATION	Install
absent	(installed)	N.A.		CLOCK THERMOSTAT	Install
absent	(installed)	N.A.		WATER HEATER INSULATION	Install
absent	installed	(N.A.)		SOLAR WATER HEATER	Install
absent	installed	(N.A.)		VENT DAMPER	Install
absent	installed	(N.A.)		ELECTRONIC IGNITION	Install
absent	installed	(N.A.)		NEW COOLING SYSTEM	Install
absent	installed	(N.A.)		SOLAR POOL HEATER	Install
absent	installed	(N.A.)		HEAT GAIN RETARDANT	Install
				OTHER	

Home Now
Btu's/Square foot × degree days: **10**

Note: The Predicted Annual Heating Cost for the house is based on the following assumptions:
Electricity: $/kwh: —   Heating Oil: $/gal: —   Natural Gas: $/ccf: **0.60**

Improved Home
Btu's/Square foot × degree days: **8**

Disclaimer: Although every effort has been made to provide accurate information on this form, neither this form nor any entries made on it constitutes any warranty, express or implied, as to, without implied limitation, the presence or lack of energy features in the house, the heating fuel used in the house and its cost, or the actual annual heating energy consumption of the house.

Exhibit 5

Building envelope: wall, floor, and ceiling insulation; doors and windows
- Opaque components: insulation measured in R-value
- Windows: measured for heat loss (U-value) and heat gain (low-E coating)

HVAC (heating, ventilation, and air conditioning) and plumbing: requirements for efficiency of equipment

Lighting: fluorescent is recommended

Compliance Procedures
Local building department requires compliance documentation

Prescriptive approach: menu of component packages with pre-approved calculations; straightforward but not flexible

Performance approach: flexible design, compliance calculated case by case, by point system or computer simulation

Two documents, Certificate of Compliance and Mandatory Measures Checklist

Energy consultants can assist with calculations and other matters

PG&E's Energy Conservation Incentives
To shift state's energy policy from increased production to conservation

PG&E saves cost of building additional power plants

New Construction Incentive Program for builders; also rebates for retrofits

Appliances labeled with energy information; rebate programs

California Comfort Homes incentives for efficient cooling systems in new homes

Demonstration homes and Pacific Energy Center for consumer and builder education

Energy efficiency facts: new refrigerator uses 50% less energy than 1973 model
- Compact fluorescent bulbs last 10 times longer, use 75% less energy
- Save 33% on heating and cooling by insulating ceiling

Energy is either primary (mostly fossil fuels) or derived (electricity)

Alternative renewable forms of energy (wind, water, solar, geothermal) represent a small but growing source of electricity

CHEERS: California Home Energy Efficiency Rating System
Nonprofit corporation of utilities, building, real estate, financial industries, consumer advocates, and state Energy Commission

Based on national program; scheduled to start in California in 1993

About 90 million of 107 million existing homes are considered energy inefficient

Rating system for energy efficiency of homes, with list of suggested improvements

Scale of 1 to 100 (100 = uses no energy at all): homes that meet Title 24 score 75 to 80

Private consultants and utility employees will perform inspections

Improvements will be voluntary; incentive is savings on energy bills

Energy Efficient Mortgages: lenders can adjust debt-to-income ratio to allow for future energy savings

Financing at time of purchase to make energy-saving improvements

CHEERS rating helps homeowners and real estate practitioners understand full cost of ownership and operation

COURSE 6
Landscaping & the Environment

INTRODUCTION

The contribution of landscaping to a residential property's value is often overlooked. Landscape design not only affects a home's aesthetics and comfort, it also directly influences environmental hazards such as landslides and fires, and the energy and water costs of maintaining the property. Licensees who are knowledgeable about the ways that landscaping affects property value will be better equipped to serve and advise their clients. This course covers the impact of landscaping on environmental hazards, and the key factors that add value to landscaping: water conserving and low maintenance plants and design, and "hardscapes" such as gates, fences, and walkways.

Disclosure Although there are no disclosure requirements specifically for landscaping except with regard to vegetation clearance in certain wildland fire hazard areas (see Course 12, Environmental Disclosures), many features of residential landscaping may be "material facts" that the licensee would be wise to look for and disclose. Although not all are specifically mentioned on the standard Real Estate Transfer Disclosure Statement, licensees will want to recognize and disclose landscaping and site features that materially affect the property's risk from flooding, settling or drainage problems, landslides, and fire.

Property Value In an appraisal or market analysis, landscape features such as site, view, and patio are often singled out and valued as distinct elements of comparison. Large trees can also be individually valued, for marketing or insurance purposes. In addition, landscaping has a powerful effect on the more subjective "curb appeal" and amenity value of a property.

Cost Savings Well thought out landscaping can save time and labor in maintenance, can save water, can save energy by regulating light and heat, and can even avert liability and result in lower insurance rates. A basic knowledge of plant care and sitework principles can head off future repair or replacement costs.

SITE AND SOIL PROBLEMS: FLOODING, LANDSLIDES, DRAINAGE

Landscaping refers not only to the plants in a yard, but to the arrangement of scenery into a pleasing ensemble. Thus landscaping includes what is done to the land as well as the arrangement of vegetation. Residential landscaping often involves modifying the natural state of the land to drain water away from the house, and this shaping of the land can either create problems or mitigate existing hazards.

Site Preparation In most residential areas, the natural grade or terrain of the land has been altered to make room for the houses and to divert the natural runoff of water away from the homes. To create most subdivisions, massive land-moving equipment cuts and fills the natural terrain into flat lots, drainage culverts, and streets. On hillsides, cuts are made into the hill to support foundations, and retaining walls are constructed to keep hillsides from sliding down into homes. Whatever the terrain, the sitework must be carefully planned and carried out in light of existing drainage patterns, the type of soil, past flooding, planned vegetation, and the placement of other homes in the area.

Flooding A licensee's responsibility to disclose flooding problems does not end once the Special Studies and Flood Hazard Disclosure form is filled out. Flood zone maps record known hazards, such as rivers with a history of flooding. This macro-level disclosure does not necessarily address micro features that may directly affect the property, such as dry creeks, artificial drainage ditches or culverts, and the like. Any number of conditions can cause one property on the street to flood or suffer water damage while others are untouched.

Localized Problems. Figure 1 illustrates flooding problems that can occur either because houses were built where they should not have been, or the land was altered incorrectly.

- Figure 1A shows what happens when homes are constructed in hollows or low areas. In heavy rains, water pools in the low spot and floods the homes.

- Figure 1B illustrates what can happen if site drainage is entirely dependent on one culvert. In storm conditions, culverts can become choked with branches and other debris and overflow. Water then accumulates in the low areas and houses built there will be flooded.

- Figure 1C illustrates another common occurrence when a culvert overflows or becomes blocked with debris: the runoff reverts to an old stream bed route, perhaps right through back yards and even living rooms.

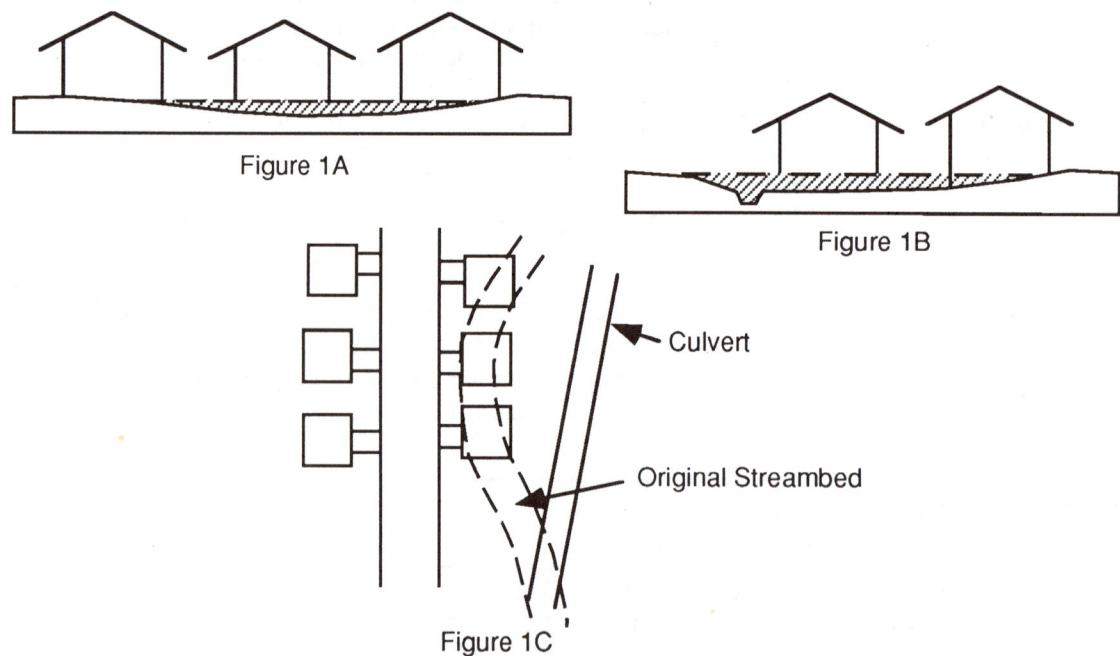

Inspection. Flood zone maps are no substitute for a visual inspection. Many California homeowners have been surprised to find the "dry creek bed" behind their house suddenly lapping at their back door when heavy rains turn it into a swollen torrent of muddy water. This can be a problem in areas that were built up long ago, since building was far less regulated and homes may have been inadvertently built in flood zones. On the other hand, as California becomes more crowded, builders are forced to use sites that earlier generations sensibly rejected as unbuildable.

Flood Insurance. Where there is a known risk of flooding and the clients choose to purchase the property with this knowledge, they may be able to obtain flood insurance as a rider to their homeowner's insurance policy.

Landslides and Slippage

Few real estate lawsuits are as messy as those involving drainage and soil slippage. Unfortunately, many homes in California have been built on or near inherently unstable hillsides. Heavy rains cause clay soils to absorb moisture and expand. With the added weight and expansion, the soil starts sliding downhill. There is usually no lack of parties to blame: the city for allowing the homes to be built, the developer, the soils engineer, the architect, the sitework contractor, the general contractor, and so on. Regardless of who ends up paying the bill, stabilizing hillsides is usually prohibitively expensive. It is wiser to avoid purchasing a home with potential landslide problems.

Homeowner Liability. Licensees should be aware that the homeowner may be held liable for part or all of the damage caused by a landslide originating on his or her property. If a property is sited on a potentially unstable hillside above other homes, this is definitely a material fact worth disclosing.

Soils Report. When a property is on a hillside or at the base of a hillside, the licensee would be wise to recommend the buyer obtain a current soils report. This will not only provide the client with useful information, but will also help protect the licensee from claims should the property suffer landslides in the future. Remember that licensees have been held liable for *potential hazards* as well as known hazards.

Site Selection. Sitework is supposed to minimize landslides and drainage problems. In general, sites that have the natural terrain and drainage left alone are the least likely to suffer drainage and slippage problems. The exceptions are homes built below inherently unstable hills. Figure 2 illustrates how a naturally occurring land formation can collect water in storm conditions and slide down into homes below. In cases such as these, there is little a builder can do to mitigate the risks; houses simply should not be built at the foot of these hills.

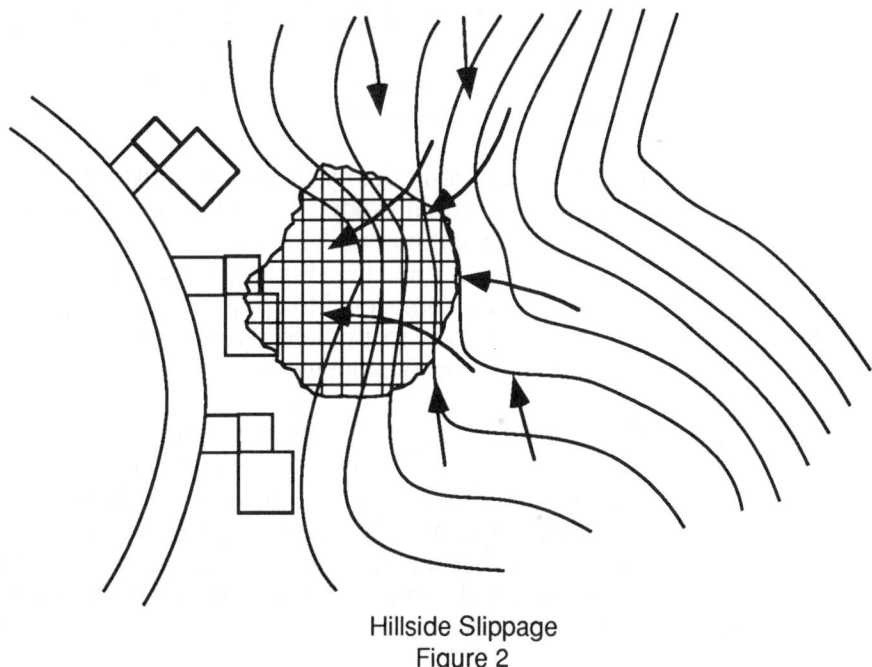

Hillside Slippage
Figure 2

Site Preparation The density of developments that respect the natural drainage and shape of the terrain is often limited, and developers find it necessary to cut into the land to produce economically feasible subdivisions. The likelihood of homes suffering landslides or water damage is directly related both to the underlying soils and geography of the neighborhood, and to the quality of the sitework performed by the developer.

Inspection. While the typical licensee is not a soils engineer, and is not expected to be, licensees should protect themselves by keeping an eye open for shoddy sitework and common-sense errors in the siting of homes. Examples include:

- Steep hillsides that have not been riprapped (stabilized with rocks and concrete)

- Hillsides with signs of slippage (broken riprap, topsoil landslides, retaining walls that have shifted or broken, etc.)

- Evidence of underground streams (soggy yards in summer, blackberry bushes, wet foundation or basement walls)

- Drainage swales or ditches that are clogged with refuse or poorly maintained

- Hillside homes with no drainage system; homes without gutters and downspouts to lead runoff to the street or to a naturally occurring drainage system like a stream bed

- House lots situated so runoff flows down onto someone else's property

- Houses sited on the edge of creeks, streams, or at the foot of narrow valleys

- Erosion or slippage caused by inadequately compacted fill.

Risk Factors. Landslides are like earthquakes in that they do not happen often, but when they do they can be catastrophic. Licensees need to be on the lookout for any natural or artificial landscape conditions that increase the potential for flooding or landslides.

Fill. A common difficulty in subdivisions where massive changes were made to the natural terrain is poorly compacted fill. To create a level lot on a slope, the bulldozer may cut into the hillside and then deposit this soil on the downslope to create a flat building site. (Figure 3.) This fill is supposed to be laid in six inch layers and then compacted to approximately 90 percent of maximum density. If the fill is dumped in thicker layers and not properly compacted, settling or slippage is bound to happen sooner or later.

Drainage. On flat lots, the potential is not so much for catastrophic flooding as for gradual water damage from poor or nonexistent drainage. Water from both the roof and the yard should drain to the street or to a culvert or creek. Water that pools up against the house may eventually damage the foundation or create settling by causing the soil to expand and contract, and may also provide moisture for dryrot, which can destroy the wood posts, floors, and joists underneath a home.

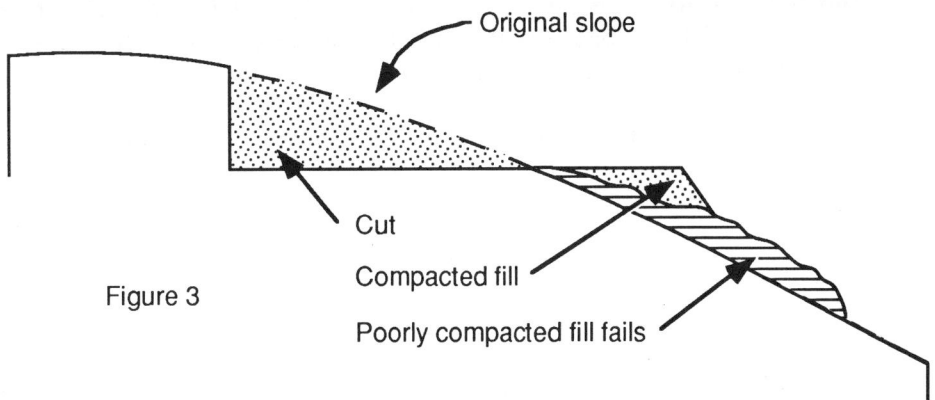

Figure 3

Effective Sitework. Most basically, proper sitework directs water from each lot to the street or to a culvert or existing stream. Water should not collect on a lot, or run through a lot onto another property. Figure 4 is an example of good landscape sitework. Note how drainage swales and underground pipes lead water away from the house to the street. These swales can be very gradual, and can be designed into the landscape so as to be almost invisible.

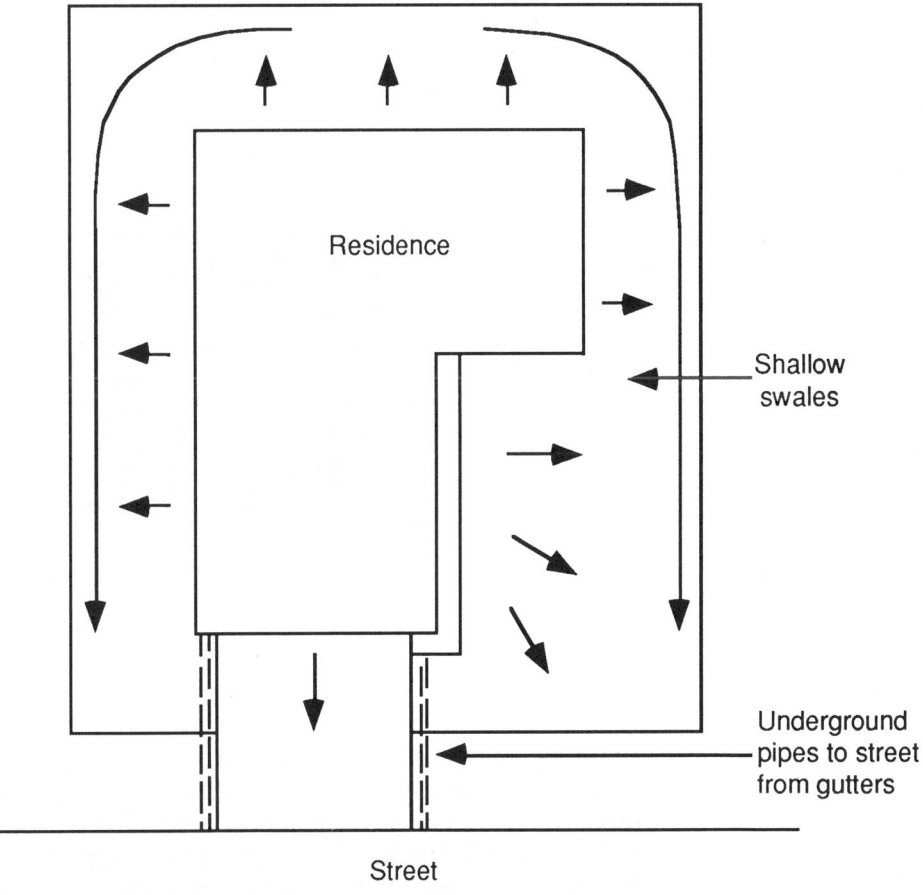

Figure 4

Landscaping & the Environment

Landscaping to Reduce Flood and Slide Hazards

Where homes are backed up against a large, unstable hillside, individual homeowners may not be able to reduce the risk of landslide since the problem is a macro-scale one. In most cases, however, the homeowner can lessen the risk of flooding and slippage with either additional sitework or appropriate planting.

Sitework. Examples of remedial sitework include:

☐ Installation of gutters and downspouts to lead run-off to the street or culvert

☐ Cutting swales into the soil to lead surface water away from the house

☐ Constructing solid concrete retaining walls to hold back hillsides

☐ Installation of subsurface drainage pipes near the house or property lines. Figure 5 illustrates a typical subsurface drainage system, which collects water and takes it to the street or a culvert. This type of drain is very effective in reducing surface water pooling and improper drainage while remaining unobstrusive.

☐ Installation of riprap or concrete and drainage pipes to hold hillsides and drain water away

☐ Installation of sump pumps or gravel sumps to collect and dissipate ground water. Where there is no way to drain water to the street or a culvert, as where the house sits below the street, then a pit, called a sump, can be dug and filled with gravel. In extreme conditions, an electric pump can be installed in the sump to pump out excess water.

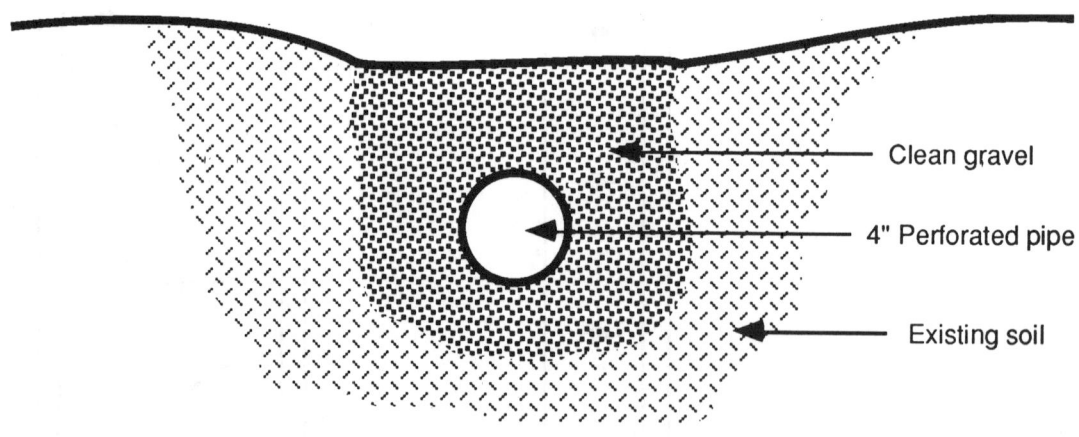

Figure 5

Planting. A second, complementary approach to lessening landslides is to use trees, shrubs, and ground cover to absorb water and help hold the hillside in place. Figure 6 is a list of plants that provide the kind of deep root structure that helps stop soil slippage. The type and quantity of such planting depends on the climate, soil type, and other local conditions, so a qualified landscape architect or designer should be consulted.

> ### Figure 6: Plants for Erosion Control
>
> **Trees**
> Aesculus californica — California Buckeye
> Agonus flexuosa — Peppermint Tree
> Celtis species — Hackberry
> Ceratonia siliqua — Carob Tree
> Ceris species — Redbud
> Pistachia chinensis — Chinese Pistache
> Quercus species — Oak
>
> **Shrubs**
> Ceanothus species — California Lilac
> Cistus species — Rockrose
> Erigonum species — Buckwheat
> Lavandula species — Lavender
> Loenotis leonurus — Lion's Tail
> Mahonia species — Holly Grape
> Rhus integrifolia — Lemonade Berry
>
> **Vines**
> Cissus antarctica — Kangaroo Ivy
> Euonymous fortunei — Winter Creeper
> Rosa banksiae — Lady Banks Rose
> Vitus vinifera — Grape
>
> **Groundcovers**
> Arctostaphylos species — Manzanita
> Baccharis pilularis — Dwarf Coyote Bush
> Coprosma species
> Gazania species
> Juniperus species — Juniper
> Lantana montevidensis
> Malephoria species — Ice Plant
>
> source: *Water Conserving Plants & Landscapes for the Bay Area,* © 1990, EBMUD

FIRE HAZARDS AND LANDSCAPING

The Oakland-Berkeley hills fire of 1991 dramatically illustrated the dangers of building houses in urban wild'and interface zones (UWIZ) and the disastrous consequences of volatile foliage being left untended in heavily forested residential areas. While experts continue to debate the causes of this fire and whether anything could have stopped it, some basic conclusions were drawn by the Mayors' Task Force on Emergency Preparedness and Community Restoration. A panel of experts brought together in the wake of the fire by Oakland Mayor Elihu Harris and Berkeley Mayor Loni Hancock concluded that the most effective ways of inhibiting fire in UWIZ areas are fire-resistant roofing (banning wood shingle roofs) and consistent vegetation control. The panel's studies indicated that the species or type of vegetation was less important than the spacing of trees and the constant removal of plant debris which fuels rapidly spreading fires.

Urban-Wildland Interface Urban-wildland interface zones are areas where residential land adjoins wildland. These low-density neighborhoods draw much of their charm from the natural trees and shrubbery on empty lots, public land, and around dwellings. The dangers inherent to UWIZ are twofold: fires that start in wildland forests or grassland can spread quickly to the nearby residential neighborhoods, and once the fire has entered the residential areas it can jump rapidly from tree to tree and from house to house, eventually spreading to more urban neighborhoods.

Landscaping & the Environment

UWIZ Hazards. Two special dangers in the UWIZ can turn a small fire into a roaring inferno. One is firebrands—burning embers that are carried aloft by the wind and land elsewhere to start another fire. Another is that the density of burnable materials in a house is very high. In a wildland fire, the fire may spread quickly but burn out just as quickly as it rapidly consumes the available fuel, which is typically small underbrush and branches. Once a fire starts in a wood frame house, however, hundreds of dry boards and shingles are available for burning, and a small fire can become a firestorm.

Risk Factors. The simple conclusion from this report is that either homes should not be built in UWIZ or strict and mandatory vegetation control measures must be enforced. The importance of UWIZ to licensees is that homes in these zones are inherently more at risk of fire than typical suburbs, and this may be considered a material fact about a property that should be disclosed.

Statewide Concern. Urban-wildland interface zones can be found throughout California, as urban sprawl has crept into the hills around cities. Although vegetation management and other precautions are especially important in UWIZ areas, they are also effective in reducing the fire risk to any neighborhood or home.

Vegetation Management

The task force warned that eradicating certain species of fire-prone trees such as eucalyptus and Monterey pine was simplistic and would not reduce fire hazards as much as preventive maintenance and cleaning of all trees and plants in fire hazard areas. These tasks should be performed on a neighborhood-wide scale to really lessen the danger of fire.

☐ Top and trim trees regularly

☐ Clear underbrush and tree debris regularly

☐ Reduce tree density

☐ Plant fire-resistant foliage

☐ Replace fire-prone trees

☐ Keep foliage away from the house.

Plant Selection. There is a common-sense relation between fire resistance and drought tolerance. The plants with the most moisture, such as succulents, are the most fire resistant, but they also require the most water—a concern in drought-prone California. Landscaping in UWIZ areas requires a balance between water-conserving and fire-resistant plants. Figures 7 and 8 are charts listing some of the common fire-prone and fire-resistant plants and trees available in California.

Disclosures. Awareness of landscaping may suggest additional areas where it is prudent to offer disclosures. For example, many experts believe Monterey pine trees pose a significant fire hazard. A home surrounded by mature Monterey pines may face a higher fire risk than a similar home surrounded less flammable plants. If the house burns down from a wind-fed fire while neighboring houses with no pines are left standing, the proximity of the fire-prone trees was obviously a material fact about the property.

Figure 7: Fire-Retardant Plants

Trees
Arbutus unedo — Strawberry Tree
Ceratonia siliqua — Carob Tree
Ceris occidentalis — Redbud
Rhus lancea — African Sumac

Shrubs
Cistus species — Rockrose
Heteromeles arbitufolia — Toyon
Nerium oleander — Oleander
Prunus ilicifolia — Holly-Leaved Cherry
Prunus lyonii — Catalina Cherry
Rhamnus californica — Coffeeberry
Rhus integrifolia — Lemonade Berry

Vines
Solanum jasminoides — Potato Vine
Tecomaria capensis — Cape Honeysuckle
Trachelospurum jasminoides — Star Jasmine

Groundcovers
Aloe species — Aloe
Arctotheca calendula — Cape Weed
Delosperma alba — Ice Plant
Duchesnea indica — Mock Strawberry
Frageria chiloensis — Wild Strawberry
Lampranthus species — Ice Plant
Rosemary

Perennials
Achillea tomentosa — Woolly Yarrow
Agapanthus — Lily of the Nile
Diplacus — Monkey Flower
Santolina species — Lavender Cotton
Tricostemma lanatum — Woolly Blue Curls

source: *Water Conserving Plants & Landscapes for the Bay Area,* © 1990, EBMUD

Figure 8: Fire-Prone Plants

Trees
Acacia species — Acacia
Cedrus species — Cedar (Deodar, Lebanon, Atlas)
Cupressus species — Cypress
Eucalyptus globulus — Blue Gum Eucalyptus
Pinus species — Pines

Shrubs
Adenostoma sparsifolium — Red Shanks
Artemesia californica — California Sage
Dononaea viscosa — Hopseed Bush
Juniperus species — Juniper
Salvia mellifera — Black Sage

Groundcovers
Hedera canariensis — Algerian Ivy

Perennials
Cortaderia selloana — Pampas Grass
Eriogonum species — Buckwheat
Pennisetum setaceum — Fountain Grass

source: Brende and Shapiro Tree and Shrub Care, Berkeley, CA, "Lists of More and Less Fire-Prone Plants"

LANDSCAPING TO CONSERVE WATER AND ENERGY

The value of a property's landscaping is much more than the replacement cost of the plants. A water conserving, low maintenance yard adds to a property's market value, as it will save money in water bills and in yard maintenance expenses year after year. Conserving water is a concern for all residents of California, and one obvious method of saving water is to reduce the need for landscape irrigation by substituting plants that require less water than thirstier varieties. Drought-tolerant landscapes, also called xeriscapes, have been popular in California since the drought of 1976–77.

Benefits **Water Savings.** By reducing lawn size, using drought-tolerant plants, and installing an efficient sprinkler or drip irrigation system, it is possible to cut irrigation water usage by half without sacrificing beauty or variety. This not only saves the homeowner money by lowering water bills, it conserves California's water supply and the electricity needed to pump vast quantities of water into urban areas.

Low Maintenance. A significant side benefit of water-conserving landscaping is that it requires much less maintenance. Replacing lawns and hedges with low maintenance plants can save a homeowner hundreds of dollars a year in yard maintenance expenses, or hundreds of hours of labor.

Aesthetics. True conservation does not require any great sacrifice; it simply means doing more with less, or doing something different. This is the guiding philosophy of water-conserving landscaping.

Figure 9: Water-Conserving Plants

Trees
Bailey's Acacia
California Buckeye
Peppermint Tree
Italian Alder
Chinese Hackberry
Bronze Loquat
Coolibah Tree
Raywood Ash
Crape Myrtle
European Olive
Chinese Pistache
Coast Live Oak
African Sumac
California Pepper Tree
Coast Redwood
Manzanita
Western Redbud

Shrubs
Blue Hibiscus
Bush Anenome
Flowering Quince
Smokebush
Forsythia
Toyon
Flannel Bush
Hollywood Juniper
Oleander
Catalina Cherry

Vines
Bougainvillea
Kangaroo Ivy
Blood Red Trumpet Vine
Giant Burmese Honeysuckle
Pink Jasmine
Cat's Claw
Potato Vine
Black-Eyed Susan
Grape
Wisteria

Groundcover
Woolly Yarrow
Sea Thrift
Dwarf Coyote Bush
Snow in Summer
Dwarf Plumbago
Chamomile
Fan Flower
Sweet Violet

(partial listing only; for more complete lists, refer to
Water Conserving Plants & Landscapes for the Bay Area, © 1990 EBMUD)

Drought Tolerant Planting Contrary to common misconceptions, xeriscapes do not have to look like a desert. There is a wide variety of trees, shrubs, vines, flowers, and groundcovers that are classified as "drought-tolerant," meaning that they have deep root systems and can thrive on infrequent rains or watering.

Native Plants. Since much of California is semiarid, plants that are native to the region are always good choices for drought-tolerant landscapes, as are those from other Mediterranean climates similar to California's in Europe, Africa, and Australia. Many native plants are disease and insect resistant as well.

Ecological Considerations. The ecological movement's call for species protection or "biodiversity" is not just a concern for remote locations like the Amazon basin. Homeowners can personally contribute to maintaining the diversity and genetic vigor of California's native plants by using some in their own landscaping. Choosing plants from one's own area is a simple way of maintaining the diversity of native plant stock.

Functional Considerations. Lawns are notoriously thirsty, and one simple way of reducing water use is to cut down the size of lawns to fit the actual needs of the household. A family with young children may want a lawn for playing in the back yard, but they may not use the front yard at all, perhaps because of street traffic or size limitations. The front lawn could be replaced with a drought-tolerant groundcover, which would not only require far less water, it would also not need mowing. Reducing the use of power lawnmowers in turn helps improve the air quality, especially in the Los Angeles basin.

Plant Selection **General Criteria.** An easily maintained, water-conserving yard has plants that meet these criteria:

- *Native to Mediterranean Climates.* The ideal water-conserving plants are those already adapted to California's climate of dry summers and occasional winter rain—either plants native to California or those native to climates similar to California's. These plants can survive with few or no summer waterings. Other water-conserving plants will need one deep watering during each dry month—still a big savings over lawns and exotics that need watering weekly or even more often.

- *Attractive Appearance*

- *Readily Available at Retail Nurseries at Reasonable Cost*

- *Resistant to Pests and Diseases.* All plant life is susceptible to disease and pest infestations, but an easy-to-maintain yard has few fragile exotics that need constant doctoring to survive.

- *Low Maintenance.* Trees, shrubs, and groundcovers mentioned in this course typically need only one thorough spring pruning and occasional maintenance during the year. An example of a high-maintenance plant to avoid is bamboo, which grows extremely quickly, spreads ferociously, and is difficult to trim.

Specific Plants. The following are selected examples of plants that meet these criteria, grouped by general types as ground covers, trees, shrubs, vines, flowers, and ferns.

- ***Ground Covers***. Low maintenance, water-saving ground covers include gazania (small yellow flowers), ice plant, silver spreading juniper, lippia, and thyme. Many are flowering and are quite attractive; others are low, ground-hugging bushes.

- ***Trees***. Many common trees are drought-tolerant. Examples include the coast live oak, the California pepper tree, the European olive, and the crape myrtle.

- ***Shrubs***. A wide variety of attractive flowering shrubs, such as the bottlebrush, blue hibiscus, bush anemone, white rockrose, oleander, mock orange, and Santa Cruz Island buckwheat, are drought resistant.

- ***Vines***. Vines like bougainvillea, pink jasmine, cat's claw, and wisteria are double-duty plants: they conserve water, and they also lower the temperature inside the home in summer if they are planted on trellises near the south, east, or west exposures of the house.

- ***Flowering Plants***. An astonishing variety of flowering plants—perennials, annuals, and bulbs—are classified as drought-tolerant, water-conserving plants. Examples include the following.

    - Perennials: aloe, African daisy, trailing geranium, English lavender, California fuchsia

    - Annuals: hollyhock, California poppy, love-in-a-mist

    - Bulbs: naked lady lily, calla lily, watsonia

- ***Ferns***. Even the cool grace of ferns can be used in a xeriscape. Not all ferns require a jungle atmosphere. Holly fern, western sword fern, and squirrel's foot fern are all drought-tolerant choices for landscaping.

Soil Preparation

Soil preparation is as important as the plants themselves in water-conserving landscaping. To conserve water, the soil must allow plants to send down deep roots, and there must be enough mulch to limit the amount of water lost to evaporation. The quality of the soil is an asset or liability that the homeowner can influence.

Assessing Soil Quality. Poor soils limit plant growth and contribute to plant diseases, which means the homeowner must constantly spend money to replace diseased or dying plants or improve the soil. Poor soils are characterized by these traits:

- Thin soil over hardpan or rock—too thin to support root structures

- Soil heavily compacted during grading or sitework—too hard for roots to penetrate, and lacking in porosity

- Low porosity—clay or compacted soils that do not absorb water

- Excessive porosity—sandy soils that do not hold water

- Low fertility—low in nutrients like nitrogen and organic matter

- High mineral content

- Excessive salinity.

Testing. Good soil is both rich in nutrients and well-percolated. The best way to ascertain the fertility and type of soil is to take several samples from different areas of the yard and have them tested by a soils laboratory. Percolation can be assessed by the homeowner.

Texture. The best soil has a crumb texture, rather like the crumb crust on a coffee cake. It is readily *friable,* that is, the particles are loose and crumble into small pieces when handled. This type of soil is rich in organic matter—mulch, composted grass and leaves, loam—and loosely structured so a hand trowel slides easily and deeply into the soil.

Percolation. The reason soil texture is so important is water percolation. A good soil will absorb about one-half inch of water per hour.

- *Too Little.* When soils have been compacted by machinery, foot traffic, or even hard rain and water from sprinklers, they no longer absorb water easily. Plants in these soils are thirsty no matter how much they are watered because the water is not penetrating down to the roots.

- *Too Much.* Soils with no body, that is, sandy, grainy soils, are equally inadequate because they cannot hold the water long enough for it to be absorbed by the roots. Plants in sandy soils are always thirsty because the water leaches away immediately. Nutrients are also washed through these high-percolation soils quickly, lessening the fertility of the soil.

- *What To Do.* If water pools up, especially in level areas, it indicates a clay-type or compacted soil, or a thin soil resting on impervious clay hardpan. The solution is to break through the impervious layers of subsoil, and then break up the clay or compacted earth and add organic materials such as mulch and compost. These light, absorbent materials will improve the texture and percolation. In severely compacted soils, relatively inert organic materials such as redwood bark chips are added to loosen and lighten the structure of the soil. In general, organic additions to the soil must be worked in at least eight inches deep, more for large shrubs and trees.

Effects of Planting. Long-time homeowners have probably noticed that the type of plant or grass affects soil compaction over time. Soil near ground covers or shrubs with deep, pervasive roots (like common ivy) is kept porous by the root structure. Open areas covered with thin grass are almost always compacted because there are no deep roots to keep the soil moist and porous.

Improving Soil. Soils do best if they are not over-worked. Excessive rototilling can actually harm soils. The recommended method of improving soil is to add organic matter regularly and build the soil over time. In porous, sandy soils, the best treatment is to add organic matter that will help hold water, and to limit sprinkler use so the nutrients are not washed out by excessive watering.

Mulch. Spreading a two- to four-inch layer of organic material such as pine needles, bark chips, leaves, or other mulched plant trimmings around trees, shrubs, and flower beds accomplishes these water-conserving goals:

- Retains moistures and keeps soil from drying out

- Reduces compaction and wind erosion
- Limits weed growth
- Adds nutrients as organic matter breaks down and enters the soil.

Watering Efficiently Drip irrigation and sprinkler systems add value to a home by making it cheaper and easier for residents to water the yard, by saving water, and by eliminating laborious hand watering. Whatever method is used, the underlying principle is to water when and where it does the most good.

Drip Systems. Drip irrigation systems save water by delivering a slow but steady flow of water directly to the plants' root zones through small plastic tubing. Drip irrigation avoids the excessive runoff and evaporation caused by overhead sprinklers. Drip systems do not require trenching and burying pipes. Drip systems reduce weed growth by not watering indiscriminately, and they save plants from the cycle of over-watering and under-watering that often occurs with sprinklers or hand watering. Timing devices can be attached to the system so that watering is done automatically and at the best time of the day. Drip systems lie on the surface, and so they are suitable for vegetable gardens as well as permanent landscaping.

Basic Principles. Efficient watering follows several simple rules. Water when needed, not by calendar day. Apply infrequent deep waterings. Prune and mulch to limit evaporation. Learn the plants' fertilizing requirements. Learn to recognize early wilting symptoms (drooping leaves or a dull grayish color) that signal a need for water.

Low Maintenance Landscaping The biggest expense in maintaining a yard is generally not the cost of the water but the labor and tools required to mow lawns, trim hedges, weed flower beds, and remove tree and shrub debris. A yard that has been designed to be easily and cheaply maintained—one without huge lawns, multiple hedges, numerous flower beds, and shrubs that need constant pruning—is an asset that will save a homeowner time and money over the years.

Trees Mature shade trees have economic as well as aesthetic value. Large shade trees on the south, east, or west exposures help lower the cost of cooling a home in hot climates. Trees are not only an energy-saving asset, they are expensive to replace. As anyone who has visited a nursery knows, the cost of a tree goes up proportionate to its maturity. The bigger and older the tree, the more it is worth.

Insurance Concerns. Appraisals often undervalue the replacement cost of mature trees. Homeowners whose property includes large trees should make sure their fire policy will pay the market or replacement value of trees and landscaping. Big shade trees thirty or more years old that were killed in the Oakland hills fire in 1991 were valued in the thousands of dollars by appraisers and insurance adjusters.

Hardscaping Hardscaping (as opposed to "soft" plant landscaping) is a catch-all term for permanent improvements on the property that are not part of the residence. This includes detached decks and patios, trellises, walkways, gates, fences, gazebos, reflecting pools, and fountains. Hardscaping such as trellises that help shade the house from direct sunlight are valuable components of an energy-saving landscape.

ENVIRONMENTAL LANDSCAPE DESIGN PRINCIPLES

While beauty may be in the eye of the beholder, no one can argue with lower utility bills and practical outdoor spaces. These are key questions for any California landscape design, whatever one's individual aesthetic preferences:

☐ Does it contribute to lower water and energy costs?

☐ Does it provide inviting, practical outdoor areas for recreation and entertainment?

☐ Does it fit the climate zone?

Energy Conserving Design As outlined above, water is conserved by using drought-tolerant plants and efficient irrigation systems. A competent landscape design will also save energy by using orientation, plant location, and selection to shade the hottest walls of the house in summer. Pacific Gas & Electric Company states that deciduous trees (trees that lose their leaves in winter) located on the south, east, and west sides of a home can cut summer air conditioning bills by thirty percent, and that vine-covered trellises protecting these exposures can lower the surface temperature of the house walls by as much as forty degrees Fahrenheit.

Orientation to the Sun The starting point for any landscape design that aims to save energy and provide practical places for recreation is the orientation of the house and yard to the sun. Landscaping should allow sunlight to warm walls and roofs in winter to help heat the home, and cut direct sunlight in summer to reduce the need for air conditioning. Decks and patios should be oriented to make use of the morning and afternoon sun, and should be surrounded by plants that help make the outdoor living space comfortable. Figure 10 is an example.

North Side: Cool. The north side of a property receives the least sunlight year round, so it is the coolest exposure. Decks located on the north side of a home will be shady and cold much of the year, and are poor design choices in much of California because they are simply not comfortable to use. Heavy evergreen foliage against the north wall of a home is also not recommended, as it will cut the already modest heat gain and may contribute to the growth of mildew, dryrot, and other destructive fungi by providing a damp, shady cover for the walls and roof of the house.

South Side: Needs Shade in Summer. The south side of a home receives the most sun and is therefore the first place to plant shade trees and shrubs, preferably species that shed their leaves in winter to let sunlight in when the house needs to be warmed. Vine-covered trellises can also shade south windows from summer sun. Decks and patios facing the south may be too warm in summer unless a trellis with vines or other landscaping is deployed to shade direct sun.

East Side: Morning Sun. Outdoor living areas facing the east are ideal for morning use, as the sun warms the eastern exposure first. In areas with hot summers, the eastern walls of the house should be protected with deciduous trees and shrubs like the south walls.

Landscaping & the Environment

West Side: Afternoon Sun. Outdoor dining areas placed on the west side of the property will be useful to homeowners who like to entertain or dine outdoors in the early evening, as these hardscapes will be warmed by the afternoon sun. In zones with hot summers, the west walls and windows of the home should be protected from direct sunlight like the south and east walls.

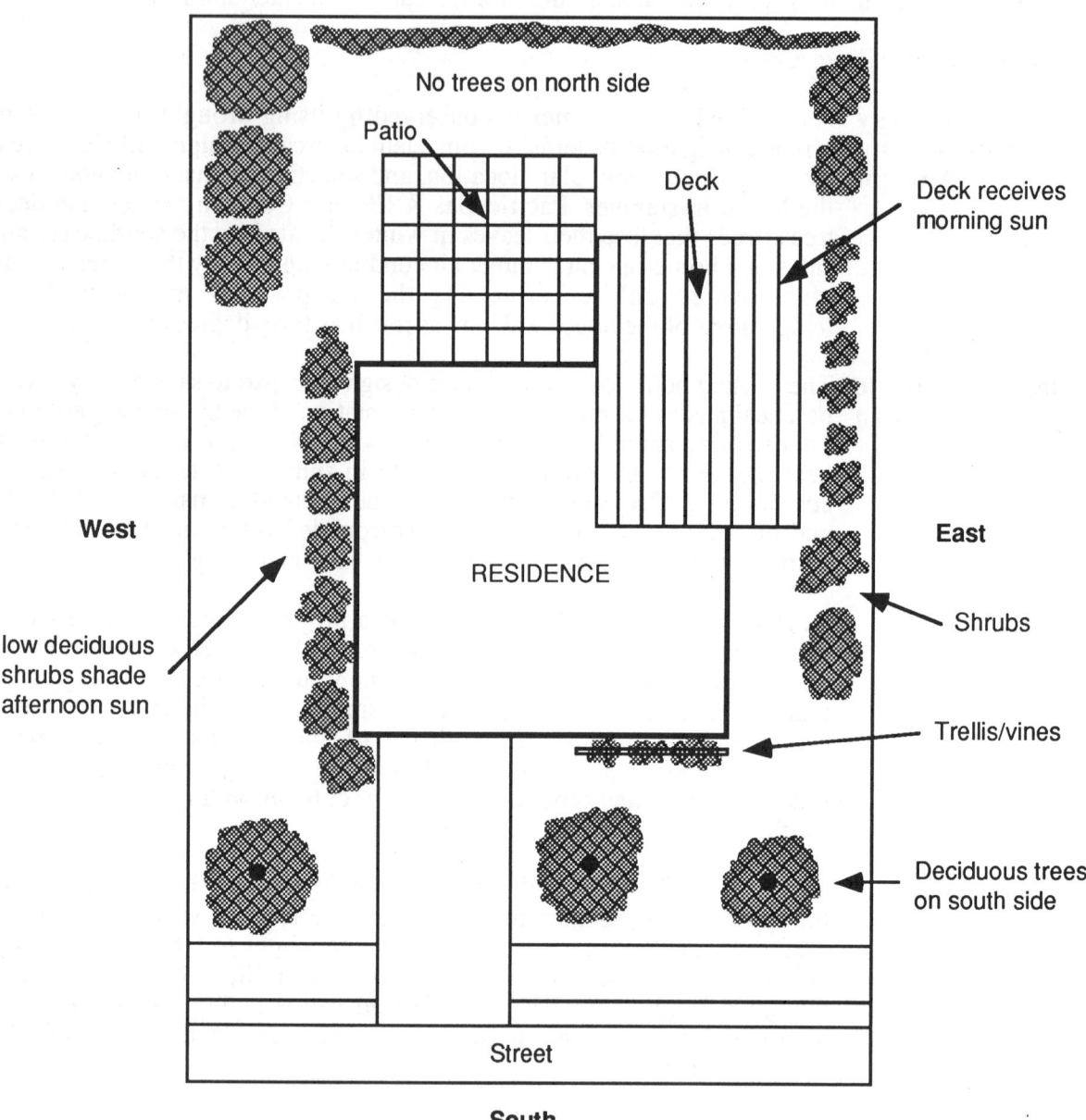

Figure 10

Functional Landscape Design Issues

Although not directly related to conservation, there are other factors that make for a successful landscape environment. A yard loaded with every conservation trick in the book will still be a liability to the property if it does not fit the climate, floor plan of the house, and rules of good design.

California's Climate Zones. Landscapes should be designed to fit the climate and topography of the area. Yet a surprising number of California landscapes are ill-suited to their climate zone. Examples include foggy Bay Area yards loaded with exotic plants that need constant tropical warmth to survive, desert yards with large, lush lawns, and homes in cold mountainous zones hidden by thick evergreen trees. A water-saving, energy-conserving landscaping plan should be built around plants that grow well in the zone's soils and weather conditions, and that provide shade and light in keeping with the extremes of temperature found in the zone. Sunset Magazine's *Western Garden Book* (© 1988 Lane Publishing Co., Menlo Park, CA) includes climate zone maps of California and is a useful resource guide. Bear in mind that every lot has its own microclimate.

Landscaping that Works with the House. Landscaping should work with the house not only aesthetically—a landscape using cactus and rocks might be jarring around a Colonial-style home—but with the floor plan. The landscaping should be designed to fit:

- The function of each room
- View corridors
- Circulation and foot traffic patterns
- Window and door locations
- Privacy and security.

Views and Privacy. If there is an attractive view to the west out of the living room, the landscaping should be designed so that it does not block the view but still reduces the amount of direct afternoon sun hitting the wall of the house. In bathrooms and bedrooms, landscaping can enhance privacy by blocking neighbors' views of windows or by creating a private fenced garden. If there is no scenic view from the house, landscaping can create one, as is done in Japanese gardens.

Security. Home security is a concern in today's world, and landscaping can enhance or impair the security of a property. Hedges and fences can provide cover for prowlers, while prickly plants such as bougainvillea and cactus under windows can inhibit burglars.

Outdoor Lighting. Well-conceived outdoor lighting can not only enhance the security of a home (especially if it is operated by motion sensors) and provide lighting for evening activities, it can also heighten the drama and interest of landscaping at night.

Design Principles

There are a number of fundamental principles that guide all landscape design. Within these principles lie an infinite number of variations.

Order and Symmetry. Landscapes without repetition, visual rhythm, or patterns seem disconnected or chaotic and lose our attention and interest.

Contrast and Asymmetry. Interest is created by occasional variations within a pattern, or asymmetry contrasting with symmetry.

Edge Characteristics. The edge or border of a landscape can be transparent, semitransparent or solid. Fences, hedges, or rows of bushes can be used for a variety of effects. Solid borders such as fences or hedges provide the most privacy.

Configuration. Landscapes and hardscapes can be described as rectangular, curved, circular, or angular in their basic shape or configuration.

Theme. Landscapes often have a stylistic theme, such as Asian, English, or Southwest, or even a color scheme. Both the hardscapes and plant selection are chosen to reflect the theme.

Views and Screening. Landscapes are designed to screen unwanted scenes (such as neighbors' houses) and frame or focus the eye onto chosen views. This is often accomplished by using trees or shrubs to bracket the view.

Elevation Changes. One method of providing visual and spatial interest in a yard is to establish more than one level. A meandering set of steps dropping down to another level or a series of multilevel flower beds rising up from the street are common elevation change techniques.

Focal Points and Grouping. Some landscapes set up a grouping of rocks, benches or plants as a focal point of a garden. Plants are sometimes grouped together for their color or to create a contrast with other sections of the yard.

Circulation. Landscapes typically have paths, and the manner in which these paths lead from entrance to exit can be flowing, indirect, or direct.

Art and Space Relationships. Like a painting or sculpture, landscapes display basic visual and spatial qualities that affect the three-dimensional look and feel of the landscape:

- Line (straight, curved, irregular)
- Texture (fine or coarse, as in leaf size and shape)
- Shape (square, round, low, tall, etc.)
- Mass (density)
- Color (foliage, flowering plants, hardscape materials).

Elements of Hardscape Design. Hardscapes may include these elements:

- Water—in reflecting pools, fish ponds, fountains, streams
- Walkways and paving—many patterns and materials are used, including bricks, paving stones, gravel, concrete, and redwood chips
- Fences—many patterns and materials, including wood, brick, concrete, lattice, and concrete blocks
- Gates—an essential element of privacy and design; gates are used to establish a visual theme to a landscape.

Drought tolerant plants have deep root systems, need water infrequently

California native plants resist local diseases and insects

Advantage of maintaining native plant stock: biodiversity

Other plants can substitute for lawns, except as household needs lawn for recreation

Plant selection: examples of native drought tolerant, low maintenance plants:

 Ground cover: gazania, ice plant, thyme

 Trees: coast live oak, California pepper, European olive, crape myrtle

 Shrubs: bottlebrush, oleander, mock orange, blue hibiscus, bush anemone

 Vines: bougainvillea, pink jasmine, wisteria, cat's claw

 Flowers: lavender, hollyhock, California poppy, calla lily

 Ferns: holly fern, western sword fern, squirrel's foot fern

Plants vary in tolerance for sun or shade, should be placed accordingly

Soil must be prepared to allow plants to send down deep roots

Drip irrigation and sprinkler systems save water and labor

Drip system: slow flow to root zones, eliminates runoff and evaporation

Low maintenance landscaping saves cost of labor and tools

Shade trees save energy and are expensive to replace: should be adequately insured

Hardscaping: improvements like patios, trellises, fences, gates, pools, paths

Environmental Landscape Design Principles

Energy conservation: mainly through shading hottest walls in summer, using sun for heat in winter

 North side: coolest exposure, prone to mildew, poor choice for decks

 South side: deciduous trees can shade in summer, allow sunlight in winter

 East side: morning sun ideal for breakfast room; may need shade in summer

 West side: afternoon sun, good for evenings outdoors; may need shading

Climate zones: planting must suit the climate and topography of the area and lot

Functional and aesthetic issues: landscaping should be compatible with house style, view corridors, room functions, circulation patterns, privacy and security

Basic design principles:

 Order and symmetry vs. contrast and asymmetry

 Emphasizing or screening views; focal points and grouping

 Stylistic or color theme

 Transparent, solid, or semitransparent edges

 Circulation and configuration: curved, angular, etc.

 Elevation changes

 Art and space relationships: line, texture, shape, mass, color

 Elements of hardscape design: water, walkways and paving, fences, gates

COURSE 7
Earthquake Safety

INTRODUCTION

This course is condensed from *The Homeowner's Guide to Earthquake Safety*, a booklet written and adopted by the California Seismic Safety Commission (© 1992 California Seismic Safety Commission; reproduced by permission). This booklet is used as an integral part of the real estate transfer disclosure process. The real estate licensee will be called upon to explain the new seismic disclosure requirements to sellers and buyers and to oversee delivery of the booklet and disclosure forms. It is therefore important to be familiar with its content. The complete book also contains photographs, an extensive bibliography, and a list of resource organizations.

Copies of the booklet are available from the Seismic Safety Commission, 1900 K Street, Suite 100, Sacramento, CA 95814-4186. The price is $2.25 each for up to five copies, which includes sales tax and delivery via first class mail. To order, send delivery address with a check or money order for the full amount to the Seismic Safety Commission. To order six or more copies, call 916-322-4917 for price and delivery information.

There is also a *Commercial Property Owner's Guide to Earthquake Safety*. It is used in commercial property transactions in the same way the *Homeowner's Guide* is used in residential transactions.

This guide has been developed and adopted by the Seismic Safety Commission as required by Assembly Bill 2959 authored by Assemblyman Johan Klehs (Chapter 1499, Statutes of 1990) and Assembly Bill 200 authored by Assemblyman Dominic Cortese (Chapter 699, Statutes of 1991). It will be updated in future years.

THE HOMEOWNER'S GUIDE TO EARTHQUAKE SAFETY: LEGAL REQUIREMENTS FOR SELLING YOUR HOME

The law requires disclosure of matters relating to earthquake safety, but does not require either seller or buyer to do any actual repairs or retrofitting. However, taking precautions such as strengthening a home can reduce the risk of earthquake damage. There are no guarantees of safety during earthquakes, but precautions can help. The Seismic Safety Commission hopes that you will act on the suggestions outlined in this booklet and make yourself, your family, and your home safer before the next damaging earthquake.

- ☐ When you sell your home, state law requires you to disclose to buyers all material defects and deficiencies that you know about. Your real estate agent or broker, or the state Department of Real Estate, can tell you about this general requirement. To comply with this law, you must disclose whether your home has earthquake weaknesses such as those described in this booklet.

- ☐ If your house was built before 1960, another state law requires you to deliver a copy of this booklet, *The Homeowner's Guide to Earthquake Safety*, to the buyer. You are also required to disclose whether your home has any of the weaknesses described in this booklet. Your real estate agent is required to supply you with a copy of this booklet.

- ☐ You are not required to hire anyone to evaluate your home.

- ☐ You are not required to strengthen your home to resist earthquakes.

How to Comply To fulfill the legal requirements for selling a home built before 1960, the seller must give the buyer a completed earthquake hazards disclosure report, like the one on the next page, and a copy of the booklet, *The Homeowner's Guide to Earthquake Safety*. The booklet describes how to identify each weakness and, in general terms, how to fix it. You are not required to fix the weaknesses before you sell your home, but you may get a better price if you do.

Disclosure. To complete the disclosure report, answer the questions to the best of your knowledge. If the item applies to part of your house—for example, if part of your house is anchored to the foundation and an older portion is not—answer the question no since a part of the house is not anchored. You are not required to remove siding, drywall, or plaster to answer the questions, or to hire anyone to inspect your house.

Seller. If you are selling a home, the following requirements and suggestions apply.

- ☐ You must disclose to the buyer any known earthquake weaknesses that your house has.

- ☐ If your house was built before 1960, you must give the buyer a copy of this booklet and disclose weaknesses listed on the disclosure form. Though you are not required to hire someone to answer the questions for you, you may want to get assistance from a home inspector, contractor, architect, or engineer.

- ☐ If you list your house for sale with a real estate broker or agent, give the agent the completed disclosure form when you sign the listing agreement. Your agent can give the booklet and the form to the buyer for you.

- ☐ Keep a copy of the form, signed by the buyer, as evidence that you have completed the earthquake disclosure requirement.

Buyer. If you are buying a home, consider the following points.

- ☐ Before you agree to buy a house, review the information disclosed by the seller. Pay special attention to any items that indicate earthquake weaknesses.

- ☐ You may wish to have a home inspector, contractor, architect, or engineer inspect the house and give you an opinion regarding any earthquake weaknesses and how much they would cost to strengthen.

- ☐ Consider the house's location: is it in or near a fault rupture zone or in an area where it might be damaged by a landslide, liquefaction, or a tsunami?

- ☐ You may wish to negotiate the cost of strengthening with the seller. The law does not require either you or the seller to strengthen the home but if these weaknesses are not fixed you may find that repair costs after a damaging earthquake amount to more than your equity in your home.

RESIDENTIAL EARTHQUAKE HAZARDS REPORT

Refer to Section 8897 *et seq.*, California Government Code

Name	Assessor's Parcel No.
Street Address	Year Built
City and County	Zip Code

Answer these questions to the best of your knowledge. If you do not have actual knowledge as to whether the weakness exists or not, answer "Don't Know:" If your house does not have the feature, answer "Doesn't Apply." The page numbers in the right-hand column indicate where in this guide you can find information on each of these features.

		Yes	No	Doesn't Apply	Don't Know	See Page
1.	Is the water heater braced, strapped, or anchored to resist falling during an earthquake?	☐	☐	☐	☐	6
2.	Is the house anchored or bolted to the foundation?	☐	☐	☐	☐	7
3.	If the house has cripple walls:					
	° Are the exterior cripple walls braced?	☐	☐	☐	☐	8
	° If the exterior foundation consists of unconnected concrete piers and posts, have they been strengthened?	☐	☐	☐	☐	9
4.	If the exterior foundation, or part of it, is made of unreinforced masonry, has it been strengthened?	☐	☐	☐	☐	10
5.	If the house is built on a hillside, answer the following:					
	° Are the exterior tall foundation walls braced?	☐	☐	☐	☐	11
	° Were the tall posts or columns either built to resist earthquakes or have they been strengthened?	☐	☐	☐	☐	11
6.	If the exterior walls of the house, or part of them, are made of unreinforced masonry, have they been strengthened?	☐	☐	☐	☐	12
7.	If the house has a living area over the garage, was the wall around the garage door opening either built to resist earthquakes or has it been strengthened?	☐	☐	☐	☐	13

If any of the questions are answered "No," the house is likely to have an earthquake weakness. Questions answered "Don't Know" may indicate a need for further evaluation. If you corrected one or more of these weaknesses, describe the work on a separate page.

As Seller of the property described herein, I have answered the questions above to the best of my knowledge in an effort to fully disclose any potential earthquake weaknesses it may have.

EXECUTED BY

_____   _____   _____
(Seller)   (Seller)   Date

I acknowledge receipt of this form, completed and signed by the Seller. I understand that if the Seller has answered "No" to one or more questions, or if Seller has indicated a lack of knowledge, there may be one or more earthquake weaknesses in this house.

_____   _____   _____
(Buyer)   (Buyer)   Date

This earthquake disclosure is made in addition to the standard real estate transfer disclosure statement also required by law.

Keep your copy of this form for future reference.

Laws Relating To Earthquake Hazard Disclosure

California's real estate disclosure laws (Civil Code, §1102 et seq.) require sellers of real property to disclose known defects and deficiencies in the property—including earthquake weaknesses and hazards—to prospective purchasers. Sellers and their real estate agents or brokers must also disclose whether the property is located in an Alquist-Priolo Special Studies Zone or earthquake fault rupture zone (Public Resources Code §2621 et seq.).

Standard Forms. The California Association of Realtors® has a form (GFD-14) for Special Studies Zone, Seismic Hazard Zone, and Flood Hazard Area disclosures. The standard Real Estate Transfer Disclosure Statement asks about soils problems and earthquake damage, as well as structural defects. These forms are based on Civil Code requirements. (They are discussed in detail in Course 12.)

Pre-1960 Homes. Since earthquakes pose a serious threat in California, and many older homes are not built to modern earthquake codes, in 1991 the California legislature specified that sellers of homes built before 1960 must deliver to the buyer, "as soon as practicable before the transfer," a copy of *The Homeowner's Guide to Earthquake Safety* (this booklet) and disclose certain earthquake deficiencies. (Government Code, Title 2, Division 1, Chapter 13.8)

Form of Disclosure. The reporting form in the booklet may be used for this disclosure. The seller's real estate agent is to provide the seller of such a home with a copy of the booklet for delivery to the buyer.

Booklet. Under Business and Professions Code, Article 1, Chapter 3, §10149, the Seismic Safety Commission is required to develop, adopt, and publish *The Homeowner's Guide to Earthquake Safety* containing information on geologic and seismic hazards, explanations of structural and nonstructural earthquake hazards, and recommendations for mitigating the hazards. This booklet is to be distributed to home sellers by real estate agents (in accordance with §8897.5 of the Government Code) and is also available to the buyer and the general public in accordance with §2079.8 of the Civil Code.

EARTHQUAKE WEAKNESSES IN RESIDENTIAL BUILDINGS

If your home has any of these weaknesses, it is more likely to be damaged in an earthquake. Strengthening your home can help reduce or prevent this damage. The following common weaknesses are almost certain to lead to earthquake damage and should be your priorities for strengthening. You can often identify and fix them yourself.

- ☐ The house has an unbraced water heater.

- ☐ The house is not adequately anchored to its foundation.

- ☐ The house has weak cripple walls, or is on a pier-and-post foundation.

Unbraced Water Heater

If the water heater is not securely attached to the wall, it can topple during an earthquake. If the gas or electrical lines are broken as it falls, this may cause a fire as well as water damage. This is a common, and serious, problem, but it is relatively easy and inexpensive to fix.

How to Identify It. Examine your water heater to see if there are metal straps or braces around it that are bolted to the wall. Make sure the bolts go into studs or into concrete, not just into drywall or plaster. Pull on them to make sure they are secure and tight.

What Can Be Done. Using metal tubing, heavy metal strapping, and lag bolts, secure the water heater to the wall. Flexible pipes for the gas and water lines are better in an earthquake than rigid pipes like aluminum or copper tubing or solid pipe.

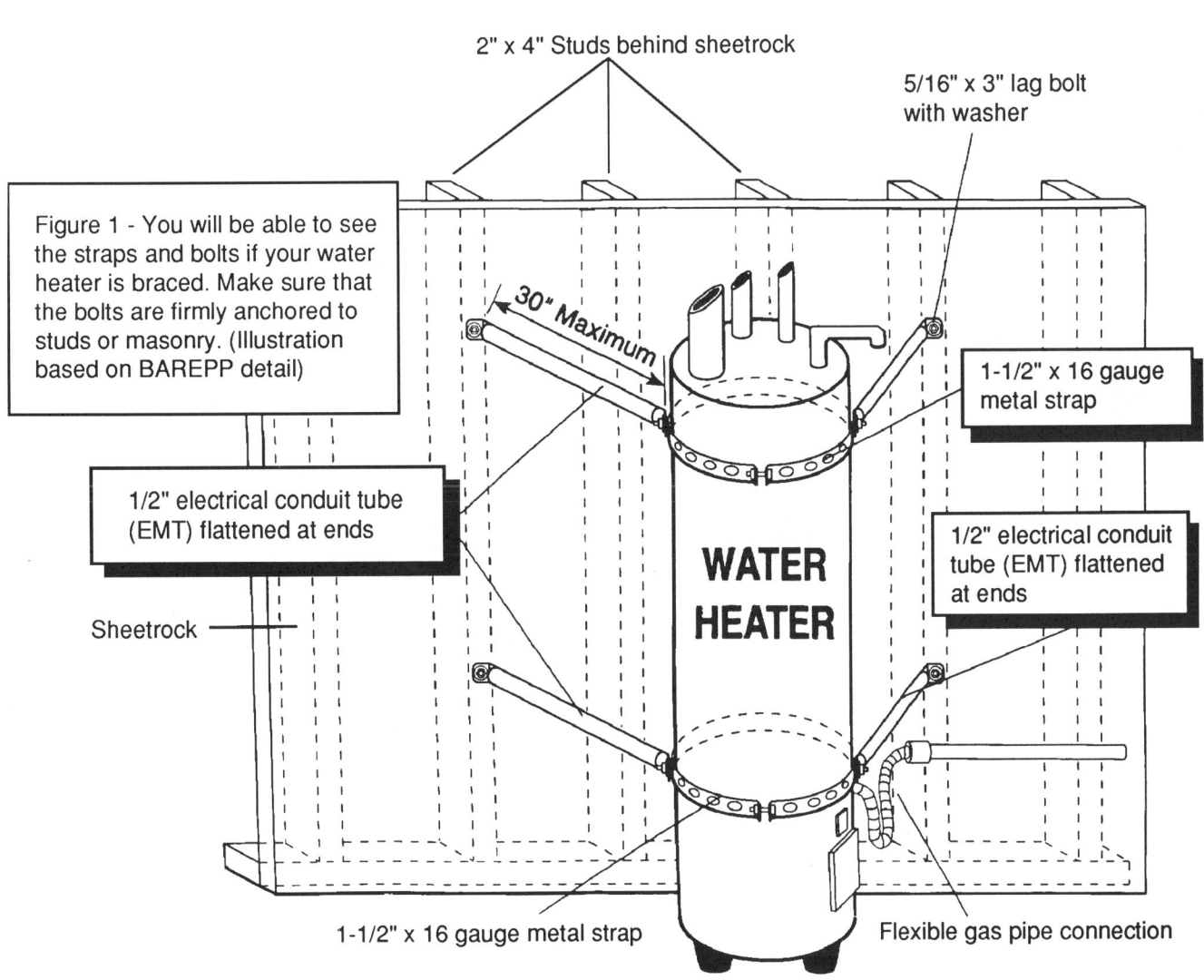

Figure 1 - You will be able to see the straps and bolts if your water heater is braced. Make sure that the bolts are firmly anchored to studs or masonry. (Illustration based on BAREPP detail)

Earthquake Safety **139**

Foundation Not Anchored When an earthquake moves a house from side to side and up and down, the house can move off its foundation if it is not anchored. This can cause a fire from broken gas lines, and damage the foundation, floors, walls, windows, and utility connections as well as the contents of the home. It is very expensive to lift a house up, put it back on its foundation, and repair this damage.

How to Identify It. If the first floor of the house is built off the ground, the area between the first floor and the ground is called the crawl space. Look in the crawl space for the heads of anchor bolts that fasten the sill plate—the wood board that sits directly on top of the foundation securely to the foundation. You should be able to see the large nuts, washers, and anchor bolts installed every four to six feet along the sill plate, or bent steel plates, connecting the foundation to the home.

What Can Be Done. Drill holes through the sill plate and into the foundation and install special bolts, or install steel plates, connecting the foundation to the sill plate of the house.

Houses Built on Concrete Slabs. Many homes do not have crawl spaces because they are built directly on concrete slabs. These houses do not have cripple walls, and they generally had foundation anchor bolts installed when they were built. If you can't tell whether your house had anchor bolts installed without removing interior plaster or drywall, which is not required by the disclosure law, you can look to see if the house has an unfinished garage with anchor bolts visible. If they are there, it is an indication that the living area of the house may have them too.

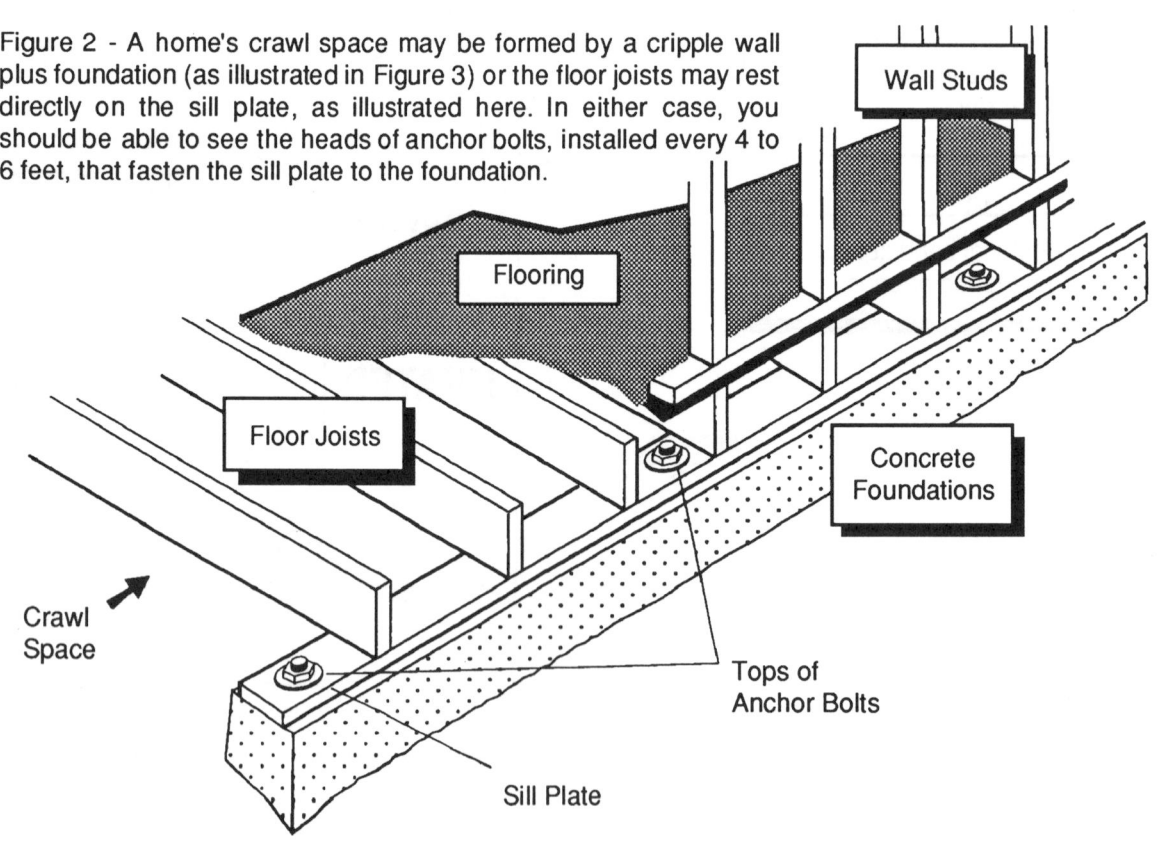

Figure 2 - A home's crawl space may be formed by a cripple wall plus foundation (as illustrated in Figure 3) or the floor joists may rest directly on the sill plate, as illustrated here. In either case, you should be able to see the heads of anchor bolts, installed every 4 to 6 feet, that fasten the sill plate to the foundation.

Weak Cripple Walls Wooden stud walls are sometimes used on top of an exterior foundation to support a house and create the crawl space. These are called cripple walls. These short walls carry the weight of the house. When the house sways from side to side in an earthquake, these walls must be braced to resist swaying. If the cripple walls are not braced, they can collapse and the house falls, causing damage to the foundation, floors, walls, windows, and utility connections as well as the contents of the home. It may also cause a fire from broken gas lines. It is very expensive to repair this damage.

How to Identify It. Go under the house to see if there are any cripple walls and, if so, whether they are braced. If you can see a cripple wall, and there is only plywood or diagonal wood sheathing, the cripple walls are probably inadequately braced or unbraced. Horizontal or vertical wood siding is not strong enough to brace cripple walls.

What Can Be Done. Plywood panels can be nailed on the inside of the studs. Notice in Figure 3 that the panels are provided with holes for ventilation.

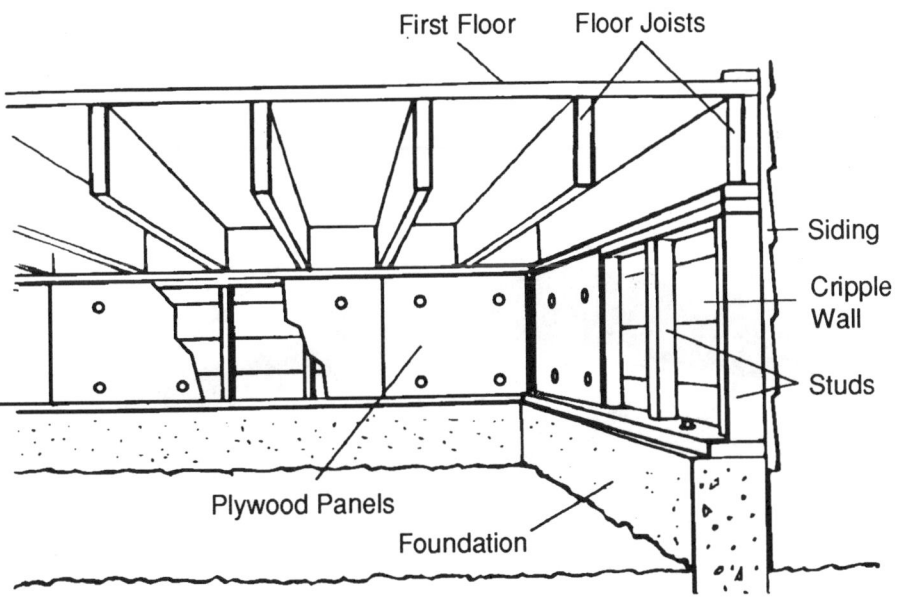

Figure 3 - If your home has a cripple wall between the foundation and the first floor, and it is not braced with plywood sheathing, the house may collapse in an earthquake.

Earthquake Safety

Pier-and-Post Foundations Pier-and-post foundations are somewhat similar to cripple walls. In this type of construction, the outside wall of the house is supported by wood posts resting on unconnected concrete piers. Siding is often nailed to the outside of the posts. If the posts are not braced against swaying, they may fall down during an earthquake.

How to Identify It. From underneath the house, if you do not see a continuous foundation under the outside walls of the house and you only see unconnected concrete piers and wood posts (or just wood posts) supporting the outside walls, your home may have this weakness. Horizontal or vertical wood siding alone is not strong enough to brace pier-and-post foundations.

What Can Be Done. This project may require the advice of an architect or engineer as well as a foundation contractor. It may be possible to make the foundation safer by bracing the posts, but you might be better off to add a new foundation and plywood walls in the crawl space to make sure that the house will not fall off its foundation in an earthquake.

Houses on Tall Walls or Posts If a house is built on the side of a steep hill, it may be set on bare posts or columns. Sometimes the downhill side will have a large unfinished space similar to, but taller than, a crawl space underneath the first floor. If such posts or walls are not properly braced, they may collapse.

How to Identify It. Examine the space underneath such a house. If you see wall studs without plywood or diagonal wood sheathing or steel bracing, or wood posts without diagonal braces, you may want to consult with an architect or engineer.

What Can Be Done. An architect or engineer can advise you on whether the posts or unbraced walls need strengthening and how to get the work done.

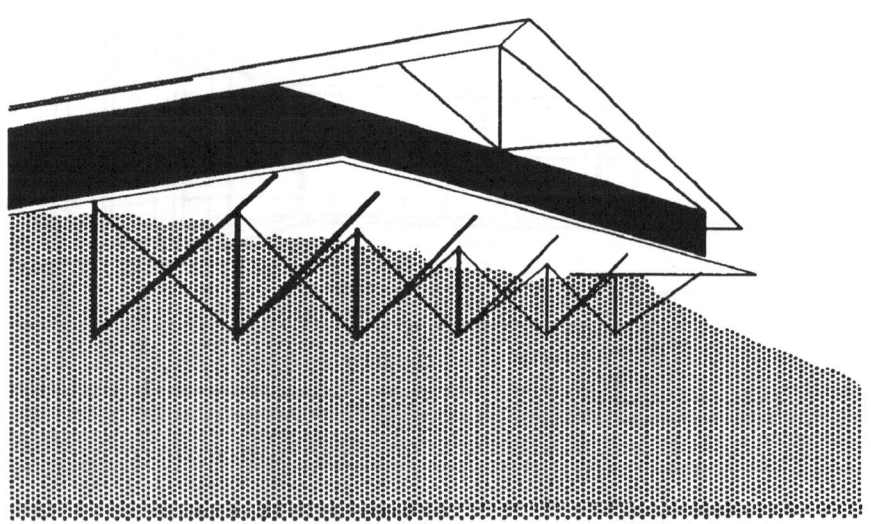

Figure 4 - A house on tall, unconnected posts is vulnerable to earthquakes unless specifically engineered for the site.

Unreinforced Masonry Foundation

Unreinforced masonry—brick, concrete block, or stone—foundations often cannot resist earthquake shaking. They may break apart, or be too weak to hold anchor bolts. Homes may shift off such foundations in an earthquake, damaging the walls, floors, utility lines, and home contents.

How to Identify It. If the outside of the foundation is covered, look underneath the house to check what your foundation is made of.

Brick or Stone. If your home's foundation is brick or stone it is probably unreinforced unless there is a space filled with grout between the inner and outer faces of a brick foundation where anchor bolts and reinforcing steel would be installed.

Concrete Block. Concrete block foundations should have steel reinforcing bars embedded in the cells of the individual blocks. Check the top of the foundation, at the sill plate, to see if there is concrete in the cells of the blocks. If the cells are hollow, the foundation is probably not reinforced.

What Can Be Done. Strengthening an unreinforced brick or stone foundation can be expensive. There are a number of ways to approach the problem; you may need the help of an architect or engineer as well as a foundation contractor. Common procedures include jacking the house off the old foundation and replacing all or part of it with a poured concrete foundation.

No Foundation

Some older houses were built on wood beams laid directly on the ground, without any foundation at all. These homes may move in earthquakes, causing structural damage and breaking utility lines. (They are also susceptible to termite damage.)

How to Identify It. If you can get under the house but cannot see any concrete or masonry around the outside walls, your house may lack a foundation.

What Can Be Done. To make a home without a foundation earthquake resistant, you may need to add a foundation. Like strengthening or replacing an unreinforced masonry foundation, this will require the advice of an architect, engineer, or foundation contractor.

Old Concrete Foundations

Some older concrete foundations were made with types of sand or aggregate that cause a chemical reaction so that the concrete eventually crumbles and becomes too soft to withstand earthquake forces.

How to Identify It. Look at the foundation to see if there are large cracks in the concrete, if concrete is crumbling off the foundation, or if the concrete crumbles when you pick at it with a screwdriver.

What Can Be Done. To fix this problem, you may need to replace some or all of the foundation. You should consult a foundation contractor or an engineer.

Room Over Garage The large opening of a garage door may make a wall too weak to withstand the shaking of a strong earthquake and the weight of a second story built over it. This is a particular concern when there are only narrow sections of wall on each side of the opening and they are not reinforced or braced. Some relatively new homes with this weakness have been damaged in past earthquakes. The problem is most serious in apartment buildings where the whole ground floor is open for parking, creating a "soft story."

How to Identify It. A room above the garage does not necessarily indicate an earthquake weakness. Check to see if there are braces or plywood panels around the garage door opening. If the garage door opening is in line with the rest of the house, additional bracing around the door is probably not needed, and may not be needed in any case. It may be hard to determine whether strengthening is needed. This is an area where you may need the help of an architect or engineer.

What Can Be Done. Install a steel frame or plywood paneling around the door opening. You should consult an architect or engineer if you have a multistory house built over a garage.

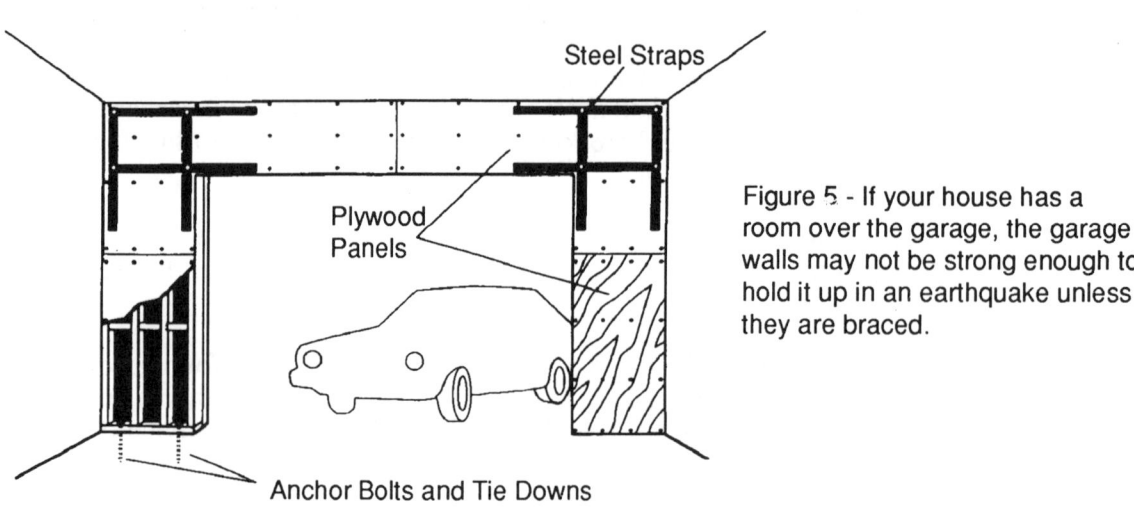

Figure 5 - If your house has a room over the garage, the garage walls may not be strong enough to hold it up in an earthquake unless they are braced.

Figure 6 - If the wall of the main house is in line with the wall containing the door of a garage with a room over it (#1), the adjoining wall will help brace the garage. If the "in-line" wall consists only of porch supports (#2), the garage may require additional bracing.

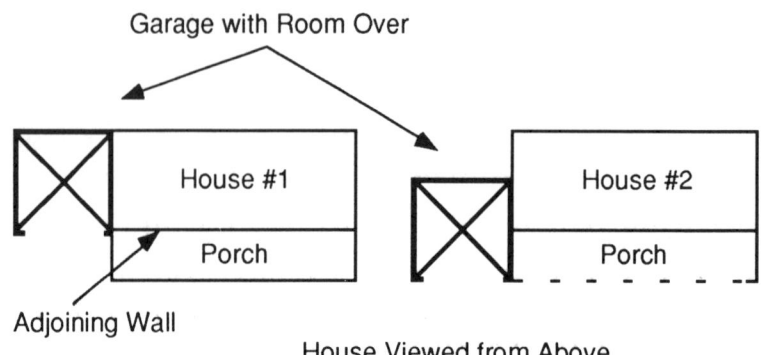

144 *Environmental Issues & Obligations*

Unreinforced Masonry Walls   Houses built of unreinforced masonry—bricks, hollow clay tiles, stone, concrete blocks, or adobe—are very likely to be damaged in a strong earthquake. The mortar holding the masonry together may not be strong enough to resist earthquake forces, and the house cannot bend a little, like a wood-frame house, and then return to its original shape.

How to Identify It. You can usually see bricks or stone from the outside unless the walls are covered with plaster. If you can't tell from the outside, you can take the cover plate off one of the electrical outlet boxes on an outside wall (turn off the power first!) and look for brick or other masonry.

Brick. If brick walls have header courses (rows of bricks turned endwise every five or six rows: see Figure 7), or if the house was built before 1940, the walls are most likely unreinforced.

Concrete. If the wall is concrete or concrete block, it is very difficult to determine whether reinforcing steel was included during construction. An experienced testing firm may tell you whether any steel is present. Otherwise, consulting the house's plans, which may be on file with the local building department, might be the only way to tell without damaging the wall.

What Can Be Done. This is another problem that requires the services of an architect or engineer. Strengthening may require tying the walls to the floor and roof or other measures. Masonry buildings are discussed further in *The Commercial Property Owner's Guide to Earthquake Safety*.

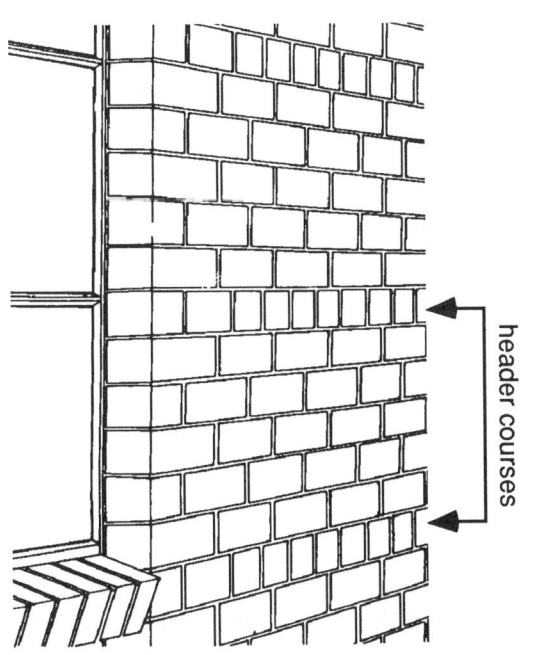

Figure 7 - Walls of unreinforced brick may not withstand earthquake shaking. Note header courses every six rows.

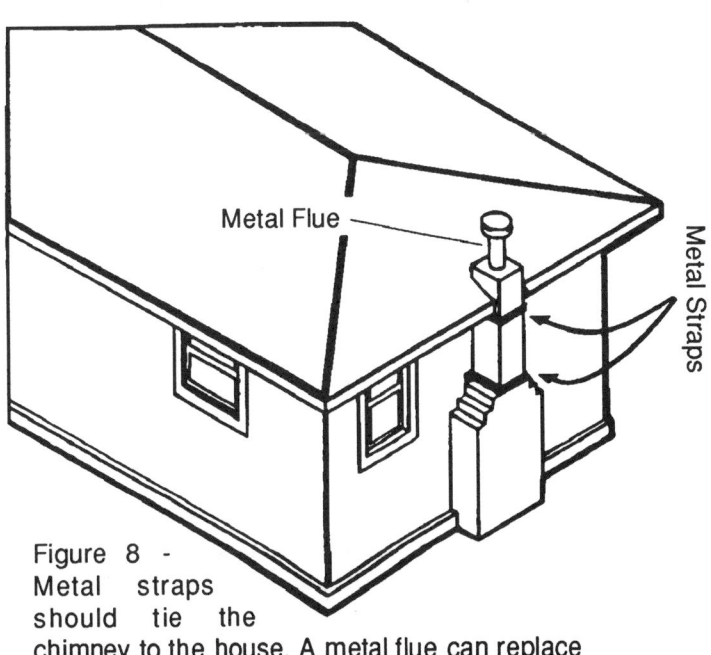

Figure 8 - Metal straps should tie the chimney to the house. A metal flue can replace the upper chimney if the mortar is good.

Earthquake Safety

Unreinforced Masonry Chimneys Many chimneys are built of unreinforced brick or stone and can collapse or fall over in an earthquake. If the chimney comes apart, the brick or stone may fall, damaging houses and cars and injuring people.

How to Identify It. Determining whether a chimney is susceptible to earthquakes is not easy. Tall, slender chimneys are most vulnerable to collapse. If the mortar between the brick or stone crumbles when you pick at it with a screwdriver, the chimney may be a hazard. Look in the attic and floor spaces to see whether you can find the metal ties that should be holding the chimney to the house (Figure 8).

What Can Be Done. You can rebuild a reinforced chimney, strap the chimney to the house, or nail plywood panels above the ceiling, in the attic, or under the shingles when you reroof, to prevent the brick or stone from falling into the house. Do not locate patios, play areas, or parking spaces near a questionable chimney. Tell family members to get away from chimneys and fireplaces during an earthquake.

Home Design Some design features can cause earthquake weaknesses if the homes are not properly planned and built. Homes with irregular shapes, large windows (which can break in an earthquake, scattering shards of glass), more than two stories, irregular walls, or porches and overhangs may suffer damage in a strong earthquake.

How to Identify It. Many homes with these features are strong enough to withstand earthquakes, and it is difficult to tell whether such a home needs strengthening. If you have doubts about one or more of these features in your home or a home you are planning to buy, you should consult an architect or engineer to check it.

What Can Be Done. The professional that you consult can advise you on how to identify and fix the problem, if needed. You can make large windows safer by applying plastic film to them.

Home Contents The contents of a home may be damaged, and can be dangerous, in earthquake. Earthquake shaking can make light fixtures fall, refrigerators and other large items move across the floor, and bookcases and television sets topple. They may injure you and your family, and it can be expensive to repair and replace items that are broken.

How to Identify It. Look around your house for things that could fall or move during an earthquake. Could your cupboard doors fly open, allowing dishes to shatter on the floor? Is your TV and stereo equipment fastened down, and are the shelves they sit on fastened to the wall? Do you have hanging plants or light fixtures that might fall? Is there a heavy picture or mirror on the wall over your bed?

What Can Be Done. You can install door latches, braces, and fasteners to fix most of these hazards yourself. Various publications can help you identify these hazards and deal with them.

GETTING THE WORK DONE

For your family's safety and financial security, you should strengthen your home to resist earthquakes. This guide can help you decide which projects to tackle first. If your home has an unanchored water heater, an unbolted foundation, or an unbraced cripple wall, these are the projects that will give you the most protection in return for your money.

Do It Yourself You may be able to do the simpler strengthening projects yourself. Your local building department can provide guidelines for the project, and a contractor may charge only a nominal fee, if any, to provide advice you may need for doing the work. You will need building permits for these projects (except perhaps for strapping the water heater). There are many publications that go into detail about how to do these strengthening projects. You should review one or two of these publications even if you do not plan to do the work yourself, to get a better idea of what your architect, engineer, or contractor is doing.

Professional Help Many homeowners will find they need the assistance of building professionals, especially for the more complex projects. They can help you assess the earthquake weaknesses of your house, estimate the costs of correcting these weaknesses, and prepare the plans and specifications needed to get a building permit. For large, complicated projects, you may wish to hire an architect or engineer to evaluate the structure and design the earthquake strengthening project, and then advise you about selecting a contractor.

Screening. When obtaining help, make sure the professionals have experience in residential earthquake strengthening, as well as the appropriate state licenses. Check references carefully. Call former customers to make sure you are contracting with reliable people, and ask for examples of previous jobs similar to yours. Talk to two or three professionals and be sure to compare their experience, ideas, and fees. Select someone you can talk to, someone who can explain what is to be done in terms that you can understand.

Bids. You should get several bids for construction work. Remember, though, that the low bid may not be the best choice. Opinions on the best way to do the job may vary.

Recordkeeping. Be sure to keep the plans, permits, and other paperwork related to your strengthening project to show future buyers as well as for tax and insurance purposes.

Historic Buildings. If your home has been designated as "historic" (for example, a local landmark or in a historic district) you may be subject to special design review requirements, and may be able to benefit from the State Historical Building Code. Your local building department can help you determine how this affects the methods and materials you use.

Costs: Strengthen or Repair? Repairing earthquake damage to a home can be very expensive. Usually it costs less to correct earthquake weaknesses than to repair earthquake damage. After an earthquake, you may have lodging costs in addition to repair costs if you cannot live in your home until the damage is repaired.

Strengthening. The following chart shows the typical range of costs to strengthen a home. The low end is the approximate cost of a simple job for materials only, assuming you do the work. The upper end is for a job done by a

Earthquake Safety **147**

professional. Costs vary from job to job; ask your architect, engineer, or contractor to explain how the cost of your job was estimated.

Repair. The repair costs given, which are based on 1991 prices, are for an average house on a level lot. Your costs may vary. But these estimates give you some idea of the risks of leaving the work undone. Usually it is far cheaper and safer to strengthen your home before the earthquake than to fix it afterward.

Earthquake Strenthening Project	Cost of Project (Range)	Cost to Repair Unstrengthened House After Earthquake
Bracing Water Heater	$25 - $200	$200 - Total*
Anchoring Foundation	$250 - $5,000	$25,000 - Total*
Bracing Cripple Walls	$500 - $2,500	$25,000 - Total*
Strengthening Foundations	$15,000 - $50,000	$15,000 - Total*
Bracing Tall Walls or Posts	$1,000 - $25,000	$1,000 - Total*
Bracing Garage with Rooms Above	$200 - $25,000	$1,000 - Total*
Bracing or Replacing Chimney	$2,000 - $12,000	$1,000 - $15,000

Total—full cost of home, which may be completely destroyed by this failure.

Earthquake Insurance The insurance company that insures your home for fire is required by law to offer you earthquake insurance. Earthquake insurance policies usually cost $80 to $400 per year in addition to your homeowners insurance premium, depending on your location, the size and type of your house, and other factors. The policies carry deductibles of 5 percent, 10 percent, or more of the house's replacement value. A 10 percent deductible means an earthquake must do more than $20,000 worth of damage to a $200,000 house before the insurance company pays for any earthquake damage; you must pay for the first $20,000 worth of repairs.

Property Tax Exemption To encourage homeowners to complete earthquake strengthening projects, the state provides a property tax exemption for such projects. If you add a swimming pool or a new den to your home, your property tax bill will increase, but a strengthening project to help your home resist earthquakes will not add to your property taxes. The chart below shows how your property tax might be affected by improvements to your home. You must file a claim form with your county assessor to receive the exemption.

TAXABLE ITEM	COST	PROPERTY TAX AMT.	TOTAL PROP. TAX
Home Purchase	$150,000	$1,500	$1,500
Addition of Swimming Pool	$10,000	$100	$1,600
Converting Garage to Den	$5,000	$50	$1,650
Strengthening Weak Foundation	$20,000	$200	$1,850
Less Exemption for Earthquake Improvement		$200	$1,650

Environmental Issues & Obligations

GEOLOGIC HAZARDS

Building damage caused by ground shaking is not the only earthquake hazard that can threaten your home. Others include ground failure (landslides or liquefaction), fault rupture (breaking of the ground's surface), tsunami (earthquake-caused sea wave), and dam failure due to earthquake damage. Strengthening your home as described in this guide will help it resist ground shaking, but you should also be aware of the actions that you and your family can take to protect yourselves against these other hazards.

Information Sources Some of the hazards described below are shown on maps that you can see at your local government planning department or get from the California Division of Mines and Geology. These hazards should also be described in the safety element of your city or county general plan, available at your local planning department. The Division of Mines and Geology is preparing a series of maps that will show areas of high earthquake hazard all over the state, but the first such maps will not be available until 1995. You might want to talk with a geologist or geotechnical engineer about your home's potential for damage due to ground shaking, ground failure, or fault rupture in an earthquake.

Ground Shaking Ground shaking causes ninety-nine percent of the earthquake damage to California homes. Homes that have the earthquake weaknesses described above, and homes that are on soft soil with shallow ground water, can be damaged by shaking from earthquakes that occur many miles away. Homes in San Francisco and Oakland were damaged by the 1989 Loma Prieta earthquake which was centered over fifty miles away. No area in California is safe from the possibility of damaging ground shaking.

How To Identify It. Geologists believe that areas near large active faults, known as Seismic Zone 4 (see Figure 9), are more likely to be shaken than areas in Seismic Zone 3. Your local planning department may have information on the intensity of ground shaking predicted for your area.

What Can Be Done. The strengthening measures suggested in this guide will reduce or prevent damage from ground shaking.

Ground Failure In addition to ground shaking, earthquakes can trigger landslides that can severely damage homes, and liquefaction, the process that occurs when earthquakes shake loose, wet, sandy soil so that the soil loses strength, allowing the house to sink.

How To Identify It. Your local government planning department or the California Division of Mines and Geology may have maps that will assist you in determining whether your house is in a hazardous area; geologic or soils reports have been prepared for many housing developments and some individual homes. There may be information in the safety element of your city or county general plan.

What Can Be Done. Consult an engineering geologist or a geotechnical engineer if you believe that your house may be in an area with potential for ground failure.

Tsunami A tsunami is a large sea wave caused by an earthquake. The wave can do considerable damage if it hits low-lying areas along the shore. Ten people were killed in Crescent City when the tsunami caused by the 1964 Alaskan earthquake slammed into the town.

How To Identify It. Tsunami damage is rare in California, but some low-lying coastal areas can experience a tsunami. Consult your city or county general plan's safety element.

What Can Be Done. If you live along the coast, be alert for news of tsunami warnings issued by the government's Tsunami Warning Center, and plan ahead how you will get to higher ground. If you see the sea level suddenly rise or fall, move to higher ground or go to the upper floors of a building and stay there until the authorities issue an "all clear," for at least several hours. Don't go down to the shore to see the sea bottom that has been uncovered—the water will come back, and it could come, suddenly, and higher than before. Low water is a warning that a high wave is coming.

Dam Failure Earthquake damage to a dam can cause a flood. A dam above the San Fernando Valley was damaged in the 1971 earthquake; if it had failed, it might have flooded the homes below, causing many deaths and injuries.

How To Identify It. City and county planning departments have maps showing the areas that would be flooded if local dams failed. Inquire if there are any dams or reservoirs nearby and if your property is down stream from them.

What Can Be Done. Dam failure is unlikely. But if you decide to buy a home in an area that might be flooded after an earthquake, be sure to be alert for announcements of damage to the dam, and make plans to move to a safer location if necessary.

Fault Rupture Fault rupture is an actual crack or breaking of the ground along a fault during an earthquake. An earthquake fault that has ruptured the surface of the ground in the last eleven thousand years is considered active and able to cause surface rupture again. A house built directly over an active fault can be torn apart if the ground ruptures. If the house is built over a creeping fault that moves in a series of small earthquakes rather than a strong shock, the damage may not be noticed for some time.

How To Identify It. The city or county planning department should have maps, called Alquist-Priolo or Special Studies Zone maps (Figure 10), that will tell you if your home is on or near a known active fault that has broken the ground's surface. The safety element of your city or county general plan may help you identify these and other faults that may cause earthquakes near your home.

What Can Be Done. Your house is far more likely to be damaged by earthquake shaking than by ground rupture, so you should take all the strengthening and planning precautions described in this booklet, whether or not your house is in a Special Studies Zone or near a known active fault. Consult a geologist if you want more information regarding whether a specific fault may rupture.

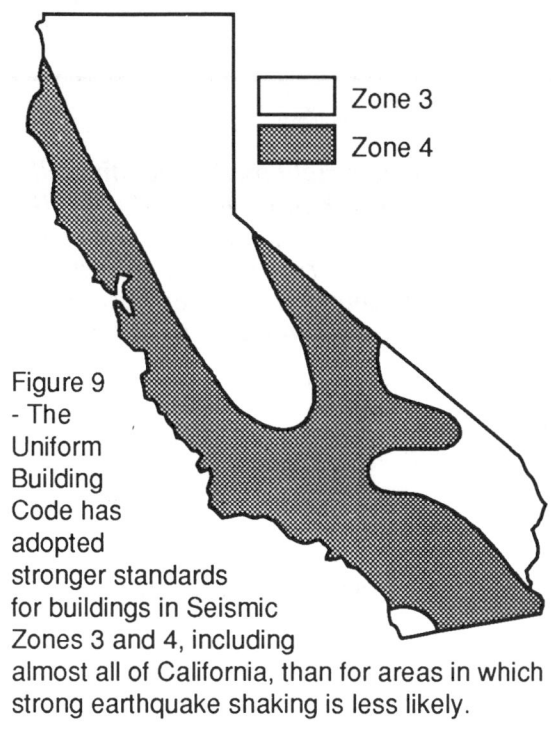

Figure 9 - The Uniform Building Code has adopted stronger standards for buildings in Seismic Zones 3 and 4, including almost all of California, than for areas in which strong earthquake shaking is less likely.

Figure 10 - This Alquist-Priolo map shows where the Hayward fault underlies part of San Pablo.

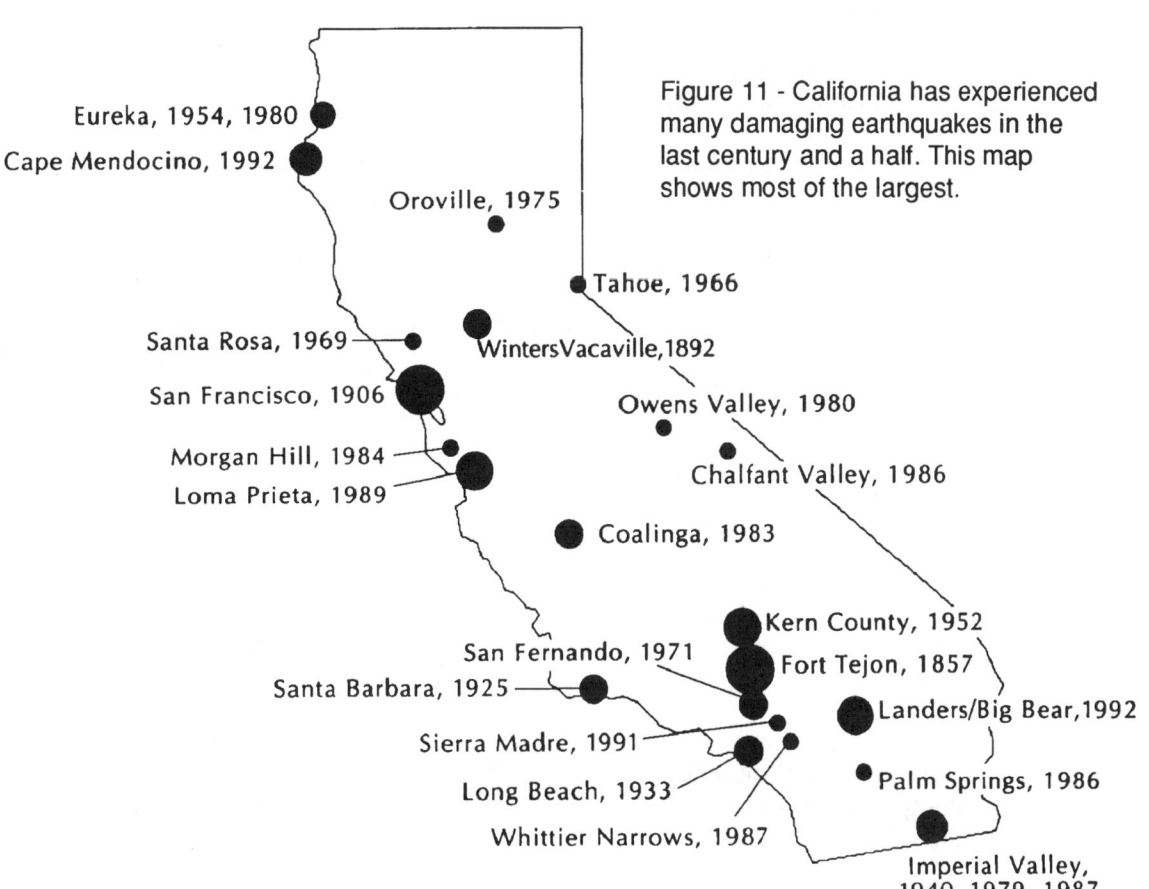

Figure 11 - California has experienced many damaging earthquakes in the last century and a half. This map shows most of the largest.

Earthquake Safety **151**

BE PREPARED FOR EARTHQUAKES

The information in this section is reprinted with the permission of the copyright owner, Pacific Bell, a Pacific Telesis Company. The full Survival Guide is available in the White Pages of Pacific Bell Directories, © Pacific Bell 1991. This information was provided by medical and emergency service authorities and published as a public service. While every reasonable effort was made to insure its accuracy, Pacific Bell is not responsible and assumes no liability for any action undertaken by any person in utilizing such information. Any person relying upon such information does so at his or her own risk.

Emergency Supplies Be sure you have these basic supplies on hand:

- Fire extinguisher.

- Adequate supplies of medications that you or family members are taking.

- Crescent and pipe wrenches to turn off gas and water supplies.

- First aid kit and handbook.

- Flashlights with extra bulbs and batteries.

- Portable radio with extra batteries.

- Water for each family member for at least three days (allow at least one gallon per person per day) and purification tablets or chlorine bleach to purify drinking water from other sources.

- Canned and packaged foods, enough for several days, and a mechanical can opener. Remember to include extra pet food.

- Camp stove or barbecue to cook on outdoors. Store fuel out of the reach of children.

- Waterproof, heavy duty plastic bags for waste disposal.

Plan Ahead Make sure each member of your family knows what to do no matter where they are when an earthquake occurs.

- Establish a meeting place where you can reunite afterward.

- Find out about the earthquake plan developed by your children's school or day care.

- Remember that transportation may be disrupted, so you may have to stay at your workplace for a day or two following a major earthquake. Keep some emergency supplies—food, liquids, and comfortable shoes, for example—at work.

- Know where your gas, electric, and water main shutoffs are and how to turn them off if there is a leak or electrical short. If in doubt, ask your utility companies. Make sure that all the adult members of your family can shut off the utilities.

- ☐ Locate your nearest fire and police stations and emergency medical facility. Remember that you probably won't be able to telephone for help after earthquakes.

- ☐ Talk to your neighbors. How could they help you, or you help them, after an earthquake?

- ☐ Take a Red Cross first aid and CPR training course.

During an Earthquake

If You Are Indoors. Stay there. Get under a desk or table and hang on to it, or move into a hallway or get against an inside wall. Stay clear of windows, fireplaces, and heavy furniture or appliances. Get out of the kitchen, which is a dangerous place in earthquakes since it is full of things that can fall. Do not run downstairs or rush outside while the building is shaking or while there is danger of falling or being hit by falling glass or debris.

If You Are Outside. Get into the open, away from buildings, power lines, chimneys, and anything else that might fall on you.

If You Are Driving. Stop, but carefully. Move your car as far out of traffic as possible. Do not stop on or under a bridge or overpass or under trees, light posts, power lines, or signs. Stay inside your car until the shaking stops. When you resume driving, watch for breaks in the pavement, fallen rocks, and bumps in the road at bridge approaches.

In a Mountainous Area. Watch out for falling rock, landslides, trees, and other debris that could be loosened by quakes.

After an Earthquake

Wear sturdy shoes to avoid injury from broken glass and debris. Expect aftershocks.

Check for Injuries:

- ☐ If a person is bleeding, put direct pressure on the wound. Use clean gauze or cloth, if available.

- ☐ If a person is not breathing, administer rescue breathing. The front pages of many telephone books contain instructions on this and other first aid measures.

- ☐ Do not attempt to move seriously injured persons unless they are in immediate danger of further injury.

- ☐ Cover injured persons with blankets to keep them warm.

- ☐ Seek medical help for serious injuries.

Check for Hazards:

- ☐ Fire or fire hazards. Put out fires in your home or neighborhood immediately. Call for help, but do not wait for the fire department.

- ☐ Gas leaks. Shut off the main gas valve only if you suspect a leak because of broken pipes or the odor of natural gas. Do not turn it back on yourself—wait for the gas company to check for leaks.

- ☐ Damaged electrical wiring. Shut off power at the control box if there is any damage to your house wiring.

- ☐ Downed or damaged utility lines. Do not touch downed power lines or any objects in contact with them.

- ☐ Spills. Clean up any spilled medicines, drugs, or other potentially harmful materials such as bleach, lye, and gasoline or other petroleum products.

- ☐ Downed or damaged chimneys. Approach chimneys with caution. They may be weakened and could topple during aftershocks. Do not use a fireplace with a damaged chimney—it could start a fire or let poisonous gases into your house.

- ☐ Fallen items. Beware of items tumbling off shelves when you open the doors of closets and cupboards.

Check Food and Water Supplies:

- ☐ Do not eat or drink anything from open containers near shattered glass.

- ☐ If power is off, plan meals to use up foods that will spoil quickly, or frozen foods. If you keep the door closed, food in the freezer should be good for at least a couple of days.

- ☐ Do not light the kitchen stove if you suspect a gas leak.

- ☐ Use barbecues or camp stoves, outdoors only, for emergency cooking.

- ☐ If water is off, you can drink water from water heaters and melted ice cubes, or liquid from canned vegetables. Try to avoid drinking water from swimming pools or spas—it may have too many chemicals in it to be safe.

Do Not:

- ☐ Do not turn on the gas again if you turned it off; let the gas company do it.

- ☐ Do not use matches, lighters, camp stoves or barbecues, electrical equipment—including telephones—or appliances until you are sure there are no gas leaks. They may create a spark that could ignite leaking gas and cause an explosion and fire.

- ☐ Do not use your telephone, except for a medical or fire emergency. You could tie up lines needed for emergency response. If the phone does not work, send someone for help.

- ☐ Do not expect firefighters, police, or paramedics to help you. They may not be available.

Getting the Work Done
- Do it yourself: water heater, cripple walls, foundation bolting are easiest and least expensive
- Hiring a contractor: get bids and references, keep records
- Special permit requirements may apply to historic buildings
- Costs are usually far less to strengthen a building before an earthquake than fix it afterward
- Earthquake insurance must be offered by homeowners insurer; costs commonly $80 to $400 a year, 5 or 10 percent deductible
- Earthquake upgrades do not add to property tax bill (must apply to assessor for exemption)

Geologic Hazards
- Hazard areas are mapped by Division of Mines and Geology and local governments
- Ground shaking causes 99 percent of earthquake damage, far from actual fault or epicenter
- Ground failure includes landslides and liquefaction
- Tsunami is a giant sea wave caused by an earthquake
- Dams may flood areas below if they are damaged by earthquake
- Fault rupture—a crack in the earth at the fault line—can split a building apart
- Special Studies maps show fault lines

Be Prepared for Earthquakes
- Telephone directory contains survival guide and first aid instructions
- Emergency supplies: food, water, medicine, tools, flashlight, radio, fire extinguisher, first aid, waste disposal
- Plan ahead: family meeting place, supplies at work, utility shutoffs, locate emergency services, organize with neighbors, learn first aid
- During a quake: stay away from falling hazards
- After a quake: check for injuries and hazards (fire, gas and electricity, falling objects)
- Use food, water, and cooking equipment cautiously
- Do not use fire or electrical equipment—including telephones—if there is any possibility of gas leaks
- Do not tie up telephone, and do not expect police and fire services to be available

COURSE 8
Hazardous Material in the Home

INTRODUCTION

This course is condensed from the booklet Environmental Hazards: Guide for Homeowners and Buyers. *This booklet may be used as part of the real estate transfer disclosure process, and licensees should be familiar with its contents. It is an independent research report developed by M.B. Gilbert Associates, under contract with the California Department of Real Estate in cooperation with the Department of Health Services. The Departments of Real Estate and Health Services offer this booklet for information purposes only, not as a reflection of the position of the administration of the State of California.*

The section on Ground Water Contamination is added from another booklet, A Home Buyer's Guide to Environmental Hazards, *published by a consortium of housing and finance industry organizations including the National Association of Realtors®. Additional information on waste disposal sites is from the California Association of Realtors® Legal Department's memorandum, "Typical Environmental Hazards in Real Estate Transactions," September 24, 1990.*

The California Departments of Real Estate and Health Services have prepared this booklet in response to the California legislative mandate (Chapter 969, Statutes of 1989, AB 983, Bane) to inform the homeowner and prospective homeowner about environmental hazards located on and affecting residential property. Although the disclosure of known hazards is required by law, an environmental survey may be conducted to obtain further information. The booklet discusses some of the most important environmental hazards which may be present on residential property. Other environmental hazards may be identified in the future. The booklet should be used only for general guidance. Homeowners and prospective homeowners may wish to obtain other literature for additional information on hazards of concern.

Disclosure Requirements Pursuant to AB 983, if the environmental hazards booklet is made available to homeowners or prospective homeowners, real estate licensees, and home sellers are not required to provide additional information on such hazards. However, delivery of this publication to homeowners or prospective homeowners does not relieve home sellers and real estate licensees of the responsibility to disclose the existence of environmental hazards when such hazards are known to them.

Waste Disposal Disposal of hazardous wastes is an issue of concern to all Californians. In the interest of reducing the use of and properly disposing of household hazardous wastes, a section on their storage and disposal is included.

ASBESTOS

Asbestos is a generic term describing a group of diverse, naturally occurring, fibrous minerals. These minerals occur as bundles of strong flexible fibers that are chemically inert, do not burn, and have good insulating properties.

Asbestos in the Home Asbestos has been used in many products in the home to provide insulation, strength, and fire protection. In 1989, the U.S. Environmental Protection Agency (USEPA) announced a phased ban of asbestos products to be completed by 1996. The most common items in the home that may contain asbestos are:

- Vinyl flooring

- Duct wrapping on heating and air conditioning systems

- Insulation on hot water pipes and boilers, especially in homes built from 1920 to 1972

- Some roofing, shingles, and siding

- Ceiling and wall insulation in some homes built or remodeled between 1945 and 1978

- Sheetrock taping compounds and some ceiling materials.

Asbestos that has been sprayed on ceilings often has a spongy, "cottage cheese" appearance with irregular soft surfaces. Asbestos troweled on walls has a textured, firm appearance. Information on the asbestos content of home products can be provided by the manufacturers. Qualified inspectors can be hired to identify asbestos in the home.

Dangers of Asbestos Intact or sealed (painted or taped over) asbestos is not harmful unless it becomes friable. Friable means the material can be easily crushed or pulverized to a powder by hand pressure. Friable materials have a higher potential to release fibers. Asbestos fibers that are released into the air and inhaled can accumulate in the lungs and pose a health risk.

Asbestosis and Cancer. This risk can be divided into two general categories: 1) risk of asbestosis; and 2) increased risk of cancer. Most persons diagnosed with asbestosis have been exposed to asbestos in the work place. Cancer is considered the main risk associated with asbestos exposure in the home.

Cancer and Asbestos Exposure. The USEPA classifies asbestos as a known human carcinogen. If asbestos fibers are inhaled, the likelihood of lung cancer or mesothelioma (cancer of the lining of the chest or abdomen) increases. As more asbestos is inhaled, the risk further increases. Smokers who are exposed to high levels of asbestos have a much greater risk of developing lung cancer than nonsmokers exposed to the same level. Symptoms of cancer may not develop until ten to forty years after the first exposure.

Safe Levels. In theory, inhalation of one fiber of asbestos can increase the risk of developing cancer. Breathing ambient air in an urban area already results in the inhalation of about 20,000 asbestos fibers per day. As a result of this exposure to asbestos in ambient air for a lifetime, it is estimated that three to thirty cases of lung cancer and four to twenty-four cases of mesothelioma will occur for every one million Americans. Those cancer cases are in addition to those due to other causes, particularly smoking. Obviously inhalation of additional asbestos fibers increases the risk of developing lung cancer and unnecessary exposure should be avoided.

Determining Asbestos Content When asbestos is suspected to be present in building materials, it is important to have the materials tested by a qualified laboratory. Visual inspection alone is not enough to identify the presence of asbestos. Testing may not be warranted if the material is in good condition, in which case it is best to leave it in place. If the material is damaged, or will be disturbed during normal household activities or remodeling, it should be tested. A list of asbestos consultants and contractors registered with the California Department of Industrial Relations (Cal/OSHA) for doing asbestos-related work may be obtained by calling (415) 737-2731.

Asbestos Removal Repair or removal of asbestos by the homeowner may be unwise, since it may result in unnecessary exposure to airborne fiber. Small repairs of pipe or duct insulation can be made with paint or duct tape, but other materials such as sprayed-on acoustical ceilings are not easily repaired by the homeowner. In cases where planned remodeling projects are expected to damage asbestos-containing materials, it is wise to hire a qualified contractor to remove the material. The homeowner should use the following guidelines in choosing a qualified contractor:

- Check to see if the contractor is licensed by the California Contractors' State License Board or registered with the California Department of Industrial Relations (Cal/OSHA) for doing asbestos work.

- Be aware that some contractors may remove material in an unsafe manner and still charge a substantial fee.

- Require references from the contractor and check them to see if the contractor's work has been satisfactory.

- Require the contractor to specify safety procedures in writing.

Removal Costs. The homeowner may expect to pay three times as much for a remodeling or repair job involving asbestos removal than if asbestos were not present. For a small job, the cost may be even more than three times the normal cost, since it is expensive for a contractor to set up all the necessary safety equipment. Consider hiring an independent asbestos consultant (contact Cal/OSHA for a list) to review safety procedures and oversee the performance of the contractor.

Removal Not Required. Asbestos mitigation is at the discretion of the homeowner. Even if the material contains asbestos, the homeowner may choose to leave it alone or if necessary repair it.

Information Hotlines:

- For information concerning the identification and abatement of asbestos hazards in the home and on the asbestos content of certain consumer products contact the Consumer Product Safety Commission, Washington, D.C. at (800) 638-2772.

- For general information concerning federal requirements about abatement projects, school programs, analytical methods, and product use restrictions contact the USEPA Toxic Substance Control Act (TSCA) Hotline in Washington, D.C. at (202) 554-1404.

Publications:

- *Asbestos in the Home*
- *The Inside Story—A Guide to Indoor Air Quality*

These publications are available at no cost from: U.S. Environmental Protection Agency, TSCA Assistance Information Service, 401 M Street SW, Washington, D.C. 20460, telephone (202) 554-1404.

FORMALDEHYDE

Formaldehyde is a colorless, pungent gas that is soluble in water and most organic solvents. It is used as a raw material in the manufacture of paints, plastics, resins, photographic materials, and in building materials such as fiberboard and some foam insulation. Formaldehyde is found in the outdoor air at levels ranging from about 0.0002 to 0.050 parts per million (ppm). (One ppm can be compared to one cent in ten thousand dollars.)

Levels in the Home Formaldehyde concentrations inside California residences range from less than 0.01 to almost 0.50 ppm. Concentrations of formaldehyde inside mobile homes are somewhat higher than those found in conventional homes.

Sources Formaldehyde is emitted from products manufactured with formaldehyde. These include pressed-wood products, urea formaldehyde foam used in insulation, and curtain and upholstery textiles treated with formaldehyde resins for crease resistance. Formaldehyde may also be emitted from improperly vented gas stoves and kerosene heaters. Pressed-wood products are probably the most significant source of formaldehyde in the home.

Pressed-Wood Products Pressed-wood products contain resins to bind together wood or wood products such as wood chips. The two most commonly used resins are urea formaldehyde and phenol formaldehyde. Pressed-wood products used in the home include:

- ☐ Particleboard, used for subflooring, shelving, and in furniture
- ☐ Hardwood and plywood paneling, used in furniture and as a wall covering
- ☐ Medium density fiberboard, used for cabinet doors, table tops, and shelving
- ☐ Waferboard and softwood plywood, for exterior use and subflooring; both are manufactured using phenol formaldehyde resins.

Of these products, medium density fiberboard typically has the highest formaldehyde emission rate.

Formaldehyde Emission In the production of the resins, not all formaldehyde is bound as urea formaldehyde or phenol formaldehyde. Unbound or free formaldehyde can be released later as a gas from pressed wood. Formaldehyde emissions are highest from new products and decrease as the product ages. Emissions ordinarily decrease to undetectable levels over time. If properly manufactured, pressed-wood products which incorporate phenol formaldehyde resins do not release significant amounts of formaldehyde. Urea formaldehyde resins have higher emission rates than phenol formaldehyde resins.

Urea Formaldehyde Foam Urea formaldehyde foam insulation (UFFI) was installed in the wall cavities of some homes during the 1970s and has been used in the manufacture of mobile homes. The Consumer Product Safety Commission banned the use of UFFI in homes and schools in 1982. Although this ban has been removed by a federal court for procedural reasons, UFFI is not currently being installed in homes in California because of the insulation standards of the California Energy Commission. Implementation of these standards effectively prohibited the use of UFFI in homes in California after 1982. Formaldehyde emissions from UFFI decline with time. Thus, in homes where UFFI was installed prior to 1982, formaldehyde concentrations are by now generally comparable to those in homes without UFFI.

Dangers of Formaldehyde The USEPA classifies formaldehyde as a probable carcinogen. This means that there is sufficient data from animal studies, and limited data from human studies, to conclude that formaldehyde is likely to cause cancer in humans. Regulation of carcinogens is based on the assumption that any exposure to a carcinogen carries with it a finite risk of developing cancer. This assumption has not been proven scientifically, but was adopted as conservative regulatory policy to protect the health of the general public. Risk is assumed to vary directly with exposure—as exposure decreases, risk decreases as well.

Safe Levels. Most persons experience eye and throat irritation when exposed to formaldehyde at levels above 0.1 parts per million. Because people differ in their sensitivity to toxic effects, it is difficult to precisely define a concentration of formaldehyde that would be harmless to all people under all circumstances. Levels in the outside air may be considered as the safest and lowest levels that can practically be achieved in the home.

Formaldehyde Detection Levels of formaldehyde can be measured by chemical analysis of air samples. The usefulness of air monitoring for a short time, for example over twenty-four hours, is limited because levels of formaldehyde change with temperature, humidity, and ventilation, and decline as the products age. A useful indicator of the presence of indoor formaldehyde is knowledge of the formaldehyde content of products. This information can be obtained from the manufacturer.

Hazard Reduction Immediate measures include opening windows to increase ventilation and reducing the number of new pressed-wood products by choosing products made from solid wood or non-wood materials. Formaldehyde emissions increase with increasing humidity and temperature. Therefore, reducing the temperature and humidity in the home will reduce formaldehyde levels. Where the source of formaldehyde is wood paneling or subflooring, these measures may not be adequate. In this case, removal of paneling and subflooring may be necessary. Local trade organizations and builders' associations may be helpful in finding a contractor to do this work. Where UFFI is the source of formaldehyde, removal has been shown to be ineffective because the wood frame support continues to emit formaldehyde absorbed from UFFI.

Information Publications:

- *Formaldehyde: Everything You Wanted to Know But Were Afraid to Ask*

This publication is available at no cost from Consumer Federation of America, 1424 Sixteenth Street NW, Washington, D.C. 20036, telephone (202) 387-6121. (A stamped, self-addressed envelope is required.)

- *A Consumers' Guide to Manufactured Housing*

- *Manufactured Housing for Families*

These publications are available at no cost from the California Department of Housing and Community Development, Division of Administration, P.O. Box 952050, Sacramento, CA 94220, telephone (916) 322-0303.

- *Exposure to Formaldehyde From Indoor Air (ARB/RD-90-01)*

This publication is available at no cost from the California Air Resources Board Research Division, Indoor Exposure Assessment Division, 1800 15th Street, Sacramento, CA 95814, telephone (916) 445-0753.

LEAD

Lead can be found in lead-based paint, lead water pipes, lead solder in plumbing systems, soils around the home, and drinking water. Lead-based paint, containing up to 50 percent lead, is of concern when it is ingested by children who chew on paint surfaces, and when it flakes and cracks to form lead particles and dust. House dust in homes where lead-based paint is not intact or has been sanded may contain up to 15 percent lead. Even when lead-based paint is intact, it can form a chalky powder and contribute to the lead dust level. Environmental sources, such as lead-emitting industries and automobiles using leaded gasoline, may also increase the lead dust level in and around a home.

Dangers of Lead Excessive exposure to lead can result in the accumulation of lead in the blood, soft tissues, and bones. This accumulation of lead may damage the kidneys, brain, and central and peripheral nervous systems. Because lead accumulates in the body, exposure even to low levels of lead may be harmful. At lead exposure levels once believed to be safe, researchers are now finding subtle neuropsychological effects such as learning disabilities, behavioral problems, and decreased I.Q.

Special Risks. Infants and children under the age of seven years are considered more vulnerable to the toxic effects of lead, as lead is more easily absorbed into growing bodies. When pregnant women absorb lead, it can be transferred to the developing fetus. Lead has also been shown to cause adverse reproductive effects in men.

Lead Paint in Older Homes In older homes, paint containing high levels of lead may have been used on both interior and exterior surfaces. The U.S. Environmental Protection Agency estimates that lead-based paint was used in about two-thirds of the houses built before 1940, in one-third of the houses built between 1940 and 1960, and in some houses built since 1960.

Restricted Use. In 1978, the federal government required the reduction of lead in house paint to less than 0.06 percent. Although homes built before 1978 are likely to contain some lead-based paint, those built before 1950 are most likely to have paint containing very high levels of lead. Since the lead content in paint has been restricted, lead-based paint is unlikely to be a problem in homes built after 1978. Some paints containing more than 0.06 percent lead, such as those legally manufactured for industrial, marine, and military uses, remain available through retail markets and may have been inadvertently applied to residential buildings.

Determining Lead Content

There are no accreditation programs in California which qualify inspectors to identify lead problems in homes. Samples of paint must be taken and analyzed in a certified laboratory by qualified persons. A list of statewide laboratories that are certified for analyzing lead in hazardous materials, including paint, is available from the California Department of Health Services Hazardous Materials Laboratory at (510) 540-2800. The U.S. Department of Housing and Urban Development (HUD) has published general guidelines for selection of inspectors, laboratories, and abatement contractors in its publication *Lead-Based Paint: Interim Guidelines for Hazard Identification and Abatement in Public and Indian Housing* ($3 from HUD Information Services, P.O. Box 6091, Rockville, MD 20850).

Removal of Lead Paint

The hazard posed by lead-based paint may be reduced by covering or replacing the painted surfaces. Covering materials should be durable, such as a layer of wallboard or paneling. Covering materials that are not permanent should be well maintained. Paint can be removed chemically, by scraping, or using a heat gun. However, all removal methods generate lead-rich dust and extensive precautions must be taken to ensure the safety of the workers, family, and community. Sanding, open-torch methods, and methylene chloride should not be used to remove lead-based paint.

Abatement Contractors. Abatement contractors should have extensive experience in building restoration and be familiar with and follow abatement guidelines included in the HUD publication mentioned above. To find qualified abatement contractors, homeowners should contact state and local health departments and local chapters of building, housing, and renovation organizations.

Precautions. The California Department of Health Services Childhood Lead Poisoning Prevention Program (CLPPP) suggests that parents remove lead from the environment of children whenever possible or reasonable. Other everyday precautions include mopping floors and window sills to remove dust which may contain lead, washing the hands before eating, and ensuring that a child eats regularly as a child's stomach absorbs more lead when empty.

Testing of Children. Because lead is everywhere in the environment and lead-poisoned children often have no symptoms, the American Academy of Pediatrics and the U.S. Center for Disease Control suggest that all children between one and six years of age be tested for lead.

Removal Requirements

In California, public housing authorities must test paint in all public housing built prior to 1978 and carry out abatement where paint is found with a lead content which exceeds 0.06 percent. In privately owned housing, testing and removal of lead-based paint is at the discretion of the homeowner.

Lead in Drinking Water

The source of lead in water is most likely to be lead water pipes, lead solder used on copper pipes, and some brass plumbing fixtures. Lead pipes are generally found only in homes built before 1930. The use of lead-based solder in plumbing applications in homes and buildings was banned in 1988. However, homes built prior to 1988 may contain plumbing systems that use lead solder. The levels of lead in water from these homes are likely to be highest during the first five years after construction. After five years there can be sufficient mineral deposit, except where the water is soft, to form a coating inside the pipe; this coating prevents the lead from dissolving.

Safe Levels. Maximum contaminant levels (MCLs) are regulatory standards developed for contaminants commonly identified in drinking water. The MCL for lead in drinking water is presently 0.050 parts per million (comparable to one cent in two hundred thousand dollars). However, recent studies on lead toxicity in children indicate that this level should be lowered and a revised MCL is currently under review by USEPA.

Testing. If lead contamination in drinking water is suspected, samples of water should be sent to a certified analytical laboratory for testing. Lists of certified laboratories can be obtained from local, county, or state health departments. Laboratories usually require two water samples: a "first draw" taken after at least twelve hours of no water use from the tap being tested, and a "fully flushed" sample taken after water has been run long enough to feel cold and then for fifteen seconds more or until about two gallons of water have been drawn.

Agencies with Information. Information on the lead concentration and the corrosivity of household water can be obtained from most municipal water companies and the regional offices of the California Department of Health Services Office of Drinking Water.

Hazard Reduction

Lead levels can be reduced by removing lead piping or lead solder, installing a home treatment system, or regularly flushing each tap before consuming the water. Another alternative is to purchase bottled water. Home treatment methods that are effective in removing some or all lead from water include distillation and reverse osmosis. The cost for a home treatment system varies depending on the type of system and whether the system is designed for a single tap or the entire house. A more detailed discussion of home treatment systems is presented in *Consumer's Guide to California Drinking Water*.

Precautions. Where there are elevated lead levels in water, homeowners who choose not to install a treatment system or use bottled drinking water should flush each tap before the water is consumed. Water that has been standing in the water pipes for more than six hours should be flushed from the tap until the temperature changes and then about fifteen seconds more. Because lead is more soluble in hot water, one should not drink or prepare food using hot water from the tap. The flushed water can be saved and used for purposes such as washing clothes or watering plants.

Information

Publications:

- *Lead Poisoning in Children—A Community Problem*

This publication is available in English and Spanish at no cost from the California Department of Health Services, Childhood Lead Poisoning Prevention Program, 5900 Hollis Street, Suite E, Emeryville, CA 94608, telephone (510) 540-3657. (A stamped, self-addressed envelope is appreciated.)

- *Manual for the Identification and Abatement of Environmental Lead Hazards*

This publication is available at no cost from The National Maternal and Child Health Clearinghouse, 38th and R Streets NW, Washington, DC 20057, telephone (202) 625-8410.

- *Lead in Your Drinking Water*

- *The Inside Story—A Guide to Indoor Air Quality*

These publications are available at no cost from U.S. Environmental Protection Agency, Public Information Center, 401 M Street SW, Washington, DC 20460, telephone (202) 475-7751.

- *Consumer's Guide to California Drinking Water*

This publication is available for $5 from Local Government Commission, 909 12th Street, Suite 205, Sacramento, CA 95814, telephone (916) 448-1198.

Hotlines: For more information on lead in drinking water and federal regulations about lead in drinking water, contact the USEPA Safe Drinking Water Hotline in Washington D.C. at (800) 426-4791.

RADON

Radon is a naturally-occurring radioactive gas formed from radioactive decay of radium and uranium. Since radon cannot be seen, tasted, or smelled, special instruments are necessary for its detection. The unit of measurement for radon is picocuries per liter of air (pCi/L).

Occurrence Radon is typically present in rocks containing uranium such as certain granites and shales. The amount of radon that can enter soils and ground water depends on the concentrations of uranium in the underlying rock. Radon can also be found in the air at very low concentrations. In California, outdoor levels of radon range from 0.1 to 0.5 pCi/L.

Indoor Levels. Radon gas can also enter and concentrate in homes and buildings. In the United States, the average level indoors is 1.5 pCi/L, but radon levels have been found to range from 0.25 to over 3,000 pCi/L.

Rare in California. Surveys in California indicate that elevated annual average radon levels are uncommon, and will occur in about 1 percent of homes. The California Department of Health Services is currently conducting studies to identify the geographic areas of potential concern.

Dangers of Radon The U.S. Environmental Protection Agency (USEPA) classifies radon as a known human carcinogen. Long-term exposure to high levels of radon may increase a person's risk of lung cancer. It is believed that tobacco smokers who are exposed to high radon levels account for a large percentage of the lung cancer deaths associated with radon exposure in the United States. The risk is believed to be substantially less for nonsmokers.

Long-Term Risk. Exposure to radon does not result in any immediate symptoms. For example, it does not result in acute respiratory effects such as colds or allergies. Any cancer resulting from inhaling radon is not likely to arise for twenty to thirty years after exposure begins, and both the level of exposure and duration of exposure are factors which determine the risk of developing lung cancer.

Safe Levels Although there is consensus that the greater the exposure to radon the greater the risk of developing lung cancer, there is insufficient data to define a radon level that is harmless. Both the length of time during which radon is inhaled and the level of radon in the air are important in determining the risk of developing lung cancer. It is also believed that smoking may be a large contributing factor to lung disease associated with radon exposure.

Sources of Radon The main source of radon is the soil from which radon gas enters the home through cracks and openings in concrete slabs, crawl spaces, floor drains, sumps, and the many tiny pores in hollow-wall concrete blocks.

Air Pressure Differences. When the pressure within a home is lowered, more radon can be drawn from the soil and enter the home. Indoor air pressure may be lower during the colder months when heated air rises from the floor level to the ceiling or second story in the house. Indoor pressure may also be lowered in tightly sealed houses through use of exhaust fans in kitchens and bathrooms.

Water. If radon is present in tap water, it can be released when water is used indoors, such as by showering, washing dishes, or washing clothes. Water as a source of radon is of most concern when water is obtained directly from a well that draws water from a source exposed to uranium or radium. Most of the radon in water obtained from a surface source, such as a reservoir or well water stored in an open tank, has been released before it reaches the home.

Building Materials. Building materials are not a significant source of radon except where they incorporate rocks rich in radium or uranium. The use of these rocks (typically granites and shales) in construction of homes in California is not common.

Radon in the Home Generally, the living area closest to the soil surface has the highest level of radon. Upper stories have lower levels of radon. Consequently, radon is rarely a concern in high rise apartment buildings, other than at ground level.

Variation from Site to Site. Because of the variability of the uranium content of soil and differences in house construction and use, it cannot be assumed that houses in the same neighborhood have the same radon levels. In order to determine radon levels in any particular house, measurements must be made.

Radon Measurement The level of radon in a house can be measured with several types of passive radon detectors. Passive detectors are devices left in place for a period of time that require no ongoing activity or power. To obtain accurate results, the homeowner should carefully follow the manufacturer's instructions. Although short-term measurements of radon levels are more convenient, health risk can be more accurately determined from measurements made over a year.

Sources of Radon Measurement. The USEPA publishes a list of companies it has determined to be proficient in the analysis of the measurement devices used for radon. Those companies that do business in California are listed in the USEPA Radon Measurement Proficiency Report, which may be obtained by calling the California Department of Health Services Radon Program Hotline at (800) 745-7236.

Reducing Indoor Radon Levels The USEPA recommends that homeowners should attempt to reduce radon levels in any home that has an annual average level of radon over 4 pCi/L. The mitigation method chosen will depend on the construction of the house, extent of radon reduction required, and cost. After installing a mitigation system, it is recommended that radon levels be monitored at regular intervals to verify that the mitigation remains effective.

Mitigation Contractors. The State of California does not issue a license for radon mitigation. A list of contractors who meet the requirements of the USEPA Radon Contractors' Proficiency (RCP) Program is available as the USEPA Proficiency Report from the California Department of Health Services Radon Program at (800) 745-7236.

Radon in Water When indoor levels of radon exceed 4 pCi/L, homeowners should consider a water test. If the water comes from a water system, information about the source of the water and any radon tests done on it can be obtained from the water company which supplies the water. For more information or assistance in interpreting test results, contact the California Department of Health Services Office of Drinking Water.

Well Water. If water comes from a private well, the radon concentration can be measured by analyzing a water sample at a laboratory certified to test for radon in water. Homeowners should consult a county health office or local water district for guidance on the type of water analysis appropriate to the area and well type. It must be emphasized that the method of sample collection is critical. Since a special sampling device and trained sampler are needed, a certified laboratory should handle the sample collection. To obtain a list of certified laboratories, call the California Department of Health Services at (510) 540-2800.

Treatment **Carbon Filter.** Radon levels in water can be reduced by 99 percent by installation of a granular activated carbon (GAC) unit on the water line entering the house. As radon accumulates in the GAC unit, the unit becomes radioactive as the radon decays. Thus GAC units installed to remove radon in household water must be shielded or located in areas remote from the house to protect occupants from radiation. The GAC filters also require special handling during replacement and disposal.

Aeration. Aeration may also be used to remove radon from water. This technique may be more costly but avoids the problem of radiation build up.

Installation. Both GAC units and aeration devices should be installed by contractors who are listed in the USEPA Proficiency Report as meeting the requirements of the USEPA Radon Contractors' Proficiency Program. This report may be obtained from the California Department of Health Services at (800) 745-7236.

Selection Criteria. Selection of the proper water treatment technology depends upon its removal efficiency (other contaminants in the water may adversely affect this), safety, initial costs, and operating and maintenance costs. Therefore, professional guidance is strongly advised.

Mitigation Requirement Mitigation of radon is not required by law and is at the discretion of the homeowner.

Information Publications:

- *Radon Reduction Techniques for Detached Houses*
- *Radon Reduction Methods: A Homeowner's Guide*
- *A Californian's Guide to Radon*
- *Radon Reduction in New Construction: An Interim Guide*
- *Removal of Radon from Household Water*

These publications are available at no cost from California Department of Health Services, Environmental Management Branch Radon Program, 744 P Street, PO Box 942732, Sacramento, CA 94234, telephone (800) 745-7236.

HAZARDOUS WASTES

Hazardous waste means a waste that has the potential to harm human health or the environment. The characteristics that make a waste hazardous are that it may be toxic, corrosive, ignitable, or reactive. Hazardous waste is generated by many different industries such as oil and gas, petrochemical, electronics, and smaller businesses such as dry cleaners and print shops. Over twenty million tons of hazardous wastes are generated in California every year.

Disposal and Spills Following the generation of hazardous waste, most of it is usually treated or disposed of at the facility where it was generated. The remainder is shipped by truck to off-site facilities for treatment, storage, or disposal into a special type of landfill designed only for hazardous waste. Hazardous waste that is not properly managed may escape into the environment and contaminate soil, ground or surface water, and air. These hazardous waste releases can occur through leaking underground storage tanks or drums, poorly contained landfills or ponds, spills, or illegal dumping directly on land.

Efforts to Locate and Clean Up The U.S. Environmental Protection Agency has targeted about a thousand sites nationwide for federal cleanup, with almost eighty identified in California. The federal Superfund law authorizes the USEPA to supervise cleanup of the sites designated under the Superfund program. California is investigating and overseeing the cleanup of hundreds of other sites under a state Superfund which is implemented by the California Department of Health Services Toxic Substances Control Program (TSCP). The TSCP works jointly with USEPA and other state agencies, such as the California Regional Water Quality Control Boards and local health departments, to eliminate the risks the sites pose to public health or the environment.

Effect of a Hazardous Waste Site If a parcel of land contains a significant deposit of hazardous waste, the California Department of Health Services may designate it a hazardous waste property after holding a hearing and determining that a potential hazard is presented by the deposit. An active hazardous waste disposal site is automatically classified as hazardous waste property and a hearing is not required.

Border Zones. Land within 2,000 feet of a hazardous waste property may be designated a border zone property following a hearing if the Department determines that an actual or potential hazard is presented by certain uses of that land. Such uses include residences, hospitals, schools, and day care centers.

Use Restrictions. For a designated hazardous waste property or a border zone property, modification of the use of the land may be prohibited unless a variance is issued by the Department.

Disclosure Real estate transfer disclosures should reveal whether a home is affected by a waste site. State law requires certain written disclosures to be made to prospective homeowners. Under state law, a seller is required to disclose whether he or she is aware that the property has or is affected by any environmental hazards such as asbestos, formaldehyde, radon, lead-based paint, fuel or chemical storage tanks, or contaminated soil or water.

Information Sources There are several sources of information on the status and location of hazardous waste sites in California. A real estate licensee does not possess the technical expertise to evaluate health risks or identify hazardous conditions that may be posed by the existence of a waste disposal site. A real estate licensee can only point out the presence of such a site to a potential purchaser.

Cortese List. The Environmental Affairs Agency Office of Hazardous Materials Data Management maintains the Hazardous Waste and Substances Sites List, popularly known as the Cortese list. This list consolidates most of the lists of hazardous waste problem sites in California, including hazardous waste sites, contaminated wells, leaking underground storage tanks, and sanitary landfills from which there is a known migration of hazardous waste. The purpose of this list is to inform local agencies of these hazardous sites identified by the state. State law requires an applicant for a development project to consult the list and to submit a signed statement indicating whether the project site is listed.

TSCP List. The Toxic Substances Control Program of the California Department of Health Services maintains a list of state and federal hazardous waste sites currently scheduled for mitigation; this list is contained in the Expenditure Plan for the Hazardous Substances Cleanup Bond Act of 1984, revised 1989. The TSCP database of potential hazardous waste sites (ASPIS) contains information on about 25,000 potential hazardous waste sites. Two-thirds of these sites have been classified as needing no further action, and the remaining sites are in various stages of review and evaluation. Many of the TSCP Expenditure Plan and ASPIS sites are included in the Cortese list.

Environmental Assessors. A homeowner or prospective homeowner may wish to hire a registered environmental assessor to further investigate a known or suspected environmental hazard at a property. To obtain a list of California registered environmental assessors, contact the Environmental Affairs Agency at (916) 324-6881.

HOUSEHOLD HAZARDOUS WASTE

Although generation of hazardous wastes is associated with industrial processes, each year Californians discard tons of hazardous wastes in trash cans or down the drain. To determine whether a product is hazardous, ask these questions.

- Is it poisonous when ingested, touched, or inhaled?
- Does it ignite easily?
- Is it corrosive?
- Could an explosion occur if it is improperly stored, spilled, or mixed with other products?

If the answer is yes to any question, then the product is hazardous.

What Products Are Hazardous Generally, information about a product's hazardous properties can be found on the container label. The words "caustic," "flammable," "toxic," and "ignitable" indicate that the product is hazardous. Some products are hazardous in more than one way. For example, bleach is poisonous by itself and when mixed with ammonia-based cleaners releases hydrazine, a poisonous gas. Other examples of household products that are hazardous are listed below. In many cases, nonhazardous materials can be used instead.

- Cleaning products: ammonia, drain cleaners, rug cleaners, oven cleaners, metal polishes, bleaches
- Garden supplies: weed and insect killers, rat poison, fertilizer, charcoal lighters, kerosene, gasoline
- Automotive supplies: antifreeze, motor oil, gasoline, batteries, brake fluid
- Paint supplies: paint, varnish, paint removers, glues, waxes.

Storing Hazardous Products Safe storage of hazardous products requires a cool, dry, and secure location. Places to store hazardous products include locked cupboards, locked drawers, or a high shelf out of reach of children and pets. To prevent spillage during an earthquake, shelves should be firmly secured to the wall and have a restraining bar along the side. The following guidelines will help in the proper storage of household hazardous products.

- Sort the products into hazardous waste categories (i.e., poisonous, flammable, corrosive, and reactive) and store them as separate categories. For example, flammable products such as charcoal lighter and waste oil should be stored apart from corrosive products such as drain cleaner and acid batteries. It is important to store reactive products in separate locations. Thus, bleach and ammonia-based cleaners should be stored in separate cupboards so that, if a spill does occur, mixing and release of poisonous gas is avoided.
- Poisonous products should always be stored apart from other products.
- Labels should be legible and securely affixed to the container.

☐ Where possible, products should be stored in the original container. Household hazardous products should not be transferred to a previously used container, in order to avoid reaction with incompatible products.

☐ Containers should be tightly sealed and regularly inspected for deterioration. Where rust or leaking is observed, the deteriorating container should be placed inside a larger container and clearly labeled.

Disposal of Household Hazardous Waste

The best way to dispose of household hazardous wastes is to sort them into categories according to their hazardous properties and take them to the community household hazardous waste collection center. Unused supplies of hazardous products should not be disposed of by pouring them down the drain. Information on the disposal of specific products can be obtained from the California Integrated Waste Management Board (CIWMB) Recycling Hotline at (800) 553-2962.

Collection Programs. Household hazardous waste collection programs are established in many communities in California. For information on household hazardous waste events in your area, call the CIWMB Recycling Hotline or your local environmental health department. Guidelines on developing a similar program are presented in the publication *Recommendations for Developing Household Hazardous Waste Collection Facilities* from CIWMB.

Automotive Waste. In California, it is illegal to dispose of used oil by pouring it down the drain, onto land, or by burning. Waste motor oil and used batteries can be recycled and should be taken to a recycling center.

Information

Publications:

- *Hazardous Household Products—A Guide to the Disposal of Hazardous Household Products and the Use of Non-Hazardous Alternatives*

The above publication is available at no cost from California Department of Health Services Toxic Substances Control Program, Program Education and Information Unit, PO Box 942732, Sacramento, CA 94234, telephone (800) 334-1697.

- *Recommendations for Developing Household Hazardous Waste Collection Facilities*

The above publication is available at no cost from California Integrated Waste Management Board, 1020 Ninth Street, Suite 100, Sacramento, CA 95814, telephone (916) 322-2930

- *Household Hazardous Waste Wheel*

The above publication is available at a cost of $3.75 from: Environmental Hazards Management Institute, 10 New Market Road, P.O. Box 932, Durham, NH 03824, telephone (603) 868-1496.

Hotlines:

To report hazardous waste violations, call the California Department of Health Services Waste Alert hotline at (800)-25TOXIC or (800) 258-6942.

For general information on hazardous waste, contact the California Department of Health Services Toxic Substances Control Program at (916) 324-1826.

GROUND WATER CONTAMINATION

Ground water contamination occurs when hazardous chemical wastes, pesticides, or other agricultural chemicals (such as fertilizer) seep down through the soil into underground water supplies. Faulty private septic systems, improperly managed municipal sewer systems, and leaking industrial injection wells can also contribute to ground water contamination. In recent years, leaking underground storage tanks also have posed a threat to ground water. Half of all Americans and 95 percent of rural Americans use ground water for drinking water.

Dangers The U.S. Center for Disease Control reports an average of approximately 7,500 cases of illness linked to drinking water in the United States each year. This estimate generally is thought to be considerably lower than the actual figures because drinking water contaminants are not always considered in the diagnoses of illnesses.

Testing The only way to know whether or not the water in a home is contaminated is to test it. Since 1977, federal law has required water suppliers to periodically sample and test the water supplied to homes. If tests reveal that a national drinking water standard has been violated, the supplier must move to correct the situation and must also notify the appropriate state agency of the violation. Customers must also be notified, usually by a notice in a newspaper, an announcement on radio or television, or a letter from the health department that supervises the water supplier. If the home is supplied with water from its own private well, laboratory testing of a water sample is the only way to determine if the water supply is contaminated. Should you suspect that water is contaminated, or if you wish to have water tested, contact local, county, or state health or environmental departments for information about qualified testing laboratories.

Homeowner's Responsibility If the home is supplied by an outside water supply source, federal law requires the provider to correct any contamination problems. When homes are supplied by private wells, analysis and treatment of the contaminated water may solve the problem.

What Will It Cost? Normally, consumers bear no direct financial responsibility for eliminating contamination from water supplied by an outside source (if the water was contaminated when it was delivered); the supplier bears the primary responsibility for correcting contamination problems. In the case of contaminated water supplied from a private well (or water from an outside source that becomes contaminated after it is received from the supplier), the cost of decontamination will depend on the kinds and amounts of contaminants present.

Information Sources. In the majority of cases, decontamination of a private water source involves technology and knowledge beyond the scope of the average homeowner. State and local environmental and water quality officials may be able to provide additional information and assistance for decontamination of private water sources.

EPA Actions The U.S. Environmental Protection Agency has the lead responsibility for assuring the quality and safety of the nation's ground water supply. The EPA's approach is focused in two areas: minimizing the contamination of ground water and surface waters needed for human consumption, and monitoring and treating drinking water before it is consumed.

Federal Law. In 1986, the U.S. Congress passed a set of amendments that expanded the protection provided by the Safe Drinking Water Act of 1974. These amendments streamlined the EPA's regulation of contaminants, banned all future use of lead pipe and lead solder in public drinking water systems, mandated greater protection of ground water sources, and authorized EPA to file civil suits or issue administrative orders against public water systems that are in violation of the act.

Standards. Working with the states, EPA has set national standards for minimum levels of a number of contaminants and is mandated to set such standards for additional contaminants. In addition, EPA and the states are working to devise a national strategy for the monitoring and management of ground water supplies.

Information Publications:

- *Is Your Drinking Water Safe?*

Available from U.S. Environmental Protection Agency Public Information Center 401 M Street SW, Washington, DC 20460, telephone (202) 475-7751.

Hotline:

- *Safe Drinking Water Hotline*

This hotline provides information and publications to help the public and the regulated community understand EPA's drinking water regulations and programs. The hotline operates Monday through Friday, 8:30 a.m. to 4:30 p.m., eastern time, telephone (800) 426-4791.

GLOSSARY OF TERMS

Aeration A technique by which air is introduced into a liquid; bubbles and aerosols are generated and dissolved gases released. For example, water aerated by passage through a shower head will release dissolved radon gas.

Activated Carbon A material made from burnt wood, used to remove organic solutes, such as pesticides, and some inorganic solutes, such as chlorine, from water. Dissolved organic solutes are removed from the water by absorption onto the activated carbon. The activated carbon must be replaced periodically when it becomes saturated and unable to absorb any more solute. Activated carbon is not effective in removing heavy metals such as lead, and salts, which make water hard.

Annual Average Level The average of measurements taken at different times over a period of one year or the level measured by a device left in place for a full year.

Biodegradable Describes a substance that can be broken down physically or chemically by micro-organisms.

Carcinogen A substance that causes cancer. Also, a substance on specific list of materials compiled by the U.S. Public Health Service which are known or suspected to cause cancer.

Certified Laboratory	A laboratory that has demonstrated that it can meet federal and state standards for accuracy and precision for a given analytical procedure.
Commercial Waste	All solid waste emanating from establishments engaged in business. This category includes, but is not limited to, solid waste originating in stores, markets, office buildings, restaurants, shopping centers, and theaters.
Distillation	A technique used to purify water by removal of inorganic contaminants such as salts through heating the solution and condensing the steam. The distilled water has a reduced salt concentration. Distillation is not effective in removing pesticides and volatile organic contaminants such as chloroform and benzene.
Domestic Waste	Solid waste, garbage and rubbish, which originates in residential areas.
Explosive	Any chemical compound, mixture, or device that has the potential for explosion, i.e., substantially instantaneous release of gas and heat.
Exposure	Contact with an agent through inhalation, ingestion, or touching. For example, exposure to radon is primarily through inhalation; exposure to lead is primarily through ingestion.
Filtration	Purification of water by removing undissolved solids or sediment by passing the water through a filter or sieve. Filtration does not remove dissolved salts or organic contaminants.
Hazardous Materials	In a broad sense, any substance or mixture of substances having properties capable of producing adverse effects on the health or safety of a human being.
Level	Another term for concentration or the amount of a substance in a given volume of air, liquid, or solid.
Liter	Metric unit of volume equivalent to 1.057 quarts of liquid. One gallon is equivalent to about 4 liters.
Milligram	A unit of weight. There are 1,000 milligrams in one gram and about 28 grams in one ounce.
Parts Per Million	A unit of concentration. Water which contains 1 part per million lead contains 1 milligram lead in 1 million milligrams (1 kilogram) of water. One part per million can be compared to one cent in ten thousand dollars.
Passive Detector	A measuring device which functions without any energy input or ongoing attention from the user. Use of a passive radon detector to measure radon requires only that the detector is left in place for a specified time.
Picocurie	A unit of amount used in measurement of radioactive substances. For example, five picocuries of radon are five trillionths of a curie and are equivalent to eleven radioactive radon atoms decaying every minute.
Radioactive	A term used to describe atoms that are unstable and break down or decay to form another kind of atom. For example, radium breaks down to form radon. In the process of decay high energy particles are emitted. The detection of these particles by special instruments indicates that a substance is radioactive. The high energy particles (alpha and beta particles) and gamma rays are called radiation.

Lead
- Found in paint, water pipes, solder, and outdoor soils
- Damages kidneys, brain, and nervous system; especially hazardous to children
- Lead restricted in house paint since 1978
- May be covered or removed; no abatement requirements for private housing
- Lead water pipes pre-1930, lead solder in plumbing until 1988; greatest hazard in first five years
- Install water treatment system, drink bottled water, or flush tap before use

Radon
- Naturally occurring radioactive gas found in certain granites and shales; rare in California
- Classified by USEPA as a "known human carcinogen" with long-term exposure
- Rises through floor when indoor air pressure is lowered by heating, or comes in with well water (can be filtered or aerated out)
- Best measured with passive detectors left in place for a year
- No legal requirements for mitigation

Hazardous Wastes
- Industrial wastes can be toxic, corrosive, ignitable, or reactive, and pollute soil, water, or air
- Superfund sites: targeted for cleanup by USEPA and state Toxic Substances Control Program
- California state lists of hazardous waste sites: Cortese, TSCP/ASPIS
- Seller must disclose known environmental hazards affecting real property
- Registered environmental assessor can inspect property

Household Hazardous Waste
- Cleaning, automotive, garden, and paint products, alone or when mixed
- Storage: secure, clearly labeled, sorted by type of hazard
- Disposal: some communities have collection programs

Ground Water Contamination
- Chemical wastes can seep into ground water: pesticides, fertilizers, leaking tanks
- Half of America's drinking water comes from underground water supplies
- Federal law imposes testing and cleanup standards on water suppliers
- Private wells may require testing and treatment

COURSE 9
Environmental Inspections: Regulatory Concerns

INTRODUCTION

The Comprehensive Environmental Response, Compensation and Liability Act of 1980 (CERCLA), under which the Superfunds were established, points the way toward cleaning up some of the worst environmental hazards in the nation, but it has also caused considerable concern in the business community and among institutional lenders because of the far reaching potential for owner liability. This concern has rapidly created a new industry of environmental inspection and assessment.

Liability for Cleanup Lenders are increasingly reluctant to extend credit without environmental clearances, since they may become subject to future liability if their lien position converts to ownership upon foreclosure. Liability may result even if owners are unaware of toxicity created by earlier users or invitees on the property. Cleanup costs can be substantial and red tape can be extensive, so informed buyers, sellers, and lenders all need to know what to expect.

Inspection Requirements Currently the Resolution Trust Corporation (RTC) is requiring environmental inspection on all properties. Other federal agencies (FDIC, OTS, FHA) as well as financial institutions are requiring these reports on selected properties. It is possible that in the near future, inspection reports will be required on all residential appraisal reports, the way many lenders are now requiring them on all commercial properties. Government agencies including FNMA and the RTC, and private professional organizations including the American Society of Testing and Materials and the Environmental Assessment Association, have developed guidelines and formats for what are called Phase I, Phase II, and Phase III environmental inspections.

Regulators' Guidelines This course presents the guidelines established by FNMA, the Office of Thrift Supervision (OTS), and RTC. Note the issues with which each is concerned (liability and property value), sequence of inspections, discussions of consultants' qualifications, and emphasis on careful documentation. Though environmental hazards and the accompanying dangers of liability and cleanup costs are the main focus, the RTC's inventory of properties with "special resource values" is a reminder of the larger environmental context.

FNMA HAZARDS MANAGEMENT PROCEDURES

In 1988 the Federal National Mortgage Association (FNMA) issued Environmental Hazards Management Procedures, which lenders must follow in order to qualify for FNMA financing. These procedures define Phase I and Phase II environmental assessments and explain their role in federally related transactions. The following section presents FNMA's procedures for lending on multifamily properties. (From *Fannie Mae Environmental Hazards Management Procedures, Multifamily, Conventional Selling,* August 1, 1988.)

Liability Issues There is increasing concern nationwide that properties involved in real estate transactions might contain unknown environmental problems that could present major liabilities to the purchaser and lenders. As a consequence, we [FNMA] require that lenders take responsible actions to manage the risk of loss from environmental damage and liability. This chapter outlines those requirements.

Lender's Duties The lender's primary responsibilities are (1) an environmental assessment of the property, which must be completed before we will issue an Offer to Commit or a Commitment, and (2) ongoing confirmation after purchase that the borrower is maintaining the property in an environmentally sound manner.

Expertise. We expect lenders to perform these functions diligently. Lenders are expected to educate themselves in the areas of environmental regulation and management and to have available qualified experts in order to make sound and appropriate judgments.

Borrower Oversight. Lenders must take responsibility also for assessing borrowers' ability to maintain the property and impressing upon them the need to protect the property asset from environmental liability and value loss.

Consultant Selection. We do not approve environmental consultants. Therefore, lenders must not give any consideration to a consultant's representation that he or she is approved or qualified by us. Lenders are responsible for the selection of environmental consultants and will be solely accountable for their performance. Lenders must take appropriate steps to ensure that a consultant is qualified to perform the required work.

Assessment Required §501. We require an environmental assessment of all properties submitted for a Commitment.

Phase I and II Assessments. In order to use resources effectively the assessments are to be conducted in two phases. The Phase I assessment is principally a screening exercise, which focuses on (1) a review of available documents, (2) interviews with people aware of site operations, and (3) an inspection of the site. In cases where Phase I is inconclusive, a Phase II assessment is required. Phase II assessments generally involve a more detailed review of the site, including specialized physical sampling. An environmental consultant qualified to perform the work must do the Phase II assessment on the lender's behalf.

Acceptable Properties. A property must be acceptable under either the Phase I or Phase II assessment for each of the specific hazards listed. If it is not acceptable as measured by any one of the hazard assessments, the property is ineligible and can not be the subject of a Commitment.

Diligence Requirement. The Phase I and II assessments represent our current standards. However, lenders must use diligence when evaluating the property and should make appropriate inspections to learn its true condition. Lenders should disclose their knowledge of actual or suspected environmental problems. Properties with obvious environmental impairments should not be the subject of a Commitment.

Time of Submission. The lender must submit a completed Phase I assessment as part of the loan application package, and is encouraged to submit any required Phase II assessment as part of the package. However, the lender may wait until later in the application review process before submitting any required Phase II assessment.

Discretionary Requirements. Upon review of the completed Phase I and/or Phase II assessments we may, at our discretion, impose additional assessments or environmental actions as a requirement or condition of the Commitment.

Phase I Assessment §501.01. The purpose of the Phase I screening assessment is to quickly determine whether information currently exists to clearly evaluate a property's environmental status.

Timing. The lender must submit a completed Phase I assessment as part of the loan application package.

Content. The assessment involves a review of records, interviews with people knowledgeable about the property, and an inspection of the property, the building, its fence line, and adjoining properties.

Format. The lender must complete the Phase I assessment, including the Phase I information checklist. While it is not expected that a lender use every information source when performing the assessment, enough information should be gathered to document each assessment decision.

May Trigger Phase II. If clear documentation exists that a property is environmentally sound in regard to a particular hazard, then no Phase II assessment is required for that hazard. If there are obvious problems or if the status of the property is uncertain, then either the property fails the test or a Phase II assessment for that hazard is required.

Phase II Assessment §501.02. Phase II assessments are required for each of those hazards for which the property was not acceptable under the Phase I assessment.

Timing. The lender may submit a Phase II assessment as part of the loan application package. Alternatively, the lender may wait for the preliminary results of our application review before performing a Phase II assessment. However, we will not consider issuing an Offer to Commit or a Commitment until after we have received and reviewed any required Phase II assessment.

Content. The Phase II assessment will involve a more detailed physical site inspection and review of historical records. The purpose of Phase II is typically to determine the presence or absence of an uncertain liability (e.g., asbestos, or leaking underground storage tanks) or to quantify the extent of an observed or suspected liability (e.g., soils or ground water contamination). Because of the specialized nature of the investigations under Phase II, these assessments must be conducted by a consultant qualified to perform the work.

Technical Studies. Work to be performed in a Phase II assessment could include:

- Bulk asbestos sampling and analysis, and, if required, development of abatement and maintenance programs

- Underground storage tank leak testing

- Soil sampling and analysis

- Ground water sampling and analysis
- Testing of suspected PCB contaminated soil and facilities
- Investigation of status of Superfund or RCRA enforcement actions related to neighboring properties.

Report Format. Lenders should complete and submit the Phase II assessment, with consultant's report attached. No specific protocol is mandatory for the Phase II consultant report. However, it should include a full description of the sampling procedures, the laboratory results, and recommendations. The consultant must certify in the report that the assessment was performed diligently and in accordance with all regulatory and good management standards, and that, to the best of the consultant's knowledge, the results are complete and accurate. The report must be signed by an officer of the consulting firm that performed the work.

Quality Control. It is essential that all regulatory standards and good management practices be followed at all times, and especially where physical sampling and laboratory analysis is involved.

Consultant's Qualifications

§501.03. Lenders must use care in choosing firms to perform environmental functions. The lender should confirm, for example, that personnel have adequate and appropriate education and training to carry out consulting duties. Membership in relevant professional associations is also encouraged.

References. Beyond training and education, consultants should be able to demonstrate successful prior experience in their areas of expertise. Lenders are therefore required to have available in the property file copies of three letters of reference and endorsement attesting to the consultant's prior work. The letters should clearly state the scope of work performed for the previous clients and the business purpose the work was intended to support. At least one of the references should be from a real estate firm that used the consultant to support a residential property transaction. Documentation of previous experience with the current lender may be substituted for one of the reference letters.

Relevant Experience. It is of utmost importance that the documented experience be relevant to the current duties both in terms of functions (e.g., physical sampling, operating and maintenance monitoring, underground tank testing) and media (e.g., air, water, specific chemicals). Previous experience removing asbestos does not qualify a firm to perform ground water tests. Lenders must demonstrate that the consultant has successfully completed work of a substantially similar nature to that currently being performed on the subject property.

Disqualification. We reserve the right at any time to refuse to accept any future environmental assessment, report, warranty, or certification from individual consultants, consulting firms, or branch offices of consulting firms. We will notify a lender that a particular consultant is no longer acceptable to us. In addition, lenders may not use people or firms to perform assessments that are excluded from participation in EPA-assisted programs. The list of such people and firms is maintained by the regional offices of the EPA and is published from time to time in the Federal Register.

Conflict of Interest. The consultant shall not be affiliated with the buyer or seller of the property, nor with a firm engaged in a business that might present a conflict of interest.

Unacceptable Conditions §501.04. The existence of one or more of the following situations or similar conditions makes the property ineligible for the Prior Approval product line:

Waste Disposal Site. Structure built over a sanitary landfill or other solid, hazardous, or municipal waste disposal site.

Asbestos. Presence of friable asbestos-containing materials, or substantial amounts of nonfriable asbestos-containing material that cannot be safely encapsulated or removed or will not be routinely inspected and maintained by the borrower.

Adjoining Contamination. Presence of high-risk neighbors with evidence of spills or soil or ground water contamination on or around their properties.

Incurable Contamination. Documented soils or ground water contamination on the subject property or a documented tank leak greater than 0.05 gallons per hour (National Fire Protection Association standard) and any of the following three situations:

- Physical constraints posed by the site-specific geology, geohydrology, or subsurface structure that render corrective actions technically impossible,

- Constraints that render treatment processes or disposal options prohibitively expensive, i.e., beyond the financial capabilities of the current owner; or

- Potentially responsible parties unwilling or financially incapable of instituting corrective actions on neighboring properties.

Soil Contaminants. Soil sampling values above the following limits, stated in parts per million:

Metals	Concentration (ppm)
Chromium	100
Zinc	350
Lead	100
Copper	170
Arsenic	20
Cadmium	3
Selenium	20
Nickel	100

Organics	Concentration (ppm)
Total volatile organics	1
Total hydrocarbons	100
Total petroleum hydrocarbons	100

Water Contaminants. Ground water sampling values above the following limits:

Parameter	Concentration (ppm)
Arsenic	.05
Boron	1.0
Cadmium	.01
Chromium	.05
Lead	.05
Mercury	.002
Selenium	.01
Silver	.05
Total organics (volatiles and base neutrals)	.1
Total petroleum hydrocarbons	1.0

PCBs. PCB contamination where:

☐ Physical constraints posed by the site-specific geology, geohydrology, or subsurface structure render corrective actions technically impossible, or

☐ Constraints render treatment processes or disposal options prohibitively expensive (i.e., beyond the financial capabilities of the current owner).

Radon. High radon levels (i.e., above 4 picocuries per liter) that can only be corrected through large capital improvements or extensive ongoing maintenance programs that are beyond the financial or technical capability of the borrower.

Violations of Law. Conditions which represent material violations of applicable local, state, or federal environmental or public health statutes and laws.

Litigation in Progress. Properties that are currently the subject of environmental or public health litigation or administrative action from private parties or public officials.

Remedial Actions §501.05. Properties that fail to meet a particular standard may in some cases be corrected through remedial actions and retested. This should only be done with the advice and written endorsement of a qualified consultant.

Completion Required. In general, remedial actions should be completed and their effectiveness confirmed by the lender before we issue an Offer to Commit or a Commitment. All actions must be taken in accordance with regulatory and good management standards.

Discretionary Requirements. In addition, we may require additional remedial actions.

Approval Before Completion. We will consider issuing an Offer to Commit or a Commitment prior to the completion of remedial work only when the following conditions are met:

- ☐ *Time Estimate.* A qualified environmental consultant must state in writing that (a) the work can be completed within ninety days after loan delivery (or a period not to exceed the time allowed for any repair or moderate rehabilitation work connected with the loan), and (b) the work will make the property eligible under the environmental standards.

- ☐ *Contract for Remedial Work.* Prior to loan delivery, the borrower must have a signed contract with a qualified firm to perform remediation services within the time frame mentioned above. The lender must secure a performance escrow (included in any repair, completion, or rehabilitation escrow) from the borrower for 150 percent of the gross contract amount.

- ☐ *Inspection Upon Completion.* When the work is finished, a qualified consultant must state in writing that the job has been satisfactorily completed and that the property meets the environmental eligibility standards.

Ongoing Operations and Maintenance §501.06. Some properties may have conditions that are currently acceptable but must be confirmed through the life of the loan with ongoing operations and maintenance (O&M) actions.

Lender's Responsibility. It is the lender's responsibility to recognize when regulatory standards and good management practices require O&M programs to maintain the environmental integrity of the property. It is also the lender's responsibility to assess the borrower's ability to carry out any such program. The loan is not eligible for the Prior Approval product line if the borrower or its agent is clearly not financially or organizationally capable of performing necessary O&M functions.

Written Plan Required. A written O&M plan must be developed by the borrower no later than the completion of remedial work. A qualified consultant, retained by either the borrower or the lender, must endorse the plan in writing, stating that the provisions, if carried out with diligence, are sufficient to maintain the property in accordance with applicable regulatory standards and sound business practice. The consultant must also confirm in writing that the borrower has the organizational and financial capacity to carry out the actions as prescribed.

Discretionary Requirements. In addition we may require additional operations and maintenance provisions.

Environmental Superlien States §501.07. We [FNMA] face increased risks from properties located in states with environmental superlien laws that may be applied to multifamily residential properties eligible for the Prior Approval product line. These laws give environmental authorities the ability to place a first priority lien on subject properties. This lien takes precedence over our mortgage and clearly threatens the value of our security collateral.

Lender's Responsibility. Currently several states have superlien statutes and other states are considering such legislation. It is the lender's responsibility to know whether the property state has an applicable superlien law, or will have one as of the anticipated Commitment date.

Additional Certification. In order to guard against the risks that these superlien laws present, we require that a qualified environmental consultant confirm in writing that, to the best of the consultant's knowledge, the Phase I assessment was performed with diligence and is complete and accurate. This is in addition to any endorsements and certifications required for any Phase II assessment, remedial action plans, or O&M plans.

Responsibilities After Loan Commitment

§502. In addition to loan servicing and accounting responsibilities, the lender must take the additional steps discussed in this section to manage the risk of loss from environmental damage and liability.

§502.01. Operations and Maintenance. The lender must make sure that the borrower has available all required resources and personnel to effectively carry out ongoing operations and maintenance activities identified during the environmental assessments and application review.

§502.02. Property Photographs. At or just prior to purchase of the loan by us (or no later than the completion of any remedial work) the lender must take a series of photographs to visually document the condition of the property. The photographs should be taken both inside the building and around the grounds (including adjacent sites). The photos should be clearly dated and labeled with a site description of the view presented. The photos become part of the loan file.

Ongoing Environmental Compliance

Section 502.03. The lender must confirm in writing from time to time that, after we purchase the loan, the borrower is maintaining the property according to any applicable O&M programs, environmental law or regulation.

Scope of Lender's Periodic Investigation. It is not expected that the lender perform a formal Phase I or II assessment. However, the lender must make an on-site inspection and inquiry in preparing the certification. The scope of the certification should include both the buildings and the grounds, and cover the activities of the borrower, tenants, sublessors, their agents, and any other third parties. These confirmations must specifically address the ongoing effectiveness and adequacy of all current remedial and maintenance actions.

Timing. For performing loans, this confirmation should normally be included as part of the annual physical inspection and report on the property. In addition, an inspection and confirmation must be made immediately following the occurrence of events which might reasonably be expected to impact the environmental condition of the property or the efficacy of prescribed remedial or maintenance actions. Such events would include fire, flood, building construction or rehabilitation, spills or leaks of hazardous wastes or materials, unusual or intense use of property facilities, or significant changes in custodial or management personnel.

Changes in Status. If the lender is unable to affirmatively confirm the property's environmental status, it must prepare a report which describes the property's current condition and the actions required to return it to, and maintain it in, its condition at the time we purchased the loan. The lender must submit this report to us. Further, upon notice by us, the lender must request the borrower to take all prescribed actions.

Remedial Actions. The lender must promptly confirm the environmental status of the property as soon as possible after implementation of any remedial actions.

Incidents and Violations

§502.04. The lender must notify us of any known or suspected environmental incidents that violate any environmental laws, regulations, or statutes.

Report to Authorities. At our direction, the lender must require that the borrower report all known violations of applicable environmental statutes to the appropriate local, state, or federal authority in full compliance with all provisions of the law.

Remedial Actions. In addition, at our direction, the lender must require that the borrower take all necessary actions to ensure that all violations are promptly corrected and that the property is bought back to and maintained in full compliance with appropriate environmental statutes and management practices.

Nonperforming Loans (Defaults)

§502.05. **Evaluation for Audit.** The lender must prepare an environmental evaluation of the property for the asset audit. The evaluation should be in the form of a written declaration that the property has been maintained according to sound environmental practice and any prescribed O&M plans, and is therefore still acceptable according to the standards of the assessment that was performed prior to our purchase of the loan.

Changes in Conditions. If the lender cannot affirmatively declare that the property is still in the original acceptable condition, it must state the nature of the new conditions, their cause, and an estimate of the actions and resources required to bring the property back to its original acceptable conditions.

Assessments. We may require a Phase I, and, if appropriate, Phase II assessment for properties in default. The emphasis in such assessments should be to quantify the scope and degree of any hazards present and to estimate the cost of bringing the property into compliance with applicable regulations and sound business practice.

Protecting the Property. Lenders should take all reasonable actions to protect the environmental integrity of the property during borrower delinquency or default. The lender should determine whether the borrower or property manager has adequate knowledge and resources to perform required remedial and maintenance activities.

Monitoring the Property. The lender must continue to confirm ongoing compliance with environmental requirements through the entire period of delinquency. If the lender cannot gain access to the property, it must inquire of state and local health and environmental authorities on at least an annual basis regarding compliance of the subject property with applicable environmental laws and regulations.

Liquidation: Documents to Close the File

§502.06. Upon final loan payment (either as scheduled or as a prepayment in full), the lender should take a series of photographs to visually document the condition of the property. The photographs should be taken both inside the building and around the grounds (including adjacent sites) and should, to the degree possible, replicate the pictures taken at loan purchase (see §502.02 above). The photos should be clearly dated and labeled with a site description of the view presented. The photos become part of the loan file.

Resolution Trust Corporation Environmental Guidelines

The Resolution Trust Corporation (RTC) was established by the Federal Home Loan Bank Act of 1989 (12 USC 14412) and authorized by §501 of the Financial Institutions Reform, Recovery, and Enforcement Act of 1989 (FIRREA) to manage and resolve insolvent savings and loan institutions, and to dispose of any acquired assets. In disposing of assets under its control, RTC's primary objective is to maximize return and minimize losses. RTC's holdings are substantial, and as of June 1990 included approximately 36,000 properties. Proper and efficient management of environmental issues associated with assets under RTC's jurisdiction is essential to fulfilling RTC's appointed role as conservator and receiver.

Scope of Environmental Issues The environmental issues addressed by these guidelines are categorized as properties with *special resource values* or *environmental hazards*. These special resource values and environmental hazards have generally been defined by federal and state laws and regulations. In addition to federal laws and regulations, each state may have its own laws and regulations governing environmental issues.

Special Resource Values. FIRREA §501 stipulates that: "The Real Estate Asset Division shall have such duties as the Corporation establishes, including the publication of an inventory of real property assets of institutions subject to the jurisdiction of the Corporation. Such inventory shall be published before January 1, 1990, and updated semiannually thereafter and shall identify properties with natural, cultural, recreational, or scientific values of special significance." These properties include:

- Sole source aquifers
- Wetlands
- Threatened and endangered species
- Wild and scenic rivers
- Coastal dunes and beaches
- Critical and unique habitat
- Archaeological resources
- Historic buildings, structures, and sites
- Designated natural landmarks
- Recreational areas.

Environmental Hazards. Environmental hazards pose a health or safety risk to workers or the public. They have been defined and regulated by a number of federal and state programs. For example, underground storage tanks are regulated under the Resource Conservation and Recovery Act (RCRA), and the cleanup of properties contaminated with hazardous wastes posing a health, safety, or environmental hazard is regulated under the Comprehensive Environmental Response, Compensation and Liability Act (CERCLA). The environmental hazards addressed by these guidelines are:

- ☐ Underground storage tanks
- ☐ Aboveground storage tanks
- ☐ Disposal sites: landfills, dumps, and surface impoundments
- ☐ Hazardous substances
- ☐ Radiological hazards
- ☐ Historic disposal and contamination
- ☐ Polychlorinated biphenyls (PCBs)
- ☐ Asbestos
- ☐ Pesticides
- ☐ Radon.

Environmental Issues and Property Values

The presence of certain special resource values such as wild and scenic rivers may enhance a property's value or may attract public or private buyers interested in conserving the resource. In contrast, the presence of an environmental hazard may decrease the value of an asset, increase RTC's management costs, and complicate disposition of the asset.

Market Study. In November 1989 a market study commissioned by Boelter Environmental Consultants (a national firm headquartered in Park Ridge, Illinois) illuminated the frequency with which environmental hazards may be associated with assets under RTC's jurisdiction. The market study examined the extent of environmental hazards in real estate projects. Based on a survey of 200 members of the Mortgage Bankers Association of America, the study found that environmental hazards affect 19 percent of all real estate projects. The most frequently cited problems (multiple mentions were accepted) were asbestos (49 percent), contaminated surface or ground water (33 percent), and underground storage tanks (23 percent).

RTC Experience. An informal survey of environmental issues that confront RTC offices conducted in June 1990 indicated that the percentages reported in the Boelter study were representative of RTC's experience to date, with asbestos and underground storage tanks being the two most prevalent problems. RTC's informal survey also indicated that the most frequently encountered special resources to date were wetlands and cultural or historic resources.

RTC Environmental Policies

The following environmental policies have been adopted by RTC. Implementation of these policies enables RTC and its representatives to properly manage environmental issues.

- ☐ All real estate owned (REO) and all real estate that is security for nonperforming loans should be screened for potential environmental issues.
- ☐ A property's appraisal should be "as is," i.e., it should properly reflect those uses that are restricted under federal, state, and local wetland and flood plain regulations.

- RTC's REO inventory shall identify properties with natural, cultural, recreational, or scientific values of special significance.

- RTC will attempt to notify interested public and private conservation organizations of properties with confirmed special resources.

- The U.S. Fish and Wildlife Service (FWS) will be provided access to RTC properties with wetlands and critical habitat to inspect the property and to develop recommendations, as appropriate, for the placement of restrictive easements for conservation purposes.

- RTC will implement FWS recommendations concerning conservation easements for wetlands and critical habitat to the extent that such easements do not significantly reduce the value of the asset or impede any sales in progress.

RTC Actions on Hazards RTC's response to environmental hazard issues (hazardous and toxic substances and wastes) will be case specific. The recommended option will be documented in a case memorandum and be approved by the appropriate delegated authority. The options available to RTC are:

Real Estate Owned: Sale As Is. This is the preferred option for REO. It means disposal of assets at a reduction to market value commensurate with the cost of remediation, with site remediation to be completed by the purchaser. RTC should utilize the appropriate instrument (e.g., contingencies on sales contract or placement of remediation funds in an escrow account) to ensure that remediation is completed by the purchaser to the satisfaction of regulatory authorities.

Real Estate Owned: Remediation Before Sale. This option involves completion of site remediation by RTC and subsequent disposal of the asset at market value. It may be appropriate for assets where remediation must be performed as quickly as possible to prevent contamination of adjacent properties (e.g., pollutants are migrating offsite). In general, it is not RTC's intent to conduct large-scale remediation projects if other alternatives exist.

REO: Special Cases. Case-by-case determination will be made for special problems in consultation with concerned federal and state agencies.

Nonperforming Loans: Foreclosure. RTC may determine to foreclose on a nonperforming loan that is secured by real estate if site remediation costs are less than the market value of the asset. If foreclosure is completed, RTC would proceed with one of the three options for REO.

Nonperforming Loans: Decline to Foreclose. RTC may determine *not* to foreclose on a nonperforming loan that is secured by real estate if site remediation costs are approximately equal to or exceed the market value of the asset. In this way RTC may limit financial and legal obligations associated with an environmental hazard and site remediation.

Note that these options parallel the choices that a private lender, buyer, or seller must also make. Phase I, Phase II, and Phase III environmental inspections are evolving as a way of making systematic disclosures and informed decisions.

INNOCENT LANDOWNER DEFENSE (CERCLA)

In 1991 H.R. 1217 was introduced in Congress as an amendment to CERCLA to define the specific actions necessary to qualify for CERCLA's "innocent landowner defense." It aimed to clarify the criteria for due diligence with regard to environmental factors, and to alleviate some of the fears that CERCLA has prompted with regard to liability for unknown and unsuspected hazards on a property. The bill died in committee and as of this writing remains in the category of proposed legislation. It seems clear that the affected industries will continue to press for some similar kind of clarification. In the meantime, though legal immunity is not guaranteed, the language of the proposed amendment provides a sound approach to documenting, with a reasonable degree of certainty, whether a property can be considered free of foreseeable environmental hazards, and whether the owner has met the intent of CERLA's requirement of "appropriate inquiry."

Innocent Landowner Defined — CERCLA provides for an innocent landowner or innocent purchaser defense—an exemption from liability for a landowner who acquires property unaware of the presence of hazardous material. The landowner must not have conducted, permitted, or contributed to the release of hazardous substances, and must have had, after appropriate inquiry, no knowledge of the pollution at the time the property was acquired.

Information Required — The amendment proposed a concrete definition of "appropriate inquiry." In effect, this would be a federal definition of a complete Phase I environmental audit. The criteria set out in the bill are:

- A visual site inspection of the real property and its facilities and improvements, and a visual inspection of immediately adjacent properties

- A title abstract for a period of fifty years

- Reasonably obtainable current and historical aerial photographs

- Recorded environmental cleanup liens against the property

- Reasonably obtainable federal, state, and local government records of waste sites or investigations about such sites.

Extensive documentary research is required. The real estate practitioner should understand that all this information may not be necessary for a competent environmental inspection on residential property. However, if the client wishes to establish an innocent landowner defense under CERCLA, all this information should be included in the report.

Excerpts from the Amendment — The proposed Innocent Landowner Defense Amendment of 1991 was presented as "A Bill to amend the Comprehensive Environmental Response, Compensation and Liability Act of 1980," to provide specific definition of the requirement that a purchaser of real property make all appropriate inquiry into the previous ownership and uses of the real property in order to qualify for the innocent landowner defense. It provided as follows:

Appropriate Inquiry. A defendant who has acquired real property shall have established a rebuttable presumption that he has made all appropriate inquiry within the meaning of CERCLA if he establishes that, immediately prior to or at the time of acquisition, he obtained a Phase I Environmental Audit of the real property which meets the requirements below.

Professional Defined. The term "environmental professional" means an individual, or an entity managed or controlled by such individual who, through academic training, occupational experience, and reputation (such as engineers, environmental consultants, and attorneys), can objectively conduct one or more aspects of a Phase I Environmental Audit.

Phase I Audit Defined The term "Phase I Environmental Audit" means an investigation of the real property, conducted by environmental professionals, to determine or discover the *obviousness of the presence* or likely presence of a *release or threatened release* of hazardous substances on the real property.

Documentary Research. Phase I research consists of a review of each of the following sources of information concerning the previous ownership and uses of the real property:

- ☐ *Title Search*. Recorded chain of title documents regarding the real property, including all deeds, easements, leases, restrictions, and covenants for a period of fifty years.

- ☐ *Aerial Photographs*. Aerial photographs that may reflect prior uses of the real property and are reasonably obtainable through state or local government agencies.

- ☐ *Liens*. Determination of the existence of recorded environmental cleanup liens against the real property pursuant to federal, state, and local statutes.

- ☐ *Government Records*. Reasonably obtainable federal, state, and local government records of sites or facilities where there has been a release of hazardous substances or activities likely to cause or contribute to a release or a threatened release of hazardous substances on the real property. These include landfill and other disposal location records, underground storage tank records, hazardous waste handler and generator records, and spill reporting records. "Reasonably obtainable" means that a copy or reasonable facsimile of the record must be obtainable from the government agency by request.

Site Inspection. Phase I includes a visual site inspection of the property and all facilities and improvements on the property, and a visual inspection of immediately adjacent properties from the property, including an investigation of any chemical use, storage, treatment, and disposal practices on the property.

Recordkeeping. No presumption shall arise of "appropriate inquiry" unless the defendant has maintained a compilation of the information reviewed in the course of the Phase I Environmental Audit.

Further Investigation. If the Phase I Environmental Audit discloses the presence or likely presence of a release or threatened release of hazardous substances on the real property to be acquired, no presumption [of "appropriate inquiry"] shall arise unless the defendant has taken reasonable steps, in accordance with current technology available, existing regulations, and generally acceptable engineering practices, to confirm the absence of such release or threatened release.

Federal Home Loan Bank System—Office of Thrift Supervision

Thrift Bulletin 16, February 6, 1989, Environmental Risk and Liability, by Darrel W. Dochow, FHLB executive director, addresses the potential risks and liabilities that thrift institutions can incur as a result of adverse environmental factors. It also contains guidelines for the development of policies of reasonable due diligence to protect lending institutions against financial risks created by environmental conditions. Further information is available from any Federal Home Loan Bank District or the Policy Analysis Division of the Office of Regulatory Activities, Washington, D.C.

Introduction Environmentally related hazards can be a source of high risk and potential liability in connection with mortgage or commercial loans and real estate investments. Potential environmental problems may exist in a myriad of forms, such as asbestos insulation, underground storage tanks, surface impoundments, septic tank systems, or oil and gas wells.

Increasing Regulations. Thrifts' problems with pollution and hazardous waste contamination have grown as federal, state, and local governments have passed comprehensive environmental regulations and laws imposing liabilities on landowners and others for cleaning up the environment.

Strict Liability. Thrifts must be aware of regulations that impose cleanup liability on an absolute or strict liability basis, and give governments the right to assign liability to persons or entities no longer holding title to the property.

Risks to Institutions There are at least eight basic categories of risk that an association can face as a result of environmentally contaminated property. These include:

Property Value. There is a risk that the collateral for a real estate loan or the property to be acquired may be drastically reduced in value after discovery of the existence of hazardous waste contamination.

Cleanup Cost. The cost for cleanup can be significant, and may exceed the institution's encumbrance on the property. The borrower may be unable to pay for cleaning up the contaminated property and also repay the loan.

Cleanup Superliens. A mortgage loan may lose priority to a cleanup lien imposed under the laws of those states that require super-priority liens for environmental cleanup. In these superlien states, a lien granted to the state securing the cost of cleaning up hazardous waste contamination may have priority over a lender's mortgage.

Liability for Debts. A lender may be liable to the extent of any credit extended to any debtor who has operated property containing hazardous wastes, has generated such waste, or has transported it in an improper manner. This risk extends to all creditors, not just those who hold as collateral the property containing the hazardous waste.

Foreclosure. The thrift may become directly liable for the cost of cleaning up a site if it forecloses on a contaminated property or becomes involved in the management of a company that owns or operates a contaminated facility, or is involved in decisions pertaining to the disposal of toxic or hazardous waste.

Loss of Security. In some cases a lender may not be able to pursue its foreclosure remedies and may have no practical alternative but to give up its loan security and the right to recover on the loan itself. This could lead to charging off the loan balance.

Improper Maintenance. The lender faces a risk that the borrower may not maintain collateral or property with an environmental risk potential in an environmentally sound manner.

Liability for Damage or Injury. Aside from the statutory liabilities that can be imposed for toxic waste contamination, there is also potential liability for personal injury or property damage.

Environmental Risk Policy To address these potential risks and liabilities, thrifts should develop internal underwriting and risk management procedures and revise their mortgages, guarantees, indemnities, contracts, and other loan documents to protect themselves against potential environmental hazards and to maintain the value of their loans and real estate investments.

Protective Purpose The most expeditious means by which a thrift institution may commence protective action against potential environmental risks and liabilities is to develop and implement a written environmental risk policy. Such a policy will serve several critical purposes.

Due Diligence Standard. It will establish a level of due diligence in all real estate transactions and support the institution's adherence to the principles of safety and soundness.

Underwriting. It will establish a means of identifying excessive environmental risk in properties being considered as collateral or for acquisition, or in properties being analyzed prior to foreclosure, or to meet standards set by buyers in the secondary market;

Property Maintenance. It will minimize environmental contamination of the borrower's property through the life of the loan by alerting institution staff to a potential problem property and providing for collateral monitoring and periodic property inspections throughout the loan term.

Documentation. It will establish guidelines for a satisfactory inquiry into the uses of property and for other protective actions as needed to qualify for CERCLA's innocent landowner defense in the event that it acquires, through foreclosure or otherwise, a contaminated property that it could not have reasonably known to be contaminated.

Policy Components The following are essential components in a lending institution's environmental risk policy:

Declaration of Intent. The policy should contain a stated assessment of potential environmental problems and liabilities (i.e., an acknowledgment of the risks cited under "Risks to Institutions" above) and a declaration that a policy of due diligence is adopted to protect the institution from such risks.

Information from Applicants. Loan applicants should be required to provide information on environmental matters pertaining to their business and facilities. Institutions should develop a form with specific questions concerning past, present, or proposed uses of the proposed collateral, potential hazards, insurance availability for the property as it pertains to environmental matters, and contacts by any federal, state, or local government agencies concerning environmental matters that must be resolved in order to obtain business and environmental permits.

Due Diligence Standards. There should be a requirement that an acquiring institution, in a purchase or participation loan, ensure that adequate due diligence regarding environmental risk matters has been met by the lead lender, and a requirement that all loans sold to Freddie Mac or Fannie Mae meet with the environmental due diligence standards imposed by those agencies.

Phase I Report for High Risks. The lender should require that all loan requests in which the proposed real property collateral has higher environmental risk potential than other types of real property, have a Phase I Environmental Risk Report prepared for the institution prior to approval of the loan.

OTS Guidelines

Risk Categories: Properties Likely to Require a Phase I Report

Most one- to four-family residential properties will not need a Phase I Environmental Risk Report. If cursory property inspection or records research discloses a high potential for environmental risk, however, a Phase I report is likely to be necessary.

Examples of properties that should have a Phase I Environmental Risk Report include:

a. Proposed construction properties (other than a one- to four-family residential property).

b. Industrial properties and properties on industrially zoned land.

c. Properties located close to industrial areas.

d. Properties that include or are close to an existing or former gas station site.

e. Commercial properties that include an automotive repair facility or a dry cleaning establishment where the work is done on the premises.

f. Properties adjacent to railroad tracks or underground pipelines (excluding one- to four-family residential properties).

g. Properties that have served as or are close to a refuse or waste disposal site.

h. Properties where the past uses or the surrounding uses include the storage of or use of hazardous or toxic substances (e.g., pesticides).

i. Properties suspected of containing asbestos material that is or may be friable (easily crumbled or crushed into powder and capable of being absorbed into the environment).

j. Properties where the emanation of radon gas from the soil may result in detrimental health effects to building occupants. (Institutions may need to consult with qualified environmental firms regarding the seriousness of radon problems in specific areas.)

k. Residential properties where there are known hazardous conditions on the property or in its immediate vicinity: where Superfund sites* exist within a one mile radius; where the site is in close proximity to oil and gas production; where there is asbestos within the building structure; where the site is a corner lot known to have been previously used as a gas station; or where the historic use of the property prior to its residential zoning is cause for concern.

* Sites identified by the EPA from which hazardous substance releases occurred or occur (e.g., hazardous waste dumps and chemical spills). The EPA is authorized to undertake removal or remedial actions at such sites.

Responsible Staff. The institution's board of directors or senior management should designate one or more qualified staff persons as the association's designated environmental risk analyst(s). These staff members should receive special training through courses or seminars in reviewing and interpreting environmental risk reports for the institution, and should assist in the development of the institution's environmental risk policy.

Qualified Consultants. Criteria should be established for the selection and retention of a roster of qualified environmental experts retained for risk analysis reports. The association should confirm that the organization or individual has appropriate education, training, and experience. The consultant should not be affiliated with the buyer or seller of the property nor with a firm engaged in any business that might present a conflict of interest.

Ordering and Reviewing Reports. The policy should state that it will be the loan officer's responsibility (after consultation with the designated environmental risk analyst) to order the Phase I Environmental Risk Report on the subject property as needed.

- ☐ The association must be the client on the environmental risk report. This provision will maximize the likelihood that the institution will receive an objective report that discloses all of the pertinent facts.

- ☐ The institution should only use environmental risk auditors from its approved roster.

- ☐ The loan officer, with assistance from the institution's designated environmental risk analyst, should have the responsibility to review the outside environmental audit report and judge the conclusions of the report after consulting with any environmental risk resources considered necessary.

- ☐ Final acceptance of environmental risk reports and decisions concerning the information in the report should be made by the institution's senior management.

Coordination with Appraisal Reports. The institution should require that appraisal reports fully disclose the findings and take into consideration any environmental risks and related costs identified in environmental risk reports.

Use in Underwriting Decisions. The policy should require that any potential environmental problems noted in an environmental risk report be considered by the institution's approval authority and senior management before the loan is approved or the property is purchased.

Unacceptable Conditions. Criteria should be stated for determining the circumstances in which loan requests may be declined due to environmental factors. *(These are essentially the same as stated in §501.04 of FNMA Procedures, above.)*

Use in Foreclosure Decisions. Procedures are needed for reviewing collateral before completion of foreclosure or acceptance of a deed in lieu of foreclosure. The procedures may include, but should not be limited to:

- ☐ A review of the existing loan file (including site inspection, leases, reports, and completion of an environmental checklist)

- ☐ A review of the loan documents and any subsequent modifications

- ☐ A determination as to whether any guarantees or indemnities were obtained on the loan

- ☐ A determination as to whether the borrower has any environmental impairment insurance or other applicable insurance that could be utilized for an environmental hazard claim

- ☐ A review of the current tenants and property uses

- ☐ Procurement of a Phase I Environmental Risk Report if conditions suggest it is necessary.

Coordination of Lender Departments. The policy should state the importance of coordination and cooperation among the institution's loan origination department, its loan servicing department, its designated environmental risk analyst, its legal counsel, and its appraisers, to carry out the environmental risk policy and to enlist the help of environmental specialists and applicable government agencies in this endeavor.

Types of Reports The following is a brief description of the various types of environmental risk reports that institutions may need to employ.

Phase I. A Phase I Environmental Risk Report is a qualitative assessment of the property. A typical Phase I report includes, but is not limited to:

- ☐ A historical review of the use and improvements made to the subject site

- ☐ A review of building, zoning, planning, sewer, water, fire, environmental, and other department records that would have information on or have an interest in the property and neighboring sites

- ☐ A review of the records and files of the Department of Health Services, Solid Waste Management Board, Regional Water Quality Control Board, Air Quality Management District, and other boards or agencies whose actions may affect the subject property and neighboring properties

- ☐ An investigation of the subject property and neighboring properties with regard to the EPA's National Priority List and Comprehensive Environmental Response, Compensation and Liability Information System (CERCLIS) list and similar state lists

- ☐ An inspection of the site and all improvements with particular attention to the use of hazardous materials in the structures or operating equipment

- ☐ A verification as to whether present or past owners or tenants have stored, created, or discharged hazardous materials or waste, and review of whether appropriate procedures, safeguards, permits, and notices are in place

- ☐ An analysis of old aerial photographs to determine the construction or destruction of buildings and the existence of ponds and disposal areas on the property over time

- Interviews with neighbors to determine prior uses of the subject property, if appropriate and only if deemed acceptable by the parties involved in the transaction (Confidentiality must be recognized.)
- A review of building records and a visual inspection of the building(s) to determine if asbestos-containing building materials may be present
- A review of scientific literature to determine the potential existence of radon in the soil
- A written report summarizing the findings.

Phase II Environmental Risk Report. A Phase II report is performed if "red flags" are apparent to the lender or if they are disclosed during the Phase I investigation. This report consists of all Phase I activities plus combinations of the following field tests and activities.

- Testing of underground storage tanks for content and integrity
- Soil gas analysis for petroleum hydrocarbons and volatile organic compounds such as industrial solvents and dry cleaning chemicals
- Bulk soil sampling
- Ground water sampling if ground water may be affected by land activities
- Limited surface water sampling if there is a pond, lagoon, or stream on the property
- A comprehensive review of the regional and local geology to determine the pathways leaked chemicals would follow in the event of a spill or leak
- A list of individual ground water wells or subsurface water bodies that may be affected by a spill or leak
- A comprehensive inspection of the building for asbestos-containing building materials. This should include collecting and analyzing samples of the building material for friable asbestos. It is strongly recommended that inspections be performed by EPA-certified inspectors and analyses be completed according to EPA guidelines
- If no listed hazardous materials or wastes are found, an appropriate verification to that effect
- A written report summarizing the findings.

Phase III Environmental Risk Report. A Phase III Environmental Risk Report is much more detailed, and consists of all of the Phase I and Phase II activities in addition to involved soils, water, and air quality analyses. As in a Phase I and Phase II report, a Phase III report also includes a written report summarizing the findings of the investigation.

Corrective Action. Based upon the Phase I, Phase II, or Phase III results, subsequent steps regarding further assessment, corrective action, or preventive programs should be recommended. This report should include gross cost estimates for correcting any discovered contamination.

Verification. Institutions should not hesitate to contact environmental firms and question the principal investigator regarding observations, conclusions, and recommendations made in the environmental assessment report.

HIGHLIGHTS TO REMEMBER

ENVIRONMENTAL INSPECTIONS: REGULATORY CONCERNS

Comprehensive Environmental, Response, Compensation and Liability Act (CERCLA), 1980, created great potential for lender liability for environmentally polluted properties

RTC requires environmental inspection on all properties; many lenders require it on all commercial properties

Government agencies and private organizations have developed guidelines for Phase I, II, and III inspections and reports as a means of risk management

FNMA Environmental Hazards Management Procedures

Required for lenders to qualify for FNMA financing on multifamily properties

Lender must provide environmental assessment before FNMA commitment and monitor the property during life of the loan

Lender is responsible for knowing environmental regulations and selecting qualified consultants

Phase I screening (documents, interviews, site inspection), followed by Phase II (physical sampling) if indicated

Properties with obvious environmental impairments should not be the subject of a FNMA commitment

Unacceptable conditions include waste disposal site, adjacent contamination, incurable contamination, asbestos, soil or ground water contaminants above stated levels, PCBs, radon, violations of law, litigation

Remediation may make property acceptable, after reinspection

When necessary, lender must require borrower to carry out ongoing operations and maintenance (O&M) to keep property acceptable

Additional certifications are required in states with environmental superlien laws

Lender must report any subsequent environmental incidents or other changes in status of the property

Nonperforming loans: lender must prepare environmental evaluation for the asset audit, and take steps to protect the property

Resolution Trust Corporation Environmental Guidelines

RTC manages and disposes of assets of insolvent thrifts under FIRREA

All REOs are screened for potential environmental issues, and appraised as is subject to hazards, regulations, etc.

Required to consider both environmental hazards and special resource values

Special resources usually enhance property value: commonest types are wetlands and cultural or historic resources

RTC contacts agencies and organizations with interests in special resources

Environmental hazards decrease value: commonest are asbestos and underground storage tanks

REOs with hazards may be sold as is or remedied before sale

RTC may decline to foreclose if remediation costs would exceed value of the asset

Innocent Landowner Defense
CERCLA allows possibility of exemption from liability for owner who acquires property unaware of hazards if "appropriate inquiry" is made

Proposed amendment would define appropriate inquiry in specific terms

> Federal definition of a complete Phase I audit: site inspection, title search, aerial photographs, recorded environmental liens, government records of waste sites

> Defines "environmental professional" and "reasonably obtainable records"

> Phase I looks for "obviousness of the presence or likely presence of a release or threatened release of hazardous substances"

May require further inquiry if Phase I indicates probable hazards

Federal Home Loan Bank/Office of Thrift Supervision Guidelines
Thrift institutions are directed to develop policies to guard against financial risks from environmental hazards

Risks include liability for cleanup, damage, or injury; loss of property value; cleanup superliens

Lender is responsible for identifying environmental risks, keeping records, providing for property maintenance, having qualified staff and consultants, insuring objectivity and coordination among lender's departments

Most 1 to 4 family residential properties will not need Phase I, unless on or near industrial, automotive, waste, or Superfund sites, or having asbestos or radon

Types of Environmental Risk Reports
Phase I includes site history and inspection, check of government toxic site lists, historic aerial photos, interviews, check of records for asbestos and radon

Phase II conducts actual physical tests of soils, tanks, ground and surface water, or building materials, where Phase I found "red flags"

Phase III conducts more detailed scientific analysis and recommends actions

COURSE 10
Phase I Environmental Inspections

INTRODUCTION

As stated in Course 9, federal regulators and financial institutions are increasingly requiring environmental screening of the properties they handle. Thus the real estate practitioner should have at least a basic understanding of what a Phase I inspection involves. Rather than considering an environmental inspection report requirement a threat to marketability, it can be seen as a valuable sales tool. It is an environmental report card for the property, so that concerns about toxicity can be evaluated and dealt with realistically.

Consumer Protection Like a title report and other forms of disclosure, the purpose of an environmental inspection report is to insure that there will be no surprises to the buyer or lender later on. It is a major consumer protection document. Documentation of present and former use of the site is a form of ecological tracking system, allowing identification of present or potential problems at the site. Historical information and site observations help the client evaluate the the site as collateral or for intended purchase. This is true whether or not the property is of a type commonly subject to pollution (e.g., a gas station site), and whether or not an inspection is mandated by law.

WHAT IS A PHASE I?

The Phase I inspection is a diagnostic screening, something like a medical checkup, designed to uncover clues to any possible environmental problems that should be tested in detail in a Phase II, or remedied in Phase III. The Phase I screening involves both a history (documentary research) and an examination (site inspection).

Documentary Research It is essential to identify the site and its present use accurately, and then to trace past uses, whose ecological effects may persist yet may not be visually apparent. Sources for this information include:

- ☐ Environmental agency databases (see below)
- ☐ Aerial photographs
- ☐ Historic maps
- ☐ Title search
- ☐ Interviews.

Field Inspection In Phase I, the inspector is basically looking for "red flags." Items commonly observed are listed below. Asbestos, lead, and radon are the hazards most commonly encountered in residential properties and are among factors that may make a property unacceptable to a lender.

- ☐ Above-ground tanks
- ☐ Asbestos
- ☐ Discarded batteries

- ☐ Lead paint
- ☐ Lead water pipes
- ☐ Neighboring uses
- ☐ Oil and gas drums
- ☐ Oil slicks
- ☐ PCBs (polychlorinated biphenyls)
- ☐ Pesticides and herbicides
- ☐ Radon gas
- ☐ Stained soil
- ☐ UFFI (urea formaldehyde foam insulation)
- ☐ Underground storage tanks
- ☐ Vegetation damage.

Relation to Phase II In a Phase I report, the inspector normally notes any visible manifestation that could indicate a hazard, and recommends a Phase II investigation to determine its toxicity. For example, discolored soil may indicate seepage to the surface of asphaltum or other hydrocarbons, or it may be the result of illegal dumping of toxic materials—or it may be harmless. It takes a trained observer, and often laboratory analysis, to differentiate between *harmful* and *harmless*.

Inspector Qualifications Because this is a new field, formal qualifications are still evolving. Private organizations like the Environmental Assessment Association (see next section) offer training and professional designations, and federal agencies like the Resolution Trust Corporation have requirements for experience and references. References from previous clients will be especially valuable. The environmental inspector should provide a resume including:

- ☐ Education
- ☐ Experience
- ☐ Professional affiliations
- ☐ Publications
- ☐ Awards or recognitions
- ☐ References.

Relevant education and experience might be in the areas of:

- ☐ Engineering
- ☐ Geology
- ☐ Chemistry
- ☐ Other physical sciences
- ☐ Building inspection
- ☐ Contracting
- ☐ Appraisal.

Scientific, building-related, and documentary research skills are all highly desirable. Often a team approach is best.

California Registered Environmental Assessor

The California Code of Regulations now provides for voluntary registration of environmental assessors, in a registry made available to potential clients. For purposes of this program, assessment includes recommendations for complying with legal requirements in areas related to hazardous substances, review of the risks resulting from exposure to hazardous substances, and any suggested management procedures or practices. Environmental assessors may include, but are not limited to, analytical chemists, engineers, epidemiologists, hydrologists, attorneys with expertise in hazardous substance law, physicians, industrial hygienists, toxicologists, and environmental program managers.

Qualifications. The applicant for registration as an environmental assessor must have:

- ☐ Five years full time experience in the applicant's general field of expertise within the last eight years.

- ☐ Two years substantial experience in performing environmental assessments within the last four years.

- ☐ A bachelor's or higher degree or appropriate professional license in a physical or biological science, engineering, or law. Five years substantial experience performing environmental assessments can be considered equivalent to such training.

- ☐ Three or more references as employers or clients.

Areas of Expertise. The assessor application includes a checklist of "specific areas of environmental assessing expertise" (below), and another checklist for experience, classified by "types of businesses assisted" (agricultural, asbestos removal, insurance companies, munitions, photo labs, real estate transfers, waste transporters, and about seventy others).

- ☐ Air Emissions Monitoring and Control
- ☐ Analytical Chemistry
- ☐ Asbestos
- ☐ Biological Studies
- ☐ Emergency Preparedness and Response
- ☐ Engineering:
  - ☐ Chemical
  - ☐ Civil
  - ☐ Environmental
  - ☐ Industrial Process
- ☐ Environmental Impact Assessment, CEQA/NEPA
- ☐ Environmental Impact Liability Insurance
- ☐ Epidemiology
- ☐ Field and Laboratory Analytical Services
- ☐ Geology
- ☐ Ground water Contamination
- ☐ Hydrology
- ☐ Indoor Air Quality
- ☐ Legal/Regulatory Compliance
- ☐ Management of Hazardous Substances or Waste:
  - ☐ Disposal
  - ☐ Recycling
  - ☐ Reduction
  - ☐ Storage
  - ☐ Treatment
- ☐ Mining
- ☐ Nuclear
- ☐ Occupational Health and Safety
- ☐ PCBs
- ☐ Permit Preparation
- ☐ Proposition 65
- ☐ Radiation/Radiology
- ☐ Radon
- ☐ Reclamation
- ☐ Remedial Investigations
- ☐ Risk Assessment and Control
- ☐ SARA Title III
- ☐ Site or Property Characterization
- ☐ Soil Contamination
- ☐ Toxicology
- ☐ Training/Communications/Management
- ☐ Underground Tank Checks and Management
- ☐ Water Discharge Monitoring and Control
- ☐ Others

RESEARCH: GOVERNMENT DATABASES

One task of the Phase I inspector is to determine, either directly from governmental agencies or through commercial services providing government environmental records, whether known or suspected contamination sites or activities are on or near the property. Because of the numerous sources that must be searched and the often slow response of government agencies, commercial services are often worth the cost. They may be located through the Yellow Pages under Environmental and Ecological Services. If one decides to search the government records directly, the following are the main sources.

Federal Government Record Systems Various lists may record the property or an adjoining property as contaminated or potentially contaminated. At the federal level, requests to consult these records are governed by the Freedom of Information Act (FOIA). FOIA requires a written request to the FOIA officer for the regional Environmental Protection Agency office for the region in which the site is located. The preparer should anticipate a response no sooner than four to eight weeks.

National Priority List. The NPL is a list of sites identified for cleanup or other remedial action by the Environmental Protection Agency (EPA).

Comprehensive Environmental Response, Compensation and Liability Information System. CERCLIS is the EPA's list of sites that it has investigated or is currently investigating for potential hazardous substance contamination and for possible inclusion on the National Priority List.

Resource Conservation and Recovery Act (RCRA) Notifier List. The RCRA Notifier List is a list of facilities that have filed notifications as required by federal law because they generate, transport, treat, store, or dispose of hazardous waste on or from their sites.

Open Dumps. Under RCRA, EPA's Office of Solid Waste maintains an inventory of open dumps in the United States. An open dump is defined as a facility that does not comply with EPA's Criteria for Classification of Solid Waste Disposal Facilities and Practices (40 CFR 257).

SARA Title III. SARA stands for Superfund Amendment and Reauthorization Act. SARA Title III, the Emergency Planning and Community Right-to-Know Act, requires facilities to inform certain state and local entities about the presence and amounts of hazardous chemicals kept on site above threshold quantities. It also requires facilities to report inventories and toxic chemical emissions.

Facility Index System (FINDS). FINDS is a master list of all facilities identified by the EPA for regulation under one or more federal environmental programs. It identifies the address of the site and the EPA program office which has responsibility over that facility.

State Record Systems States also keep lists of properties contaminated or potentially contaminated or associated with generation, transportation, treatment, storage, or disposal of hazardous substances.

Cleanup Lists (State Superfund Lists). State environmental agencies maintain lists of sites targeted for cleanup or other remedial action, the state agency equivalent to NPL or CERCLIS.

Leaking Underground Storage Tank (LUST) List. This is a list of sites containing one or more underground storage tanks identified as having leaked or potentially leaking their contents into the ground or ground water. These sites may also be involved in a state cleanup program.

Underground Storage Tank (UST) Registration List. This is a list of all underground storage tanks for which registrations have been filed with the responsible state office. Information varies from state to state but generally includes location, number, size, age, and contents of tanks.

Solid Waste/Landfill Facilities. The Solid Waste/Landfill Facilities List includes sites that currently accept, or have accepted in the past, waste of any kind for disposal on site. Records are typically obtained through a state office of solid waste management, which is usually a division of the primary state environmental agency.

Environmental Liens. Records of environmental liens are on file where land title records are ordinarily kept for the jurisdiction in which the property is located—usually the county recorder's office.

SITE INSPECTION:
ENVIRONMENTAL ASSESSMENT ASSOCIATION RESIDENTIAL PHASE I REPORT

The Environmental Assessment Association (EAA) is a private professional organization offering the professional designation CEI—Certified Environmental Inspector. It has developed an environmental inspection report form for Phase I site inspections of residential properties. The form is designed as a series of checklists with comments, covering the common "red flags" for hazards and contaminants. In the conclusion, the inspector evaluates each as "Acceptable" or "Suggest Phase II Audit." This form is designed for field inspection of fairly uncomplicated properties; the more extensive documentary research mandated by the RTC guidelines and likely to be necessary for a successful innocent landowner defense under CERCLA (aerial photos, databases, title search) would be a separate report, covered in the following section of this course.

The form and instructions are reprinted by permission of Environmental Assessment Association, 8383 East Evans Road, Scottsdale, AZ 85260-3614. Instructions are supplemented from EAA's *Basic Guide for Environmental Inspections*. Contact EAA for further information on training, certification, and data services.

ENVIRONMENTAL ASSESSMENT ASSOCIATION FORM 510
INSTRUCTIONS

The Environmental Assessment Association (EAA) has produced Form 510, the Phase I Environmental Inspection Report. Completion of the form is based on basic information that can be obtained by visual inspection of the property. This form has been reviewed by the United States Environmental Protection Agency (EPA) and they have expressed their desire that this type of form be used on every residential real estate transaction.

When filling out Form 510, keep in mind who your client is and the type of information the client will require. When initially contacted to perform the inspection, ask your client if there are any known or suspected problems. Parties involved in the transaction may have knowledge that will make your job easier.

With this form you are providing information that parties in a real estate transaction will rely on to make lending or purchase decisions. Keep in mind the extent of any problems you notice and the effect these problems will have on the property. It is important that you fill out the form completely before submitting it to your client.

The exhibit shows an example of a completed Form 510. In this example some problems were noted, and comments explain the extent of the problems and the inspector's suggestions.

Inspection Data. Indicate in this section the basic information about the property.

1. The property address, city, county, state, and zip code need to be included here. The legal description also should be provided. If the legal description is too long to fit in the space provided, the inspector should include an addendum. Information as to whether the property is occupied or not, and if so, by whom, is important and should be included.

2. "Prepared for" should list the person and/or company that contracted for the report. This is the client, and it is important to remember that the information contained in the environmental inspection report should be treated as confidential between the client and the inspector.

3. "Environmental Inspector" should be only the person who actually visited the property and filled out the form based on direct observations. Make sure that the date of the inspection is written in the appropriate spot.

Property Description and Analysis

4. Current and past use of the property should be checked or described. If the property is presently residential, note if there is a business being run from the home that may use or produce quantities of hazardous materials.

5. The "Comments" section should have a description of the property based on direct observation. The land and any buildings should be briefly described. Remember that this is an environmental inspection and that environmental aspects need to be observed.

General Field Observation

6. In this section the inspector, through a visual inspection, should note any general signs of possible environmental hazards. Use all your senses, but handle nothing that may be hazardous, and use appropriate safety equipment (safety glasses, latex gloves, respirators). A yes or no in this section indicates the overall presence or lack of environmental problems. Any specifics should be noted in the following sections of the report.

Storage Tanks

7. "Underground Storage Tanks." USTs should be noted here. Look for visible signs of possible past or present existence of underground storage tanks, such as vent or fill pipes. There are currently 37 states that have registrations for USTs which have been installed in recent years, have been voluntarily registered, or have been reported as leaking (LUSTs). This registration information is available from EAA.

8. "Above Ground Storage Tanks." ASTs should be easily observable when inspecting the property. They can be just about any size and may be concealed behind vegetation or some other barrier. Note that there are many types of tanks in common use that present no hazard, such as propane tanks for gas barbecues, tanks used for pool heating, etc. Describe the tanks in the comment section so the reader will understand what type of tanks exist.

Waste

9. "Waste Sites" can be a pile of old junk, or neatly stored containers or materials. Solid waste can be found in barrels, loose, buried, or dispersed.

10. "Comments." This comment section should be used to explain any concerns the inspector has with regard to the observations of the property. This is where questionable storage containers or evidence of containers on or near the property should be described. Remember, people save a lot of things, and most pose no environmental risk whatsoever.

Water Analysis

11. "Drinking Water." Determine the sources of water for the property and the system of delivering water located on the property. There are many old or abandoned wells that are no longer in use due to other supplies of water being available. These wells may or may not be capped, and could seem to be just a hole in the ground.

Most modern wells will have a mechanized pumping and filtration system located on the property. Some homes will have a storage tank, if water must be delivered to the property. If this is the case, determine where the water is coming from, i.e., city water, a neighbor's well, etc. Look for signs of lead or lead soldered pipes, wells, well pumps, municipal or county water supplies, etc. Water pipes have problems of reacting with the soil (electrolysis) as well as mineral content in the pipes themselves (lead, in particular). In addition, many of our water delivery systems are old and outmoded. Even after treatment impurities may be added to the water from the pipes that transport it. Laboratory analysis is necessary to detect these conditions.

"Comments." Use the comments section to explain observations and any concerns that may arise.

PHASE 1 ENVIRONMENTAL INSPECTION REPORT *(Residential)*

INSPECTION DATA

Property Address: 2012 West Baker Road
City: Morristown   County: Johnson   State: Iowa   Zip: 47562
Legal Description: Pt of SW Tract. 1/4, NW 14 S 173' OF W250' Thereof
Property Is: ___ Vacant Land X Improved   Occupied By Whom: M. Owen   Phone: (411) 555-6246
Prepared For: Mid-Country National Bank, Des Moines, Iowa
Environmental Inspector: Louis M. Morgan, CEI   Date: 3/27/91

PROPERTY DESCRIPTION AND ANALYSIS

Current Use of Property: X Residential ___ Commercial ___ Industrial ___ Undeveloped Land ___ Other
Past Use of Property (If Known): ___ Residential ___ Commercial ___ Industrial ___ Undeveloped Land X Other Agricultural
Comments: Property was developed from part of an existing farm in 1983. Prior to 1982 the land was used to grow corn. This is a one acre property.

GENERAL FIELD OBSERVATION

Were there any physical signs of the following observed on the property? X Yes ___ No

- ___ Underground Storage Tanks
- ___ Stained Soil
- ___ Vegetation Damage
- ___ Oily Sheens on Water
- ___ Streams, Lakes or Ponds
- ___ Discarded Batteries
- ___ Oil/Gas Drums
- X Above Ground Tanks
- ___ Lead Paint
- ___ Asbestos
- ___ Other

STORAGE TANKS

Underground Storage Tanks (UST's)

___ Yes X No   Were any Below Ground Storage Tanks observed on the property?
___ Yes X No   Was any evidence of soil or groundwater contamination observed on the property?
___ Yes X No   Were any chemical manufacturing plants, gas stations or petroleum delivery/storage facilities observed on surrounding properties?

Above Ground Storage Tanks (AST's)

 X Yes ___ No   Were any Above Ground Storage Tanks observed on the property?

Waste Sites

___ Yes X No   Is the subject or any neighboring property engaged in storing, transporting or producing waste, chemicals or hazardous substances?

Comments: The home used propane for heating, stored in an approved tank approximately 100 feet from the house.

WATER INSPECTION

Drinking Water

 X Yes ___ No   Were any water wells, in use or abandoned, observed on the property?
___ Yes X No   Are these wells the primary or sole source of drinking water?
___ Yes X No   Are lead or lead soldered pipes visible on the property?

Comments: A security capped well pipe, previously used for field watering, exists on the property.

Chemical/Gas/Mineral Analysis

12. "Asbestos." This may be present in many homes built before 1980 and some built after. Look carefully for signs of asbestos, especially for the more common uses such as pipe insulation, floor tiles, window putty, air duct lining, sprayed-on acoustical ceilings, heat reflectors, and general fireproofing. Even though asbestos was phased out in the 1970s, it is still available for use in materials produced before its restriction. Keep in mind that you are looking for "friable" or readily crumbled asbestos. Studies indicate that asbestos which is not friable poses no threat to occupants.

13. "Urea Formaldehyde Foam Insulation." UFFI is often hard to spot without opening a wall. If possible, look in garages and basements where finishing may not be as complete as in the main part of a structure, or behind light switch covers.

14. "Lead Paint." This can be seen as cracked or peeling paint on walls and ceiling or as chips which collect on floors. Some lead paint may still be available and used in newer homes, but this is rare. Lead paint was banned in 1972. Homes built prior to 1972 have a higher chance of lead paint being present. Other types of paint may crack and peel with age, so it may be difficult to determine whether lead is present.

15. "Pesticides and Herbicides." These can be evidenced by the actual containers of the substances or by signs of their use, such as dead vegetation. Some use is normal. The inspector should look for severe overuse or very large quantities stored on the property.

16. "Polychlorinated Biphenyls." PCBs are seen as the oil in which they are suspended. This oil is found in electrical transformers, hydraulic equipment, and fluorescent light ballasts. Note if any of these types of equipment are present on the property. Spills or leaks will appear as oily spots on the ground or floor under or near the equipment.

17. "Radon" is a colorless, odorless radioactive gas that can be detected only by special measuring procedures. An inspector may wish to check an EPA radon map to determine if there is a high probability that the property is an area affected by radon.

18. "Comments." In this comments section summarize and explain observations and concerns relating to the substances listed in this section.

General

19. This is where the inspector notes if anything else was observed that deserves mention. Any suspicious substances, containers, objects, etc., that the inspector feels may pose a potential environmental threat should be noted.

20. Nearby properties might pose a risk potential for the subject property. This is especially important for adjacent properties, and observations should be noted here.

21. This comment section will explain any general observations of the site and nearby properties which were not covered in previous sections.

Environmental Databases

A number of federal and state databases contain information about specific problems that might be located on the property or within a one mile radius. These reports should be part of every Phase I Environmental Inspection on commercial property and offered as an option on residential inspections. Reports are available through EAA for a fee, or from government agencies.

Summary and Conclusion of Inspection

22. The inspector should go through this list and check whether, in his or her opinion, the hazard potential for each category listed is acceptable or requires further testing.

23. The inspector's signature is placed here and the form is dated. The inspector's name should be typed or printed on the last line.

24. The Certification and Statement of Limiting Conditions accompanies the form.

CHEMICAL, GAS & MINERAL INSPECTION

Asbestos

_X_ Yes ___ No Were signs of asbestos observed on the property?

___ Yes _X_ No Was the structure constructed before 1979?

___ Yes _X_ No Were any suspected asbestos containing materials observed such as sprayed materials on fireproofing areas, pipe insulation, floor tile, etc?

UREA Formaldehyde Foam Insulation (UFFI)

___ Yes _X_ No Was any evidence of Formaldehyde Foam Insulation observed on the property?

Lead Paint

___ Yes _X_ No Was any visible evidence of peeling, cracking or flaking paint observed?

___ Yes _X_ No Was any visible evidence of lead paint on the ceilings, walls or floors of any structures observed on the property?

Pesticides/Herbicides

___ Yes _X_ No Does it appear pesticides or herbicides have been used in excess of normal household use?

___ Yes _X_ No Is the property used for agricultural purposes?

___ Yes _X_ No Are there any noticeable pesticide odors?

Polychlorinated Biphenyl (PCB's)

___ Yes _X_ No Were any transformers, electrical devices or hydraulic equipment observed on the property labeled as containing PCB's?

___ Yes _X_ No Was evidence of PCB contamination to the soil or groundwater observed on the property?

___ Yes _X_ No Were any fluorescent light ballasts labeled as containing PCB's observed?

Radon

_X_ Yes ___ No Is there reason to suspect that radon may be a problem in the dwelling or the immediate property's locality?

___ Yes _X_ No Has radon screening been conducted which indicates that the property may have elevated levels of radon?

Comments Asbestos heat reflector on decorative stove, not friable. Suggest removal. U. S. EPA radon map indicates problem area, home well ventilated with circulating outside air.

GENERAL

_X_ Yes ___ No Are there any conditions present not mentioned above that need to be corrected to remove any potential risks?

___ Yes _X_ No Activities of adjacent properties may pose potential environmental risks to the subject property.

Comments Open metal drum appears to contain some old motor oil, no staining on ground. Recommend removal.

SUMMARY & CONCLUSION OF INSPECTION

Underground Storage Tanks (UST's)
_X_ Acceptable
___ Suggest Phase II Environmental Audit

Above Ground Storage Tanks (AST's)
_X_ Acceptable
___ Suggest Phase II Environmental Audit

Waste Sites
_X_ Acceptable
___ Suggest Phase II Environmental Audit

Drinking Water
_X_ Acceptable
___ Suggest Phase II Environmental Audit

Asbestos
_X_ Acceptable
___ Suggest Phase II Environmental Audit

UREA Formaldehyde Foam Insulation (UFFI)
___ Acceptable
___ Suggest Phase II Environmental Audit

Lead Paint
_X_ Acceptable
___ Suggest Phase II Environmental Audit

Pesticides/Herbicides
_X_ Acceptable
___ Suggest Phase II Environmental Audit

Polychlorinated Biphenyl (PCB's)
_X_ Acceptable
___ Suggest Phase II Environmental Audit

Radon
___ Acceptable
_X_ Suggest Phase II Environmental Audit

I certify that to the best of my knowledge and belief the facts and data used in this inspection are true and accurate, based on currently accepted and available information as of the inspection date; I personally inspected the subject property; and I have no undisclosed interest, present or prospective therein.

Environmental Inspector's Signature _____ Date 3/27/91

Name Louis M. Morgan, CEI

Environmental Assessment Association
CERTIFICATION
AND
STATEMENT OF LIMITING CONDITIONS

Certification: The Environmental Inspector certifies to the Buyer, Seller and/or lender in a transaction as named in the inspection report "Principal Parties"; and the Inspector and the Principal Parties agree that:

1. The Environmental Inspector has no present or contemplated future (a) partnership with Principal Parties nor (b) an interest in the property inspected which could adversely affect the Inspector's ability to perform an objective inspection; and neither the employment of the inspector to conduct the inspection, nor the compensation for it, is contingent on the results of the inspection.

2. The Environmental Inspector has no personal interest in or bias with respect to the subject matter of the inspection report or any parties who may be part of a financial transaction involving the property. The conclusions and recommendations of the report are not based in whole or in part upon the race, color, creed, sex or national origin of any of the Principal Parties.

3. The Environmental Inspector has personally inspected the property, both inside and out and has made visual inspection of adjacent properties, to the extent possible by readily available access. The inspection does not include the removal of any soil, water or air samples, the moving of furniture or fixtures, or any type of inspection that would require extraordinary effort to access.

4. All contingent and limiting conditions are contained herein (imposed by the terms of the inspection assignment or by the undersigned affecting the conclusions and recommendations contained in the report).

5. This Environmental Inspection report has been made in conformity with and is subject to the requirements of the Code of Professional Ethics of the Environmental Assessment Association.

6. All opinions, conclusions and recommendations concerning the inspected property that are set forth in the inspection report were prepared by the Environmental Inspector whose signature appears on the report. No change of any item in the report shall be made by anyone other than the Inspector, and the Inspector shall have no responsibility for any such unauthorized change.

Contingent and Limiting Conditions: The certification of the Environmental Inspector appearing in the environmental inspection report is subject to the following conditions and to such other specific and limiting conditions as are set forth by the Inspector in the report.

1. The Inspector assumes no responsibility for matters of a legal nature affecting the property inspected or the title thereto. The property is inspected assuming responsible ownership.

2. Any sketch appearing in or attached to the inspection report, or any statement of dimensions, capacities, quantities or distances, are approximate and are included to assist the reader in visualizing the property. The inspector has made no survey of the property.

3. The Inspector is not required to give testimony or appear in court because of having made the inspection with reference to the property in question, unless arrangements have been previously made therefor.

4. This report is not intended to have any direct effect on the value of the property inspected but simply to provide a visual Environmental Assessment solely for the benefit of the Principal Parties.

5. The Inspector assumes that there are no hidden, unapparent, or latent conditions or defects in or of the property, subsoil, or structures, other than those noted on the inspection report or any addendum to the report which the Inspector has included. The Inspector assumes no responsibility for such conditions, or for the inspection, engineering or repair which might be required to discover or correct such factors.

6. Information, estimates and opinions furnished to the Inspector, and contained in the report, were obtained from sources considered reliable and believed to be true and correct. However, the Inspector has made no independent investigation as to such matters and undertakes no responsibility for the accuracy of such items.

7. The Inspection and Inspection Report are made by the Inspector solely for the benefit and personal use of the Principal Parties. Disclosure of the contents of the Inspection Report is governed by the Bylaws and Regulations of the Environmental Assessment Association. No disclosure may be made of the Inspection Report without the prior written consent of the Inspector and the Inspector undertakes no responsibility for harm or damages to any party other than the Principal Parties.

8. Neither the Inspection Report, any part thereof, nor any copy of the same (including conclusions or recommendations, the identity of the Inspector, professional designation, reference to any professional organization, or the firm with which the Inspector is connected), shall be used for any purposes by anyone but the Principal Parties. The report shall not be conveyed by anyone to the public through advertising, public relations, news, sales, or other media, without the prior written consent and approval of the Inspector.

© 1991 Environmental Assessment Association. No part of this document may be reproduced or used in any form, or by any means (graphic, electronic, or mechanical, including photocopying, recording, typing or information storage and retrieval systems) without permission in writing from the Environmental Assessment Association, 8383 East Evans Road, Scottsdale Arizona 85260 USA.

Major Hazardous Substances: Field Guide

The following information from EAA's *Basic Guide for Environmental Inspections* supplements the instructions accompanying the Phase I report form. The emphasis is on visual clues to look for in a field inspection. Refer to Course 8 for additional information on these and other hazards.

Asbestos

Asbestos is a mineral fiber found in rocks. Although the dangers associated with the use of asbestos have been evident for some time, its superior fire resisting and insulating qualities kept it in use. By some estimates, 75 percent of all residential properties that are more than thirty years old or are heated with steam or hot water contain asbestos in some form. Between 1900 and 1980, it has been estimated that more than 30 million tons of asbestos were used in the United States. Uses of asbestos to look for are:

- To cover hot water pipes, ducts and boilers
- In vinyl floor tiles and rolled linoleums
- Siding on both residential and commercial buildings
- Roofing shingles and felts
- Spray-on insulation or paint on walls and ceilings
- Acoustical ceiling tiles
- Window putty
- Fuse boxes
- Heat reflectors, such as found on wood stoves
- Air duct lining.

Visual Clues. There are three common types of materials that can contain friable asbestos and may signal the need for further inquiry. These are:

- A fluffy, sprayed-on material used for fireproofing ceilings or walls (sometimes it looks like cotton candy) or a sprayed or troweled-on material that resembles a granular, cement-like plaster and is usually used for fireproofing and soundproofing on walls and ceilings.
- Nonfriable asbestos wall board (presents no threat unless it is broken) with sprayed or troweled-on material behind as insulation.
- Asbestos-based pipe or boiler insulation which may resemble felt, cement, or fibrous wrapping paper.

Precautions. Friable asbestos-containing material can be easily crumbled by hand pressure. If you suspect asbestos, or have accidentally crumbled material that may be asbestos, take care to not breathe in the fibers or get them near your face. Keep away from any dust in a suspected area. Exercise due care to insure that the material is not disturbed (scraped, sanded, drilled, etc.), and recommend that a Phase II inspection be made.

Radon Radon is a radioactive gas produced when certain natural radioactive minerals break down or decay. Radon gas further decays into smaller particles known as radon "daughters" or progeny. These can be deposited on the lining of the lung and subsequently decay or emit radioactive particles, causing cellular changes that may transform normal cells into cancer cells.

Visual Clues. There are none. Radon cannot be seen or smelled; only testing will determine if it is present in dangerous amounts.

Distribution. There are certain areas of the country where the incidence of radon in very high. In Pennsylvania, for example, of over 30,000 homes tested, 55 percent had levels of radon considered potentially dangerous. Local, state, and federal environmental and health officials can often provide information about general areas of radon occurrence. The EPA produces a radon map of the entire United States that shows areas with proven high probability for radon gas. Interview current or former owners to determine if they are aware of any EPA radon tests performed on the property, and check water and gas utility records for reports of radon on or near the property.

Testing. The major types of radon testing are charcoal canister, liquid scintillation, alpha tracking, E-perm, and continuous monitoring. Alpha tracking is a long term test, up to one year. The E-perm and continuous monitoring tests can be used for varying amounts of time, from a few minutes to many days. A preliminary radon test is available that involves exposing a small canister in the lowest part of the structure for several days and mailing it to a laboratory for testing; these test kits are available through EAA for around $30.

Lead-Based Paint The presence of old lead-based paint in homes represents the most significant hazard for lead poisoning today, particularly for young children. The most common means of exposure is children swallowing peeled and flaking pieces of paint, especially where housing is older and poorly maintained.

Visual Clues. Look for chipped or peeling paint anywhere on the inside or outside of a building. If the building was constructed before 1980 lead paint should be suspected.

Testing. There are presently only two ways lead-based paint can be tested. These are laboratory analysis of paint chips and by means of portable X-ray fluorescence analyzers.

Tanks Tanks can be above ground or under the ground. Soil contamination is the primary concern with both kinds of tanks. If the inspection reveals evidence of leakage (quite common as seals weaken in older tanks), processing of the soil on the site may be required. In extreme cases, underground waters may need to be treated in order to be safe for human consumption.

Visual Clues: Underground. You will be able to find USTs that are currently in use by locating their fill and vent pipes. These may be small pipes sticking a few inches out of the ground, open or covered with caps. Any recessed boxes, such as often used to house sprinkler control systems, should be examined. USTs that have been abandoned may have had their fill and vent pipes removed and are hard to locate. Professional testing equipment may be needed to locate these USTs.

Visual Clues: Above Ground. Faulty valves, seams that lack structural integrity, and poor construction can all lead to discharge from above ground tanks, and may be visible in a walk-through inspection.

Remediation. Any tank having held regulated substances (including all petroleum products) needs a site assessment and proper closure. This means an investigation into the ground below the tank and any connected pipelines, and the filling of the tank with an inert material or removal (with inspection) to a proper safe location. Any materials held in the tanks must also be properly disposed of.

Information Sources. Interview current owners, former owners, or neighbors to determine if they are aware of any tanks now or previously on the property. Refer to records to see if the property was ever used for any activity which involves the storage of petroleum or other chemicals in tanks, or was ever heated by fuel oil. Check with the appropriate state agency to see if any USTs have been registered on the property. In some states underground storage tank (UST) registration is required for all underground tanks containing regulated substances that are not already listed as hazardous waste sites or LUSTs.

Polychlorinated Biphenyls (PCBs)
Polychlorinated biphenyls are toxic molecules that attach themselves to human fat tissue and act as possible carcinogens. There is little evidence that PCBs are harmful to humans unless they are ingested.

Distribution. Most often PCBs are found in electrical equipment, such as transformers, ballasts in fluorescent lighting, circuit breakers, and switch gears. PCBs may also exist in hydraulic fluids used in heavy equipment. The danger from PCBs develops when the oils or fluids containing the PCBs leak out and contaminate the soil and ground water. If the equipment is in good condition and the PCBs are contained within it, there is little danger to humans. When a building with PCB-containing electrical equipment suffers fire or other damage, there is an increased probability of PCBs leaking.

Visual Clues. Look for fluorescent lights and electrical transformers along with other PCB-containing products. Spills or leaks will appear as oily spots below or near the cquipment. PCB regulations were not issued until 1979 and PCBs have been used since 1929. Buildings constructed or renovated between these two dates have a high probability of having PCB-containing products.

Miscellaneous Waste
Even if there is no noticeable leaking, discharge, or spills, the presence of containers or materials may indicate the storage of hazardous materials. Dead or dying vegetation or bare or discolored patches of ground may also indicate something amiss. Determine if materials or containers pose a potential or obvious environmental hazard by observation only.

Judgment Needed. Many waste materials such as wood are unlikely to pose an environmental threat. Keep in mind that it is often only large numbers of quantities of objects or materials that constitute a hazard. Three abandoned cars are probably not going to cause a severe environmental problem. On the other hand, if they are abandoned right next to a well that supplies the property's drinking water, further investigation is probably required.

RTC Environmental Guidelines: Phase I Outline

(In contrast to the EAA form's visual inspection, the RTC's guidelines focus more strongly on historical research, as likely to be required to establish an innocent landowner defense under CERCLA.)

The material presented below outlines the typical scope of work for a Phase I environmental site assessment (ESA). The scope of work includes three tasks required for all Phase I ESAs: a review of historical records, a review of readily available files and databases maintained by regulatory agencies, and a field reconnaissance of the subject site and adjacent properties. A fourth task, characterization of the environmental setting, may be added if potential contamination sources are identified. Each task description identifies information requirements and potential data sources. The level of effort that should be placed on each task and the scope of work for each Phase I ESA will vary on a site-by-site basis. Therefore, the scope of work for individual Phase I ESAs must be developed by the RTC representative's environmental specialist and the environmental contractor.

Introduction The introduction should state the purpose and objectives of the Phase I ESA, identify the subject property, and briefly outline the scope of services provided. A site location map should be provided, identifying the property location with respect to local and regional roads, significant landmarks, and other points of interest. The map should include a scale, source, date, and north arrow.

Historic Site Conditions Understanding the historic use of a property is one of the most important aspects of a Phase I ESA. Because most existing environmental problems are the result of historic practices or activities, investigation into past activities is essential. The main avenues to the identification of historic activities are review of historic aerial photographs, review of ownership records, and personal interviews.

Historic Aerial Photographs. Historic aerial photographs of the site and vicinity should be obtained. Obtain photographs at approximately five- to ten-year intervals, as far back as possible.

- *Information Content*. Attempts should be made to obtain photographs before and after suspected or documented land use changes. The photographs should be observed for activities with a potential for environmental contamination as exhibited by ground disturbances, stained soils, waste piles, drums, etc.

- *Interpretation*. If available, the photographs should be purchased as stereo pairs and viewed stereoscopically by a trained photointerpreter. Stereoscopic interpretation is important because it allows for three-dimensional viewing, and features such as depressions, piles, or mounds can be distinguished.

- *Sources*. Potential sources of aerial photographs include the U.S. Geological Survey, U.S. Department of Agriculture, and private firms that specialize in aerial photography.

Previous Ownership. Previous ownership records can be traced from the property's chain of title report. These reports are available from title companies.

Historical Research. In addition, insight into the activities of previous owners, tenants, or occupants can sometimes be obtained from building and demolition permits, tax assessment records, historic city directories (the predecessors of modern phone books), and historic insurance maps.

Personal Interviews. Individuals familiar with the subject site and adjacent properties should be interviewed. These individuals may include current or previous site owners, tenants, and employees. Individuals occupying nearby properties may also provide valuable information on past activities.

Potential Environmental Threats

Environmental threats include active or abandoned operations, facilities, or land uses that may have an impact on the environmental quality of the subject site and its environs. Potential environmental threats should be identified by the review of environmental databases and contacts with regulatory agencies.

National Databases. The following databases are available on a nationwide basis and can be obtained from the appropriate regional office of the U.S. Environmental Protection Agency. These databases may already have been reviewed by the RTC during the initial screening phase to identify potential environmental issues. If these databases have not been reviewed within the past six months, they should be reviewed by the environmental contractor during the Phase I ESA to determine if the subject site or nearby properties are listed.

- CERCLIS
- RCRA Notifiers
- SARA Title III
- Open Dumps

State Lists. State environmental agencies also maintain databases that should be reviewed. These databases may address underground storage tank notification records, state-permitted landfills, and other solid waste disposal sites.

Relevance to Site. Significant threats, such as CERCLIS sites and state-listed uncontrolled hazardous waste sites, located within a one-mile radius of the subject property are normally evaluated in a Phase I ESA. The radius of evaluation may be reduced to approximately a quarter mile for other sites (e.g., RCRA and SARA Title III notifiers), because they generally pose a less significant threat. These distances can be adjusted up or down, depending on whether the threats are upgradient or downgradient of the property, the type of past and current land uses in the vicinity of the property, the likely significance of individual threats to the property, and other site-specific factors.

Other Inquiries. Regulatory agencies should also be contacted to further determine whether there are any outstanding environmental violations or issues related to the subject property or off-site regulated businesses that may pose a threat to the property, and to verify any allegations related to environmental contamination. Government agencies normally contacted include the local fire department, health department, and local, county, state, and federal environmental agencies.

Note: While telephone inquiry to these regulatory agencies is the most direct method, many agencies will only reply to written Freedom of Information Act requests. Because replies to written requests can take up to three months, it may be appropriate to avoid relying heavily on regulatory agency replies when developing conclusions for a site.

Site Reconnaissance The site reconnaissance should focus on signs of potential contamination and assess the site in relation to surrounding property uses and natural surface features. The site reconnaissance should be conducted by an experienced environmental professional whose evaluation emphasizes the identification of:

- Past or present hazardous material usage and waste disposal practices

- Visible signs of stressed vegetation or soil or water contamination

- Site conditions or activities that could potentially result in soil or ground water contamination

- Presence of surface and subsurface storage tanks, drums, barrels, and other storage containers

- Waste generated on site and hazardous material handling practices (including, but not limited to, pesticides)

- Electrical or hydraulic equipment that may contain PCBs

- Building materials that may contain asbestos.

It is particularly important to investigate waste and wastewater disposal practices at sites that have handled chemicals. Inappropriate disposal (e.g., dumping down the septic system) could have occurred.

Surrounding Properties. After the subject property has been evaluated, the surrounding properties should be surveyed to visually identify those that may potentially affect the environmental integrity of the subject property. Surrounding properties that may pose potential environmental threats include gasoline stations, junk yards, manufacturing facilities, or sites identified in the environmental database review.

Interviews. Since many sites are not strictly regulated, the environmental professional should attempt to interview adjacent or hydrologically upgradient property owners to obtain information about historic site conditions, as well as to inquire whether any environmental incidents, such as leaking tanks or chemical spills, are known to have occurred in the past.

Other Sources. Other site records that may be located or identified during the site reconnaissance should also be reviewed. For example, existing reports on geotechnical borings should be reviewed to determine the presence and cleanliness of any fill material.

Environmental Setting The environmental setting of the property is characterized to evaluate potential routes of exposure to, or the migration pathways of, contaminants, and to assist in the development of recommendations for Phase II ESAs. For example, if a leaking underground storage tank is suspected to be on site, ground water contamination will be a concern. Information on the depth to ground water and directions of ground water flow will be important in the assessment of contaminant fate and exposure.

Method. Characterization of the general environmental setting is accomplished through the collection and review of readily available references, reports, and maps. Detailed field investigations, which are typically beyond the scope of a Phase I ESA, would be required to characterize site-specific environmental conditions.

Topics. Components of the environmental setting to be addressed, and potential sources of information, are listed below.

- *Topography*. Discuss the range of site elevations, overall site topography or slope, and significant physiographic features such as ridges and stream valleys. In the absence of site-specific hydrogeologic data, surface topography can be used to infer the direction of ground water flow (and therefore the direction of flow of contaminated waters) in near-surface aquifers. The U.S. Geological Survey's (USGS) 7.5 minute topographic maps can be used for most areas of the country.

- *Soils*. Identify soil types and general characteristics such as drainage, permeability, soil mantle, and depth to bedrock. Soils data assist in determining the ease with which contaminants may migrate laterally and downward, depth to ground water, and suitability for underground storage tanks (some soils are highly corrosive to metals and may speed the failure of steel tanks). Soil data can be obtained from county soil surveys. Surveys are published by the U.S. Department of Agriculture (USDA) Soil Conservation Service, and are available for most counties.

- *Geology*. Geologic data may be limited for some sites. If possible, local geologic formations should be described (e.g., rock types, impermeable layers, bedrock characteristics). These characteristics assist in determining the susceptibility of ground water to contamination. For example, aquifers or water-bearing zones located beneath impermeable layers of rock or soil are somewhat protected from contamination by near-surface contaminant sources such as leaking underground storage tanks. Potential data sources include the USGS and state and local environmental agencies.

- *Hydrology*. Hydrologic data may not be readily available for all sites, but should be addressed to the extent possible. Determine approximate depth to ground water, ground water quality, direction of flow, aquifer productivity, and suitability for use or consumption. For surface water, describe site drainage and water quality. Hydrologic data are important in assessing the significance of water contamination. For example, contaminated ground water in a naturally poor quality aquifer with no withdrawal for human use would generally not be considered significant. Potential sources of hydrologic data include the USGS and state and local environmental or water resource agencies.

Conclusions and Recommendations Upon completion of the Phase I ESA, conclusions should be presented concerning key observations and findings. The conclusions should emphasize any environmental threats or suspect activities (current or historic) identified at the subject site and vicinity. Appropriate recommendations for additional investigations or environmental sampling and analysis under a Phase II ESA should be made.

RESOLUTION TRUST CORPORATION
Suggested Phase I Report Format

1. **Introduction**
    1.1 Purpose and Organization of Report
    1.2 Site Background
        1.2.1 Site Description
        1.2.2 Site History

2. **Study Area Investigation: Physical Characteristics**
    2.1 Topography
    2.2 Soils/Geology
    2.3 Surface Water Hydrology
    2.4 Hydrogeology

3. **Historic Site Conditions**
    3.1 Interviews
    3.2 Historical Aerial Photographs
    3.3 Historical Document Review (including previous owners and site uses)

4. **Current Site Conditions**
    4.1 Description of Current Property Use
    4.2 Description of Adjacent Land Use

5. **Review of Regulatory Agency Records**
    5.1 Hazardous/Regulated Wastes
    5.2 Underground Storage Tanks
    5.3 Discharge Incidents
    5.4 Discharge Permits
    5.5 Transformers

6. **Review of Environmental Databases**
    6.1 Comprehensive Environmental Response, Compensation and Liability Information System (CERCLIS)
    6.2 RCRA Notifiers
    6.3 SARA Title III Notifiers and Report
    6.4 Open Dumps

7. **Summary and Conclusions**
    7.1 Summary
        7.1.1 Nature and Extent of Contamination
        7.1.2 Fate and Transport
    7.2 Conclusions and Recommendations
        7.2.1 Data Results and Limitations
        7.2.2 Recommendations Concerning Additional Investigations

Appendixes
    A. Technical Memoranda on Field Activities
    B. Summaries of Interviews
    C. Documentation of Assets Search

PCBs: polychlorinated biphenyls, used in electrical equipment (transformers, ballasts, etc.); leaks look like oil

Miscellaneous wastes

Resolution Trust Corporation Environmental Guidelines: Phase I Outline

Focuses more strongly on documentary research: "appropriate inquiry" to establish innocent landowner defense under CERCLA

Introduction: site identification, map, purpose, objective, and scope of services

Historic site conditions: documented in aerial photos, ownership records, interviews, and other sources

Potential environmental threats known to government databases and regulatory agencies: CERCLIS, RCRA, SARA Title III, open dumps, state lists

- One-mile radius for major threats (CERCLIS), quarter mile for lesser hazards
- Local fire department, health department; federal, state, county, and local environmental agencies

Site reconnaissance

- Visible signs of potential contamination, relation to surrounding uses and natural features
- Tanks, vegetation damage, electrical equipment (PCBs), hazardous material use or disposal, asbestos

Environmental setting

- Topography, geology, and hydrology affect migration patterns of contaminants
- USGS and USDA maps and soil surveys provide information

Conclusions and recommendations: note any potential threats and recommend further study or sampling in Phase II if appropriate

COURSE 11
Phase II & III Environmental Inspections

INTRODUCTION

Especially on nonresidential properties, further examination beyond the Phase I inspection is sometimes required. If a Phase II report is recommended by the Phase I environmental inspector, samplings will be taken and analyzed, and corrective recommendations may be developed in Phase III. Phase II and III analyses are highly technical, and the property owner, lender, or real estate practitioner will normally be involved as the client of a specialized environmental consulting firm. The purpose of this course is to outline the steps involved in each stage.

Value of Inspections A well-prepared environmental inspection report serves as the client's first line of defense in a business and political climate that is becoming increasingly protective of the environment and increasingly concerned about liability. Early inspections will head off unanticipated cleanup costs imposed after the client has acquired the property.

Nonresidential Properties Since these additional inspection phases are most likely to occur for commercial, industrial, and special purpose properties, this course will be of particular interest to licensees engaged in the leasing, sale, or hypothecation of these property types. A real estate practitioner dealing in commercial and industrial properties should develop an awareness of site characteristics that could signal an environmental hazard, and the possible costs and timelines involved in investigation and remedial action.

PHASE II AND III OVERVIEW

A Phase II report is normally recommended if the Phase I inspection shows that hazardous materials are or have been located on the property and may threaten the health of people or the environment. A variety of situations might suggest evaluation past the Phase I stage; examples include the following:

- Older industrial facilities with insufficient capacity to deal adequately with wastes

- Abandoned gasoline stations where soil oxidation causes potential underground tank leakage

- Agrarian sites where there is evidence of extensive pesticide use

- Older structures with potential asbestos exposure

- Undocumented underground tanks with no evidence of soundness

- Property already identified as a hazardous waste site on RCRA, CERCLA, or other lists

- Proximity to any form of mining or extractive activity or solid waste landfill

Phase II: Technical Analysis Phase II site assessment is normally handled as a phased series of samplings and analyses, divided into *initial* and *expanded* categories. Some situations suggest an immediate expanded Phase II study, where hazards are already known from previous studies.

Costs. Laboratory analysis costs are likely to be the largest Phase II expense, ranging from a few thousand dollars to several hundred thousand dollars. Fieldwork collecting samples involves labor, materials, and equipment, and is usually the second largest cost in a Phase II assessment. Remediation costs, most dramatically for soil contamination at abandoned gas station sites, can reach millions of dollars, sometimes far exceeding the value of the site.

Initial Phase II The main purpose of initial Phase II investigation is to determine *whether a hazardous materials release has occurred* that could result in health and environmental hazards. It involves three basic steps:

- Determine what samplings are initially required. This is done based on the observations in Phase I (suspicious ground water, chemical vats, underground tanks, faulty insulation, older transformers, etc.).

- Arrange and conduct site inspection and sampling.

- Recommend further site assessment or determine that further analysis is unnecessary.

Sampling. This involves examination and gathering of contaminants from the soils, air, water, or improvements on the site to verify toxicity and other hazards. The extent of sampling varies with results obtained in Phase I.

- *Precautions.* It is extremely important that workers and the general public be protected with appropriate safety equipment and procedures, and that properly identified and uncorrupted samples are sent to the testing laboratory.

- *Scheduling.* Since analysis often takes a long time, it is important to begin sampling early, and some form of Gantt or critical path tracking method may be appropriate.

Recommendations. The initial phase might result in recommendations for expanded study, notification of environmental agencies of severely impacted sites, or initiating interim measures to deal with site conditions.

Expanded Phase II If the initial Phase II has confirmed the presence of hazards, the expanded Phase II examines and describes the contaminants in detail, as to type, amount, effects, and recommendations.

Phase II Report Format The appropriate format varies with the environmental hazards at a given site. The data must be organized in a logical fashion that the client can comprehend. A sample format might be:

- Introduction: scope of the report, site location and history, prior site assessments

- Field investigation

- Physical characteristics of site

- Nature and extent of site contamination

- Contaminant dispersion, migration, and persistence, within the site and to adjoining areas

- Risk assessment for potential dangers to human health

- Summary, conclusions, recommendations

- Technical appendixes, including detailed description of field work, analytical data, and the like.

Phase III Environmental Site Assessment: Remediation

Once the findings from Phase II have been collected, evaluated, and reported, remedial alternatives are developed and screened. The EPA has procedures for screening remedial alternatives, somewhat similar to the investigation of alternatives in an Environmental Impact Report.

Alternative Solutions. Through a careful sifting of the results of both laboratory and field work, a list of alternative solutions to neutralize the site's environmental problems is compiled. Alternatives on this list are then compared for the potential of:

- Accomplishing benchmarks for site cleanup geared to existing regulations

- Lessening adverse environmental and health impacts

- Cost containment, particularly through innovative technology.

Choices of Alternatives. Following this filtering process, the next stage of Phase III reduces the alternatives and reaches a final conclusion as to the remedial action required. In certain instances "no action" may be an appropriate recommendation. A detailed analytical report addresses the following:

- Cost estimates including a time frame (e.g., decontamination expenditure of $150,000 annually for five years)

- Engineering or structures required in the remedial process (e.g., erection of a water treatment plant)

- Effects on the environment and on public health and safety.

Feasibility Study. After duly weighing the remedial alternatives in accordance with state and federal guidelines, the Phase III feasibility study analyzes the ultimate recommendation and formulates a plan of action.

Report Format. An outline similar to Phase II is used that includes:

- Introduction and executive summary: review of report's objective and of site characteristics

- Technologies: remedial objectives and available treatment responses (e.g., removal of oil pollution from water by use of phosphates, or some form of filtering instead of phosphates)

- Screening of alternatives: comparative examination of a full range of alternatives

- Detailed analysis of selected alternatives: rationale for selection of the single alternative which most exemplifies adherence to state and federal standards, community acceptance, cost effectiveness, and the least impact on public health and safety

- Recommendations: proposing the most effective alternative for removing the hazards on the site.

Action. From this stage on, action is initiated to implement the recommendations of the feasibility study, challenge them, or, in extreme cases, abandon the site.

PHASE II ENVIRONMENTAL SITE ASSESSMENT: RTC GUIDELINES

The RTC (Resolution Trust Corporation) has the most highly developed environmental assessment guidelines, because it has been the recipient of a variety of environmentally impacted sites through foreclosure. The RTC's Phase II and Phase III guidelines, including suggested report formats, are presented here.

Phase I Results At the completion of the Phase I environmental site analysis (ESA), the RTC representative will have made a preliminary evaluation concerning the likelihood that hazardous materials are or have been located on the property, the likelihood that releases of such materials have occurred or are occurring, and the likelihood that the past, present, or future releases have resulted or will result in exposures that may threaten the health of humans or the environment.

Recommendation for a Phase II ESA The recommendation to implement a Phase II ESA depends on several important factors, including the nature of the property under investigation, the quantity and quality of information gathered during the Phase I ESA, and the strength of the evidence that human or environmental exposures have occurred or are occurring. No specific guidelines exist, however, to calculate when Phase II ESA sampling and analysis should be conducted.

Judgment Required. The professional judgment of the RTC environmental specialist is the most important factor in assessing the need for a Phase II ESA. Certain situations that strongly suggest the need for the sampling and analysis associated with a Phase II ESA can be anticipated, including manufacturing and gas station sites and known hazardous waste sites according to EPA's RCRA or CERCLA programs.

Types of Phase II ESAs The findings of the Phase I ESA may indicate that sampling and analysis of materials or environmental media is required to assess the suspected presence of contamination that may be hazardous to human health or the environment. Such a recommendation for sampling and analysis will form the basis for the scope of the Phase II ESA. Phase II ESAs will differ from one property to another depending on the timing of the Phase II ESA and the scope of the Phase I ESA.

Phased Approach. Due to the limited scope of Phase I ESAs and the uncertainties they leave regarding the magnitude of any known or suspected contamination and health risk, Phase II ESAs generally consist of a phased approach of study involving multiple rounds of sampling and analysis. In practice, this phased approach is often referred to as an Initial Phase II ESA and an Expanded Phase II ESA. The following sections discuss typical rationales for selecting an Initial or Expanded Phase II ESA and their respective scope and components.

Selection Rationale   At all but the most exceptional properties, an Initial Phase II ESA would be initiated before an Expanded Phase II. Possible exceptions would be where the equivalent of an Initial Phase II ESA has already been conducted. Obviously, the availability of such preexisting data does not always mandate an Expanded Phase II ESA, because it is possible that it documents the *absence* of the suspected hazardous materials.

Preexisting Data. Examples of preexisting data comparable to an Initial Phase II ESA include:

- Asbestos survey results for commercial buildings

- Radon monitoring results for residential buildings, affordable housing units, and commercial buildings

- Results of leak testing of underground storage tanks

- Contamination survey results in conjunction with the Environmental Protection Agency's RCRA or CERCLA programs.

Notorious Sites. In rare circumstances an Expanded Phase II ESA might be recommended at a property in the absence of any preexisting hazardous materials monitoring data. Such properties are becoming rare today due to the enforcement of strict environmental regulations over the past decade, but examples of such circumstances would include:

- A property such as a rural gasoline station that has leaking underground storage tanks evidenced by obviously degraded ground water (determinable by taste and odor) as reported by adjacent property owners.

- A property for which a consensus exists among the local property owners that it is a well-known (albeit unofficial) source of risk to human health. Such a property might be an abandoned former manufacturing facility known to have had severe hazardous materials spills or disposal facilities such as open lagoons.

Initial Phase II Components   Initial Phase II ESAs are necessary at properties where, based on the judgment of the RTC representative, the information from Phase I indicates that a hazardous materials release has occurred, resulting in potential human health or environmental hazards. The principal objective of the Initial Phase II ESA is to *confirm whether a release has occurred* by implementing a *limited* program of collection and analysis of appropriate site samples.

Scope. The key characteristic of the Initial Phase II is its limited scope; it is only intended to confirm the occurrence of hazardous materials. Efforts to *characterize* the release fully in terms of extent, magnitude, and migration potential are beyond the scope of the Initial Phase II. There are four principal components of an Initial Phase II ESA:

- Development of a sampling plan
- Preparations for the site visit
- Conducting the sampling visit
- Making recommendations for further action or no action.

Development of the Sampling Plan

The sampling plan clearly states the objectives of the sampling effort in terms of the types of samples, the number of samples, the analytical parameters, and the rationale for why the sampling is required. Additionally, the sampling plan provides details concerning methods of sample collection, preservation, transportation, and analysis.

Scope. The scope of an Initial Phase II ESA is generally small enough that the required sampling plan components can be presented in a single document. This contrasts with the sampling plan for an Expanded Phase II, which may be so extensive as to require separately bound documents dedicated to individual topics (Sampling and Analysis Plan, Quality Assurance and Quality Control Plan, etc.).

Complexity. Routine sampling plans (simple plans that address very limited scopes such as collection of a few asbestos or radon samples) can usually be standardized, prepared, and administered by RTC staff. In contrast, subcontractors who specialize in quantitative environmental assessments may be used to prepare nonroutine sampling plans for more involved Initial Phase II ESAs. More involved Initial Phase II ESAs may, for example, call for ground water and soil monitoring.

Extent and Locations of Sampling

At a minimum, one sample of each environmental medium suspected to be a source of hazardous material (air, soil, floor wipes, etc.) should be collected. If different classes of contaminants are suspected (i.e., metals and organics) for which different analytical procedures are required, more than one sample (a soil sample for metals analysis and a second soil sample for organics analysis) would be necessary. In general, this stage requires no more samples than are necessary to confirm whether the suspected environmental medium is a source of hazardous material.

Types of Tests. If the investigator does not know the type of hazardous materials that may be on site, but suspects their presence, indicators such as total organic halogens (TOX), total petroleum hydrocarbons (TPH), specific conductivity, pH, etc., may be appropriate initial parameters. However, it is preferred that specific analytical parameters be identified.

Laboratory Procedures. Typically, laboratories that specialize in the analysis of environmental samples classify the constituents or contaminants of interest into broad classes of compounds for which class-specific analytical procedures are available. The most common classes are listed below, although there are many other less common classes:

- Volatile organic compounds (VOCs)

- Base-, neutral-, and acid-extractable compounds (BNAs)
- Pesticides and PCBs
- Anions and cations
- Metals
- Miscellaneous constituents or contaminants (i.e., cyanide, phenols).

Plan Format and Content The sampling plan should present a concise synopsis of the required sampling and associated procedures and analytical methods. The following points summarize the information that should be contained in the sampling plan under RTC guidelines.

Quality Assurance and Quality Control. Identify the number and type of quality assurance samples, specifically the number of blanks, duplicates, or spikes that will be taken. The specific QA/QC guidelines to be followed in this program are to be stipulated by each RTC Region.

Equipment Decontamination. Identify the reagents and any special procedures associated with equipment decontamination.

Chain of Custody. All samples collected (including blanks and spikes) must be maintained under chain of custody procedures. Chain of custody minimizes the potential for damaging or losing samples before they are analyzed. Chain of custody tracks the possession of a sample from the time of collection, through all transfers of custody, to when it is received in the laboratory, where internal laboratory chain of custody procedures take over. Investigators should generally follow regional protocols for chain of custody procedures.

Field Operation. Discuss the sequence for conducting the field activities.

Sampling Locations and Rationale. As precisely as possible, identify the location of each sample. A site map should be prepared to guide the investigator to the appropriate locations. Specific sampling methods, the number of samples, the parameters being sampled, and a description of the objectives for each sampling activity should be included in the sampling plan.

Analytical Requirements. Discuss the technique and level of detection that will be used to analyze each sample.

Handling. Describe sample preservation and other handling practices.

Preparing for Sampling If required resources exceed those available, the sampling plan may be revised. Prior to actual sampling and analysis at the property, the following steps must be taken:

Ensure Access to the Property. The sampling team must make sure that they have access to the property and that they are capable of identifying the locations and media to be sampled. If sampling is to be conducted at adjacent properties, they need to secure permission and access.

Community Relations. If sampling is to be conducted in areas where bystanders are anticipated (especially residential areas), particularly if health and safety equipment such as respirators will be used, procedures for reassuring the public and maintaining community relations should be established.

Health and Safety Plan. A health and safety plan should address the following issues:

- Suspected hazards and risks
- Levels of protection to be worn
- Decontamination procedures
- Documentation of health and safety training given to the sampling crew.

Conducting the Sampling Visit The actual sampling visit involves:

- Reviewing the sampling plan
- Documenting the visit with photographs
- Tracking sampling activities with a field logbook
- Factual descriptions of structures and features
- Sketches of the property layout and sample collection locations.
- Decontamination and demobilization
- Sample shipment and analysis

Decontamination and Demobilization. Decontaminate persons and equipment, as necessary, prior to rest breaks and departure from the property.

Sample Shipment and Analysis Careful tracking should ensure that the samples are analyzed for the appropriate parameters, that all samples sent to the laboratory are actually received, and that the samples are analyzed within the prescribed holding times. Analysis may require from several days to several weeks (sometimes months for Expanded Phase IIs). This time lag must be considered when making projections of the amount of time necessary to determine the disposition of a property.

Recommendations The final task of the Initial Phase II is to make recommendations concerning the need for further actions at the property. These may include:

- No further action
- Conducting an Expanded Phase II to more fully characterize contamination confirmed by the Initial Phase II
- Planning and implementing interim measures at the property
- Notifying environmental regulatory personnel about particularly severe environmental contamination.

Expanded Phase II The components of an Expanded Phase II ESA are identical to those of an Initial Phase II except for the scope of the investigation.

Media. As a general rule, an Expanded Phase II will concentrate on the sampling and analysis of *environmental* media such as soil, ground water, and surface water, while the Initial Phase II ESA usually will have focused on the sampling and analysis of *building* materials, indoor air, materials spilled within the confines of buildings, and the like.

Analysis. While the purpose of the Initial Phase II is to confirm the *presence* or *absence* of hazardous materials, the objective of the Expanded Phase II is to *characterize* the contamination. Characterization refers to:

- *Type.* Specifying the *type* of contamination present, particularly if its presence was confirmed using generic indicator tests such as TOX, TPH, etc.

- *Occurrence.* Assessing three-dimensional *occurrence* (distribution) of the contamination by increasing sampling frequencies both horizontally and vertically.

- *Migration.* Assessing *migration* rates, directions, and possible human and environmental receptors and the risks posed to them, in relation to natural environmental conditions such as climate and ground water occurrence and flow direction.

- *Monitoring.* Establishing a *data base* as a basis for documentation of changes in the occurrence of the contamination.

Endangerment Assessment. The Phase II ESA evaluates the potential impacts, if any, of the property on public health and the environment by conducting an endangerment assessment. The potential exposure of people and sensitive environmental systems is estimated. Exposure pathways and points of possible human and environmental exposure are identified, and populations, if any, that may be at risk are characterized. Environmental concentrations of significant constituents are calculated at all exposure points and compared to applicable standards and criteria.

Scope. There is an almost unlimited range of scope and complexity for Expanded Phase II ESAs; each one is determined on the basis of the existing data. Scope requirements for the Expanded Phase II ESA are best developed by individuals experienced in the interpretation of Initial Phase II ESAs and having a working knowledge of regulations.

Report Format The following outline is the Resolution Trust Corporation's suggested Phase II format. It summarizes site history and previous investigations, field methods and findings, nature and extent of contamination, natural features of the site as they relate to migration of contaminants, and degree of risk to human health and the environment. Some but not all of the subjects listed under each heading will be addressed, depending on the particular site.

Resolution Trust Corporation
Suggested Phase II Report Format

Executive Summary

1. Introduction
   1.1 Purpose and Organization of Report
   1.2 Site Background
      1.2.1 Site Description
      1.2.2 Site History
      1.2.3 Previous Investigations

2. Study Area Investigation
   2.1 Includes field activities associated with site characterization. These may include physical and chemical monitoring of some, but not necessarily all of the following:
      - Surface Features (topographic mapping, etc.): natural and manmade features
      - Contaminant Source Investigations
      - Meteorological Investigations
      - Surface Water and Sediment Investigations
      - Geological Investigations
      - Soil and Vadose Zone Investigations
      - Ground Water Investigations
      - Human Population Surveys
      - Ecological Investigations
   2.2 If technical memoranda documenting field activities were prepared, they may be included in an appendix and summarized in this report chapter.

3. Physical Characteristics of the Study Area
   3.1 Includes results of field activities to determine physical characteristics. These may include some, but not necessarily all of the following:
      - Surface Features
      - Meteorology
      - Surface Water Hydrology
      - Geology
      - Soils
      - Hydrogeology
      - Demography and Land Use
      - Ecology

4. Nature and Extent of Contamination

    4.1 Present the results of site characterization, both natural chemical components and contaminants, in some but not necessarily all of the following media:
    - Sources (lagoons, sludge, tanks, etc.)
    - Soils and Vadose Zone
    - Ground Water
    - Surface Water and Sediments
    - Air

5. Contaminant Fate and Transport

    5.1 Potential Routes of Migration (air, ground water, etc.)

    5.2 Contaminant Persistence

        5.2.1 If applicable (for organic contaminants), describe estimated persistence in the study area environment and physical, chemical, or biological factors of importance for the media of interest.

    5.3 Contaminant Migration

        5.3.1 Discuss factors affecting contaminant migration for the media of importance (sorption onto soils, solubility in water, movement of ground water, etc.)

        5.3.2 Discuss modeling methods and results, if applicable.

6. Baseline Risk Assessment

    6.1 Human Health Evaluation

        6.1.1 Exposure Assessment

        6.1.2 Toxicity Assessment

        6.1.3 Risk Characterization

    6.2 Environmental Evaluation

7. Summary and Conclusions

    7.1 Summary

        7.1.1 Nature and Extent of Contamination

        7.1.2 Fate and Transport

        7.1.3 Risk Assessment

    7.2 Conclusions

        7.2.1 Data Limitations and Recommendations for Future Work

        7.2.2 Recommended Remedial Action Objectives

Appendixes

A. Technical Memoranda on Field Activities (if available)
B. Analytical Data and Quality Assurance/Quality Control Evaluation Results
C. Risk Assessment Methods

PHASE III ENVIRONMENTAL SITE ASSESSMENT: RTC GUIDELINES

The Phase III ESA is intended to *evaluate in detail* the data compiled during the Phase II ESA, as well as all applicable geologic and hydrogeologic conditions, environmental and public health risks, etc. Based on this evaluation, the Phase III ESA develops, screens, and provides a cost estimate for one or more *remedial alternatives* to address contamination on the property.

General Approach The approach to analyzing remedial alternatives conforms, in general, to the approach outlined under Subpart F of the National Contingency Plan (NCP), as described in 40 CFR Part 300 (§300.68). The NCP is the document that outlines response powers, responsibilities, and authorities under CERCLA.

Two-Stage Approach. The NCP provides a general framework for evaluation of possible remedial options and for identifying remedial alternatives that are "consistent with permanent remedy to prevent or mitigate the migration of a release of hazardous substances into the environment." The procedures can be divided into two parts:

☐ Development and preliminary screening of alternatives (general response actions)

☐ Detailed analysis of selected alternatives.

Part 1: Preliminary Screening The initial phase involves the development of a comprehensive list of general remedial actions to be considered. Data from the Phase I and II ESAs are reviewed to identify general categories of response actions and broadly define the nature of the required response.

Range of Responses. Selected response actions appropriate to various property problems are presented in USEPA documents. These are to be considered in the elimination process, supplemented by knowledge of workable, property-specific procedures. By eliminating inapplicable responses at this stage, emphasis can be placed on alternatives with greater potential applicability to the problems under consideration.

Performance Standards. The first phase of remedial alternatives analysis for the property includes the establishment of appropriate performance standards or cleanup criteria as a basis for the evaluation of remedial alternatives. Standards may be presented in the form of cleanup levels (concentrations) for specific contaminants, where such levels are available, or goals for contamination control (prevention of further contaminant migration).

Preliminary Screening of Alternatives. The assembled list of remedial alternatives is screened according to specified environmental, public health, legal, regulatory, and cost criteria. Innovative as well as established technologies should be carried through this screening process if the analysis demonstrates that there is a reasonable probability that they will provide better treatment, fewer adverse impacts, or lower costs than demonstrated treatment technologies.

Part 2: Detailed Evaluation of Selected Alternatives After applying the technical, environmental and public health, legal and regulatory, and cost screens, the remaining remedial alternatives are examined in greater detail. A "no action" (no further study or remediation) alternative should always be included in the detailed analysis.

Level of Analysis. The NCP states that the analysis should include "detailed cost estimation, including distribution of costs over time; evaluation in terms of engineering implementation or constructability; an assessment of each alternative in terms of the extent to which it is expected to . . . provide adequate protection of public health, welfare, and the environment; and analysis of any adverse environmental impacts, methods of mitigating these impacts, and costs of mitigation." Detailed technical, economic, environmental, legal, regulatory, and public health evaluations should be conducted.

Technical. Each remedial alternative should undergo detailed evaluation of technical factors including performance and reliability. The ability to construct each remedial technology under the site conditions and the time required to implement each alternative should be assessed. In addition, the safety of workers and the public during and after construction should be considered.

Public Health and Environment. Potential impacts, if any, of each remedial alternative on public health and the environment are evaluated in detail to assess potential exposure of people and sensitive environmental systems, potential exposure pathways, and populations at risk. Environmental concentrations of the "indicator chemical" identified by the Phase II ESA should be estimated at all exposure points and compared to applicable standards and criteria.

Comparative Table. The results of the detailed analyses are summarized in a tabular format that compares cost, health risks, environmental impacts, performance, technical reliability, and other important factors. This table will facilitate the selection of a preferred alternative.

Selection Criteria. Under the NCP, the alternative selected should be the "lowest cost alternative that is technologically feasible and reliable and which effectively mitigates and minimizes damage to and provides adequate protection of public health, welfare, or the environment." The selected remedy should:

- Be protective of human health and the environment

- Be cost effective

- Attain "applicable, relevant, and appropriate requirements" (ARARs) that have been identified by federal and state public health and environmental agencies for a National Priorities List (NPL) site

- Utilize permanent solutions and alternative treatment or resource recovery technologies to the maximum extent practicable.

Exceptions. SARA provides exceptions to the attainment of ARARs for six circumstances:

- Balancing of the Superfund

- Technical impracticability

- Selection of an interim remedy

- Greater risk to health and the environment

- Equivalent standard of performance
- Inconsistent application of state standards.

Additional Study. If analysis up to this point does not indicate a single alternative clearly preferred as the optimum choice, additional analyses (such as cost-benefit and decision-risk analyses) may be recommended.

Feasibility Study Report The feasibility study (FS) report should consist of the following major elements:

- Executive summary
- Introduction, including site background information, data on the nature and extent of problems, and objectives of remedial action
- Discussion and results of the preliminary screening of remedial alternatives
- Descriptions of alternatives selected for detailed analysis
- Discussion of the detailed analysis of alternatives, based on technical engineering feasibility, health and environmental, legal and regulatory, and cost considerations
- Summary of analysis results
- Detailed description of the recommended corrective alternatives
- Appendixes supporting documentation of screening and detailed analyses, including cost, technical and engineering feasibility, public health and environmental assessments, legal and regulatory analysis, discussions of the sampling and analysis program, and other items as appropriate.

COSTS ASSOCIATED WITH PHASE II AND III ESAs

The costs for conducting environmental investigative and remediation efforts vary depending on the project. The most costly aspect of any contamination investigation effort is associated with the laboratory. The second is costs associated with fieldwork, including labor and equipment. The following list provides a rough indication of what these costs can be for sites with soil and ground water contamination. Actual costs will vary from case to case, but these estimates provide an order of magnitude.

Field and Laboratory Work The average cost for an initial Phase II ESA to identify types of contaminants and the extent of contamination ranges from $20,000 to $50,000. If more extensive sampling is required to better identify the extent, the cost can be as high as several hundred thousand dollars.

Field Work. Field sampling costs vary depending on the number of samples and depth of sampling; some expected basic costs include:

- $5,000 a day for a geophysics survey
- $200 per sample (including lab fees) for soil gas samples; most soil gas sampling programs will cost in the $7,000 to $15,000 range

- $1,000 to $2,000 for boring installation and sample collection
- $1,500 to $3,000 for monitoring well installation

Laboratory Fees. These will vary depending on the attributes selected for analysis, and can range from $10 to $600 per attribute. An all-encompassing analysis for priority pollutants generally costs $800 to $1,200 per sample.

Corrective Action

Remediation of contaminated soils varies greatly depending on the types of contaminants, the extent of contamination, and the accessibility of feasible treatment and disposal methods and equipment. Remediation costs vary from several tens of thousands of dollars to several million dollars.

Tanks. Removal and disposal of an empty tank generally costs a minimum of $1,500 to $2,500 for tanks under 1,000 gallons. Tanks greater than 1,000 gallons will cost an extra $1,000 to $1,500 per thousand gallons. If a tank still contains material, the cost to remove and dispose of the waste materials can range from $.50 per gallon to $1.50 per gallon. If soils or ground water have been affected by a leaking tank, investigation generally costs tens of thousands of dollars and correction costs several hundred thousand dollars.

Transformers. Retrofilling is the process of removing contaminated dielectric fluids from a transformer or other equipment and replacing the fluid with a non-PCB or oil type fluid. Retrofilling a PCB-contaminated transformer can range in cost from $10 to $100 per gallon of fluid. Retrofilling costs are generally 30 to 70 percent less than cost of disposal and replacement with new transformers.

Hazardous Waste Identification, Disposal, and Treatment. The cost to characterize and identify a waste stream is approximately $1,000 for each waste stream. Disposal of wastes varies depending on the type of contaminant, but can range from $300 to $1,500 per 55-gallon drum.

Radon. Depending on the sophistication of the measuring equipment, a radon testing program can cost $10 to $50 per sample, including analysis but not including labor costs. For single family homes, a radon mitigation system can cost $1,000 to $3,000.

Asbestos. A survey to locate and identify asbestos through bulk sampling methods is frequently required prior to the sale of a building. Building alterations, repairs, or demolition require both a survey to locate asbestos-containing materials and abatement or removal in affected areas. Survey costs range from $0.05 to $0.50 per square foot, depending upon whether a comprehensive or screening (preliminary) survey is conducted. Removal, repair, enclosure, or encapsulation costs vary from $5 to $50 or more per square foot. In addition, operation and maintenance (O&M) programs are a generally low but ongoing building operation expense. The EPA provides recommended procedures for O&M and recommends such a program even if the asbestos is in good condition.

**Resolution Trust Corporation
Suggested Phase III Report Format**

Executive Summary

1. Introduction
   1.1 Purpose and Organization of Report
   1.2 Background Information (summarized from Phase I and II reports)
      1.2.1 Site Description
      1.2.2 Site History
      1.2.3 Nature and Extent of Contamination
      1.2.4 Contaminant Fate and Transport
      1.2.5 Baseline Risk Assessment

2. Identification and Screening of Technologies
   2.1 Introduction
   2.2 Remedial Action Objectives

      Presents the development of remedial action objectives for each medium of interest (ground water, soil, surface water, etc.) relative to the following issues:
      - Contaminants of interest
      - Allowable exposure based on risk assessment
      - Allowable exposure based on ARARs
      - Development of remedial action objectives

   2.3 General Response Actions

      For each medium of interest, describes the estimation of areas or volumes to which treatment, containment, or exposure technologies may be applied

   2.4 Identification and Screening of Technology Types and Process Options

      For each medium of interest, describes:
      2.4.1 Identification and Screening of Technologies
      2.4.2 Evaluation of Technologies and Selection of Representative Technologies

3. Development and Screening of Alternatives
   3.1 Development of Alternatives

      Describes rationale for combination of technologies and media into alternatives

   3.2 Screening of Alternatives
      3.2.1 Introduction
      3.2.2 Alternative 1
         - Description
         - Evaluation
         - Effectiveness
         - Implementability

- Cost
    3.2.3 Alternative 2
    - Description
    - Evaluation
    3.2.4 Alternative 3
    3.2.5 Summary of Screening
4. Detailed Analysis of Alternatives
    4.1 Introduction
    4.2 Alternative Analysis
        4.2.1 Alternative 1
            4.2.1.1 Description
            4.2.1.2 Assessment
                - Short-Term Effectiveness
                - Long-Term Effectiveness and Permanence
                - Reduction of Mobility, Toxicity and Volume
                - Implementability
                - Cost
                - Compliance with ARARs
                - Overall Protection
                - State Acceptance
                - Community Acceptance
        4.2.2 Alternative 2
            4.2.2.1 Description
            4.2.2.2 Assessment
        4.2.3 Alternative 3
        4.2.4 Summary of Alternatives Analysis
    4.3 Comparison Among Alternatives
        4.3.1 Short-Term Effectiveness
        4.3.2 Long-Term Effectiveness and Permanence
        4.3.3 Reduction of Toxicity, Mobility, and Volume
        4.3.4 Implementability
        4.3.5 Cost
        4.3.6 Compliance with ARARs
        4.3.7 Overall Protection
        4.3.8 State Acceptance
        4.3.9 Community Acceptance
        4.3.10 Summary of Comparisons Among Alternatives
    4.4 Summary of Detailed Analysis

Glossary of Terms: Phase II and III Inspections

Abatement. Reducing the degree or intensity of pollution.

Adsorption. A way of treating wastes in which carbon removes organic matter.

Aerosol. A suspension of fine solid or liquid particles in the air. Particulates under 1 micron (millionth of a meter) in diameter are generally called aerosols.

Air Monitoring. The continuous sampling for and measuring of pollutants present in the atmosphere.

Aquifer. Geological formation, group of formations, or part of a ground formation that is usually gravel or porous, and capable of yielding water to wells or springs.

Biological Hazardous Wastes. Any substance of a human or animal origin other than food wastes which is to be disposed of and could harbor or transmit pathogenic organisms. Includes but is not limited to medical wastes such as tissues, blood elements, excreta, secretions, bandages, and related substances.

CERCLA. Comprehensive Environmental Response, Compensation and Liability Act (also referred to as Superfund). Federal law that imposes joint, several, and strict liability for individuals, corporations, and owners or operators for any site which has been declared to be an "imminent hazard" to human health or the environment.

Closure. Actions taken by the owner or operator of a hazardous waste facility to prepare the site for long-term care and to make it suitable for other uses after it has stopped accepting waste.

Combustible Liquid. Any liquid having a flash point above 100 degrees Fahrenheit as determined by tests.

Commercial Waste. All solid waste emanating from establishments engaged in business. This category includes but is not limited to, solid waste originating in stores, markets, office buildings, restaurants, shopping centers, and theaters.

Compliance Monitoring Program. A program used to determine whether ground water, air quality, or other performance standards are exceeded.

Contamination. The degradation of natural water, air, or soil quality by foreign substances, to the extent that its usefulness is impaired.

Contingency Plan. A document setting forth an organized, planned, and coordinated course of action to be followed in order to prevent pollution in case of fire, explosion, or discharge of hazardous waste constituents which could threaten human health and the environment.

Cover Material. Soil or other suitable material that is used to cover wastes daily or periodically in a properly operated sanitary or secure landfill.

Cradle-to-Grave. The tracking of the source, quantity, concentration, and type of hazardous waste from generation through final disposal.

Decontamination. The process of making any person, object, or area safe by absorbing, destroying, neutralizing, or removing biological or chemical agents.

Discharge. The accidental or intentional spilling, leaking, pumping, pouring, emitting, emptying, or dumping of hazardous waste into or on any land or water.

Disposal Facility. A collection of equipment and associated land area which serves to receive waste and dispose of it.

DOT. U.S. Department of Transportation. Regulates transportation of chemicals and other substances, to aid in the protection of the public and assist fire, law enforcement, and other emergency-response agencies when transportation incidents occur involving hazardous materials. Detailed DOT classification lists specify appropriate warnings, such as Oxidizing Agent or Flammable Liquid, which must be used for various substances.

Dump. A land site at which waste is disposed of in a manner which does not protect the environment, is susceptible to open burning, or is exposed to the elements, vermin, or scavengers.

Dust. Any solid particulate matter over 1 micron (millionth of a meter) in size.

Effluent. Solid, liquid, or gas wastes that enter the environment as a byproduct of various processes; discharge or outflow of water from ground or sub-surface storage.

Electrodialysis. A treatment by which electricity attracts or draws the mineral salts from sewage.

Encapsulation. The complete enclosure of a substance in another material in such a way as to isolate it from external effects such as those of water or air, or from contact with humans or the environment.

Feasibility Study. A detailed examination of the technical, environmental, engineering, economic, legal, and practical suitability of a proposed facility or technology for use at a specific location.

Filter Collector. A mechanical filtration system for a moving particulate matter from a gas stream, for measurement, analysis, or control. Also called bag collector.

Fluorides. Gaseous or solid compounds, containing fluorine, emitted into the air from a number of industrial processes. Fluorides are a major cause of vegetation and livestock damage.

Final Closure. The measures that must be taken to render a facility environmentally harmless when it determines that it will no longer accept waste for treatment, storage, or disposal.

Fume. Solid particles under 1 micron (millionth of a meter) in diameter, formed as vapors condense or as chemical reactions take place.

Grabsample. A single sample of wastewater taken at neither set time nor flow.

Ground Water. Water within the earth that supplies wells and springs.

Heavy Metals. High-density metallic elements (including mercury, chromium, cadmium, arsenic, and lead) which are generally toxic to plant and animal life in low concentrations.

Hydrocarbon. Any of a vast family of compounds containing carbon and hydrogen in various combinations; found especially in fossil fuels. Some of the hydrocarbon compounds are major air pollutants: they may be carcinogenic or active participants in the photo-chemical process.

Hydrology. The science of the properties, distribution, and circulation of water on and under the surface of the earth, and in the atmosphere.

Identification Code (EPA). The individual number assigned each generator, transporter, and treatment, storage, or disposal facility by state or federal regulatory agencies.

Ion. An electrically charged atom or group of atoms formed by loss or gain of one or more electrons. An anion has an overall positive charge, while a cation has an overall negative charge.

Mitigation. The process of removing or eliminating an environmental problem.

Monitoring Well. A well used to obtain water samples for water quality analysis or to measure ground water levels.

Non-Point Source. Source from which pollutants emanate in an unconfined and unchannelled manner. Examples include fertilizers and pesticides on farmland, and oil and other contaminants on roads, that get into runoff, precipitation, drainage, or seepage.

Oxidation. The consuming or breaking down of organic wastes or chemicals by bacteria and chemical oxidants.

Particulate. A particle of solid or liquid matter.

Point Source. A confined and identifiable source such as a pipe, ditch, channel, container, or other location or operation from which pollutants are or may be discharged.

Precipitators. Device using mechanical, electrical, or chemical means to collect particulates. Used for measurement, analysis, or control.

Reportable Quantity. When hazardous waste is generated as a result of a discharge or spill, the minimum quantity that must be reported to EPA or the National Response Center.

Salts. Minerals that water picks up as it passes through the air, over and under the ground, and through household and industrial uses.

Smoke. Solid or liquid particles under 1 micron (millionth of a meter) in diameter.

Soot. Very finely divided carbon particles clustered together.

Sorption. A term including both adsorption and absorption. Sorption is basic to many processes used to measure, analyze, and remove both gaseous and particulate pollutants.

Surface Impoundment. A natural or artificial topographic depression, designed to hold an accumulation of liquid wastes. Examples of surface impoundments are holding, storage, settling, and aeration pits, ponds, and lagoons.

Tape Sampler. A device used in the measurement of gases and fine particulates. It allows air sampling to be made automatically at predetermined times.

Topography. The configuration of a surface including its relief and the position of its natural and artificial features.

Toxic Substances. Chemicals that are subject to the regulations issued under the Toxic Substances Control Act by the U.S. Environmental Protection Agency; also used in a generic sense to mean "toxic chemicals" or "toxic agents."

TSDFs. Hazardous waste treatment, storage, and disposal facilities.

Vadose Zone. A zone of intermittent saturation above the water table. The water table is recharged largely by downward percolation of water through the overlying vadose zone.

Waste Treatment Plant. A series of tanks, screens, filters, and other processes by which pollutants are removed from water.

Water Table. The upper surface of the zone of permanent ground water saturation. The depth of the water table varies according to the season and climatic factors, the overlying topography, and the nature of the bedrock.

Highlights to Remember

Phase II and III Environmental Inspections

Phase II and III Overview

If recommended in Phase I, samplings are taken and analyzed in Phase II, and corrective recommendations developed in Phase III

Most often occurs with commercial and industrial properties; important for licensees in these fields

Situations calling for Phase II: industrial, gas station, landfill, mining, or agrarian sites; sites on cleanup lists; tanks, asbestos

Costs: laboratory analysis, fieldwork, remediation

Initial Phase II: sampling to determine whether a hazardous materials release has occurred

Expanded Phase II: detailed analysis of contaminants—type, amount, effects, recommendations

Phase III: remedial alternatives are studied for cost and feasibility, and action is recommended

Phase II Environmental Site Assessment: RTC Guidelines

Need for Phase II is a professional judgment based on likelihood of dangers to humans or the environment

Approach and content varies from site to site; usually phased as Initial and Expanded

Exceptions: immediate Expanded Phase II where other studies have already confirmed toxics, or pollution is obvious and notorious

Initial Phase II: limited sampling to confirm presence of toxics, through sampling plan, site visit, and recommendations for further action

Sampling Plan: states questions and methods; may be routine (radon, asbestos) or more complex (soils, ground water)

- Samples of environmental media that may be contaminated: air, soil, floor wipes
- Order tests for specific materials if known, or general classes of compounds
- Provide for quality control, decontamination, chain of custody, handling practices

Prepare for sampling visit: access, community relations, health and safety plan

Document sampling visit with photos, logbook, maps, sketches, and narrative

Recommendations: no further action, Expanded Phase II, interim measures at the site, notifying regulators about severe contamination

Expanded Phase II: Repeats Initial Phase II procedures in more detail, to characterize type, amount, and spread of contamination

- Often deals with natural environment while Initial Phase II deals with buildings
- Endangerment assessment: identifies likely points of human and environmental exposure to hazards, and degree of danger

Phase III Environmental Site Assessment: RTC Guidelines

Evaluates Phase II data in detail and develops, screens, and estimates cost of remedial alternative(s)

- Comprehensive list of possible responses, including innovative as well as established technologies
- Tested against performance standards for cleaning up or confining the hazard
- Preliminary screening narrows list based on technical, public health, legal, and cost considerations; best are analyzed in detail
- "No action" alternative is always considered
- Detailed analyses compared in table format for cost, health risk, environmental impact, performance, technical reliability
- Selected remedy attains ARARs—applicable, relevant, and appropriate requirements—permanently and cost-effectively
- Alternative analysis reported in Feasibility Study (FS) report

Costs Associated With Phase II and III ESAs

- Initial Phase II lab and sampling costs average $20,000 to $50,000; remediation costs extra
- Examples: General lab analysis for priority pollutants $800–$1200 per sample; geophysics survey $5000 a day
- Soil or ground water cleanup can cost hundreds of thousands of dollars
- Tank removal roughly $1500 per thousand gallons
- Transformer retrofilling (PCBs) $10–$100 per gallon
- Asbestos survey 5 to 50 cents a square foot, removal or enclosure $5–$50 a square foot plus continuing O&M
- Characterizing and identifying a waste stream, about $1000; disposal $300–$1500 per drum

COURSE 12
Environmental Disclosure Requirements

INTRODUCTION

The seller and the seller's agent in a real estate transfer are required to disclose to the buyer all "material facts" known to them pertaining to the property—facts that might reasonably be expected to have an impact on the buyer's decision whether, or on what terms, to purchase the property. This course presents environmental and other conditions that have been held by statute or case law to constitute material facts. This list should not be considered exhaustive, as any fact about the property may, under certain circumstances, be considered material.

Material Facts: Structural Defects
The most obvious type of material fact that must be disclosed is any structural defect in the property. Examples include flaws in roofs and windows, sagging or cracked foundation, termites, seismic weaknesses, and plumbing, sewer, or electrical problems. Nondisclosure can include physical acts to conceal flaws, such as painting over cracks that might indicate structural defects.

Example. In a recent Vermont case, a seller was convicted of involuntary manslaughter after the buyers died of carbon monoxide poisoning from a leaky boiler he had neglected to mention—"a reminder to sellers that the more they disclose the better." (*Los Angeles Times,* November 16, 1992).

Environmental Concerns
A growing number of laws require sellers of real estate to disclose any environmental hazards or potential for disasters associated with a property. Subjects for disclosure include location in a flood zone or seismic zone, toxics on or near the property, adjoining hazardous uses, and airport noise.

Legal Restrictions
Zoning and building codes, taxes and assessments, easements, CC&Rs, liens, and any other public or private legal conditions affecting the property must be disclosed. Proposed legislation or taxes should probably be disclosed.

History of the Property
Significant facts about the history of the property should be disclosed. This can include events and reputation, as well as actual structural and physical matters.

Environmental. A history of flooding, mudslides, soil subsidence, or other geological problems must be disclosed. So must past uses of the site that might have left harmful residues, such as a service garage or cleaning plant.

Notoriety. In *Reed vs. King*, a 1983 Court of Appeals case, the court held that the fact that multiple murders had occurred in a house might be considered a material fact about the property's history, which could affect the value of the property and therefore had to be disclosed. Facts that must be disclosed are those known to the seller or agent, or which through reasonable diligence should be known to an agent who practices in the area.

Exclusions. Civil Code §1710.2 says no cause of action arises against an owner or real estate agent for failure to disclose an occupant's death upon real property or the manner of death where the death has occurred more than three years before, or that an occupant of the property had or died from AIDS.

However, this law does not immunize an owner or agent against "intentional misrepresentation in response to a direct inquiry."

EVOLVING DISCLOSURE REQUIREMENTS

"It is *required* that a broker disclose" is not always the same as "It is *wise* that a broker disclose." While it is relatively easy to keep aware of disclosure requirements established by law, the real estate broker must also be aware that disclosure requirements are constantly changing through court decisions. A few years ago it would have been difficult to imagine that a broker could be held liable for failing to disclose information which was unknown to the broker, but which could have been discovered by physical inspection of the property. The legal environment is changing around us as well as the physical environment. A prudent broker will be aware of both kinds of changes.

Necessity of Written Disclosures   In any real estate transaction the possibility exists that a disappointed party may, rightly or wrongly, sue the agent. The most common legal action against licensees is for failure to disclose defects or other material facts concerning the property. Thus, from a listing broker's point of view, there is no substitute for a written disclosure. Such a disclosure protects the licensee in several ways.

Information Received by Buyer. It ensures that the buyer has actually received the information disclosed. If a listing broker simply makes oral disclosures to a cooperating broker, the cooperating broker may forget to relay the information to the buyer, or may relay it inaccurately. Inaccurate information relayed to the buyer may be worse than no information at all.

Seller Takes Responsibility. By incorporating written disclosures in the contract executed by the seller, the listing broker receives some assurance that the seller is accepting responsibility for the disclosures being made.

Evidence in Legal Action. If the agent is sued for nondisclosure, the written disclosures will constitute physical proof that the disclosures were made, so that the evidence will not consist solely of the broker's word against the buyer's. The very existence of written disclosures may discourage a disgruntled buyer from bringing a groundless lawsuit, since allegations of nondisclosure can easily be proven false.

Clarifying Licensee's Role. Disclosures help establish good public relations and a full understanding by the parties of the real estate agent's role in the transaction. Many people believe that, because one is licensed by the state to participate in real estate transactions, one is an expert in all phases of soil engineering, construction, development, and investment. It is important that agent and principal reach an understanding as to what is expected in the particular transaction.

- A *buyer's* agent should assume that the principal is unaware of both the existence and the significance of information such as structural pest control and title reports. The agent, therefore, must *affirmatively suggest* that the principal obtain such reports, *review* the reports with the principal, and point out any problems. Failure to suggest acquiring reports, or failure to review them, may violate the agent's fiduciary duty to the principal (see Course 14), resulting in civil liability and disciplinary action.

- If a licensee represents the *seller,* failure to disclose to the buyer any problems uncovered by the reports could result in liability.

Affirmative Duty The obligation of disclosure is not just a prohibition against false statements, but also an affirmative obligation to inform the buyer of real property about all "material facts" known to the seller or seller's agent, even if the buyer does not ask about them. Half-truths also qualify as nondisclosures, as would failures to disclose changes when information previously given becomes false. The California Real Estate Transfer Disclosure Statement contains a series of questions designed to elicit disclosure of the most common categories of material facts.

Legal Principles Depending upon the type of transaction involved (sale, long-term lease, development, transfer of title), seller and agent may be jointly and severally required to give written disclosure to buyer, lessee, developer, or transferee, of all material facts known to them pertaining to the property—facts that might reasonably be expected to influence a decision about the transaction. This includes environmental and other property conditions, and government regulations.

Licensee's Special Duties. A real estate licensee has two special sets of duties: those imposed by regulatory statutes, and those arising from the general law of agency. (2 Witkin, *Summary of Cal. Law,* 9th Ed., 1987, Agency & Employment, §253, pp. 245-246)

Care and Skill. Whether a legal duty of care and skill does or does not exist in a given situation is a "question of law to be determined by the court, not a jury." (*Ballard vs. Uribe,* 41 Cal. 3d 564, 572 (1986))

Professional Standards. Where a duty is found to exist, a real estate agent must fulfill it by exhibiting the degree of care and skill ordinarily exhibited by professionals in the industry, as measured by known facts, knowledge, education, and experience of the licensee. (2 Miller & Starr, *Agency* §3:17, pp. 94-95; *Montoya vs. McLeod,* 176 Cal. App. 3d 57, 65 (1985))

Role of Expert Testimony. The "degree of care and skill required" to fulfill a professional duty ordinarily is a "question of fact" and may require testimony by professionals in the field if the matter is within the knowledge of experts only. (*Carson vs. Facilities Development Co.,* 36 Cal. 3d 830, 844-845 (1984)) However, expert testimony is incompetent on the question of whether the duty exists, because this is a question of law for the court alone. (*Clarke vs. Hoek,* 174 Cal. App. 3d 208, 214 (1985))

Modification by Agreement. The existence and extent of the duties of inspection and disclosure may also be determined by terms of the agreement between the parties, except to the extent that fraud, duress, illegality, or incapacity of one or both of the parties deprives it of legal effect. (Rest. 2d Agency, 3 Cal. Jur. 3d Agency)

Professional Limitations. The California legislature has mandated that buyers and sellers of residential property up to four units be told: "A real estate agent is a person qualified to advise about real estate. If legal or tax advice is desired, consult a competent professional." (Civil Code §2375) While brokers hold themselves out to the public as possessing special knowledge in real estate transactions, public policy does not require them to recognize, or advise clients on, matters that require advice from other competent professionals. Express exculpatory disclaimer language to this effect in agreements, disclosure statements, and purchase contracts is permissible and binding. (*Ernest Carleton vs. Mary Tortosa,* 93 C.D.O.S. 2228 et seq. (March 1993))

Knowledge After Inspection. An affirmative duty may arise based upon the agent's visual inspection of accessible areas of the property. If the agent's education, experience, and knowledge would lead the agent to reasonably believe there may be toxics or contaminants and that tests are advisable, this must be disclosed. Should the agent procure a written report confirming toxics or contaminants on the property, the agent then has an affirmative duty to convey that report and its contents to the principal and all interested parties.

Obligations of Buyer or Lessee. A buyer or lessee is not relieved of any self-created negligence as a result of a failure to conduct a personal visual inspection of easily accessible areas, when it leads the buyer or lessee to reasonably believe there may be toxics or contaminants. (Civil Code §2079, §1102 et seq.)

Professionalism

The following statements regarding professionalism, from the California Department of Real Estate's *Reference Book*, have particular relevance to the ever increasing responsibilities imposed under the disclosure laws.

Meeting the Obligations. Clearly, real estate agents must be prepared to meet the duties and obligations imposed upon them by law. Failure to do so may result in civil, penal, or administrative action and penalties. Courts and legislatures around the country are continuing to impose more and more responsibility upon the professional for knowing what and how to disclose, when, where, why, and to whom.

Staying Informed. Real estate licensees need to make strong personal efforts to stay current with changing real estate laws, technological changes, and trends in today's "information society."

Consumer Protection. The real estate broker who is uninformed or stale in matters affecting business activities has great vulnerability to court action in today's climate of consumerism. Consumer groups and jurists are rejecting the once universally accepted *caveat emptor*—"let the buyer beware"—as being too harsh in modern social and economic settings. Real estate agents, then, must obtain and maintain currency of knowledge in this evolving field.

Caveat Who? As modern society changes, so does the law. This explains much of the steady growth of consumerism and the resultant erosion of *caveat emptor*. It has been said that the one thing that is permanent is change. The following statements by jurists in contemporary real estate cases characterize the climate in which real estate professionals may operate in the future:

- "Law, as an instrument of justice, has infinite capacity for growth to meet changing needs and mores.... Ancient distinctions which make no sense in today's society and tend to discredit the law should be readily rejected."

- "The doctrine of *caveat emptor* is one of the less admirable hand-me-downs of our Anglo-Saxon common law heritage and is a doctrine which exalts deceit, condemns fair dealing, and scorns the credulous."

Natural Hazard Disclosures

Californians enjoy their justly famed scenery and climate at the cost of a significant amount of natural risk from earthquakes, fire, landslides, and floods. In a broad sense, we implicitly accept these risks by choosing to live in the state. On a more practical level, there are a number of required or suggested disclosures related to these potentially disastrous acts of nature.

Earthquakes **Special Studies Zone.** Under the Alquist-Priolo Act (Public Resources Code §§2621-2630), a potential buyer must be informed if property is in an area of a "potentially [or] recently active" earthquake fault (known as a special studies zone). Zones are shown on index maps prepared by the State Division of Mines and Geology. California Association of Realtors® has a standard form for the special studies and flood hazard zone disclosures (Exhibit 1).

Applicability. If property is situated in a special studies zone, construction or development of any structure for human occupancy may be subject to the findings of a geologic report prepared by a state registered geologist, unless waived by the city or county. California Public Resources Code §§2621.5-2621.8 excludes structures in existence prior to May 4, 1975, conversion of existing apartment houses into condominiums, and alterations and additions under 50 percent of the value of the structure from this requirement.

Disclosure Law: Residential. Seismic disclosure laws cover both geologic and structural aspects. A state law effective January 1, 1993, requires sellers of homes built before 1960 to disclose seismic weaknesses in the building, for example:

- House is not bolted to the foundation
- Crawl space or basement walls are not adequately strengthened
- Walls are made of unreinforced masonry, brick, or stone.

The law requires real estate agents to give each seller the state Seismic Safety Commission's *Homeowner's Guide to Earthquake Safety*. The guide includes a disclosure form that is given to the buyer along with the book itself. Unlike a termite report, this disclosure form does not include a cost estimate for correcting seismic weaknesses. Some two-thirds of all home sales in California—about 550,000 a year—will fall under this law.

Commercial Buildings. Transfer of certain masonry or precast concrete buildings built before 1975 requires delivery of the Seismic Safety Commission's *Commercial Property Owner's Guide to Earthquake Safety,* as well as disclosure of any specific known earthquake hazards.

Seismic Retrofit Requirements. Retrofit regulations vary enormously from one jurisdiction to another. The buyer, seller, and their agents should obtain copies of local ordinances, find out how they apply to the property in question, and disclose findings fully. In addition to the new law on residential buildings, state and local laws passed after the 1989 Loma Prieta earthquake require identification and often upgrading of unreinforced masonry buildings.

Fill. If the land is composed partially or completely of fill, this fact must be disclosed. This is one of the standard questions on the Real Estate Transfer Disclosure Statement.

Environmental Disclosure Requirements

GEOLOGIC, SEISMIC AND FLOOD HAZARD DISCLOSURE
CALIFORNIA ASSOCIATION OF REALTORS® STANDARD FORM

The paragraph(s) below, when initialled by both Buyer and Seller, are hereby incorporated in and made a part of the ☐ Real Estate Purchase Contract and Receipt for Deposit, ☐ Investment Purchase Contract and Receipt for Deposit, ☐ Commercial Real Estate Purchase Contract and Receipt for Deposit, ☐ Business Purchase Contract and Receipt for Deposit, ☐ Lots and Land Purchase Contract and Receipt for Deposit, ☐ Mobile Home Purchase Contract and Receipt for Deposit, ☐ Other _____,
dated _____ 19___, on property known as _____,
in which _____ is referred to as Buyer
and _____ is referred to as Seller.

Buyer's Initials   Seller's Initials
___ / ___   ___ / ___   **1. FLOOD HAZARD AREA DISCLOSURE:** Buyer is informed that the Property is situated in a "Special Flood Hazard Area" designated by the Federal Emergency Management Agency (FEMA) in a "Flood Insurance Rate Map" (FIRM) or "Flood Hazard Boundary Map" (FHBM). The law provides that as a condition of obtaining financing on most structures located in a Special Flood Hazard Area, lender(s) may require flood insurance where the Property or its attachments are security for a loan.
The extent of coverage and the cost may vary. For further information consult the lenders or insurance agents. No representation or recommendation is made by the Seller and the Broker(s) in this transaction as to the legal effect or economic consequences of the National Flood Insurance Program and related legislation.

Buyer's Initials   Seller's Initials
___ / ___   ___ / ___   **2. GEOLOGIC, SEISMIC HAZARD DISCLOSURE:**
(a) Buyer is informed that the Property is situated in the zone(s)/area(s) designated below:
☐ Special Studies Zone (SSZ) designated under Public Resources Code §§2621-2625.
☐ Seismic Hazards Zone (SHZ) designated under Public Resources Code §§2690-2699.6.
☐ Locally designated zone(s)/area(s) where disclosure is required by local ordinance:
  ☐ _____
  ☐ _____
  ☐ _____

☐ Local ordinance additionally requires disclosure of the following information:
_____
_____
_____

(b) The construction or development of any structure for human occupancy located within one of these zone(s)/area(s) may be subject to the findings of a geologic report prepared by a geologist registered in the State of California unless such report is waived by the City or County under the terms of those statute(s)/ordinance(s). Disclosure of SSZs or SHZs are required only where the respective maps, or information contained in the maps, are "reasonably available."

3. **This paragraph applies only if the above referenced contract DOES NOT CONTAIN a provision for Buyer's disapproval or approval of the applicable flood, geologic or seismic hazards information:**
(a) Buyer is allowed _____ calendar days after receipt of the above disclosure(s) to make further inquiries at appropriate governmental agencies, lenders, insurance agents, or other appropriate entities concerning use of the Property under local building, zoning, fire, health and safety codes as may be applicable under the Special Studies Zone Act, Seismic Hazards Mapping Act, local geologic ordinances, or National Flood Insurance Program. Buyer shall provide written notice to Seller of any items disapproved within this time period.
(b) If Buyer gives written notice of disapproval of items under the above paragraph(s), Seller shall respond in writing within _____ calendar days after receipt of such notice. If Seller is unwilling or unable to correct items reasonably disapproved by Buyer, then Buyer may cancel this Agreement by giving written notice of cancellation to Seller within _____ calendar days (after receipt of Seller's response, or after expiration of the time for Seller's response, whichever occurs first), in which case Buyer's deposit shall be returned to Buyer. BUYER'S FAILURE TO GIVE WRITTEN NOTICE OF DISAPPROVAL OF ITEMS OR CANCELLATION OF THIS AGREEMENT WITHIN THE SPECIFIED TIME PERIODS SHALL CONCLUSIVELY BE DEEMED BUYER'S ELECTION TO PROCEED WITH THE TRANSACTION WITHOUT CORRECTION OF ANY REMAINING DISAPPROVED ITEMS WHICH SELLER HAS NOT AGREED TO CORRECT. Buyer and Seller may agree in writing to extend these time periods.

The undersigned acknowledge receipt of a copy.

Date _____   Date _____

Buyer _____   Seller _____

Buyer _____   Seller _____

This form is available for use by the entire real estate industry. The use of this form is not intended to identify the user as a REALTOR®. REALTOR® is a registered collective membership mark which may be used only by real estate licensees who are members of the NATIONAL ASSOCIATION OF REALTORS® and who subscribe to its Code of Ethics.

The copyright laws of the United States (17 U.S. Code) forbid the unauthorized reproduction of this form by any means including facsimile or computerized formats.

Copyright© 1991, CALIFORNIA ASSOCIATION OF REALTORS®
525 South Virgil Avenue, Los Angeles, California 90020

FORM GFD-14

OFFICE USE ONLY
Reviewed by Broker or Designee _____
Date _____

Exhibit 1   Reprinted with permission, California Association of Realtors®
Endorsement not implied

California Mandatory Earthquake Insurance Offer Law. Obtaining insurance is a concern when property is transferred, especially if seismic concerns have been disclosed. Dwelling forms do not automatically cover losses caused by earthquake, but earthquake coverage may be added by endorsement. Effective January 1, 1985, no policy of residential property insurance may be issued or initially renewed in California unless the insured has been offered coverage for loss or damage by earthquake. This applies to individually owned residential structures of not more than four units, condominium units, and mobile homes, as well as tenants' policies insuring personal contents. The responsibility for making the offer rests on the insurer.

- *Timing.* The offer of coverage may be made prior to, concurrent with, or within sixty days following issuance or renewal. If the offer is not accepted within thirty days it is presumed that the insured elected not to accept the coverage.

- *Coverage.* Coverage may be provided in the policy of residential property insurance itself, either by specific policy provision or endorsement, or in a separate policy or certificate of insurance. Every policy must clearly disclose the deductible. At a minimum, coverage must include the dwelling, personal property, and additional living expenses of no less than $1,500 while the dwelling is uninhabitable due to the earthquake. Coverage for engineering or demolition costs is optional.

- *Discounts.* The insurer may offer discounts for earthquake hazard reduction measures such as tying or bracing the structure to the foundation, reinforcing the chimney, or securing the water heater.

Flood Hazard Area The National Flood Insurance Program (NFIP) requires lending institutions to notify purchasers of real property, in writing, if the property is located within a designated flood hazard area, unless the seller has made this disclosure. While the program does not establish any similar disclosure requirement for sellers, this is the type of item that could be considered a material fact, and should be disclosed. The CAR form for geologic and seismic disclosure also includes flood hazard disclosure (Exhibit 1).

Wording of Disclosure. The wording of the Flood Hazard Area Disclosure is prescribed by law, as follows:

The subject property is situated in a "Special Flood Hazard Area" designated by the Federal Emergency Management Agency (FEMA) in a "Flood Insurance Rate Map" (FIRM) or "Flood Hazard Boundary Map" (FHBM). The law provides that as a condition of obtaining financing on most structures located in a "Special Flood Hazard Area," lender(s) may require flood insurance where the property or its attachments are security for a loan.

Effect of Disclosure: Flood Insurance Requirement. The law requires purchase of flood insurance as a condition of approval of any form of federal financial assistance for acquisition or construction of buildings and mobile homes in FEMA-identified flood hazard zones, where such flood insurance has been made available. For loans and loan insurance, coverage is required during the term of the loan in an amount equal to the outstanding principal balance or the available limits of coverage under the act, whichever is less.

National Flood Insurance Program. Floods cause more property damage in the United States than any other form of natural disaster. Traditional homeowner policies do not cover flood or earthquake losses because insurers are reluctant to assume catastrophic risks. Disaster relief is so costly to taxpayers that the federal government had strong incentives for stepping in, with the National Flood Insurance Act of 1968. Flood insurance may be written directly with the NFIP or with participating private insurers who are underwritten by the program. The Federal Insurance Administration (FIA) sets rates, coverage limits, and eligibility requirements.

Eligibility. All communities having flood-prone areas are notified of that fact by the FIA. If the community agrees to adopt flood control measures and restrict building in the most hazardous areas, it may participate in the NFIP. Any property owner who fails to buy flood insurance if it is available is not eligible for full disaster relief funds in the event of a flood.

Coverage. The FIA conducts a detailed study of the area, resulting in a detailed Flood Insurance Rate Map (FIRM) establishing zones and rates for the entire area. Areas having the greatest potential for flooding are designated Special Flood Hazard Areas. Once this information is published, owners become eligible for insurance. Single family dwellings other than mobile homes may be insured on a replacement cost basis. All other buildings and all contents are insured on an actual cash value basis.

Fire Hazards Public Resources Code §§4125, 4136, and 4291 provide for clearance of fire hazards on public and private property (weeds, leaves, etc.), particularly in rural and recreational areas, and define areas in which the financial responsibility for preventing and suppressing fires belongs primarily to federal, state, or local agencies. Disclosure requirements are included in this law, as follows (effective July 1, 1991):

Seller's Disclosure Responsibility in SRA. A seller of real property located within a state responsibility area (SRA) must disclose to any prospective purchaser the fact that the property is located in a wildland area which may contain substantial forest fire risks and hazards and is subject to the requirements of §4291 on flammable vegetation clearance. The seller shall also disclose to any prospective buyer that it is not the state's responsibility to provide fire protection services to any building or structure located within the wildlands unless the Department of Forestry has entered into a cooperative agreement with a local agency for such purposes.

Form. Disclosures required under this section may be made on the disclosure form prescribed by §1102.6 of the Civil Code, that is, the standard Real Estate Transfer Disclosure Statement.

Effect of Disclosure. Properties in these zones are subject to Board of Forestry regulations relating to construction and development in California's wildlands. Each county has the option of implementing regulations or local standards that meet the intent of these regulations, and specific requirements should be obtained from the local planning and building departments.

- *Emergency Access Standards.* Road and street networks, whether public or private, unless exempted, must be adequate to accomodate safe access for emergency wildland fire equipment and civilian evacuation concurrently, and must provide unobstructed traffic circulation during a wildfire emergency.

- *Signing and Addressing Standards.* To facilitate locating a fire and to avoid delays in response, roads, streets, and buildings must be designated by names or numbers, posted on signs clearly visible and legible from the roadway.

- *Emergency Water Supply Standards.* Emergency water for wildfire protection must be available and accessible in quantities and locations specified, in a fire agency mobile water tanker, or in a naturally occurring or artificial containment structure.

- *Defensible Space around Structures.* Any person that owns or occupies any building or structure in a mountainous area or on forest, brush, or grass-covered lands, or any land that is covered with flammable material, must at all times maintain a fire break around each structure by clearing all flammable vegetation thirty feet on each side or to the property line, or for one hundred feet in extra hazardous conditions.

- *Spark Arresters.* Protection is required on every chimney or stovepipe and on any internal combustion engine operated on any forest, brush, or grass-covered land.

- *Fire Resistive Roofing.* Roofs on all new buildings in state responsibility areas must have at least a Class C fire resistive or noncombustible roof covering. A Class C or noncombustible roof covering is also required when 50 percent or more of the roof area is reroofed. A local jurisdiction may apply more stringent standards. The installer of the roof covering shall provide certification classification to the building owner and, when requested, to the inspection authority.

Urban Areas. In light of recent urban-wildland fires in Oakland, Santa Barbara, and elsewhere, local governments are increasingly establishing fire prevention and suppression programs that may involve many of the same requirements as outlined above for state responsibility areas (brush clearance, roofing, etc.) and special assessments. These can be material facts that should be investigated and disclosed.

HAZARDOUS SUBSTANCES

Real estate licensees and their clients are increasingly affected by hazardous substances, such as asbestos, radon, and other natural and artificial pollutants. Not only can the presence of such substances significantly limit the value, salability, and use of real property, but, if removal is required, the cost of removal may exceed the value of the property. Increasingly, real estate licensees and their clients are subject to litigation as a result of the presence or discovery of hazardous conditions or substances. Financing and title insurance are in some cases being conditioned on inspections for, and the absence of, hazardous substances or conditions. Hazardous substance problems may also arise when the real estate professional is managing, appraising, or syndicating property.

Practitioner Issues

The presence of environmental hazards in and about a property, neighborhood, or community presents a classic example of potential liability. The *known* proximity of environmental hazards is a material fact requiring disclosure in virtually any real property transaction. But what about *unknown or latent* environmental hazards? If there is reason to suspect them, this should be disclosed. On the other hand, it is important to balance the possibility that disclosure without adequate investigative data may cause potential liability to the licensee for impairment to value resulting from uninformed disclosures.

Types of Hazards. Hazardous substances in the home can include asbestos, radon, cleaning chemicals, paint, agricultural and garden chemicals, and a variety of indoor air pollutants that can accumulate in improperly ventilated buildings. Hazardous conditions outside the home include substances found in contaminated ground water, landfills and other disposal sites, industrial air and water emissions, and uses involving noise or threat of accident, such as airports and explosives plants.

Red Flags. In California, depending on the particular facts, a real estate licensee's duty normally encompasses disclosure of all known material facts and disclosure of the results of a reasonably competent, diligent, visual inspection of the property. Even if a licensee does not know of the presence of an environmental hazard, if an inspection would reveal *suggestions* of any defect, these "red flags" must be disclosed to the buyer. Liability standards are the same for environmental hazards as for any other physical defect that exists on the property. However, the expertise required to identify even the red flags of a latent environmental hazard, much less the hazard itself, is often beyond the typical, competent real estate licensee.

Expertise. Real estate licensees are engaged by sellers and buyers to assist in the marketing, sale, and purchase of property. Licensees are not, nor should they be expected to be, experts in the area of toxic or hazardous materials. *It is important that licensees not set themselves up as experts in this matter.* Licensees should never attempt to make determinations regarding the presence or absence of environmental hazards; rather, they should recommend that their clients employ environmental experts.

Disclosure. The booklet *Environmental Hazards: A Guide for Homeowners and Buyers* was prepared by the California Departments of Real Estate and Health Services in response to the 1989 California legislative mandate to inform the homeowner about environmental hazards located on and affecting residential property. As stated in the introduction to this booklet: "If this environmental hazards booklet is made available to homeowners or prospective homeowners, real estate licensees and home sellers are not required to provide additional information on such hazards. However, delivery of this publication to homeowners or prospective homeowners does not relieve home sellers and real estate licensees of the responsibility to disclose the existence of environmental hazards when such hazards are known to them."

Toxic Disclosures Act

Industrialization has meant extracting natural resources from the ground in the form of oil, metals, and minerals, increasingly manipulated to form unnatural combinations in plastics, paints, resins, lubricants, pesticides, fertilizers, and thousands of other products. It is estimated that as many as one thousand new chemicals go into production every year. Many of these create environmental problems in production, disposal, or consumption. The law is now addressing these consequences.

New Disclosure. Chapter 171, §1102.6 et seq. of the California Civil Code (1992) establishes a requirement to warn real estate transferees if the seller knows of any environmental hazard affecting the property (fuel or chemical storage tanks, hazardous materials, or other forms of contaminants). This legislation adds to the standard Real Estate Transfer Disclosure Statement (Part II, C, Item 1) the following new question:

> C. Are you (Seller) aware of any of the following:
>
> 1. Substances, materials, or products which may be an environmental hazard such as, but not limited to, asbestos, formaldehyde, radon gas, lead-based paint, fuel or chemical storage tanks, and contaminated soil or water on the subject property? ___ Yes ___ No

Asbestos Hazard Disclosure Act

Health and Safety Code §25915 et seq. deals with asbestos contamination of structures. The owner of any public or commercial building constructed prior to 1979, who knows that the building contains asbestos, must provide notification to all employees of that owner working in the building, including test results, safety procedures, potential health risks, and details of any asbestos abatement or management plan. This provision does not apply to residential buildings.

Timing. Notice shall be provided in writing to each individual employee, and to co-owners, within fifteen days of the first receipt by the owner of information identifying the presence of asbestos-containing construction materials. Notice shall be provided annually thereafter.

New Owners. Notice shall be mailed to any new owner within fifteen days of the effective date of the agreement under which a person becomes a new owner.

Common Interest Developments. Owners of a building or part of a building within a residential common interest development (CID) need not mail written notification to other owners if a large sign in a prominent location informs persons entering the building that the association knows the building contains asbestos.

CID Transfers. The owners or association must disclose to the transferee, as soon as practicable before the transfer of title of a separate interest in the CID, the existence of asbestos-containing material. Failure to comply does not invalidate the transfer of title, however.

Multiple Owners. When there is more than one owner, the owners may agree in writing to designate one owner to prepare any notice required, and may rely on that owner's notice to satisfy the requirements of the law.

Restricted Use of Hazardous Waste Sites

Under §25202.5 et seq. of the Health and Safety Code, properties on or bordering hazardous waste disposal sites have restrictions on use, imposed by means of recorded easements. There may be restrictions on activities on, over, or under the land, including prohibitions against building, filling, grading, excavating, or mining. They run with the land from the date of recordation and are binding on all owners of the land, their heirs, successors, and assignees, and their agents, employees, and lessees.

Buffer Zone. Any land containing a hazardous waste disposal facility shall be surrounded by a minimum buffer zone of two thousand feet, unless the State

Department of Health Services determines that more is necessary or the owner proves to the satisfaction of the Department that a buffer zone of less than two thousand feet is sufficient.

Form of Disclosure. Recordation constitutes constructive notice to buyers, lenders, and the public. Explicit disclosure should still be made, however.

Hazards to Renters Various required disclosures concern toxics, safety, fitness for habitation, and the condition of the premises in general.

- ☐ If formaldehyde, radon, methane, or other potentially lethal gas is known to be present, it must be disclosed.

- ☐ If the property is in an area designated as seismically active, disclosure must be made.

- ☐ If the property is near an ammunition dump (§§1102.15 and 1940.7 of the Civil Code) tenants must be notified of this hazard.

Asbestos. Under the asbestos hazard disclosure law, the known existence of asbestos on the premises must be disclosed to tenants. Pre-1970 housing is especially likely to have asbestos as insulation and as exterior siding.

Airport Noise Disclosure Brokers who negotiate the sale of real property in the vicinity of an airport must be aware of Public Law 96-193, the Aviation Safety and Noise Abatement Act, which requires a disclosure of "yearly day-night average sound level."

SELLER'S DISCLOSURE RESPONSIBILITIES—CALIFORNIA LAW

The California Civil Code, in §§1102 et seq., establishes comprehensive disclosure requirements for sellers in real property transfers. It applies to any sale, real property sales contract, lease-option, or ground lease coupled with improvements, of one- to four-unit dwellings. Exempted are transfers to or from governmental entities, between spouses, co-owners, or relatives, transfers pursuant to court order, and transfers subject to the Subdivided Lands Act.

Seller's Written Disclosure Form The Real Estate Transfer Disclosure Statement form (Exhibit 2) includes disclosures of the property's description, condition, and restrictions, and the agent's inspection disclosure.

Responsibility for Accuracy. The seller and real estate agent are not liable for any mistakes or omissions that are not within their personal knowledge, as long as the disclosures:

- ☐ Are based on information timely provided by public agencies, if the transferor exercised ordinary care in obtaining and transmitting it, or

- ☐ Are based on information provided by experts acting within their expertise (such as land surveyor, geologist, pest control operator), if

    - Information was timely provided,
    - The transferor or agent exercised care in obtaining and transmitting the information, and
    - The information was provided to the transferee at the request of the transferor or agent.

Duplicate Information. If any required information has been provided to the buyer by some other person or public agency, the seller and agent are not required to provide the same information again. If the buyer has obtained a report about the electrical system from an electrician prior to presentation of the disclosure form by the seller, the seller does not need to provide duplicate information.

Delivery Requirements. The transferor must deliver the disclosure statement to the prospective transferee as soon as practicable before transfer of title, and prior to the execution of any real property sales contract, lease-option, or ground lease coupled with improvements. The transferor must indicate on the face of the deposit receipt, or on a separate document, that the disclosure requirement has been fulfilled.

Right of Rescission. If any disclosure or amendment is delivered after execution of the purchase offer, the transferee may cancel in writing up to three days after personal delivery or five days after mailing of the disclosure statement.

Buyer's Rights after Discovery of Nondisclosure. Failure to disclose subjects the licensee to potential civil liability for damages and disciplinary action by the Real Estate Commissioner. There should be some acknowledgment of receipt of the disclosure by the transferee prior to close of escrow as a matter of mutual protection for the agent as well as the recipient of the disclosure. The right to commence an action for damages continues two years from the date of possession, which means the date of recording, the escrow closing date, or the date of occupancy, whichever comes first.

Inspection and Disclosures by Seller's Agent to Buyer

Prior to 1984, the traditional rule was that the listing agent was obligated to disclose to the buyer only facts actually known. In the 1984 case of *Easton vs. Strassburger*, the Court of Appeals rendered a decision that was seen by much of the real estate profession as significantly expanding the listing agent's duties of disclosure to buyers. The California Supreme Court declined to review the Court of Appeals decision, and subsequent legislation essentially codified the holding in *Easton*, effective January 1, 1986.

Facts. Plaintiff Easton purchased a home from Strassburger. During the three years preceding the sale, there had been two landslides on the property. Strassburger had taken action to prevent further subsidence, but did not tell listing broker Valley Realty of the problem. The evidence showed that Valley's agents had inspected the property and noticed certain "red flags" that should have indicated to them that soil problems existed. After Easton's purchase, landslides destroyed the property.

Ruling. Easton sued Valley, charging negligence. The Court of Appeals upheld the verdict against Valley, stating: "A real estate broker is a licensed person or entity who holds himself out to the public as having particular skills and knowledge in the real estate field. He is under a duty to disclose facts materially affecting the value or desirability of the property that are known to him or *which through reasonable diligence should be known to him.*"

REAL ESTATE TRANSFER DISCLOSURE STATEMENT
(CALIFORNIA CIVIL CODE 1102, ET SEQ.)
CALIFORNIA ASSOCIATION OF REALTORS® (CAR) STANDARD FORM

THIS DISCLOSURE STATEMENT CONCERNS THE REAL PROPERTY SITUATED IN THE CITY OF _____, COUNTY OF _____, STATE OF CALIFORNIA, DESCRIBED AS _____
THIS STATEMENT IS A DISCLOSURE OF THE CONDITION OF THE ABOVE DESCRIBED PROPERTY IN COMPLIANCE WITH SECTION 1102 OF THE CIVIL CODE AS OF _____, 19____. IT IS NOT A WARRANTY OF ANY KIND BY THE SELLER(S) OR ANY AGENT(S) REPRESENTING ANY PRINCIPAL(S) IN THIS TRANSACTION, AND IS NOT A SUBSTITUTE FOR ANY INSPECTIONS OR WARRANTIES THE PRINCIPAL(S) MAY WISH TO OBTAIN.

I
COORDINATION WITH OTHER DISCLOSURE FORMS
This Real Estate Transfer Disclosure Statement is made pursuant to Section 1102 of the Civil Code. Other statutes require disclosures, depending upon the details of the particular real estate transaction (for example: special study zone and purchase-money liens on residential property).
  Substituted Disclosures: The following disclosures have or will be in connection with this real estate transfer, and are intended to satisfy the disclosure obligations on this form, where the subject matter is the same: _____

(LIST ALL SUBSTITUTED DISCLOSURE FORMS TO BE USED IN CONNECTION WITH THIS TRANSACTION)

II
SELLER'S INFORMATION
The Seller discloses the following information with the knowledge that even though this is not a warranty, prospective Buyers may rely on this information in deciding whether and on what terms to purchase the subject property. Seller hereby authorizes any agent(s) representing any principal(s) in this transaction to provide a copy of this statement to any person or entity in connection with any actual or anticipated sale of the property.

THE FOLLOWING ARE REPRESENTATIONS MADE BY THE SELLER(S) AND ARE NOT THE REPRESENTATIONS OF THE AGENT(S), IF ANY. THIS INFORMATION IS A DISCLOSURE AND IS NOT INTENDED TO BE PART OF ANY CONTRACT BETWEEN THE BUYER AND SELLER.

Seller ☐ is ☐ is not occupying the property.

A. The subject property has the items checked below (read across):

☐ Range	☐ Oven	☐ Microwave
☐ Dishwasher	☐ Trash Compactor	☐ Garbage Disposal
☐ Washer/Dryer Hookups	☐ Window Screens	☐ Rain Gutters
☐ Burglar Alarms	☐ Smoke Detector(s)	☐ Fire Alarm
☐ T.V. Antenna	☐ Satellite Dish	☐ Intercom
☐ Central Heating	☐ Central Air Conditioning	☐ Evaporator Cooler(s)
☐ Wall/Window Air Conditioning	☐ Sprinklers	☐ Public Sewer System
☐ Septic Tank	☐ Sump Pump	☐ Water Softener
☐ Patio/Decking	☐ Built-in Barbeque	☐ Gazebo
☐ Sauna	☐ Pool	☐ Spa ☐ Hot Tub
☐ Security Gate(s)	☐ Automatic Garage Door Opener(s)*	☐ Number of Remote Controls ____
Garage: ☐ Attached	☐ Not Attached	☐ Carport
Pool/Spa Heater: ☐ Gas	☐ Solar	☐ Electric
Water Heater: ☐ Gas	☐ Solar	☐ Electric
Water Supply: ☐ City	☐ Well	☐ Private Utility ☐ Other____
Gas Supply: ☐ Utility	☐ Bottled	

Exhaust Fan(s) in _____ 220 Volt Wiring in _____
Fireplace(s) in _____ ☐ Gas Starter
☐ Roof(s): Type: _____ Age: _____ (approx.)
☐ Other: _____
Are there, to the best of your (Seller's) knowledge, any of the above that are not in operating condition? ☐ Yes ☐ No If yes, then describe. (Attach additional sheets if necessary): _____

B. Are you (Seller) aware of any significant defects/malfunctions in any of the following? ☐ Yes ☐ No If yes, check appropriate space(s) below.
☐ Interior Walls ☐ Ceilings ☐ Floors ☐ Exterior Walls ☐ Insulation ☐ Roof(s) ☐ Windows ☐ Doors ☐ Foundation ☐ Slab(s) ☐ Driveways ☐ Sidewalks ☐ Walls/Fences ☐ Electrical Systems ☐ Plumbing/Sewers/Septics ☐ Other Structural Components
(Describe: _____)

If any of the above is checked, explain. (Attach additional sheets if necessary): _____

*This garage door opener may not be in compliance with the safety standards relating to automatic reversing devices as set forth in Chapter 12.5 (commencing with Section 19890) of Part 3 of Division 13 of the Health and Safety Code.
Buyer and Seller acknowledge receipt of copy of this page, which constitutes Page 1 of 2 Pages.
Buyer's Initials (_____) (_____) Seller's Initials (_____) (_____)

OFFICE USE ONLY
Reviewed by Broker or Designee _____
Date _____

Copyright 1990, CALIFORNIA ASSOCIATION OF REALTORS®
525 South Virgil Avenue, Los Angeles, California 90020
IN COMPLIANCE WITH CIVIL CODE SECTION 1102.6 / EFFECTIVE JULY 1, 1991.
SELLER'S COPY
M-PM-8/92

REAL ESTATE TRANSFER DISCLOSURE STATEMENT (TDS-14 PAGE 1 OF 2)

Exhibit 2.1 Reprinted with permission, California Association of Realtors®
Endorsement not implied

Subject Property Address: _____, 19 ____

C. Are you (Seller) aware of any of the following:

1. Substances, materials, or products which may be an environmental hazard such as, but not limited to, asbestos, formaldehyde, radon gas, lead-based paint, fuel or chemical storage tanks, and contaminated soil or water on the subject property. ☐ Yes ☐ No
2. Features of the property shared in common with adjoining landowners, such as walls, fences, and driveways, whose use or responsibility for maintenance may have an effect on the subject property. ☐ Yes ☐ No
3. Any encroachments, easements or similar matters that may affect your interest in the subject property ☐ Yes ☐ No
4. Room additions, structural modifications, or other alterations or repairs made without necessary permits. ☐ Yes ☐ No
5. Room additions, structural modifications, or other alterations or repairs not in compliance with building codes. ☐ Yes ☐ No
6. Landfill (compacted or otherwise) on the property or any portion thereof. ☐ Yes ☐ No
7. Any settling from any cause, or slippage, sliding, or other soil problems. ☐ Yes ☐ No
8. Flooding, drainage or grading problems. ☐ Yes ☐ No
9. Major damage to the property or any of the structures from fire, earthquake, floods, or landslides. ☐ Yes ☐ No
10. Any zoning violations, nonconforming uses, violations of "setback" requirements. ☐ Yes ☐ No
11. Neighborhood noise problems or other nuisances. ☐ Yes ☐ No
12. CC&R's or other deed restrictions or obligations. ☐ Yes ☐ No
13. Homeowners' Association which has any authority over the subject property. ☐ Yes ☐ No
14. Any "common area" (facilities such as pools, tennis courts, walkways, or other areas co-owned in undivided interest with others). ☐ Yes ☐ No
15. Any notices of abatement or citations against the property. ☐ Yes ☐ No
16. Any lawsuits against the seller threatening to or affecting this real property. ☐ Yes ☐ No

If the answer to any of these is yes, explain. (Attach additional sheets if necessary.): _____
_____
_____

Seller certifies that the information herein is true and correct to the best of the Seller's knowledge as of the date signed by the Seller.

Seller _____ Date _____

Seller _____ Date _____

III
AGENT'S INSPECTION DISCLOSURE
(To be completed only if the seller is represented by an agent in this transaction.)
THE UNDERSIGNED, BASED ON THE ABOVE INQUIRY OF THE SELLER(S) AS TO THE CONDITION OF THE PROPERTY AND BASED ON A REASONABLY COMPETENT AND DILIGENT VISUAL INSPECTION OF THE ACCESSIBLE AREAS OF THE PROPERTY IN CONJUNCTION WITH THAT INQUIRY, STATES THE FOLLOWING:
_____
_____

Agent (Broker
Representing Seller) _____ By _____ Date _____
                        (PLEASE PRINT)   (ASSOCIATE LICENSEE OR BROKER-SIGNATURE)

IV
AGENT'S INSPECTION DISCLOSURE
(To be completed only if the agent who has obtained the offer is other than the agent above.)
THE UNDERSIGNED, BASED ON A REASONABLY COMPETENT AND DILIGENT VISUAL INSPECTION OF THE ACCESSIBLE AREAS OF THE PROPERTY, STATES THE FOLLOWING:
_____
_____

Agent (Broker
obtaining the Offer) _____ By _____ Date _____
                        (PLEASE PRINT)   (ASSOCIATE LICENSEE OR BROKER-SIGNATURE)

V
BUYER(S) AND SELLER(S) MAY WISH TO OBTAIN PROFESSIONAL ADVICE AND/OR INSPECTIONS OF THE PROPERTY AND TO PROVIDE FOR APPROPRIATE PROVISIONS IN A CONTRACT BETWEEN BUYER AND SELLER(S) WITH RESPECT TO ANY ADVICE/INSPECTIONS/DEFECTS.

I/WE ACKNOWLEDGE RECEIPT OF A COPY OF THIS STATEMENT.

Seller _____ Date _____ Buyer _____ Date _____

Seller _____ Date _____ Buyer _____ Date _____

Agent (Broker
Representing Seller) _____ By _____ Date _____
                        (PLEASE PRINT)   (ASSOCIATE LICENSEE OR BROKER-SIGNATURE)

Agent (Broker
obtaining the Offer) _____ By _____ Date _____
                        (PLEASE PRINT)   (ASSOCIATE LICENSEE OR BROKER-SIGNATURE)

A REAL ESTATE BROKER IS QUALIFIED TO ADVISE ON REAL ESTATE. IF YOU DESIRE LEGAL ADVICE, CONSULT YOUR ATTORNEY.

This form is available for use by the entire real estate industry. The use of this form is not intended to identify the user as a REALTOR. REALTOR is a registered collective membership mark which may be used only by real estate licensees who are members of the NATIONAL ASSOCIATION OF REALTORS and who subscribe to its Code of Ethics.

Copyright © 1990, CALIFORNIA ASSOCIATION OF REALTORS
525 South Virgil Avenue, Los Angeles, California 90020

BUYER'S COPY

Page 2 of _____ Pages

OFFICE USE ONLY
Reviewed by Broker or Designee
Date _____

M-PM-8/92

REAL ESTATE TRANSFER DISCLOSURE STATEMENT (TDS-14 PAGE 2 OF 2)

Exhibit 2.2 Reprinted with permission, California Association of Realtors®
Endorsement not implied

DISCLOSURE

Sellers of real property should be aware of their disclosure obligations under the California Court Cases, Statutes and Real Estate Law commentaries excerpted or paraphrased below:

SELLER DISCLOSURE OBLIGATIONS
UNDER CIVIL CODE SECTION 1102, ET SEQ.

Effective January 1, 1987, a transferor (seller) of real property including a residential stock cooperative containing 1 to 4 residential units (unless exempted under §1102.1) must supply a transferee (buyer) with a completed Real Estate Transfer Disclosure Statement in the form prescribed in Civid Code §1102.6.

EXEMPTED TRANSFERS: Summary of exempted transfers (Civil Code Section 1102.1) where Real Estate Transfer Disclosure Statement is **not** required:

a. Transfers requiring "a public report pursuant to §11018.1 of the Business & Professions Code" and transfers pursuant to §11010.4 of Business & Professions Code where no public report is required;
b. "Transfers pursuant to court order" (such as probate sales, sales by a bankruptcy trustee, etc.);
c. Transfers by foreclosure (including a deed in lieu of foreclosure and a transfer by a beneficiary who has acquired the property by foreclosure or deed in lieu of foreclosure);
d. "Transfers by a fiduciary in the course of the administration of a decendent's estate, guardianship, conservatorship, or trust."
e. "Transfers from one co-owner to one or more co-owners."
f. "Transfer made to a spouse" or to a direct blood relative;
g. "Transfers between spouses" in connection with a dissolution of marriage or similar proceeding;
h. Transfers by the State Controller pursuant to the Unclaimed Property Law;
i. Transfers as a result of failure to pay property taxes;
j. "Transfers or exchanges to or from any government entity."

TIMING OF DISCLOSURE AND RIGHT TO CANCEL (CIVIL CODE SECTION 1102.2):

a. In the case of a sale, the disclosures to the buyer shall be made "as soon as practicable before transfer of title."
b. "In the case of transfer by a Real Property Sales Contract, (Installment Land Sales Contract)...or, by a lease together with an option to purchase, or ground lease coupled with improvements, as soon as practical before...the making or acceptance of an offer."

"If any disclosure, or any material amendment of any disclosure, required to be made by this article, is delivered after the execution of an offer to purchase, the transferee shall have three days after delivery in person or five days after delivery by deposit in the mail, to terminate his or her offer by delivery of a written notice of termination to the transferor or the transferor's agent."

SUBSTITUTED DISCLOSURES: (CIVIL CODE SECTION 1102.4)

a. Neither the transferor nor any listing or selling agent shall be liable for any error, inaccuracy, or omission of any information delivered pursuant to this article if the error, inaccuracy, or omission was not within the personal knowledge of the transferor or that listing or selling agent, was based on information timely provided by public agencies or by other persons providing information as specified in subdivision (c) that is required to be disclosed pursuant to this article, and ordinary care was exercised in obtaining and transmitting it.
b. The delivery of any information required to be disclosed by this article to a prospective transferee by a public agency or other person providing information required to be disclosed pursuant to this article shall be deemed to comply with the requirements of this article and shall relieve the transferor or any listing or selling agent of any further duty under this article with respect to that item of information.
c. The delivery of a report or opinion prepared by a licensed engineer, land surveyor, geologist, structural pest control operator, contractor, or other expert, dealing with matters within the scope of the professional's license or expertise, shall be sufficient compliance for application of the exemption provided by subdivision (a) if information is provided to the prospective transferee pursuant to a request therefor, whether written or oral. In responding to such a request, an expert may indicate, in writing, an understanding that the information provided will be used in fulfilling the requirements of Section 1102.6 and, if so, shall indicate the required disclosures, or parts thereof, to which the information being furnished is applicable. Where such a statement is furnished, the expert shall not be responsible for any items of information, or parts thereof, other than those expressly set forth in the statement.

OTHER DISCLOSURE REQUIREMENTS

I "...Where the seller knows of facts materially affecting the value or desirability of the property which are known or accessible only to him and also knows that such facts are not known to, or within the reach of the diligent attention and observation of the buyer, the seller is under a duty to disclose them to the buyer." Lingsch v. Savage, 213 Cal. App. 2d 729.
II "Concealment may constitute actionable fraud where seller knows of facts which materially affect desirability of property and seller knows such facts are unknown to buyer." Koch v. Williams, 193 Cal. App. 2d 537, 541.
III "Deceit may arise from mere nondisclosure." Massei v. Lettunich, 248 Cal. App. 2d 68, 72.
IV Failure of the seller to fulfill such duty of disclosure constitutes actual fraud. [Civil Code Section 1572(3)]
V **California Civil Code: §1709. Deceit—Damages** One who willfully deceives another with intent to induce him to alter his position to his injury or risk is liable for any damages which he thereby suffers. **§1710. Elements of Actionable Fraud** A deceit, within the meaning of the last section, is either: (1) The suggestion, as a fact, of that which is not true, by one who does not believe it to be true; (2) The assertion, as a fact, of that which is not true, by one who has no reasonable ground for believing it to be true; (3) The suppression of a fact, by one who is bound to disclose it, or who give information of other facts which are likely to mislead for want of communication of that fact; or (4) A promise, made without any intention of performing it
VI "The maker of a fraudulent misrepresentation (seller) is subject to liability...to another (buyer) who acts in justifiable reliance upon it if the misrepresentation, although not made directly to the other (buyer), and that it will influence his conduct..." [parenthetical material added]. Restatement (2d) or Torts §533.
VII "The Seller may have an affirmative duty to disclose certain significant facts regarding the condition of his property. It is not enough for the seller to say nothing because he is not asked." California Real Estate Sales Transactions, §12.2, p.463 (Cal. C.E.B. 1967).
VIII "A buyer who has been defrauded by the seller has the choice of either: (A) Using the seller's fraud as a defense when and if the buyer refuses to follow through with his obligation under the contract; or (B) Using the seller's fraud as a basis for an action for affirmative relief in the form of an action for damages or for recission of the contract."
IX Exculpatory Clauses: "It is better for the seller to disclose the specific condition than to attempt to exculpate himself against its nondisclosure. In general, the exculpatory (e.g., "as is") clause provides little, if any, protection." California Real Estate Sales Transactions p.483 (Cal. C.E.B. 1967).

[The Above is a general statement of the seller disclosure obligations. Other disclosure may be required].

Exhibit 2.3 Reprinted with permission, California Association of Realtors®
Endorsement not implied

Legislation. Civil Code §2079 states: "It is the duty of a real estate broker . . . to a prospective purchaser of residential real property comprising one to four dwelling units . . . to conduct a reasonably competent and diligent visual inspection of the property offered for sale and to disclose to that prospective purchaser all facts materially affecting the value or desirability of the property that such an investigation would reveal, if that broker has a written contract with the *seller* to find or obtain a buyer or is a broker who acts in cooperation with such a broker to find and obtain a buyer."

General Rule. If a licensee fails to disclose a material fact the licensee *should have* known, even though not actually known, the licensee can be held liable to the buyer for any damages caused by this failure. The court decision stressed the responsibility inherent in the licensee's professional status, and the need for consumer protection. The legislature spelled out the licensee's disclosure responsibilities.

Court's Rationale. "If a broker were required to disclose only known defects but not also those that are reasonably discoverable, he would be shielded by his ignorance of that which he holds himself out to know. The rule thus narrowly construed would have results inimical to the policy upon which it is based. Such a construction would not only reward the unskilled broker for his incompetence, but might provide the unscrupulous broker the unilateral ability to protect himself at the expense of the inexperienced and unwary who rely upon him."

Legislature's Rationale. "It is the intent of the Legislature that this act codify and make precise the holding in *Easton vs. Strassburger* . . . . The Legislature finds that the imprecision of terms in the Easton case and the absence of a comprehensive declaration of duties, standards, and exceptions has caused insurers to modify professional liability coverage of real estate licensees and has caused confusion among real estate licensees . . . . The Legislature finds that it is desirable to facilitate the issuance of professional liability insurance as a resource for aggrieved members of the public, and declares that the provisions of this act are, and shall be interpreted as, a definition of the duty of care found to exist by *Easton vs. Strassburger* . . . ."

Scope of Licensee's Duty. Under Civil Code §2079, standards are established which protect consumers from concealment and incompetence on the part of the seller or licensee, and also protect the licensee from liability for matters beyond his or her reasonable knowledge.

- *Standard of Care.* The care required is that which would be exercised by a "reasonably prudent real estate licensee" in light of the education and experience required to obtain a license.

- *Scope of Inspection.* A licensee need not inspect areas that are inaccessible. If the property is a condominium, stock cooperative, or unit in a planned development, the licensee is required to inspect only the unit offered for sale, not the entire complex.

- *Buyer's Responsibility.* "Nothing in this article relieves a buyer . . . of the duty to exercise reasonable care to protect himself . . . including those facts which are known to or within the diligent attention and observation of the buyer."

> **Example**
>
> Because of a defective roof, a house has extensive water damage, which is obvious upon any visual observation of the ceiling. In going through the house, neither the listing agent nor the buyer looked at the ceiling and noticed the damage. Since the facts were equally apparent to both buyer and licensee, the licensee probably would not be held liable, or would be held only partially liable, for failure to disclose the leaky roof. In the Easton case the licensee, because of his special expertise, should have spotted the soil-retaining netting, while the untrained buyer would not necessarily be expected to know what it meant.

Disclosure Chart The California Association of Realtors® Legal Department has published a useful summary of California real estate disclosures in its "Legal Q&A" series. This eight-page chart summarizes disclosure trigger (e.g., sale), disclosure requirement, and law citation for 16 different topics. Both existing and proposed requirements are summarized; the latter include home energy ratings and a lead hazard pamphlet. The California Real Estate Law Disclosure Chart is reproduced in full in the Appendix, by permission of C.A.R.

Pest Control Disclosures Special disclosure requirements apply to every real property transfer or real property sales contract in which a pest control certification or report is a condition of the transfer or of any financing.

Disclosure Requirements. Under Civil Code §1099:

- ☐ A copy of any structural pest control inspection report must be delivered to the buyer as soon as practicable before transfer of title or execution of the sales contract.

- ☐ The transferor, fee owner, or agent is responsible for compliance.

Licensee Responsibilities. Commissioner's Regulation 2905 assigns responsibility for making disclosures and keeping records.

- ☐ If Civil Code §1099 is applicable, the broker acting as agent in the transaction must be the one to deliver the report, certification, or notice of work completed.

- ☐ If more than one broker is involved, the one who obtained the offer (the selling broker) must make the disclosure, unless the seller has, in writing, directed another broker acting in the transaction to make the delivery.

- ☐ If the responsible broker cannot obtain either the required documents or the transferee's assurance that they have been received, the broker must advise the transferee in writing of the transferee's rights under §1099.

- ☐ The broker must keep a record of the action taken to comply with this regulation.

Disclosure Must Be Full. In the 1982 case of *Godfrey vs. Steinpress*, the sellers and their agent obtained two different pest control reports, hoping to obtain one that would call for only minimal repairs. The second report showed more damage and a higher repair estimate than the first. The sellers and their agent showed the buyers only the first report, and the repairs were done in accordance with that report. Buyers discovered, after moving into the house, that much additional work was necessary. Buyers sued, and the broker was held liable for over $80,000 in damages, including punitive damages as well as actual damages for both fraud and emotional distress.

PUBLIC AND PRIVATE RESTRICTIONS

Material facts include any restrictions that affect the purchaser's legal ability to use the property. Restricted use of hazardous waste sites (see above, Environmental Hazards) is one such restriction, since it is enforced by means of a recorded easement. Other restrictions are imposed by law or by private agreement.

Zoning and Building Codes A seller should disclose whether the property is in violation of any local zoning law or building code, including energy conservation and safety retrofit requirements. Disclosure should also be made if the property will *subsequently* be in violation of regulations. For example, if an area has been rezoned, existing nonconforming uses may be permitted only for a specified period of time, or until the ownership changes.

Building Codes and Permits. Failure to determine whether significant remodeling and additions have been done in accordance with applicable building codes and pursuant to valid building permits may subject the agent to liability and disciplinary action. Civil Code §1134.5 requires the transferor of property of up to four residential units to deliver a written statement of whether any structural additions or alterations have been made.

Zoning. As a real estate professional, the licensee is expected to verify whether the current condition and use of the property, or any proposed use, complies with applicable zoning ordinances. Item C.10. on the Real Estate Transfer Disclosure Statement specifically inquires about zoning violations.

> **Example**
> A broker, acting as seller's agent, represented to the buyer that a property was zoned for commercial use when, in fact, it was only *partially* zoned for such use. The seller was obliged to repurchase the property from the buyer, and the broker was held liable for the client's expenses in connection with both the original sale and the repurchase, including the broker's commission.

Retrofit Ordinances. State law (Health and Safety Code §13113.8) requires that smoke detectors must be installed in all residential properties sold, and a disclosure statement given to the purchaser (Exhibit 3). In addition some municipalities require retrofits such as tempered glass in sliding glass doors and various energy and water conservation measures.

Assessments The seller should disclose whether there are any assessments that have not yet been made against the property (and therefore do not yet show up in title reports), although the improvements have been made and will be assessed. In the wake of Proposition 13, localities are increasingly turning to special assessments to support services and infrastructure, such as parks, fire suppression, and undergrounding utilities. Thus it is important to inquire into possible new assessments.

SMOKE DETECTOR STATEMENT OF COMPLIANCE
(As required by Health and Safety Code §13113.8(b))

CALIFORNIA ASSOCIATION OF REALTORS® STANDARD FORM

Property Address _____ ("Property")

Seller represents that the Property is in compliance, as of the date below, with Health and Safety ("H&S") Code §13113.8, by having operable smoke detector(s) approved and listed by the State Fire Marshal and installed in accordance with State Fire Marshal's regulations, and with applicable local ordinance(s). H&S Code §13113.8 applies only to single family dwellings or factory-built housing, as defined in H&S Code §19971.

The undersigned acknowledge receipt of a copy, including the provisions of H&S Code §13113.8, as set forth on the reverse hereof.

Date _____   Date _____

Buyer _____   Seller _____

Buyer _____   Seller _____

THIS STANDARD DOCUMENT HAS BEEN APPROVED BY THE CALIFORNIA ASSOCIATION OF REALTORS® IN FORM ONLY. NO REPRESENTATION IS MADE AS TO THE LEGAL VALIDITY OF ANY PROVISION OR THE ADEQUACY OF ANY PROVISION IN ANY SPECIFIC TRANSACTION.

A REAL ESTATE BROKER IS THE PERSON QUALIFIED TO ADVISE ON REAL ESTATE TRANSACTIONS. IF YOU DESIRE LEGAL OR TAX ADVICE, CONSULT AN APPROPRIATE PROFESSIONAL.

This form is available for use by the entire real estate industry. The use of this form is not intended to identify the user as a REALTOR®. REALTOR® is a registered collective membership mark which may be used only by real estate licensees who are members of the NATIONAL ASSOCIATION OF REALTORS® and who subscribe to its Code of Ethics.

The copyright laws of the United States (17 U.S. Code) forbid the unauthorized reproduction of this form by any means including facsimile or computerized formats.

Copyright© 1991, CALIFORNIA ASSOCIATION OF REALTORS®
525 South Virgil Avenue, Los Angeles, California 90020

OFFICE USE ONLY
Reviewed by Broker or Designee _____
Date _____

EQUAL HOUSING OPPORTUNITY
M-SC-JAN-92

FORM SDC-11

Exhibit 3.1   Reprinted with permission, California Association of Realtors®
Endorsement not implied

HEALTH AND SAFETY CODE
SMOKE DETECTORS REQUIRED; NOTICE TO BE GIVEN TO TRANSFEREE.

Section 13113.8.

(a) On and after January 1, 1986, every single-family dwelling and factory-built housing, as defined in Section 19971, which is sold shall have an operable smoke detector. The detector shall be approved and listed by the State Fire Marshal and installed in accordance with the State Fire Marshal's regulations. Unless prohibited by local rules, regulations, or ordinances, a battery-operated smoke detector shall be deemed to satsify the requirements of this section.

(b) On and after January 1, 1986, the transferor of any real property containing a single-family dwelling, as described in subdivision (a), whether the transfer is made by sale, exchange, or real property sales contract, as defined in Section 2985 of the Civil Code, shall deliver to the transferee a written statement indicating that the transferor is in compliance with this section. The disclosure statement shall be either included in the receipt for deposit in a real estate transaction, an addendum attached thereto, or a separate document.

(c) The transferor shall deliver the statement referred to in subdivision (b) as soon as practicable before the transfer of title in the case of a sale or exchange, or prior to execution of the contract where the transfer is by a real property sales contract, as defined in Section 2985. For purposes of this subdivision, "delivery" means delivery in person or by mail to the transferee or transferor, or to any person authorized to act for him or her in the transaction, or to additional transferees who have requested delivery from the transferor in writing. Delivery to the spouse of a transferee or transferor shall be deemed delivery to a transferee or transferor, unless the contract states otherwise.

(d) This section does not apply to any of the following:

  (1) Transfers which are required to be preceded by the furnishing to a prospective transferee of a copy of a public report pursuant to Section 11018.1 of the Business and Professions Code.

  (2) Transfers pursuant to court order, including, but not limited to, transfers ordered by a probate court in the administration of an estate, transfers pursuant to a writ of execution, transfers by a trustee in bankruptcy, transfers by eminent domain, or transfers resulting from a decree for specific performance.

  (3) Transfers to a mortgagee by a mortgagor in default, transfers to a beneficiary of a deed of trust by a trustor in default, transfers by any foreclosure sale after default, transfers by any foreclosure sale after default in an obligation secured by a mortgage, or transfers by a sale under a power of sale after a default in an obligation secured by a deed of trust or secured by any other instrument containing a power of sale.

  (4) Transfers by a fiduciary in the course of the administration of a decedent's estate, guardianship, conservatorship, or trust.

  (5) Transfers from one coowner to one or more coowners.

  (6) Transfers made to a spouse, or to a person or persons in the lineal line of consanguinity of one or more of the transferors.

  (7) Transfers between spouses resulting from a decree of dissolution of a marriage, from a decree of legal separation, or from a property settlement agreement incidental to either of those decrees.

  (8) Transfers by the Controller in the course of administering the Unclaimed Property Law provided for in Chapter 7 (commencing with Section 1500) of Title 10 of Part 3 of the Code of Civil Procedure.

  (9) Transfers under the provisions of Chapter 7 (commencing with Section 3691) or Chapter 8 (commencing with Section 3771) of Part 6 of Division 1 of the Revenue and Taxation Code.

(e) No liability shall arise, nor any action be brought or maintained against, any agent of any party to a transfer of title, including any person or entity acting in the capacity of an escrow, for any error, inaccuracy, or omission relating to the disclosure required to be made by a transferor pursuant to this section. However, this subdivision does not apply to a licensee, as defined in Section 10011 of the Business and Professions Code, where the licensee participates in the making of the disclosure required to be made pursuant to this section with actual knowledge of the falsity of the disclosure.

(f) Except as otherwise provided in this section, this section shall not be deemed to create or imply a duty upon a licensee, as defined in Section 10011 of the Business and Professions Code, or upon any agent of any party to a transfer of title, including any person or entity acting in the capacity of an escrow, to monitor or ensure compliance with this section.

(g) No transfer of title shall be invalidated on the basis of a failure to comply with this section, and the exclusive remedy for the failure to comply with this section is an award of actual damages not to exceed one hundred dollars ($100), exclusive of any court costs and attorney's fees.

(h) Local ordinances requiring smoke detectors in single-family dwellings may be enacted or amended. However, the ordinances shall satisfy the minimum requirements of this section.

(i) For the purposes of this section, "single-family dwelling" does not include a manufactured home as defined in Section 18007, a mobilehome as defined in Section 18008, or a commercial coach as defined in Section 18001.8.

(j) This section shall not apply to the installation of smoke detectors in dwellings intended for human occupancy, as defined in and regulated by Section 13113.7 of the Health and Safety Code, as added by Senate Bill No. 1448 in the 1983-84 Regular Session.

Exhibit 3.2   Reprinted with permission, California Association of Realtors®
Endorsement not implied

Private Restrictions The seller should disclose any private restrictions on the property, such as significant homeowners' association policies or unrecorded easements.

Deed Restrictions. Deeds or other private contracts may be drafted to restrict the use of land, as long as the purpose is lawful. A subdivider may establish rules for use, character, cost, and siting of buildings in order to create a particular type of neighborhood. The restrictions are recorded and incorporated into all deeds in the subdivision. There may be a property owners' association to administer the restrictions. These rules are commonly referred to as CC&Rs—covenants, conditions, and restrictions. (Real Estate Transfer Disclosure Statement, C.12.)

Davis-Stirling Common Interest Development Act. For condominiums and similar projects, Civil Code §§1350 et seq. requires a declaration (disclosure) setting forth the restrictions on the use or enjoyment of any portion of the common interest development. A prospective purchaser must be given copies of:

☐ The declaration

☐ Bylaws

☐ Articles of incorporation

☐ A statement concerning any delinquent assessments and penalties

☐ Current financial statements.

Easements. An easement (Real Estate Transfer Disclosure Statement, C.3.) is the right to use another's property for some special purpose. Easements are most commonly created by express statement in the grant deed (and are thus recorded), but they can also be created by contracts between parties, and without any formal agreement at all by operation of law or by virtue of long use. The most familiar type of easement is a right of way across one property for access to another. Other types are for public utilities to run pipes or wires through or over private land, public paths, and conservation easements where a protective interest in a natural or historic resource is granted to a government agency or conservation organization.

HIGHLIGHTS TO REMEMBER

ENVIRONMENTAL DISCLOSURE REQUIREMENTS
Material facts must be disclosed: any facts which might reasonably affect buyer's decision
- Stuctural defects
- Environmental concerns
- History of property
- Legal restrictions

History includes the fact that murders have occurred on the property (*Reed vs. King*)

Exclusions: 3 year limit on required disclosures about deaths; AIDS not a material fact

No immunity for intentional misrepresentation in response to a direct inquiry

Evolving Disclosure Requirements
Written disclosures protect all parties by providing documentation and clarifying responsibilities

Affirmative duty to disclose material facts even if not asked

Responsibilities imposed by general law of agency, Real Estate Law, and court decisions

Professional competence required is that prevailing in the industry

Consumer protection is bringing about changes in the law: practitioner must keep informed

Natural Hazards
Earthquakes
- Location in Alquist-Priolo Act "special studies zone" must be disclosed by seller's broker
- Maps from State Division of Mines and Geology
- Seismic disclosure law (1993) for pre-1960 homes: seismic weaknesses in construction
- Retrofit requirements: not currently in state law, but may exist locally
- Insurance: must be offered by residential property insurer

Floods
- Location in FEMA hazard area must be disclosed by lender under federal law; seller or broker should disclose if known
- Flood insurance required for federally-related financing: National Flood Insurance Program

Fire
- State law establishes disclosure and prevention requirements in state responsibility areas (wildland): vegetation clearance, roofing, water, access
- Similar local requirements may apply in urban areas

Environmental Hazards
Increasingly important area of potential licensee liability

Hazardous substances include asbestos, radon, air and water pollutants

Known and "red flagged" potential hazards must be disclosed to buyer

Environmental experts should be consulted when needed

Toxic Disclosures Act (1992): new question on Transfer Disclosure Statement
- Asks if seller is aware of toxics on property (asbestos, radon, formaldehyde, lead paint, tanks, contaminated soil or water)

Asbestos: owner of pre-1979 building containing asbestos must inform employees and new owners

Environmental Disclosure Requirements

Restricted Use of Hazardous Waste Sites: surrounding buffer zones, by recorded easement

Hazards to Renters: parallel to sales disclosures—asbestos, seismic, toxic gases, ammunition dumps

Airport Noise Disclosure: required for property in vicinity of an airport

Seller's Disclosure Responsibilities—California Law
One- to four-unit residential properties; applies to sale, sales contract, lease-option, ground lease coupled with improvements

Seller's Written Disclosure:
Real Estate Transfer Disclosure Statement standard form available from California Association of Realtors®

Property description, condition, and restrictions

Responsibility for disclosure rests primarily on seller and agent

Personal knowledge or responsibly obtained

Certain information may be provided by parties other than the seller and agent

Delivery required before transfer of title or execution of sales contract, option, or lease

Right of rescission if not timely; damages for nondisclosure discovered within two years

Easton vs. Strassburger
Licensee's obligation defined by California Supreme Court and statute

Inspection and disclosures by seller's agent to buyer

Duty to investigate with reasonable diligence and disclose material facts

Facts which "should be known" to competent licensee

Civil Code §2079 applicable only to residential property, one to four units

Licensee is not required to inspect areas that are innaccessible

Pest Control Disclosures
Required when pest control certification or report is a condition of transfer or financing

Disclosure required before transfer; broker must provide disclosure or advise buyer of rights

Copy of report, certification, or notice of work completed must be delivered to buyer

Broker must keep record of compliance

Contents of all inspections are material facts

Public and Private Restrictions
Actual as well as potential future violations of zoning law or building code

Assessments not yet made

Private restrictions: CC&Rs, easements

Common interest development disclosures (Davis-Stirling Act)

Environmental Issues & Obligations

COURSE 13

Taxes, Real Estate & the Environment

INTRODUCTION

Complex tax issues affect every industry in the United States. As taxation increases to cover government programs and the national debt, the tax system must constantly undergo revision to balance adequate revenue and fair distribution of the tax burden, and to balance the burden between businesses and the individual.

TRA '86 The first part of this course presents current federal and state income tax laws that affect the real estate industry, including changes created by and since the passage of the Tax Reform Act of 1986 (TRA '86). The Tax Reform Act of 1986 made sweeping changes to our tax system. Overall, it provided for a more equitable system by broadening the tax base (limiting deductions) and eliminating many tax shelters. Changes have occurred since its passage, however, requiring one to keep apprised each year of the current guidelines. The state of California also changed its income tax rules to conform with the fundamental changes of TRA '86. Areas where state income tax changes differ from the federal changes will be noted.

Green Fees Part Two of this course deals with certain recent proposals designed to generate government revenues while preserving the environment and stimulating the economy. These proposed "green fees" were outlined in a 1992 report by the World Resources Institute, titled *Green Fees: How a Tax Shift Can Work for the Environment and the Economy*. It is not the intent of this course to influence the reader towards or against these proposals. Rather, it is to inform the reader of their existence, and illustrate the ways taxes interrelate with other aspects of public policy.

CONTINUING EFFECTS OF TRA '86

In 1986 Congress passed the Tax Reform Act. This act resulted in the greatest change to the Internal Revenue Code since 1954. The objectives of this change were to create a fairer system of taxation, remove tax shelters, simplify the tax brackets, and maintain a revenue neutral position; that is, TRA '86 would neither increase nor decrease net tax revenues for the government. The changes highlighted in this course are those which directly affect the real estate industry. A complete publication on all changes created by TRA '86 is available from the Internal Revenue Service, and from the Franchise Tax Board for state income tax changes, for those who need more information. Real estate licensees should refer clients to professional tax accountants or attorneys for tax advice.

Continuing Revisions Besides the monumental changes to the Internal Revenue Code which became effective in January of 1987, the code has been amended every year since. Some might say that ever since the passage of TRA '86, there has been a gradual change back to the old system. Regardless of viewpoint, legislation from 1986 on has made many changes in how certain real estate events are taxed, and others are subject to change each year as the new system continues to be amended. Such volatility in both federal and state tax systems make it imperative for the real estate professional to keep abreast of current regulations.

State Law. In California the legislation that brought state income tax laws into conformity with the federal changes is entitled the California Personal Income Tax Fairness, Simplification, and Conformity Act of 1987. This state legislation created base-broadening changes that directly conform to those in the federal law, including passive loss limits, limits on home mortgage interest deductions, and repeal of income averaging. Some areas of state law continue to differ from the federal, such as California's exemption for unemployment and social security benefits, and lottery winnings. In the following highlights of tax changes, state income tax changes are mentioned only when they differ from federal law.

Major Tax Changes

Tax Brackets Reduced. The number of federal tax brackets was reduced: from seven prior to 1986 down to three today. For California state income tax, the number of brackets was reduced from eleven down to six.

Lower Tax Rates. The tax rates in the three federal brackets are currently 15%, 28%, and 31%, increasing progressively as taxable income increases. For California state income tax, the rates in the six tax brackets are currently 1%, 2%, 4%, 6%, 8%, and 9.3%.

Capital Gains. Capital gain is the profit that a person realizes upon disposition of an asset. Capital gain can be short-term (property owned for a year or less) or long-term (property owned for more than a year prior to disposition). The IRS has traditionally treated long-term capital gain differently from other income. The manner of treatment of capital gain has changed many times over the years, but generally long-term capital gain has been taxed at a lesser rate than other income.

- *Long-Term Gain.* TRA '86 eliminated this advantage for capital gain. In the past only a portion of the gain was subject to taxation. Today, all of the gain is taxable. A recent amendment, however, establishes a 28% maximum rate on long-term capital gain.

> **Example**
> If a person's entire income including a long-term capital gain does not exceed the 15% tax bracket, this capital gain is taxed at 15% along with the taxpayer's other income. However, if a long-term capital gain when added to other income would push the taxpayer into the top bracket (31%), then the gain would be taxed separately from the other income at a maximum rate of 28%.

- *Short-Term Gain.* Short-term capital gain treatment remains unchanged, taxed at the same rate as other income without any beneficial treatment. California legislation conforms to the federal rules.

Capital Losses. Capital loss is loss from the disposition of an asset. Though capital gain is frequently combined with other income in computing taxable income, capital loss is always kept separate. It is not deductible against other income. It is only deductible against capital gain, if any. If there is no capital gain to be offset by the capital loss in a given year, resulting in a net capital loss for the taxpayer, this *excess* capital loss is treated as follows:

- Excess capital losses are no longer reduced by 50% prior to treatment, as they were before TRA '86.

- Up to $3,000 of net capital loss ($1,500 if married filing separate returns) may be deducted against ordinary income.

- The balance of capital loss after the $3,000 deduction is carried forward and used in future years to offset capital gain. Up to $3,000 of loss may also be deducted against ordinary income in future years. This process may continue indefinitely year by year until all the excess capital loss has been used up.

Gain on Sale of a Principal Residence. Rollover gains (Section 1034 of the IRS Code) still allow a deferment of gain upon the sale of a principal residence if it is replaced within a two year period. Replacement may occur within two years *either before or after* the sale of the former residence. A principal residence is defined as the personal residence where a taxpayer resides most of the time. Only *one* principal residence per taxpayer is permitted at any time, though that taxpayer may possess more than one *personal* residence. Exceptions to the two-year limit for rollover treatment of gain are:

- Involuntary conversions (nonvoluntary sales)—three years

- Military personnel on active duty—four years; under certain circumstances eight years.

Senior Exclusion. The *one-time* $125,000 exclusion of gain from the sale of a principal residence is still in effect for taxpayers who are 55 years or older.

INCOME AND DEDUCTIONS

Income or loss has always been classified by the IRS as either *ordinary* or *capital*. Simply put, ordinary income (or loss) is money earned or received (or lost) from the course of one's work, business, or investments while they are owned. Capital gain or loss is any profit or loss from an asset (investment) after it is sold. These two classifications still exist; however, they are now further divided into four categories of income or loss for tax calculations. For the most part, the income or loss from these four categories must be kept separate when reporting them; that is, a loss from one category cannot automatically offset an income from another one.

Active Activity This category comprises ordinary income (or loss) that is derived from active participation in the operation which produces the income. Such income includes wages, commissions, and profits (or losses) from owner-operated businesses.

Portfolio Activity This category includes income or loss derived "passively" from investments. It comprises ordinary income not included in the "active" category as well as capital gain or loss. Ordinary income in this category would include interest, royalties, stock dividends, etc., from investments *while they are owned*. Capital gain or loss is the profit or loss upon the sale or other disposition of the investment. Income or loss from rental properties is not included in this category; it falls into one of the next two categories.

Offset Rules. Ordinary income can be offset by ordinary loss, even if one is active and the other is portfolio, although an ordinary loss is virtually limited to owner-operated businesses. Capital loss cannot offset ordinary income.

Passive Activity This covers income or loss from most income producing real estate properties *while they are owned*. This category comprises limited partnership-owned real estate and other rental properties that are not actively managed or operated by the owners themselves.

Purpose. This new category of income was created in line with the goal of fairness in TRA '86. Many investor-owned properties show "paper losses" (tax shelters) to reduce other taxable income, while the properties are actually creating a long-term profit (capital gain) for the owners. The revised law provides that passive activity loss cannot offset other taxable income of the owner, thereby preventing such paper losses.

Process. Net annual losses from passively held properties are deductible only against net annual income from other passive properties. Once that deduction is made, any net (remaining) annual loss from the passive activity properties is "suspended"; that is, it is calculated and totaled every year, but it is not applied until the property is sold. Upon sale or other disposition of the property, all suspended loss accumulated during ownership may then be deducted from the capital gain realized. The remaining capital gain or loss is then treated as previously discussed.

Example

Mr. Smith owned an apartment complex and did not actively participate in its operation. While he owned it, the complex showed a net loss on paper of $5,000 per year for ten years. He sold it for $75,000 more than he had invested in it. What was his net capital gain?

$5,000 "suspended" loss per year

x 10 years

$50,000 total "suspended" loss

gain: $75,000 profit upon sale

minus $50,000 "suspended" loss while owned

equals $25,000 net realized capital gain

Passive Activity with Active Owner Participation This category of income is the same as passive activity except that the owner "actively participates" in the operation of the property. The tax treatment is the same except that up to $25,000 ($12,500 if married and filing separately) of annual loss *can* offset other income in any year. Any loss in excess of the $25,000 limit per year is "suspended" to future years in the same manner as passive activity treatment.

Definition. "Active participation in the operation" does not require the owners to do everything themselves. They merely have to perform at least some management-type decisions or duties while they own the property. Limited partnership-owned property is by definition excluded from this category, since limited partners are not allowed to participate in the operation.

Income Limits. The $25,000 per year loss limit is gradually phased out for higher income taxpayers. It begins to phase out for adjusted gross incomes of $100,000 and is totally gone for incomes above $150,000. For married people filing separately, these income limits are $50,000 to $75,000.

Depreciation The law permits taxpayers to recover the cost of property that they use to produce income. The cost of the property is recovered by depreciating it, that is, taking deductions for the cost over a period of years. Only the improvement portion of real property (buildings or structures) can be depreciated, since land does not deteriorate.

Longer Recovery Periods. TRA '86 made substantial changes to the depreciation rules that apply to rental property put into use after 1986. For residential income property, the recovery period has been expanded to 27.5 years (an increase of at least ten years). The depreciation period for nonresidential property is now 31.5 years. This results in a smaller annual deduction for depreciation, since the total amount must be spread over a longer period.

Straight-line Method. The depreciation deduction is now figured using only the straight-line method (an equal amount taken each year). Only certain farm structures and fruit and nut bearing trees are still allowed to use an accelerated method.

Forty-Year Option. An investor may elect a depreciation period of 40 years, instead of the 27.5 or the 31.5 year schedules. This choice must be made in the first year of ownership, and it must be maintained without change throughout the ownership. A taxpayer who cannot make use of a large annual depreciation deduction would probably choose the longer period, since it would result in a smaller deduction for a longer time.

Interest Deductions Prior to 1987 virtually all interest paid on loans was tax deductible. Today, few categories of interest are still deductible. Personal interest and mortgage interest were the most affected.

Personal Interest. Before 1987, personal interest was fully deductible as an itemized deduction. Personal interest is interest paid on nonbusiness loans that are not secured by real estate, such as car loans, personal loans, and credit cards. These personal interest deductions were phased out from 1987 through 1990. Today no deduction is allowed for personal interest.

Mortgage Interest. Before 1987, mortgage interest was fully deductible as an itemized deduction. Mortgage interest is interest paid on any loan secured by real estate. Business mortgage interest remains for the most part treated as before, but home mortgage interest and investment mortgage interest are now treated as follows:

Home Mortgage Interest. This is interest paid on one's personal residences. It is deductible (with limitations) on first and second mortgages (including home equity lines of credit) on first and second homes only. This deduction is limited by the amount of home acquisition indebtedness up to a total of one million dollars, and by the amount of home equity indebtedness (nonpurchase money loan) up to a total of $100,000.

- *Acquisition.* Home acquisition indebtedness is the indebtedness one incurred at the time of acquiring (purchasing) the home. It can be increased only by the addition of home improvements. It includes purchase money, construction, and home improvement loans as well as refinancing loans (nonpurchase money) that do not exceed the original indebtedness at the time of acquisition. Interest on indebtedness over one million dollars is not deductible.

- ☐ ***Equity Loans.*** Home equity indebtedness is a loan secured by the owner's equity in the home, for any reason other than to purchase the home. Homeowners are allowed to deduct the interest paid on these loans up to a maximum of $100,000 of equity loan. Interest paid on an amount of loan in excess of the $100,000 limit is not deductible.

- ☐ ***Old Loans.*** Interest on home loans that originated prior to August 17, 1986, continues to be deductible to the extent that the amount of debt is not more than the fair market value of the residence, so long as the debt does not increase after August 17, 1986.

Investment Interest. This is interest on loans secured by investment (or income) property. Prior to 1987, investment interest was fully deductible against investment income, and any interest paid in excess of the income was deductible up to $10,000. This interest deduction in excess of income was phased out from 1987 through 1990. Currently excess investment interest deductions are treated the same as excess passive activity deductions; that is, they are suspended to future years and may be used to offset future investment income only.

REPORTING AND TAXATION

TRA '86 has changed many of the rules regarding the reporting of certain real estate transactions to the IRS, as well as the taxation resulting from the reports. Money is required to be withheld in some instances. Some taxpayers must submit two entirely different calculations of their taxable income. The following are highlights of the pertinent changes in real estate reporting.

Alternative Minimum Tax This is a "straight tax" calculation of income tax required of certain individuals as an alternative to the "progressive" tax structure. The purpose of Alternative Minimum Tax (AMT) is to ensure that everyone with income above a certain level pays some income tax. AMT provides a formula for tax computation which, in effect, ignores certain preferential tax treatments that are allowed under present law. By eliminating these preferential deductions, a tax liability may be created for a taxpayer who would otherwise pay little or nothing.

Calculation. The current rate for AMT is a flat 24% of taxable income as figured by the AMT formula. The taxpayer must also calculate taxable income according to the normal IRS guidelines, and calculate the income tax using the progressive rate (15%, 28%, and 31%). The taxpayer then owes the higher of the two different tax computations. AMT calculations are required when the taxpayer has a significant amount of portfolio losses that provide for preferential tax treatment.

State Tax. California has enacted an Alternative Minimum Tax in conformity with the federal AMT. For California, the AMT rate is a straight 7%.

Real Estate Reporting All real estate transactions involving a transfer of ownership must now be reported to the IRS on Form 1099-S, giving the following information:

- ☐ The name, address, and taxpayer identification number (TIN—usually the social security number) of the transferor (seller)

- A description of the real estate transferred
- The settlement date (close of escrow)
- The gross proceeds of the transaction, which includes cash, amount of liabilities taken over by the transferee (buyer), and notes received from the buyer. If the total consideration includes other property or services, then the reporting person must indicate this in accordance with the instructions on the form
- The reporting person's name, address, and TIN.

Responsibility for Reporting. The primary responsibility for reporting the transaction to the IRS falls on the person responsible for closing the transaction, normally the escrow agent. If such an agent is not used, the people responsible for reporting are in order as follows:

- The primary mortgage lender, then
- The seller's broker, then
- The buyer's broker.

Delivery of Copies. Once the form is properly completed and sent to the IRS by the appropriate reporting person, copies must be given to the seller and the buyer in the transaction.

FIRPTA The Foreign Investment in Real Property Tax Act (FIRPTA) states that every buyer of United States real property must, unless an exemption applies, deduct and withhold from the seller's proceeds 10% of the gross sales price, and report and pay it to the IRS within 20 days after close of escrow. Exemptions to this requirement are:

- The seller provides an affidavit that the seller is not a "foreign person"
- A "qualifying statement" from the IRS specifies that no withholding is necessary
- The buyer purchases the property for use as a personal residence, and the purchase price is not over $300,000.

Penalties. Failure to comply with FIRPTA could result in the buyer being held liable to the IRS for the lesser of the seller's actual tax liability or the 10% of the sales price that should have been withheld, plus penalties and interest. Should a real estate licensee be an agent in a transaction that did not comply with FIRPTA (as agent of the seller or of the buyer), then that agent can be held liable for the least of the following, plus penalties and interest:

- The 10% of seller's proceeds that should have been withheld
- The seller's actual tax liability
- The amount of commission received by the agent.

California Law. In California, the state requires an additional 3.33% to be withheld from the proceeds of all sellers who are not residents of California, whether they are U.S. citizens or not. The only exemptions are proof of seller's California residency, or verification that the buyer is purchasing the property for use as a personal residence and the purchase price is not over $100,000. Payment is due in 20 days.

Tax Deferred Exchanges

Tax deferred exchanges (Section 1031 of the IRS Code) have long been used to allow an investor to dispose of one real estate investment and acquire another without having to pay capital gains tax on the first property. This allows the investor to use the value of the one to purchase the other without paying a part to the government. All or part of this gain can be deferred indefinitely, so long as the investor keeps *exchanging* one investment for another instead of *selling*. When the investor *sells* a property, then all deferred capital gains taxes associated with the property become due.

Delayed Exchange. Some years ago a variation of the tax deferred exchange was tested in the U.S. District Court in Portland, Oregon. In the Starker case, the IRS objected to the fact that the exchange was delayed; that is, Starker disposed of one property but did not acquire the exchange property until some time later. The court held that this delay would not necessarily defeat the tax deferred status of the exchange, provided certain conditions were met that perfected the intent of creating a tax deferred exchange.

New Rules. Subsequent cases showed considerable uncertainty over the conditions that would allow a tax deferred delayed exchange. In 1991 the IRS established a new ruling that better defined the bounds of an acceptable delayed exchange. In order to qualify as tax deferred, the exchange property must be identified within 45 days from the date that the disposed property is transferred. In addition, the exchange transaction must close within 180 days from the date that the disposed property transaction closed.

Elimination of Tax Credits

Virtually all tax credits associated with real estate investment that were allowed prior to TRA '86 have been abolished, such as investment tax credits and residential energy credits. However, two new tax credits have been created.

Low Income Housing Credit. This credit is allowed for owners of residential rental property which provides low income housing.

Rehabilitation Credit. This is allowed on qualified expenditures for the rehabilitation of certified historic structures and also on some other rehabilitated buildings first placed in service before 1936.

State Credits. California eliminated all tax credits except a minimal renter's credit. California has created tax credits for research and development projects, as well as low income housing projects (paralleling the federal program). The state has also re-enacted solar tax credits for commercial solar projects.

GREEN FEES: SHIFTING THE TAX BURDEN TO SUPPORT THE ENVIRONMENT

In late 1992, the World Resources Institute formulated several environmentally oriented tax proposals based on studies, program models, and trial programs that have been ongoing in various communities. These proposals introduce the idea of environmental charges, called *green fees*. Unlike traditional forms of taxation (income and sales taxes on the general public), environmental charges are more like a *user fee*, designed specifically to tax those products or activities that are harmful to the environment. Proponents say these fees could reduce the existing tax burdens that are harming the economy, generate needed revenue to preserve and protect the environment, and serve as a deterrent to environmentally harmful activities. The Institute argues that providing a better framework of market incentives by restructuring our revenue system can simultaneously improve environmental quality and make the American economy more competitive.

Current Tax System To appreciate the possible benefits of shifting tax burdens from current methods to alternative ones, one must examine the effects of our current trends in taxation. Between 1972 and 1990, average personal income taxes and social security payroll taxes together have risen from 17.5% to 19.2% of personal income. In 1991, 41% of federal tax revenue came from personal income tax, 9% from corporate income tax, and 42% from payroll taxes.

Effect on the Economy. Increasing this tax burden to cover increases in governmental expenditures tends to discourage the economy in a variety of ways. These effects create what is termed a "marginal excess burden" of taxes, which is the *additional* loss of income due to reductions in effort and investment.

- Workers withdraw or work fewer hours, seeing little difference in their net income.

- Labor becomes too expensive for employers, so cheaper labor is sought, resulting in layoffs of skilled workers and flight of jobs to lower-paid areas in or outside the country.

- Cheaper labor results in less tax revenue to government, which turns to increased taxes to make up for the decrease in revenue.

- Studies indicate that if tax on capital income (investment) is raised 10 percent, then total savings fall by 4 percent.

Effects on Investment. For every extra dollar of tax revenue collected, the *marginal excess burdens* of payroll taxes are about $0.30; of individual income taxes, they are about $0.40; and of tax on investment income, they are about $0.60. This effect tends to reduce investment capital, and that income which continues to be invested will seek only those investments which offer tax shelters to offset these effects. This quest for tax-sheltered investments has already caused changes in the tax guidelines that have eliminated shelters.

Possible Alternatives The overall result is that government's current revenue needs are met through taxes that are extremely costly to the United States economy in terms of lost work and savings. How, then, can additional revenue be raised in a way that is less burdensome than taxes on income, profits, and payrolls? User fees and environmental charges may be such an alternative.

State Programs. Many state governments are already using this alternative. In 1993, over half of new tax revenues for the states are to come from increases in alcohol and tobacco taxes, gasoline taxes, motor vehicle registration fees, and other user fees. Louisiana, South Carolina, and New Jersey have already proposed environmental charges, including fees on hazardous waste processing facilities, fees on solid waste facilities, and fees for emissions discharge inspections and control.

Benefits. Environmental charges could result in improved cost-effectiveness in U.S. environmental regulations. Unit charges on environmentally sensitive activities create an incentive to the extent that it costs less to reform than to pay the charge incurred. Currently, the total cost of administering and complying with environmental regulations in the United States is around $120 billion per year, which is 2 percent of the entire Gross Domestic Product (GDP). Studies of specific programs indicate that costs could be much less if cleanup and control responsibilities were reallocated in this manner.

Method of Assessment. Without incentive-based policies in force, environmental costs cannot readily be collected from those whose activities cause the damage. This is especially true because air and water are used in common. When the air or water is impaired through a contaminating discharge, a per unit charge would allow an incentive for control and a method of collecting the charge assessed. The circumstances under which environmental charges work particularly well include:

- When the problem is being caused by many different sources, which are difficult to regulate

- When each party's actions contribute proportionately to the overall problem

- When the overall damages resulting from the activity are reasonably understood and regular

- When the relevant behavior of each party can be monitored accurately at reasonable cost, so that charges are enforceable.

Example: Carbon Tax. Everyone who burns fossil fuel or uses electricity generated with fossil fuels contributes carbon dioxide to the growing concentration in the atmosphere. Since the amount of carbon dioxide emitted per unit of each fossil fuel burned is known with reasonable accuracy, the obvious way to regulate emissions is to impose a tax on the carbon content of each fuel. It is not yet possible to quantify accurately the potential economic damages from climate change caused by emissions, but some studies suggest that they are substantial, perhaps as much as 1 to 2 percent of the GDP. Thus a tax on carbon fuels could yield net economic savings along with revenues that could be used to reduce other taxes that now have distorting effects on the economy.

Proposed Fees. Three environmental charges under serious consideration today, outlined in detail in the next section, are solid waste charges, congestion tolls on urban highways, and carbon taxes. The first reportedly could generate at least $5 billion in annual revenues for federal, state, and local governments. The second could raise another $40 billion, and the third over $30 billion in annual revenues.

Economic Benefits. Using just these three revenue sources would allow governments to reduce marginal rates of economically crippling taxation (income, profit, and payroll) and produce over $45 billion in annual net economic benefits, while improving the environment by spending some congestion toll revenue on public transportation, and investing some revenues from solid waste charges in recycling.

Proposals for Environmental Charges

Three main programs for environmental user fees are under consideration by federal, state, and local governments. As of this printing, the federal Department of Energy under the Clinton administration has outlined a proposed carbon tax, which is expected to be instituted in some form within this presidential term. There are many other proposed "green fees"; however, the three most prominent ones are solid waste charges, highway congestion tolls, and carbon taxes.

Solid Waste Charges Landfills are filling up faster than new disposal facilities can be created. Community resistance to developing new dumps has toughened, as have the environmental standards required of them, such as methane gas extraction, leachate collection, surface and ground water monitoring, and installing impermeable liners. As a result, landfill disposal costs are dramatically higher than in the past, while controversies over interregional and international shipments of waste have intensified.

- *Increasing Waste.* Between 1960 and 1988, the volume of municipal solid waste more than doubled, from 88 to 180 million tons. This averages to 4.5 pounds of trash discarded daily per person, which is a world record. Over half of this waste volume consists of categories that are readily recyclable, such as yard waste, newspapers, corrugated cardboard, and beverage containers; yet only about 13 percent is actually recycled, and even that percentage has created a glut on most secondary markets.

- *Decreasing Disposal Capacity.* Nearly three-quarters of all municipal waste is landfilled, and the remaining unrecycled fraction is incinerated. Despite this huge and increasing need for landfills, the number of new landfill openings fell from 381 in 1970 to only sixty-two in 1986. A recent EPA survey found that approximately 80 percent of existing landfills will reach capacity within the next twenty years. Twenty-eight states report less than ten years of remaining capacity, and ten states have less than five years.

Solution. The first step to any solution in this area is to reduce the amount solid waste that could be recycled but is now entering landfills. The reason it is not being recycled is that communities offer no financial incentives for households to discard less solid waste and recycle more. Since most households pay for rubbish collection through property taxes—a flat annual amount completely unrelated to the volume or composition of trash they discard—the incremental cost or reward to them of varying the amount or composition of their rubbish is exactly zero.

- *Fees and Incentives.* Incentives can be created by charging households the full incremental costs of waste collection and disposal through a "pay-by-the-bag" system, and, where necessary, adjusting fees to reflect disposal costs more accurately. This incentive would be furthered by an enhanced recycling program. The pay-as-you-discard approach gives households incentives to recycle, compost, and adjust their purchasing habits to reduce the volume of waste. In turn, consumer demand signals producers and retailers to reduce the amount of packaging and to increase its recyclability.

- *Statistics.* The experience of ten communities across America with pay-by-the-bag systems over periods up to nine years was analyzed statistically for the effect of pricing on the tonnage of waste sent to landfills. A typical community that raised its collection fee per 32 pound bag from zero to

$1.50—in line with incremental costs—would probably induce about an 18 percent reduction in the volume of solid waste it had to landfill. If the community introduced a curbside recycling program at the same time, its landfill volume would fall about 30 percent.

Benefits. By charging households for the volume of wastes they discard instead of financing waste management services through property taxes or other uniform flat-rate collection fees, communities can arrest the growth of the solid waste stream, reduce collection and disposal costs, extend the lifetimes of existing landfills, and encourage recycling, while generating the revenues and cost savings needed to pay for recycling programs.

Congestion Tolls on Urban Highways

Traffic congestion is a serious problem in American cities. Between 1970 and 1989, the total miles traveled by motor vehicles increased by 90 percent and the number of vehicles registered increased by over 70 percent, but urban road capacity increased by less than 4 percent. Nearly 70 percent of rush-hour travel endures stop-and-go conditions—a 30 percent increase since 1983. Nevertheless 74 percent of all drivers commute alone in their cars, and only 15 percent carpool.

Costs. Increasing urban traffic congestion means longer delays, more accidents, wasted fuel, and more smog, acid precipitation, and greenhouse gas emissions. Congestion reduces productivity directly by lengthening the time it takes to get people, goods, and services to their destinations and indirectly by imposing added stress on all drivers.

- *Time and Fuel.* A study of twenty-nine western cities found that in 1986 the costs of time delays and excess fuel consumption due to congestion was $17.5 billion. In Los Angeles, these costs total almost $6 billion a year—$3 a day per vehicle on the road. In 1984, 1.25 billion hours were lost in road delays; by 2005, the Federal Highway Administration predicts 6.9 billion hours will be lost. This would waste an additional 7.3 billion gallons of fuel per year and increase drivers' costs by $40 billion annually.

- *Incremental Costs.* The Bay Area Economic Forum of 1990 concluded that one additional car can cause an extra hour in delay, when summed over all drivers already on the Bay Area highways during rush hour. But that additional driver is oblivious to these extra costs imposed on fellow travelers. Drivers ignore this "external" cost, thinking only of the cost of their own time. The "price" of travel is too low in that it does not reflect its full incremental costs.

Solution. For over thirty years, economists have advocated congestion tolls to deal with this problem. Such tolls would be based on the costs that an additional car imposes on all others during congested periods, and would force drivers to make decisions that more accurately reflect their overall economic consequences. Road space during rush hour is a scarce commodity. If drivers faced all of the costs of using it, to others as well as to themselves, then road capacity could be allocated more efficiently among users.

- *Current Examples.* Soon this idea will be tested. Two private toll roads under construction in Orange County and another in San Diego County may all be subject to congestion pricing. Three government-owned toll roads are under construction in Orange County, and the county government is exploring the idea of incorporating peak and off-peak pricing.

☐ *Effect of Fees*. Congestion tolls will influence many driving decisions: the amount of travel, the timing, the route and destination, and the choice between public and private transportation. The "right" price will induce the optimal number of trips and types of travel, where the *marginal social cost* of an extra trip equals the *marginal social benefit* it produces.

Benefits. To say that rush-hour travel is harmful means that the social costs of driving exceed the private costs, since each additional vehicle also imposes delay costs on all other vehicles. Congestion tolls, unlike most taxes, have the potential to generate revenues and simultaneously to improve economic and general welfare by discouraging undesirable activity. The authors of the recent book *Road Work* conclude that "plausible congestion tolls would reduce peak traffic volumes 10 percent to 25 percent on many congested highways."

☐ *Incentives to Change*. Reducing peak demand can be much cheaper than providing extra capacity that will only occasionally be used. This is what phone companies and utility companies do by giving discounts during evenings and weekends, which are off-peak demand periods.

☐ *Targeted Users*. Rush-hour trips that are not work related have been increasing much faster than commuter trips. Indeed, such journeys now account for most rush-hour traffic and approximately 75% of all weekday car trips. Morning rush-hour travel for nonwork reasons increased by 42.1% between 1977 and 1983, while work related trips increased by only 2.7%. Since nonwork trips are probably more flexible and thus more sensitive to cost than work trips are, congestion tolls could encourage people to schedule nonwork trips outside of rush hours.

☐ *Air Quality*. A study of a toll scheme in Boston estimated that carbon monoxide concentrations would be reduced by 7% overall, and up to 60% in the central business district. In the Los Angeles area, a joint study by the Environmental Defense Fund and the Regional Institute of Southern California found that congestion tolls could decrease carbon monoxide emissions by 12%, carbon dioxide by 9%, and nitrogen oxides by 8%.

Carbon Taxes The National Energy Strategy estimates that, in the absence of policy changes, U.S. energy use will increase by 64% by the year 2030. Coal, which now accounts for 22% of total energy use, could increase to 38% in 2030.

Greenhouse Effect. While some pollutants from the burning of fossil fuels—sulfur dioxide, volatile organic compounds, particulates, and nitrogen oxides—are regulated by federal, state, and local governments, one major pollutant, carbon dioxide, remains unconstrained. Carbon dioxide emissions have no immediate effects on health and the environment, and their full environmental impacts take decades to unfold. But there is a theory that average global temperatures may increase as atmospheric concentrations of greenhouse gases rise, and there may be potential environmental risks.

Variables. Any serious effort to reduce atmospheric concentrations of greenhouse gases will involve reducing carbon dioxide emissions. Fossil fuel use is affected by consumer choices about how much heat, light, and other energy services they want to consume, how efficient their appliances are, and which type of energy their appliances use. Manufacturers can typically choose whether to use relatively more labor and capital or relatively more energy in production, and they can choose among energy types. Electric utilities can choose which fuels to use in generating power and, in many states, can also choose to buy or subsidize energy-efficient products for their consumers rather than generate more power. All these options have different costs.

- *What to Tax*. The cost of imposing charges on the huge number and wide variety of emitters of carbon dioxide would be overwhelming. However, the carbon content of the fuels that generate carbon dioxide when burned can serve as the tax basis without distorting the economic intent. This is true for two important reasons. First, virtually all the carbon in fossil fuels is released during combustion as carbon dioxide. Second, there is no economically feasible way of removing carbon dioxide from emissions the way sulfur dioxide can be "scrubbed" from the emissions of a coal-fired power plant. Thus, it is fair to assume that the carbon in a ton of coal, a barrel of oil, or a thousand cubic feet of natural gas will be released as carbon dioxide upon combustion. A charge on the carbon content of the fuel is equivalent to a charge on emissions.

- *At What Point*. Following this logic, a carbon tax is defined as an excise tax on the producers of raw fossil fuels (primary energy) based on the relative carbon content of the fuels. Such a tax would fall more heavily on coal than oil, which in turn would be taxed more than natural gas. To be most effective, the tax would be applied at the point that the fuel enters the economy—at the wellhead for natural gas, the mine mouth for coal, and the well or dockside for oil. Taxing carbon early in the production chain could influence all decisions concerning fossil fuel use.

- *Downstream Effect*. Carbon taxes would appear to consumers and manufacturers as energy price increases. But since one fuel can in many cases be substituted for another, overall price increases would not be as large as the initial tax. If a carbon tax were applied to each fuel at the point where it is produced or imported into the United States, it would influence virtually all of the downstream energy choices of producers and consumers of carbon-based fuels.

- *How Much Tax*. If environmental considerations alone are the measure, the ideal tax rate is set at the point at which the benefits from the last ton of carbon removed equal the cost of eliminating that ton. But this point is very difficult to find. It is also impossible to quantify economic damages from global warming. The most common alternative method is to estimate the tax level necessary to achieve a desired level of carbon dioxide emissions. For example, a tax rate can be chosen to stabilize emissions at 1990 levels by the year 2000. Virtually all economic analyses of carbon-reduction possibilities suggest that substantial early reductions, say over the next ten or fifteen years, can be achieved quite inexpensively, so a fairly low tax would be sufficient. But as time goes on, sustaining or extending these reductions may become harder and harder, requiring a significantly higher tax.

Results. Since a carbon tax makes fossil fuels more expensive, the theory is that it will alter the use of capital, labor, energy, and other economic resources. In response, businesses and households will try to lower their tax payments by reducing their use of fossil fuels and increasing their use of capital, labor, and nonfossil energy. Consumers might respond to higher electricity prices by buying more efficient appliances, or by less use of the ones they have. The net effect of these switches will be to reduce the production of some goods and services. The way the revenues from the carbon tax are used, however, might offset any negative effect on the GDP.

- ☐ ***Effect on Tax Structure.*** Using the carbon tax in part to lower other tax burdens can improve the nation's overall economic performance, by:
  - Returning the revenues to consumers by lowering personal income tax payments
  - Reinvesting them to promote economic growth through an investment tax credit.

  Any number of tax reform options could also be financed through a carbon or other pollution tax. The choice depends on which public policy goals are considered most important.

- ☐ ***Environmental Effects.*** A charge that reduced the use of fossil fuels would also reduce the amount of other pollutants—for example, sulfur dioxide, nitrogen oxides, carbon monoxide, heavy metals, hydrocarbons, and particulate emissions. A study by the World Bank suggests that the sulfur dioxide and nitrogen oxides reductions alone resulting from a $26 per ton carbon tax could be in the range of 2,766,000 tons per year. The economic benefits of these reductions might be in the range of $1.5 billion per year.

Other Green Fees Though the three taxes discussed above are still proposals, many similar charges are already in operation. Proposed and existing environmental charges and user fees fall into five categories: emissions charges, charges on environmentally damaging activities, product charges, deposit-return charges, and reduction of existing tax benefits and subsidies.

Emissions Charges. Charges imposed on the basis of the volume and toxicity of emissions are called effluent charges, or emission taxes. Such charges include fees on such substances and activities as:

- ☐ Water effluents
- ☐ Toxic releases
- ☐ Vehicle emissions
- ☐ Solid waste collection and disposal.

Charges on Environmentally Damaging Activities. These taxes cover activities that are themselves environmentally damaging, rather than producing a damaging by-product or incidental damage ("sin taxes").

- ☐ Recreational user fees on public lands
- ☐ Highway congestion tolls
- ☐ Noise charges on airport landings
- ☐ Impact fees on installation of septic systems, underground storage tanks, construction projects with environmental impacts, etc.

Product Charges. Product charges are not levied on the environmentally harmful activity, but on the product whose use is involved in that activity. Such products and the fees that go with them include the following:

- Taxes based on the carbon content of fossil fuels
- Gasoline taxes
- Excise taxes on ozone-depleting substances
- Taxes on agricultural chemicals
- Taxes on virgin materials (resources that have been extracted as opposed to recycled).

Deposit-Return Charges. These are related to "product charges" but with significantly different revenue implications. Charges are refunded when the product is returned to a designated collection point. They are appropriate when the policy objective is not primarily to discourage use of the product, but to encourage its proper disposal, including recycling.

- Beverage containers
- Vehicles
- Lead-acid and nickel-cadmium batteries
- Vehicle tires
- Lubricating oil.

Reduction of Tax Benefits and Subsidies. Current law allows oil and gas producers, hardrock mining companies, and some other enterprises that extract nonrenewable resources to deduct certain percentages of gross revenues from taxable income as depletion allowances. Hardrock mining on public lands remains subject to the Mining Law of 1872, which allows claimants to obtain rights to mineral exploitation—without payment of royalties—at a nominal cost of $2.50 to $5 per acre. It is argued that these policies amount to a large subsidy to the extractive industries, raising returns to investors and increasing production of such toxic materials as asbestos, lead, mercury, cadmium, and uranium, while depressing markets for recycled metals, subsidizing production of fossil fuels, and depriving the Treasury of considerable revenues. Changes in existing tax deductions and subsidies that could benefit the Treasury and the environment include:

- Elimination of depletion allowances for energy and other minerals
- Elimination of depletion allowances for ground water extraction
- Charging royalties for hardrock mining on public lands
- Eliminating below-cost timber sales
- Charging market rates for grazing rights on public lands
- Charging market rates for state and federal irrigation water
- Charging market rates for federal power.

Green Fees: Arguments For
Green fees, or environmental charges, are proposed as an attempt to solve two major problems facing the country today: how to generate new governmental revenues without injuring the economy, and how to preserve and protect the environment.

Present Tax System Is Not Working. Increasing traditional forms of taxation will continue to produce negative effects on the economy, such as:

- Personal income tax increases, which reduce consumer spending power and cause recession

- Payroll tax increases, which increase labor costs and cause layoffs and a search for cheaper labor

- Investment tax increases, which greatly reduce the availability of investment capital which in turn supports many industries

- Sales tax increases, which reduce commodity sales and cause a recessionary trend in the economy.

Environmental Charges Can Help. Environmental charges are proposed as one solution to both problems. Environmental improvements result from these fees primarily as follows:

- Taxes on pollutants reduce their use, lessening harm to the environment

- Tolls and fees on harmful activities generate revenue and discourage the harmful acts

- User fees cover costs of operation without government's having to subsidize solid waste management and recycling programs

- Refundable deposit charges encourage recycling

- Rethinking depletion allowances and subsidies will discourage the extraction of virgin resources.

Opposing Arguments

Few oppose the idea of protecting and preserving the environment, but many people fear that "green fees" would just be added to existing taxes, not shift the burden. Specific doubts and objections include the following:

Competitive Disadvantage. Taxes on products that require carbon in their production will make domestically produced items more costly than the same items produced in foreign countries, and make U.S. items less competitive in a world market.

Regressive Taxation. Environmental charges are likely to be a regressive form of taxation; that is, people with lower incomes pay the same amount of tax as those with higher incomes, consuming a larger percentage of their income. This could be a greater tax burden on the average person than traditionally progressive forms, such as income taxes.

Increased Bureaucracy. Implementing environmental charges could create worse problems than they were designed to alleviate, especially collection systems for congestion tolls.

Increased Taxes. Though green fees are presented as a way to relieve the burden of existing taxation, most people fear giving the government yet another way to tax them. Governments rarely let go of any form of taxation once adopted, even if other revenues become available.

HIGHLIGHTS TO REMEMBER

TAXES, REAL ESTATE, AND THE ENVIRONMENT

Continuing Effects of TRA '86
The Tax Reform Act of 1986 (TRA '86) made sweeping changes in the Internal Revenue Code

California changed state tax code to conform with TRA '86

Federal tax brackets reduced to three: 15%, 28%, and 31%

Deductions reduced to widen the tax base; changes made by TRA '86 are "revenue neutral"

Capital Gains and Losses
Maximum 28% tax on long-term capital gain

Capital losses are fully deductible against capital gains only, not against ordinary income

$3,000 excess capital loss may be deducted from other taxable income in a year; balance of loss carried forward for use in future years

Transfer of principal residence: Rollover of gains (§1034) and one-time exclusion of gain for persons 55 and older remain in place

Income and Deductions: Four Categories of Income
Active activity—wages, commissions, bonuses, profits from business operations

Portfolio activity—investment income, such as interest, royalties, stock dividends, capital gains, but not income from rental properties

Passive activities—income from real estate properties while they are owned (rental income)

Passive activities with owner participation—same as passive activities except owner participates in the operation or management of the property

Loss Treatment
Ordinary loss may offset ordinary income (active or portfolio)

Capital loss may offset only capital gain, except up to a $3,000 annual excess capital loss may offset other income

Passive activity cannot deduct a net loss; excess loss is suspended until property is sold, when it is used to offset capital gain

Passive activity with owner participation allows up to a $25,000 annual loss from the operation; any additional loss must be suspended

Depreciation
Depreciation schedules extended to 27.5 years for residential income property, 31.5 years for non-residential

With few exceptions, only straight-line method of calculating depreciation is allowed

Interest Deductions
Personal interest deductions—none

Home mortgage deductions—first and second loan interest on no more than two personal residences up to the amount of "home acquisition indebtedness" (maximum $1 million)

Environmental Issues & Obligations

Home equity loan maximum of $100,000

Investment interest deductions—deductible only against investment income; excess deduction over income is "suspended" as with excess passive activity loss

Alternative Minimum Tax (AMT)
To ensure that everyone with income above a certain level pays some income tax

Flat tax (24%) based on a different taxable income calculation

Some taxpayers must calculate their income tax both ways and pay the higher amount

1099-S Reporting
All real estate transfers must be reported on IRS Form 1099-S by the person responsible for closing the transaction

Foreign Investment in Real Property Tax Act (FIRPTA)
Buyer's responsibility to see that 10% of seller's gross proceeds are withheld unless seller is a U.S. citizen or buyer is purchasing as a personal residence for less than $300,000

Agent may be liable up to amount of commission if proceeds are not properly withheld

In California, 3-1/3% of seller's gross proceeds must be withheld unless seller is a California resident or buyer is purchasing as a personal residence for less than $100,000

Delayed Exchanges
Delayed tax-deferred exchanges have been restricted

Second property in the exchange must be identified within 45 days from closing of the first property, and conveyed within 180 days

Tax Credits
TRA '86 abolished most tax credits for real estate investment

Two new federal credits: low income housing and rehabilitation of pre-1936 (historic) buildings

GREEN FEES: SHIFTING THE TAX BURDEN TO SUPPORT THE ENVIRONMENT

Proposal by World Resources Institute
Traditional methods of taxation (on income, profit, payroll, and investment) are harmful to economic growth, through "marginal excess burdens"

User fees and environmental charges are proposed as a cost-effective alternative

Environmental Benefits
Environmental charges provide an incentive to reduce environmentally harmful activities

Environmental costs are distributed fairly among those whose activities harm the environment

Revenues can be used to further enhance environmental programs

Taxes, Real Estate, & the Environment

Proposals for Environmental Charges
    Solid Waste Charges
- Landfills are filling up faster than new sites can be created
- Pay-by-the-bag fees can address costs of garbage disposal and future waste sites

    Congestion Tolls on Urban Highways
- Highway congestion is costly to the environment and the economy
- Tolls could reduce rush-hour traffic and repair the societal costs created by congestion
- Fees influence people's decisions about how, when, and where they travel

    Carbon Taxes
- Many polluting emissions are regulated or controlled, but not carbon dioxide, the leading cause of greenhouse effect
- Fees on products that contain carbon or activities that involve burning of fossil fuels
- Tax rate based on amount of carbon content in fuel

    Other Green Fees:
- Five main categories existing and proposed
- Emission charges
- Fees on environmentally damaging activities (sin taxes)
- Charges on products resulting from such activities
- Deposit-return charges
- Reduction or elimination of depletion allowances and tax subsidies for harmful activities

Green Fees: Pro and Con
    Objectives
- Discourage, reduce, or prevent environmentally damaging activities
- Restructure tax system to revitalize the economy

    Opposition
- U.S. products could become more expensive and less competitive with foreign goods
- Regressive tax, hitting lower incomes harder than higher ones
- Bureaucracy involved in controlling and collecting fees
- Public opposition to yet another tax

COURSE 14
Agency in Real Estate

INTRODUCTION

The basic law that governs the relationships between a broker, salesperson, and buyer or seller in a real estate transaction is agency law. The idea behind the agency relationship is that two persons agree that one (the agent) is to act for the benefit of the other (the principal). The principal has the right to control the conduct of the agent, and since the agent has the power to affect the legal relations of the principal, the principal trusts and depends upon the agent to be faithful and use reasonable skill in the performance of duties. The relationship should function smoothly, but when it does not, as when losses occur as a result of mistake, negligence, or fraud, controversy arises and the duties, rights, and liabilities of the parties must be examined. The duties and liabilities imposed upon the California real estate licensee because of the agency relationship become more stringent each year.

Statutory Basis There are four laws that apply to agency relationships in California. All apply to real estate licensees in their activities as agents. This course reviews the principles contained in all of these laws.

Law of Agency. Civil Code, Title IX, §§2295, 2513. The Law of Agency defines agency and identifies the ways in which the various types of agency can be created. It also describes the duties and liabilities of the parties (the principal and the agent) in their relationship with each other, and describes their duties and liabililties to third parties. This law applies to all agency relationships, not just in real estate.

Real Estate Law. Business and Professions Code, §10176(d). This section of the Real Estate Law provides that the Real Estate Commissioner may suspend or revoke the real estate license of a person who has been guilty of "acting for more than one party in a transaction without the knowledge or consent of all parties thereto." Such an agency in considered an "undisclosed dual agency," or "divided agency," and such a person is acting as a "double agent." This is a violation of the Law of Agency and of the Real Estate Law.

Statute of Frauds. Civil Code §1624. The Statute of Frauds requires that certain contracts must be in writing to be enforceable, including "an agreement authorizing or employing an agent . . . to purchase or sell real estate, or to lease real estate for a longer period than one year . . . ." Because of this requirement, a broker could be held to be an agent under the Law of Agency, but be unable to enforce payment of the commission if the listing was not reduced to writing and signed by the principal.

Agency in Residential Real Property Transactions. Civil Code §2373 et seq. The agency disclosure law for residential real estate transactions requires that a licensee dealing in residential property issue a disclosure statement to both buyer and seller, explaining what agency means, disclosing whose agent the licensee is, and obtaining the buyer's and seller's consent.

PRINCIPAL-AGENT RELATIONSHIP

The general definition of agency, in California Civil Code §2295, states that "An agent is one who represents another, called the principal, in dealings with third persons. Such representation is called an agency." In real estate, a broker can be the agent of a seller or a buyer, of a lender or a borrower, of a landlord or a tenant.

Legal Effect of Relationship — The agent's actions, whether intentional, negligent, or innocent, are deemed to be the actions of the principal. Any knowledge or notice possessed by the agent is imputed (attributed) to the principal, and vice versa.

Types of Agency — **General vs. Special.** One who is employed by a principal as an agent for a particular transaction is called a special agent; all other agents are general agents. Real estate licensees are special agents, employed for the specific purpose of procuring a buyer or seller for a parcel of real property. (Civil Code §2297)

Dual vs. Single. Dual agency results when an agent, with the knowledge and consent of all parties, represents both sides in a transaction, as opposed to single agency, in which an agent represents only one of the parties.

Divided Agency. This results when an agent attempts to represent both sides to a transaction without their mutual knowledge and consent. Such an attempt represents neither side faithfully, and is a breach of the fiduciary duty an agent owes to a principal. Divided agency can subject a real estate licensee to disciplinary action by the Real Estate Commissioner. (B&P Code §10176(d))

Gratuitous Agency. No consideration (payment) is required to establish an agency relationship. An agency which does not involve payment is called a gratuitous agency.

Creation of Agency — An agency relationship is created when one person authorizes another to act on his or her behalf in transactions with others. The agent is authorized to act as the substitute for the principal, and may be empowered to do all things the principal could do except certain things to which the principal is bound to give personal attention. The agency can be created in any of three ways:

- By agreement between the parties, express or implied
- By the principal's ratification of an agent's previously unauthorized act
- By "estoppel," sometimes called "ostensible agency."

Contract Not Required. An agency relationship does not depend on the existence of a contract. While a broker's right to collect a commission requires a written agreement, an agency relationship may be created without a written agreement. Thus a broker who acts with no written listing agreement (and thus no enforceable claim to a commission) may still be subject to all the fiduciary obligations imposed by the principal-agent relationship.

Express or Implied Agreement — Although no formal contract is required to create an agency relationship, there must be an intention by the parties, either expressed or implied, that such a relationship exist. This intent may be manifested by the parties' words or conduct or by the surrounding facts and circumstances.

> **Example**
>
> When a seller and broker execute a listing agreement, a principal-agent relationship is created. If the broker assists the buyer in obtaining financing after the purchase contract has been negotiated, the broker may also become the buyer's agent, at least for purposes of all matters surrounding the financing.

Equal Dignities Rule. Although no writing is required to create an agency relationship, the "equal dignities rule" (Civil Code §2309) mandates that if a certain type of contract is required to be in writing, such as a contract to purchase real estate, then any agreement authorizing an agent to enter into such a contract on the principal's behalf must also be in writing. Brokers are rarely authorized by their principals to enter into contracts to sell or purchase real estate, but, under property management agreements, they frequently enter into rental agreements (leases) on behalf of owners.

Power of Attorney. This is a written instrument by which a principal appoints an "attorney in fact" as agent and confers upon the agent the authority to act on behalf of the principal. The authority may be general (to transact all business) or special (limited). (Civil Code §2400 et. seq.)

Ratification An agency may also be created by the principal's ratification of a previously unauthorized action by another individual (Civil Code §2307). Ratification normally results when the purported agent has held himself or herself out as representing the principal, and the principal then accepts the benefits of the purported agent's actions.

> **Example**
>
> A real estate licensee, purporting to act as an owner's agent to sell land, received a portion of the purchase price from a prospective purchaser. The owner tendered a conveyance to the purchaser and notified the licensee in writing not to return the money received. The court held that the owner's actions constituted ratification of the licensee's status as an agent.

Estoppel Agency by estoppel, or ostensible agency, results when the principal, either intentionally or negligently, allows a third party to believe that another person is the principal's agent and the third party relies on that belief. The principal's statements, actions, or inactions lead the third party to believe that the person is acting as an agent. When this happens, the principal will be "estopped"—prohibited—from later asserting that the agent was not acting on the principal's behalf. (Civil Code §2300)

> **Example**
>
> A seller advertised a property for sale through a particular realty firm. The broker who received the deposit in response to the ad was not a member of that firm, but did occupy office space in the firm's offices. When the broker disappeared with the money, the court allowed the prospective purchaser to recover her lost money from the realty firm, on the theory that the firm had allowed the plaintiff to believe the absconding broker was its agent.

Judicial Interpretation California courts are quick to find the existence of an agency relationship when they perceive a need to protect the interests of a buyer or seller by imposing a fiduciary obligation on the licensee. The California Supreme Court in *Skopp vs. Weaver*, 16 Cal. 3d 432, wrote: "Whenever the acts or omissions of a licensee cause injury in a real estate transaction, there is a compelling reason to find him an agent.... No California decision has held a licensee exempt from fiduciary obligation to the seller when the licensee has in fact acted to the seller's detriment." Thus, courts will make a special effort to find an agency relationship if a party to the transaction has been injured by some action or inaction of the licensee.

Termination of Agency An agency may be terminated in four ways: by *expiration* of its term or extinction of its subject, *death or incapacity* of either the agent or the principal, *renunciation* by the agent, or *revocation* by the principal.

Revocation. Although the principal usually has the *power* to revoke the agency, he or she may not have the *right* to do so. This means that a principal who revokes the agency without cause or reason may be held liable for breach of contract. For example, a principal who revokes a listing may be liable for payment of the broker's commission. Nevertheless, the revocation terminates the agency and cuts off the rights and duties of the agent.

Death. Listing agreements are personal contracts between parties and do not descend to the heirs. A broker's death cancels all listings held by him or her. For this reason many real estate companies elect the corporate form of ownership, with more than one qualifying broker. The corporation holds the real estate broker's license and the agency relationships with clients, which can then survive the human broker.

Authority of the Agent The authority of the agent is to do everything necessary and proper to achieve the object of the agency and to make representations of facts concerning any transaction.

Actual Authority. Authority which the principal has intentionally conferred on the agent is the agent's *actual* authority.

Ostensible Authority. Authority which the principal, either intentionally or by want of ordinary care, causes a third party to believe the agent possesses is the agent's *ostensible* authority (agency by estoppel).

Emergency Authority. An agent has expanded authority in an emergency. This can mean authority to disobey instructions of the principal when, because of the emergency, it is clearly in the best interest of the principal to do so.

Liability of Principal. Under Civil Code §2330, "An agent represents his principal for all purposes within the scope of his actual or ostensible authority, and all the rights and liabilities which would accrue to the agent from transactions within such limit, if they had been entered into on his own account, accrue to the principal." In other words, the acts of the agent are the acts of the principal when the agent is acting within the scope of the agency. Therefore, the principal is liable for those acts of his or her agent.

Notice to Either, Notice to Both. Both principal and agent are deemed to have notice of whatever either has notice of, and ought, in good faith and the exercise of ordinary care and diligence, to communicate to the other.

Torts of the Agent. A principal is responsible to third persons for negligence of the agent in the transaction of the business of the agency, including wrongful acts committed by the agent in transaction of such business, and for the agent's willful omission to fulfill the obligations of the principal. (Civil Code §2338)

Delegation of Duties A person to whom an agent delegates agency powers is a *subagent*. (Civil Code §2373(o). The most common subagency relationship in real estate is through the authorized multiple listing.

Limits on Delegation. Business and Professions Code §10137 forbids brokers to delegate to third parties, except other brokers and sales agents employed by the broker, any duties for which a real estate license is required. These duties are specifically listed in §10131.

Common Practice. The principal normally expects that the agent will perform all duties of the specific employment which is the subject of the agency relationship. However, the principal by implication authorizes the agent to delegate duties for which the agent is not competent or trained, such as making loans and performing escrow functions.

Employee or Independent Contractor The determination that a licensee is an agent of the principal does not complete the task of defining the legal relationship between the two. The question remains whether the agent is an employee of the principal, or an independent contractor.

Employee. An employee is subject to the employer's control over not only the final result but also how the result is to be achieved. Like an independent contractor, an employee may or may not be authorized to act as an agent.

Example

If a broker's secretary is subject to the broker's supervision and control as to the time, place, and way the secretarial work is done, the secretary is an employee.

Independent Contractor. The principal does not exercise control over how the independent contractor accomplishes the job; the independent contractor is engaged by the principal to accomplish a particular task, for which the contractor will be compensated. Like an employee, an independent contractor may or may not be an agent.

Example

An owner engages a general contractor to build a house. The owner does not tell the contractor how to accomplish the construction; he hires the contractor to build in accordance with plans and specifications in the manner the contractor deems proper. The building contractor will probably act as the agent of the owner in negotiating with building materials suppliers and with subcontractors.

Respondeat Superior. A major distinction between an employee relationship and an independent contractor relationship is the employer's liability for the employee's acts. Under the principle of "respondeat superior," the employer is liable for acts the employee commits in the course and scope of performance of the services for which the employee was engaged. In contrast, the employer is not liable for an independent contractor's acts, unless the independent contractor is also an agent of the employer.

- ☐ ***Broker and Client***. Under California law, a broker is normally considered both an agent of the client and an independent contractor. California law is clear that a real estate broker acting for a principal is an agent, and the principal is liable for the agent's acts.

- ☐ ***Broker and Salesperson***. The relationship between a broker and salesperson contains elements of both employer and employee, and employer and independent contractor. An independent contractor agreement will not allow the broker to escape responsibility for the acts and omissions of salespersons.

Independent Contractor Agreement. It is common in the real estate industry to identify a salesperson as an independent contractor in the written employment contract between broker and salesperson. Such a contractual designation, however, is not controlling; for some purposes a salesperson is considered the broker's employee, regardless of their characterization of the relationship.

- ☐ ***Taxes***. An independent contractor designation may be accepted by taxing authorities from the standpoint of both broker and salesperson.

- ☐ ***Liability for Salesperson's Actions***. The broker is required by the Real Estate Law to exercise reasonable supervision over salespersons, and is subject to disciplinary action for failing to do so. (Business and Professions Code §10177(h)) Not only does the salesperson act as the *agent* of the employing broker, this requirement makes the salespersons *employees* of the broker, and not independent contractors, for purposes of Real Estate Law and civil liability.

- ☐ ***Associate Licensees***. A real estate salesperson, or a real estate broker employed by another broker, is an associate licensee under the broker and acts as the agent of the employing broker.

WHOSE AGENT ARE YOU?

Because the agent's duties to the principal are fiduciary in nature and therefore more extensive than those owed to third parties, it is important for a licensee to know at all times which party to a transaction is considered his or her principal: the buyer, the seller, or both. Unfortunately, identification of the principal(s) is not always easy. Neither the existence of a listing agreement, nor the fact that one party is paying the broker's commission, completely determines who is the principal. The difficulty is compounded by the fact that once a buyer has approached a broker to assist in finding a home, the buyer often believes that he or she is the party being represented by the broker.

General Rules Usually the licensee will have a contractual relationship only with the seller. No agency with the buyer, or dual agency, will exist unless it is expressly or implicitly created by the parties. However, if a broker's actions or words inadvertently lead a buyer to believe that the broker is representing the buyer, a divided agency may result.

Listing Broker: Seller's Agent A broker who has a written listing agreement with a seller will always be considered the seller's agent, by virtue of the written contract. No selling agent may act as an agent for the buyer only, when the selling agent is also the listing agent. (Civil Code §2376)

Possibility of Dual Agency. If the listing agent also procures the buyer, or is approached directly by the buyer, the broker may in some circumstances be deemed to be functioning as a dual agent, despite the fact that the seller is paying the broker's full commission. (Civil Code §2295) However, the fact that a broker acts as both the listing agent and the selling agent does not, of itself, create a dual agency.

Selling and Cooperating Brokers A selling or cooperating licensee runs the risk of being considered a fiduciary of both seller and buyer separately—an impossible obligation to meet. Prospective purchasers tend to believe that the cooperating broker is working for the buyer's interests, when in fact California case law generally holds that the cooperating broker is a subagent, and therefore a fiduciary, of the seller.

Subagency. When a listing is filed with a Board of Realtors® Multiple Listing Service, the listing agent is extending an offer of subagency to all other members of that MLS to find a ready, willing, and able buyer on the terms of the listing or other terms acceptable to the seller. When a selling agent accepts the listing agent's offer of subagency, the selling agent becomes an agent of the seller and owes the seller the same fiduciary duties as the listing agent. (*Agency Legislation Compliance Manual,* an Office Policy Guide for Realtors®, prepared by the California Association of Realtors® Legal Department.)

Rejection of Subagency. A selling agent can reject a listing agent's offer of subagency through an MLS. However, California law is unclear on exactly how or when a selling agent has accepted an offer of subagency. Therefore, the earlier subagency is rejected, the more likely the rejection will be successful.

Judicial Rule. The courts consistently state that the existence of an agency relationship is a "question of fact"—meaning the answer will depend on the particular circumstances of a given case.

Examples

In *Kruse vs. Miller*, 143 Cal. App. 2d (1956), the sellers employed a broker, Garrity, to assist in the sale of their house. Garrity enlisted the cooperation of broker Miller, who showed the house to buyers and also made misrepresentations to them. Buyers sued the sellers for the misrepresentation. Sellers paid the judgment and in turn sued Miller for reimbursement, based on the theory that, as fiduciary agent of the sellers, Miller should have informed them of his misrepresentation to buyers. The court held that Miller was a subagent of the sellers, because he had cooperated with the sellers' broker.

In the more recent case of *Walters vs. Marler*, 83 Cal. App. 3d 1 (1978), buyer Walters, looking for a house, contacted agent Leseman, with Lampliter Realty. Leseman worked with the seller's broker in the transaction, and a court of appeal later held that "Leseman and Lampliter, as real estate agents for Walters, undeniably owed a fiduciary duty to buyer Walters...."

Present Law. Since January 1, 1988, a written disclosure is required of any real estate licensee acting as an agent or subagent in a residential real property transaction. (Civil Code §§2373-2382) This law and the required disclosure form are presented in full in the last section of this course.

Buyer's Broker It is possible for a broker who has no listing on a property to represent only the buyer. This buyer's broker, in a legal misnomer, is termed a "selling broker."

LICENSEE'S DUTIES TO PRINCIPAL IN A REAL ESTATE TRANSACTION

Once an agency relationship has been established, the agent owes a number of *fiduciary* duties to the principal. The term fiduciary is derived from the Latin *fidelis* meaning faithful. A fiduciary relation exists "where there is a special confidence in one who in equity and good conscience is bound to act in good faith and with due regard to interests of one reposing the confidence."

General Fiduciary Duties Fiduciary duties are duties of the highest good faith, loyalty, and diligent and faithful service to the principal. These duties are imposed by general agency law in all agency relationships, not only those involving real property. Specific fiduciary duties include:

Duty to Act for Principal's Benefit. All the agent's actions must be aimed at accomplishing for the principal the purpose for which the agent was employed. It is improper for an agent to act for his or her own benefit in an agency situation.

Example

Seller asks agent to list seller's house. After surveying recent sales in the area and inspecting the property, agent determines that it will probably sell for $100,000. However, agent personally wants a quick sale, and suggests the principal list the house for $90,000. It sells for that price on the first day. In this case, the agent has breached the fiduciary duty and will be subject to liability, unless (1) the seller expressed an interest in a quick sale and (2) the agent explained all the facts, including that the house would probably sell for $100,000 even though it might take longer.

Accounting. The agent has a duty to account for all profits arising out of the employment.

Undivided Agency. The agent may not act on account of an adverse party without the principal's consent.

Not Competing. The agent may not compete with the principal on the agent's own account, or for another, in matters relating to the subject of the agency.

Duties Under Real Estate Law The California Real Estate Law imposes on real estate licensees additional duties to their principals while acting as agents in real estate transactions. These duties are set forth as grounds for license revocation or suspension in Business and Professions Code §§10176, 10177, and 10177.5. These duties are established by the California Legislature, acting through the Department of Real Estate in its capacity as the regulatory authority for real estate licensees. Some are similar to the duties imposed on agents by general agency law, while others are more stringent and apply only to real estate licensees.

Full Disclosure. The agent must disclose all material facts known to the agent concerning the subject of the agency, which might influence the principal with respect to the transaction or the principal's willingness to enter into it. This is true whether the facts are to the principal's benefit or detriment, whether the agent knows the facts at the beginning of the agency relationship or learns them later, and even if disclosure will "kill the deal." Written disclosures protect licensees by ensuring that information has actually reached a buyer, by constituting hard evidence of disclosure in case of a lawsuit, and by discouraging groundless lawsuits.

> **Example**
> An agent knows at the time a seller lists property that a major department store is likely to want to buy the property. The agent must disclose this fact to the principal (seller) even if the purchase is not definite. To the extent that the department store's interest will affect the listing price, the principal is entitled to know the facts the agent knows.

Accounting. The agent has the duty at all times to account to the principal for all funds received or held by the agent on the principal's behalf. The failure to account will subject the agent to disciplinary action, and any loss arising from such failure will subject the agent to civil liability to the principal.

Secret Profits. The agent may not make a secret profit in a transaction involving the subject matter of the agency. If the agent plans to make a profit from the transaction, he or she must disclose this fact to the principal and obtain the principal's consent in order to retain the profit. (Business and Professions Code §10176(d))

Disciplinary Action. Any secret profit clearly subjects the licensee to disciplinary action by the DRE. In addition, upon discovery by the principal, the agent may be made to disgorge the profit to the principal. This is true even if the transaction was otherwise fair to the principal and even if the principal received the full asking price.

Care, Skill, and Diligence

"Reasonable" care, skill, and diligence is required of an agent in the performance of all duties for the principal's benefit. Negligence is interpreted as the failure to use the amount of care, skill, and diligence the law would expect of a "reasonable" real estate agent in similar circumstances.

Standard of Care. If the agent has not met the standard expected of the "reasonable" licensee, he or she is negligent, has breached a duty to the principal, and may be held liable. Whether the agent's care, skill, and diligence were reasonable will ultimately be determined by the judge or jury in a civil action or by the Real Estate Commissioner in a disciplinary action.

Contractual Duties Undertaken. When an agent is employed by the seller, he or she undertakes contractual duties set forth in the listing agreement: to use due diligence and best efforts to find a purchaser ready, willing, and able to purchase on the terms and conditions set forth in the listing agreement or other terms and conditions acceptable to the seller. Failure to perform these duties may subject the agent to liability for breach of contract.

> **Example**
>
> An agent lists a property, but then makes no effort to market it. The agent has breached the duty of due diligence and may be subject to civil liability and DRE disciplinary action.

Licensee's Duty to Investigate The licensee purports to be a knowledgeable practitioner in the real estate field. He or she is a professional licensed by the state and deals daily with matters about which the general public is less knowledgeable. Like any other expert, the licensee is required to know certain facts concerning the subject matter of the agency. Expanding case law and education requirements impose even greater duties of knowledge on the licensee. If a licensee does not know the answers to certain questions, the law requires that he or she inquire to discover them. If questions never arise, the licensee may nevertheless have a duty to investigate certain matters concerning the property.

Level of Knowledge. The principal assumes that the licensee is an expert in real estate, familiar with aspects of real estate transactions about which the principal is less knowledgeable. If the licensee feels that his or her knowledge is inadequate in any given area, the licensee should so inform the principal before undertaking the agency relationship. A good rule of thumb is that the licensee is required either to know or to learn about any fact that would reasonably affect the principal's decision to sell or buy on the terms being negotiated.

Duty to Interrogate Principal. Because the principal will often assume that the licensee as a professional knows all there is to know about a transaction, the principal may not always disclose all material facts unless directly asked by the licensee. If a principal is allowed to assume that the licensee has sufficient knowledge to protect the principal's interest, the principal may believe that if certain questions are not asked, then the facts are not relevant.

Material Facts. Facts that might influence the principal's decision to buy or sell include circumstances affecting the buyer's ability to perform (if the principal is the seller), or any information concerning a potential change in the property value (such as imminent rezoning or environmental hazards).

Education. As educational requirements for licensees expand, the matters about which they are expected to be knowledgeable will also increase. It is to the licensee's advantage to use every available source to stay informed about current developments in real estate law and practice.

DUTIES TO PARTIES OTHER THAN PRINCIPAL

The agent's duty is co-extensive with the principal's duty. A licensee's disclosure duty to third parties has generally been viewed as being the same as the duty of the principal to those third parties. To the extent that the law requires the principal to disclose all known facts material to the other party's decision, the licensee must also disclose all material facts known to the licensee.

Caveat Emptor is Dead The principle of *caveat emptor* ("let the buyer beware") no longer applies in real estate transactions. This change in real estate law is part of a widespread phenomenon in the commercial context generally—the emphasis on seller accountability and consumer protection.

Disclosure to Buyer. Even if the licensee is considered the agent of the seller, he or she nevertheless has a duty to disclose to potential buyers all facts known to the licensee which might be material to the buyer's decision to buy, even with a risk that such disclosure might "kill the deal."

Source of Licensee's Duty. This duty of disclosure by the agent is imposed by the Real Estate Law and by the Civil Code (§2079 et seq.), and is not necessarily a principle of general agency law.

Traditional Rule Traditionally, the licensee has been required to disclose all facts actually known to him or her which are material to the transaction. However, the licensee's duty to third parties in the past has not been as broad as the duty to the principal, in that the duty to third parties has required disclosure only of actually known facts, and has not required investigation or disclosure of facts which the licensee ought to know.

Expanded Rule In 1984, the California Supreme Court upheld (by declining to review) the Court of Appeals decision in *Easton vs. Strassburger*, 152 Cal. App. 3d 90, which has been seen as significantly expanding the duties of listing agents to buyers in real estate transactions.

Case Law. The Court of Appeals upheld the original verdict against the broker stating: "A real estate broker is a licensed person or entity who holds himself out to the public as having particular skills and knowledge in the real estate field. He is under a duty to disclose facts materially affecting the value or desirability of the property that are known to him or which through reasonable diligence should be known to him."

Legislation. Civil Code §§2079-2079.5 codified the principles established in *Easton vs. Strassburger*, requiring a real estate broker to "conduct a reasonably competent and diligent visual inspection of the property offered for sale" and disclose the facts that such an investigation would reveal.

Secret Profits The California Supreme Court has held that because of the real estate licensee's special relationship with the public, he or she may not make a secret profit in a transaction with a third party even though the third party is not the agent's principal and therefore no fiduciary duty is involved.

Example

A broker falsely represented to a potential buyer that he had an exclusive listing on a property. After the buyer made an offer of $500 per acre, the broker secretly purchased the property for $400 per acre and resold it to the buyer at a profit of $100 per acre. The Supreme Court, holding to the maxim that "no one should profit from his own wrong," required the broker to disgorge to the buyer the $100 per acre "secret profit."

Effect of Professional Status. If the broker in this example had simply been dealing with the buyer as an ordinary seller in an arm's length transaction, rather than in the capacity as of broker, he would be entitled to take as much profit as he could, without disclosing his purchase price to the buyer.

LICENSEE'S OBLIGATIONS IN DUAL AGENCY RELATIONSHIP

Agency law permits an agent to represent two principals, but requires *disclosure* of the fact to both principals, and *consent* of both. An undisclosed dual agency is a "divided agency," and violates the Real Estate Law. Once a dual agency has been established, the agent owes to *each* principal good faith, honesty, and loyalty to their mutual interests. The agent must respect and protect the confidentiality of information received from each principal and is prohibited from disclosing such information received from one principal to the other.

Example: Escrow Escrow is the most frequent dual agency in real estate. The escrow handler represents both parties as a neutral third party, and can carry out only the mutual or concurring instructions of seller and buyer or of lender and borrower.

Changing Roles The identity of principal may change within a single transaction. A licensee may be an agent of the seller during one stage of a transaction, and an agent of the buyer during another stage. A listing agent may represent the seller in negotiating a sale of real property, and then assist the buyer in obtaining financing, thus representing the buyer in negotiating the loan. There is no conflict of interests in these roles.

"No Listing" Transactions The existence of a listing agreement is not a necessary prerequisite to the existence of an agency, even with the seller. It is not the existence of a written agreement that creates an agency, but rather the intention of the parties, as disclosed by their written or oral agreement or by their conduct.

Example

A potential seller may be unwilling to negotiate a listing agreement, but may nevertheless authorize a licensee to solicit purchase offers, and may furnish the licensee with information concerning the property. In making representations concerning the property and soliciting offers, the licensee would be acting as the seller's agent. The seller could be liable for the licensee's tortious acts in connection with these activities, and the licensee owes fiduciary duties to the seller just as if a written contract existed.

Commission. A licensee's ability or inability to enforce payment of a commission without a written agreement is an entirely different issue, not based on general principles of agency. The California Statute of Frauds (Civil Code §1624) specifies that "an agreement authorizing or employing an agent, broker, or other person to purchase or sell real estate, or to lease real estate for a longer period than one year" must be in writing.

Effect of Who Pays Commission. The payment of compensation or the obligation to pay compensation to an agent by the seller or buyer does not necessarily define a particular agency relationship between an agent and the seller or buyer. A listing agent and a selling agent may agree to share any compensation or commission which arises from a real estate transaction, but the terms of such an agreement will not necessarily establish an agency relationship.

> **Example**
>
> Buyer engages a licensee to approach a third-party owner and present an offer containing a provision for a seller-paid commission. The licensee may be found to be an agent of both seller and buyer unless the agreement clearly provides that the agent represents the buyer only, and does not purport to have any kind of fiduciary relationship with the seller.

BREACH OF DUTIES

Once an agency relationship has been established, all the duties discussed above apply. The agent's failure to perform those duties is termed a "breach of duty." A breach can occur intentionally, negligently, or innocently.

Intentional Breach When an agent intentionally commits a tortious act, agency is not a defense. In other words, a real estate licensee is liable for his or her own intentional tortious acts against members of the public; and the fact that one is acting as an agent for another will not shield the agent from liability.

> **Example**
>
> Seller as principal instructs licensee to sell unimproved property for residential purposes and licensee does so, although both seller and licensee are aware that applicable zoning ordinances prohibit residential use. The fact that the seller instructed the licensee to represent the property as suitable for residential use would not exempt the licensee from liability for fraud.

Fraud. Civil Code §1710 lists four types of actual fraud:

- *Suggestion*. Suggestion, as a fact, of that which is not true, by one who does not believe it to be true

- *Assertion*. Assertion, as a fact, of that which is not true, by one who has no reasonable ground for believing it to be true

- *Suppression*. Suppression of a fact by one who is bound to disclose it, or who gives information of other facts which are likely to mislead for want of communication of that fact

- *Promises*. Promising something without any intention of performing it.

Constructive Fraud. Both general fiduciary principles and the Real Estate Law require a licensee to make full disclosures and to deal fairly with the parties to a transaction. Civil Code §1573 states that constructive fraud is any breach of duty which, without an actually fraudulent intent, gains an advantage to the person at fault, by misleading another to his prejudice.

- *Definition*. "In its generic sense, constructive fraud comprises all acts, omissions, and concealments involving a breach of legal or equitable duty, trust, or confidence, and resulting in damage to another. Constructive fraud exists in cases in which conduct, although not actually fraudulent ought to be so treated—that is, in which such conduct is a constructive or quasi fraud, having all the actual consequences and all the legal effects of actual fraud." (*Estate of Arbuckle*, 98 Cal. App. 2nd 562, 1950.)

☐ *Application to Real Estate Licensees.* Since real estate licensees have a fiduciary responsibility to their principals, thus establishing a "legal or equitable duty, trust, or confidence," and since lack of fraudulent intent is no defense to a claim of constructive fraud, it is imperative that a licensee deal "above board," and document his or her good faith with appropriate letters, reports, and other memoranda, whenever there is a possibility that the licensee may gain an advantage in the course of dealing with a principal.

Negligent Breach Negligence is defined as the failure to do what a reasonable person would do under similar circumstances. The "reasonable person" standard is a standard imposed by law, against which to measure whether an act is negligent. The standard is objective rather than subjective: the conduct required is the supposed conduct, under similar circumstances, of a hypothetical person representing a community ideal of reasonable behavior.

Real Estate Expertise. One of the circumstances to be considered in determining whether a licensee's conduct meets the reasonable person standard is the fact that a licensee is presumed to have a certain degree of knowledge about real estate transactions, superior to that of the lay person. Thus the standard of knowledge, skill, and diligence against which a licensee's conduct will be measured is not that of the ordinary "person on the street," but that of a reasonable real estate licensee—a more demanding standard.

☐ *Statutes and Regulations.* The ideal conduct which forms the basis for determining the reasonableness of a licensee's conduct in a given situation may be established by statute or by the Commissioner's Regulations.

☐ *Special Expertise.* If a licensee claims to have some particular skill greater than other licensees (e.g., in environmental inspections or large commercial property transactions), and clients rely on that claim in choosing the licensee as their agent, the agent will be held to this higher standard and not just to the basic standard of other licensees.

Reasonable Skill and Knowledge. In the absence of any representation as to special expertise, the standard of skill and knowledge required of a licensee is that which is commonly possessed by other practicing licensees of good standing in the same community. It is not that of the most highly skilled licensee; nor is it even that of the average member of the profession, since those with less than median or average skill may still be competent and qualified. On the other hand, the standard is not that of the charlatan, the quack, or the incompetent. The standard is that which is common to those recognized in the profession itself as qualified and competent to engage in professional real estate activities.

Application of Standard. The "reasonable" standard of competence will apply to all activities in which the licensee engages in the day-to-day operation of a real estate practice. In advising the seller regarding property value or which disclosures the seller should make to buyer, in making representations to the buyer concerning the quality and suitability of financing, and even in a broker's hiring of salespersons, the licensee will be expected to possess the knowledge and skill common to members of the profession. Once the agent undertakes to advise the principal or a third party with respect to real estate matters, the failure to do so properly may result in liability.

> **Example**
>
> In one case, a broker represented to a prospective buyer that an income property would yield a certain monthly income. The representation was based solely on the current owner's unverified statements. In fact, the monthly income failed to cover fixed expenses. The court held that since the broker purported to give advice and did so negligently, he could be held responsible for the damages. (*Ford vs. Cournale*, 36 Cal. App. 3d 172.)

Torts Against the Public. A licensee's liability for negligent damages to members of the public is based not on any special principles applicable to real estate agents, but on the general tort principle that each person has a duty to exercise reasonable care to prevent foreseeable damages to others, and is liable for damages caused by a breach of this duty.

Agency Is Not a Defense. As in situations involving intentional breach of duty, agency is not a defense to a licensee's liability for negligent torts committed against a third party.

> **Example**
>
> A broker holding an open house negligently places an object to hold open a door. If a visitor trips and is injured, the broker is liable under general negligence principles; the fact that he was holding the open house as agent for the seller is no defense.

Innocent Breach Courts have limited tort liability for innocent misrepresentations to cases involving property (real or personal) rather than sale of services. An innocent misrepresentation involved in the sale of services may, however, constitute a basis for rescission of a contract.

Tortious Acts of Subagents A subagent's tortious acts may be considered "innocent" acts of the principal or agent, in that the principal or agent may not have been aware of, or authorized, such acts. Whether the principal or the agent is nevertheless liable for such acts (in addition to the subagent's own liability) depends upon whether the principal authorized the subagency. If the subagency was authorized, the principal, and not the agent, is liable for the subagent's acts. If the principal did not authorize the subagency, the agent alone is liable. (Civil Code §§2350, 2351)

> **Examples**
>
> A seller as principal hires a broker and authorizes the broker to hire an advertising agency to help sell the house. Ordinarily any misrepresentation by the advertising agency would subject the principal, and not the broker, to liability.
>
> If the seller merely hired the broker to sell the house, and it was the broker's normal practice to obtain the advertising agency's assistance in marketing the house, any misstatement by the advertising agency would probably subject the broker, rather than the principal, to liability.

AGENCY RELATIONSHIPS IN MODERN BROKERAGE PRACTICE

The question "Whose agent are you?" has been a confusing one to many licensees, who are expected to understand the law of agency. It has been even more confusing and often misleading to the general public. "In the usual residential real estate transaction, the involvement of a cooperating (selling) licensee introduces confusion and uncertainty which legislators, judges, lawyers and legal writers have thus far failed to dispel." ("Dilemma of the Cooperating Agent," *Real Estate Bulletin*, Fall 1979) In an effort to dispel this confusion and uncertainty, the California Legislature added Civil Code §§2373-2382, effective January 1, 1988. Because of the great significance of these code sections to real estate licensees, they are included here nearly in entirety:

Civil Code §§2373-2382 Article 2.5. Agency Relationships in Residential Real Property Transactions

Definitions 2373. As used in this article, the following terms have the following meanings:

(a) "Agent" means a person acting under provisions of this title in a real property transaction, and includes a person who is licensed as a real estate broker and under whose license a listing is executed or an offer to purchase is obtained.

(b) "Associate licensee" means a person who is licensed as a real estate broker or salesperson ... and who is either licensed under a broker or has entered into a written contract with a broker to act as the broker's agent in connection with acts requiring a real estate license and to function under the broker's supervision in the capacity of an associate licensee.

The agent in the real property transaction bears responsibility for his or her associate licensees who perform as agents of the agent. When an associate licensee owes a duty to any principal, or to any buyer or seller who is not a principal, in a real property transaction, that duty is equivalent to the duty owed to that party by the broker for whom the associate licensee functions.

(c) "Buyer" means a transferee in a real property transaction, and includes a person who executes an offer to purchase real property from a seller through an agent, or who seeks the services of an agent in more than a casual, transitory, or preliminary manner, with the object of entering into a real property transaction. "Buyer" includes vendee or lessee.

(d) "Dual agent" means an agent acting, either directly or through an associate licensee, as agent for both the seller and the buyer in a real property transaction.

(e) "Listing agreement" means a contract between an owner of real property and an agent, by which the agent has been authorized to sell the real property or to find or obtain a buyer.

(f) "Listing agent" means a person who has obtained a listing of real property to act as an agent for compensation.

(g) "Listing price" is the amount expressed in dollars specified in the listing for which the seller is willing to sell the real property through the listing agent.

(h) "Offering price" is the amount expressed in dollars specified in an offer to purchase for which the buyer is willing to buy the real property.

(i) "Offer to purchase" means a written contract executed by a buyer acting through a selling agent which becomes the contract for the sale of the real property upon acceptance by the seller.

(j) "Real property" means any estate ... in property which constitutes or is improved with one to four dwelling units, any leasehold in this type of property exceeding one year's duration, and mobilehomes, when offered for sale or sold through [a licensed real estate] agent ....

(k) "Real property transaction" means a transaction for the sale of real property in which an agent is employed by one or more of the principals to act in that transaction, and includes a listing or an offer to purchase.

(l) "Sell," "sale," or "sold" refers to a transaction for the transfer of real property from the seller to the buyer, and includes exchanges ... real property sales contract ... [and] creation of a leasehold exceeding one year's duration.

(m) "Seller" means the transferor in a real property transaction, and includes an owner who lists real property with an agent, whether or not a transfer results, or who receives an offer to purchase real property of which he or she is the owner from an agent on behalf of another. "Seller" includes both a vendor and a lessor.

(n) "Selling agent" means a listing agent who acts alone, or an agent who acts in cooperation with a listing agent, and who sells or finds and obtains a buyer for the real property, or an agent who locates property for a buyer or who finds a buyer for a property for which no listing exists and presents an offer to purchase to the seller.

(o) "Subagent" means a person to whom an agent delegates agency powers .... However, "subagent" does not include an associate licensee who is acting under the supervision of an agent in a real property transaction.

Disclosure Form 2374. Listing agents and selling agents shall provide the seller and buyer in a real property transaction with a copy of the disclosure form specified in Section 2375, and, except as provided in subdivision (c), shall obtain a signed acknowledgment of receipt from that seller or buyer, except as provided in this section or Section 2374.5, as follows:

(a) The listing agent, if any, shall provide the disclosure form to the seller prior to entering into the listing agreement.

(b) The selling agent shall provide the disclosure form to the seller as soon as practicable prior to presenting the seller with an offer to purchase, unless the selling agent previously provided the seller with a copy of the disclosure form pursuant to subdivision (a).

(c) Where the selling agent does not deal on a face-to-face basis with the seller, the disclosure form prepared by the selling agent may be furnished to the seller (and acknowledgment of receipt obtained for the selling agent from the seller) by the listing agent, or the selling agent may deliver the disclosure form by certified mail addressed to the seller at his or her last known address, in which case no signed acknowledgment of receipt is required.

(d) The selling agent shall provide the disclosure form to the buyer as soon as practicable prior to execution of the buyer's offer to purchase, except that if the offer to purchase is not prepared by the selling agent, the selling agent shall present the disclosure form to the buyer not later than the next business day after the selling agent receives the offer to purchase from the buyer.

2374.5. In any circumstance in which the seller or buyer refuses to sign an acknowledgment of receipt pursuant to Section 2374, the agent, or an associate licensee acting for an agent, shall set forth, sign, and date a written declaration of the facts of the refusal.

2375. The disclosure form required by Section 2374 shall have this article, excluding this section, printed on the back and on the front of the disclosure form . . . .

Agency Relationships

2375.5 (a) As soon as practicable, the selling agent shall disclose to the buyer and seller whether the selling agent is acting in the real property transaction exclusively as the buyer's agent, exclusively as the seller's agent, or as a dual agent representing both the buyer and the seller and this relationship shall be confirmed in the contract to purchase and sell real property or in a separate writing executed or acknowledged by the seller, the buyer, and the selling agent prior to or coincident with execution of that contract by the buyer and the seller, respectively.

(b) As soon as practicable, the listing agent shall disclose to the seller whether the listing agent is acting in the real property transaction exclusively as the seller's agent, or as a dual agent representing both the buyer and seller and this relationship shall be confirmed in the contract to purchase and sell real property or in a separate writing executed or acknowledged by the seller and the listing agent prior to or coincident with the execution of that contract by the seller.

(c) The confirmation required by subdivisions (a) and (b) shall be in the following form:

_____ (Name of Listing Agent) is the agent of (check one):

☐ the seller exclusively ☐ both the buyer and seller

_____ (Name of the Selling Agent if not the same as the Listing Agent) is the agent of (check one):

☐ the buyer exclusively; or ☐ the seller exclusively; or ☐ both the buyer and seller.

(d) The disclosures and confirmation required by this section shall be in addition to the disclosure required by Section 2374.

2376. No selling agent in a real property transaction may act as an agent for the buyer only, when the selling agent is also acting as the listing agent in the transaction.

2377. The payment of compensation or the obligation to pay compensation to an agent by the seller or buyer is not necessarily determinative of a particular agency relationship between an agent and the seller or buyer. A listing agent and a selling agent may agree to share any compensation or commission paid, or any right to any compensation or commission for which an obligation arises as the result of a real estate transaction, and the terms of any such agreement shall not necessarily be determinative of a particular relationship.

2378. Nothing in this article prevents an agent from selecting, as a condition of the agent's employment, a specific form of agency relationship not specifically prohibited by this article if the requirements of Section 2374 and Section 2375.5 are complied with.

2379. A dual agent shall not disclose to the buyer that the seller is willing to sell the property at a price less than the listing price, without the express written consent of the seller. A dual agent shall not disclose to the seller that the buyer is willing to pay a price greater than the offering price, without the express written consent of the buyer.

This section does not alter in any way the duty or responsibility of a dual agent to any principal with respect to confidential information other than price.

2380. Nothing in this article precludes a listing agent from also being a selling agent, and the combination of these functions in one agent does not, of itself, make that agent a dual agent.

2381. A contract between the principal and agent may be modified or altered to change the agency relationship at any time before the performance of the act which is the object of the agency with the written consent of the parties to the agency relationship.

Liability **2382.** Nothing in this article shall be construed to either diminish the duty of disclosure owed buyers and sellers by agents and their associate licensees, subagents, and employees, or to relieve agents and their associate licensees, subagents, and employees from liability for their conduct in connection with acts governed by this article or for any breach of a fiduciary duty, or a duty of disclosure.

Consumer Protection The Legislature finds that it is desirable to, and that by enactment of Section 2 of this act that it intends to, do the following:

(a) Further the education of consumers on the existence of various types of agency relationships which may occur in residential real property transactions covered by this act.

(b) Require disclosure to the parties by the agent or agents of the various types of agency relationships which may occur in residential real property transactions covered by this act in a manner which explains in simple, comprehensible, and nontechnical terms, the elements of these relationships.

(c) Afford protection to consumers involved in residential real property transactions covered by this act by requiring the disclosure set forth in this act.

(d) Require uniformity of this disclosure as a means of clarifying consumer understanding of these terms, usages, and relationships.

(e) Make clear that associate real estate licensees act as agents of brokers under whom they are licensed and who, in turn, are agents of buyers, sellers, or buyers and sellers in residential real property transactions covered by this act. However, by this enactment, the Legislature does not intend to diminish any liability to buyers and sellers which may exist for tortious conduct in connection with these real property transactions.

(f) Provide an explicit basis for maintaining the confidentiality of price information provided by the consumer to a dual agent on a residential real property transaction covered by this act and an explicit method for modifying that confidentiality, while at the same time retaining without change the existing law with respect to confidentiality of other information.

(g) Delay the requirements of this act until January 1, 1988, in order to provide sufficient time to familiarize consumers and agents with the provisions of this act.

DISCLOSURE REGARDING
REAL ESTATE AGENCY RELATIONSHIPS
(As required by the Civil Code)
CALIFORNIA ASSOCIATION OF REALTORS® (CAR) STANDARD FORM

When you enter into a discussion with a real estate agent regarding a real estate transaction, you should from the outset understand what type of agency relationship or representation you wish to have with the agent in the transaction.

SELLER'S AGENT
A Seller's agent under a listing agreement with Seller acts as the agent for the Seller only. A Seller's agent or a subagent of that agent has the following affirmative obligations:
To the Seller:
  (a) A Fiduciary duty of utmost care, integrity, honesty, and loyalty in dealings with the Seller.
To the Buyer & the Seller:
  (a) Diligent exercise of reasonable skill and care in performance of the agent's duties.
  (b) A duty of honest and fair dealing and good faith.
  (c) A duty to disclose all facts known to the agent materially affecting the value or desirability of property that are not known to, or within the diligent attention and observation of, the parties.

An agent is not obligated to reveal to either party any confidential information obtained from the other party which does not involve the affirmative duties set forth above.

BUYER'S AGENT
A selling agent can, with a Buyer's consent, agree to act as agent for the Buyer only. In these situations, the agent is not the Seller's agent, even if by agreement the agent may receive compensation for services rendered, either in full or in part from the Seller. An agent acting only for a Buyer has the following affirmative obligations:
To the Buyer:
  (a) A fiduciary duty of utmost care, integrity, honesty, and loyalty in dealings with the Buyer.
To the Buyer & Seller:
  (a) Diligent exercise of reasonable skill and care in performance of the agent's duties.
  (b) A duty of honest and fair dealing and good faith.
  (c) A duty to disclose all facts known to the agent materially affecting the value or desirability of the property that are not known to, or within the diligent attention and observation of, the parties.

An agent is not obligated to reveal to either party any confidential information obtained from the other party which does not involve the affirmative duties set forth above.

AGENT REPRESENTING BOTH SELLER & BUYER
A real estate agent, either acting directly or through one or more associate licensees, can legally be the agent of both the Seller and the Buyer in a transaction, but only with the knowledge and consent of both the Seller and the Buyer.

In a dual agency situation, the agent has the following affirmative obligations to both the Seller and the Buyer:
  (a) A fiduciary duty of utmost care, integrity, honesty and loyalty in the dealings with either Seller or the Buyer.
  (b) Other duties to the Seller and the Buyer as stated above in their respective sections.

In representing both Seller and Buyer, the agent may not, without the express permission of the respective party, disclose to the other party that the Seller will accept a price less than the listing price or that the Buyer will pay a price greater than the price offered.

The above duties of the agent in a real estate transaction do not relieve a Seller or a Buyer from the responsibility to protect their own interests. You should carefully read all agreements to assure that they adequately express your understanding of the transaction. A real estate agent is a person qualified to advise about real estate. If legal or tax advice is desired, consult a competent professional.

Throughout your real property transaction you may receive more than one disclosure form, depending upon the number of agents assisting in the transaction. The law requires each agent with whom you have more than a casual relationship to present you with this disclosure form. You should read its contents each time it is presented to you, considering the relationship between you and the real estate agent in your specific transaction.

This disclosure form includes the provisions of article 2.5 (commencing with Section 2373) of Chapter 2 of Title 9 of Part 4 of Division 3 of the Civil Code set forth on the reverse hereof. Read it carefully.

I/WE ACKNOWLEDGE RECEIPT OF A COPY OF THIS DISCLOSURE.

BUYER/SELLER_____ Date_____ TIME_____ AM/PM

BUYER/SELLER_____ Date_____ TIME_____ AM/PM

AGENT _____ By _____ Date _____
     (Please Print)   (Associate Licensee or Broker-Signature)

CONFIRMATION
REAL ESTATE AGENCY RELATIONSHIPS

Subject Property Address_____

The following agency relationship(s) is/are hereby confirmed for this transaction:

LISTING AGENT: _____ **SELLING AGENT:** _____
  is the agent of (check one):   (if not the same as Listing Agent)
  ☐ the Seller exclusively; or   is the agent of (check one):
  ☐ both the Buyer and Seller   ☐ the Buyer exclusively; or
                                                 ☐ the Seller exclusively; or
                                                 ☐ both the Buyer and Seller

I/WE ACKNOWLEDGE RECEIPT OF A COPY OF THIS CONFIRMATION.

Seller_____ Date_____   Buyer _____ Date_____

Seller_____ Date_____   Buyer _____ Date_____

Listing Agent_____ By _____ Date_____
            (Please Print)   (Associate Licensee or Broker-Signature)

Selling Agent_____ By _____ Date_____
            (Please Print)   (Associate Licensee or Broker-Signature)

A REAL ESTATE BROKER IS QUALIFIED TO ADVISE ON REAL ESTATE. IF YOU DESIRE LEGAL ADVICE, CONSULT YOUR ATTORNEY.

This form is available for use by the entire real estate industry. The use of this form is not intended to identify the user as a REALTOR®. REALTOR® is a registered collective membership mark which may be used only by real estate licensees who are members of the NATIONAL ASSOCIATION OF REALTORS® and who subscribe to its Code of Ethics.

OFFICE USE ONLY
Reviewed by Broker or Designee _____
Date _____

Copyright© 1987, CALIFORNIA ASSOCIATION OF REALTORS®   FORM AD-11/AC-6
525 South Virgil Avenue, Los Angeles, California 90020   (combined)

SF-Jan-90

Reprinted with permission, California Association of Realtors®
Endorsement not implied

HIGHLIGHTS TO REMEMBER

AGENCY IN REAL ESTATE

Principal-Agent Relationship

Agent is one who represents principal in dealings with third persons
- Special agent is employed for particular transaction (real estate sale), other agents are general
- May represent both sides with their consent (dual agency) or without (divided agency, subject to disciplinary action)

Agency created by agreement between parties (express or implied); principal's ratification of agent's act (acceptance of benefits); estoppel (ostensible agency).

Does not depend on existence of written contract (but right to collect commission does)

California courts are quick to find existence of agency when necessary to protect consumer

Terminates by expiration of term or extinction of subject, death or incapacity of agent or principal, renunciation by agent, or revocation by principal

Authority of the agent may be actual or ostensible (principal allows third party to believe it)

Acts of the agent are acts of the principal; notice to either is notice to both

Principal is liable to third persons for torts committed by agent within the scope of the agency

Licensee may not delegate to an unlicensed party any activity for which license is required

Principal impliedly authorizes agent to delegate duties for which agent is not qualified

Employee or Independent Contractor

Employee is subject to principal's control in accomplishing assigned tasks

Independent contractor responsible to employer only for results, not method of achieving

"Respondeat superior": principal or employer is liable for agent's or employee's actions

Employer is not responsible for contractor's actions unless contractor is also agent

Under real estate and liability law, salesperson is employee of broker; may be independent contractor for tax purposes

Broker acting for principal is agent and independent contractor

Whose Agent Are You?

Existence of listing or commission payment agreement is not always determinative

Usually licensee has contractual relationship with seller only

A dual agency may be expressly or impliedly created with consent of both sides

Licensee dealing with buyer as well as seller may be guilty of divided agency if buyer is misled

Listing broker is always seller's agent; may be dual agent if also acts as buyer's agent with consent of both parties

Selling or cooperating broker usually deemed to be seller's subagent (always, in MLS)

May also be considered buyer's agent, with consent of both parties

Buyer's broker ("selling broker") may represent the buyer only

Licensee's Duties to Principal in a Real Estate Transaction

General fiduciary duties: utmost good faith, loyalty, faithful service
- Act primarily for principal's benefit
- Account for profits
- Not act on account of adverse party without consent
- Not compete

Duties Imposed by Real Estate Law
- Full disclosure of all material facts
- No secret profits (penalties: disciplinary action, disgorging profit)
- Accounting for funds held on principal's behalf
- Care, skill, diligence
- Contractual duties
- Duty to investigate and interrogate principal

Duties To Parties Other Than Principal
- "Caveat emptor" (let the buyer beware) no longer applies; seller accountability and consumer protection
- Seller's agent is required to disclose known material facts to buyer, plus duty to investigate
- Licensee's duty to disclose to third parties at least as extensive as principal's duty
- Traditionally applied only to known facts, not facts licensee "should" know
- *Easton vs. Strassburger* and Civil Code: licensee must investigate and disclose reasonably discoverable facts
- Licensee may not make secret profit in transaction with third parties when acting as agent

Licensee's Obligations In Dual Agency
- Licensee must first disclose to, and obtain consent from, both parties
- Agent owes duties of good faith, honesty, and loyalty to their mutual interests, and confidentiality to both parties
- Escrow is a common dual agency
- Identity of principal may vary during a single transaction, e.g., negotiate sale for seller, then financing for buyer
- Intention of parties, not existence of listing, determines whether agency exists
- Intention may be shown by written agreement, oral agreement, or conduct
- Identity of payer of commission does not affect who principal is if agency is clear and express
- If agency is unclear, court will consider commission as factor in identifying principal(s)

Breach of Duties
- Intentional breach: licensee is liable for intentional torts; agency is not a defense
- Intentional fraud: assertion or suggestion as fact of something not true, suppression of fact, promise made with no intention to perform
- Constructive fraud: gaining advantage by misleading another, even without fraudulent intent
- Licensee must be careful to deal "above board" with principal and document good faith
- Negligent breach: reasonable person standard for defining negligence
- Licensee's presumed expertise is considered in determining reasonable conduct
- Standard of "reasonable" licensee skill and knowledge: not that of most highly skilled or "average" licensee; standard common to licensees recognized as competent
- Licensees are liable for negligent torts against public (agency not a defense)
- Innocent breach: liability possible in sale of property, rescission of contract in sale of service
- Tortious acts of subagents: principal is liable if subagency was authorized by principal, agent is liable if it was not

COURSE 15
Ethics of Real Estate

INTRODUCTION

Professional ethics can be defined as *the rules or standards governing the conduct of a profession*. In the classical definition of a profession, the profession itself defines and enforces these standards, which typically address education and training, standards of competence, service to the community, and the profession's good name. In the modern world, professions are also regulated by governments, both through the general civil and criminal laws that apply to all personal and business conduct, and through special laws and administrative regulations applying to particular professions and industries. Government regulation and professional self-regulation are parallel and complementary. The former's realm is *law* and the latter's is *ethics*.

The Department of Real Estate — For the real estate industry in California, the governmental agency in charge is the Department of Real Estate (DRE). Its primary power is to license individuals to practice the profession of real estate, and to regulate their conduct through the power to suspend or revoke licenses for illegal conduct.

Applicable Laws and Regulations. The rules established and enforced by the Department of Real Estate and its Commissioner are contained in the California Business and Professions Code (the Real Estate Law) and in the Code of Regulations, formerly entitled the Administrative Code (the Commissioner's Regulations, which includes the Code of Professional Conduct). These laws and regulations apply to all brokers and salespersons licensed by the state of California.

Revised Code of Conduct. Commissioner's Regulation 2785, formerly known as Code of Ethics and Professional Conduct, was revised as of 1990 as a Code of Professional Conduct. The new Code consists of two major parts: a review of unlawful activities as defined by the Real Estate Law, and a set of Suggestions for Professional Conduct to "encourage real estate licensees to maintain a high level of ethics and professionalism in their business practices."

Professional Organizations — Professional associations are the usual agency for self-regulation, through their power to grant or withhold membership. Membership requirements typically include adherence to a code of ethics, and unethical conduct is discouraged by the possibility of censure or expulsion by one's peers. Professional organizations address aspects of ethics, public service, and professionalism which are not strictly within the realm of law.

Examples. For California licensees, the most widely known and followed code is that of the National Association of Realtors.® Other professional associations have their own codes. These include the National Association of Real Estate Brokers (Realtists), the California Escrow Association, and the Appraisal Institute, the organization that resulted from unification of the American Institute of Real Estate Appraisers and the Society of Real Estate Appraisers.

Law and Ethics The realms of law and ethics overlap, of course. Philosophically and practically, conduct which is "right" is probably both legal and ethical according to accepted codes, and conduct which is intuitively perceived as "wrong" is probably prohibited by both law and ethics. Gray areas exist where conduct considered by a profession or by the public to be unethical is not specifically forbidden by the law, and possibly also where an obsolete or unjust law violates society's current standards of ethics.

Public-Private Partnership. The standards governing California's real estate professions illustrate a public-private partnership between law and ethics. Most professional associations include observance of the law in their ethical requirements, and the Real Estate Commissioner encourages all licensees to abide by not only the Commissioner's Suggestions for Professional Conduct and the Code of Professional Conduct but also the Code of Ethics of any organized real estate industry group of which the licensee is a member.

Litigious Atmosphere. For many clients, decisions involving real estate constitute the largest single transactions of their lives. Real estate is a business of expectations. Whether the expectation is untold thousands of dollars of enhanced equity, or simply a house free from all maintenance problems and nuisances, the client's first impulse in today's world may be to sue if the expectation does not come true. The suit may charge that the particular disappointed expectation was represented to the client as fact. It is important that licensees choose their words carefully, and document all transactions, to avoid future liability.

DRE's Major Concerns The Department of Real Estate's main concerns regarding unethical behavior are conflicts of interest, misrepresentation of positive features of a property, nondisclosure of negative features, and mishandling of clients' funds.

Conflict of Interest. According to the Real Estate Commissioner's quarterly reports, the principal complaints leading to suspension or revocation of licenses fall into the broad category of conflict of interest. They involve such violations or evasions of the fiduciary relationship as fraudulent conduct, dual representation without disclosure, failure to disclose a financial interest in a transaction, undisclosed special relationships with buyer or seller, and commingling of funds. It is obvious that a practitioner concealing a hidden profit has a conflict of interest. In some cases, however, a conflict may be unwitting. In the recent case of *Blackburn vs. McCoy* (37 P.2d 153, 1 C.A. 2d 48), a licensee sold a property where other associates in his office were receiving a secret profit without his knowledge. The licensee was acquitted of any wrongdoing, but it took a court trial to clear him of liability.

Misrepresentation or Puffery. There is a fine line between actual misrepresentation and sales jargon. ("This is the best house around.") The courts have addressed this question over the years. The representation that a property would double in value due to its proximity to a motion picture studio was not considered actionable in the 1936 case of *Title Guarantee & Trust Co. vs. Stahler* (50 P.2d 515, 1 C.A. 2d 230). In a 1960 case, an agent in the sale of a ranch property who represented the availability of well water was held liable since he had personal knowledge that the facts were other than as represented (*Crawford vs. Nastos,* 6 Cal. Rptr. 425, 182 C.A. 2d 59). In a

1933 case, a salesperson indicated that only one trust deed existed on the land, without knowledge of a second encumbrance, and was not held liable since he had no knowledge of the second lien (*Graham vs. Ellmore,* 26 P.2d 696, 135 C.A. 129). The key element in these cases is knowledge of misrepresentation. In recent years, however, the standard has been expanded to what a practitioner "should" know. Commissioner's Regulation 2785 (a)(10) prohibits both "knowingly making a false or misleading representation" and "representing, without a reasonable basis for believing its truth."

Failure to Disclose Material Facts Affecting Value. The courts have been sympathetic to consumers where value is distorted by failure to be completely truthful. In a 1958 case, *Doran vs. Milland Development Co.* (323 P.2d 702, 19 C.A. 2d 322), that plaintiff charged that the salesperson had represented that a home's foundation was sound, when in fact the house was infested with wood-destroying fungus. The court found that she had indeed been damaged by this nondisclosure. Since *Easton vs. Strassburger,* the licensee has some obligation to investigate as well as disclose adverse factors reasonably apparent to someone with real estate expertise.

Mishandling of Funds. A major concern of Department of Real Estate auditors is the mishandling of clients' funds—both simple carelessness and diversion to personal use. A review of escrow activities of real estate licensees revealed that the Department was not even aware of all the licensees who were conducting their own escrows. Licensees should establish checks and balances in the handling of trust accounts, to preserve the integrity of clients' funds.

CAR's Ethical Concerns

The California Association of Realtors® reports three principal areas of concern over violations of their Code of Ethics: conflict of interest, misrepresentation or concealment of facts, and advertising. Boards of Realtors® have their own distinctive concerns and procedures.

Disciplinary Powers. Hearings are held at the local Board of Realtors® level. Accusations of unethical conduct by one member firm against another are heard and judged by fellow members. Disciplinary action usually consists of an order to cease and desist.

Multiple Listing Violations. Some members may attempt to withhold listings from the multiple over the prescribed presentation period (typically forty-eight hours) in order to get both listing and selling commissions. Another practice is to take "pocket" listings, again bypassing the multiple. Both practices violate the intent of Board membership, since Multiple Listing Services are designed to provide maximum exposure for the client and equal opportunities for licensees.

Favored Access to Information. Some members, due to their standing in local Board politics, may have access to listings that have not yet reached the multiple book, and may work on them before other members know of their existence, giving themselves almost the same advantage as the listing broker.

Pressure for Income in Hard Times. When the real estate cycle reaches a trough, as in the early 1990s, the temptation to "create" transactions can be overwhelming. It is a time for particular caution with regard to anything that might be perceived as self-dealing, deception, or overstated advertising.

COMMISSIONER'S CODE OF PROFESSIONAL CONDUCT: UNLAWFUL CONDUCT IN SALE, LEASE, AND EXCHANGE TRANSACTIONS

In order to enhance the professionalism of the California real estate industry, and maximize protection for members of the public dealing with real estate licensees, whatever their area of practice, the following standards of professional conduct and business practices are adopted:

(a) Unlawful Conduct in Sale, Lease and Exchange Transactions. Licensees when performing acts within the meaning of §10131 (a) of the Business and Professions Code shall not engage in conduct which would subject the licensee to adverse action, penalty, or discipline under §§10176 and 10177 of the Business and Professions Code including, but not limited to, the following acts and omissions:

Misrepresenting Market Value — Commissioner's Regulation 2785 (a)(1) prohibits knowingly making a substantial misrepresentation of the likely value of real property to:

- ☐ Its owner either for the purpose of securing a listing or for the purpose of acquiring an interest in the property for the licensee's own account.

- ☐ A prospective buyer for the purpose of inducing the buyer to make an offer to purchase the real property.

Case Study: *Rattray vs. Scudder* 28 Cal. 2d 214 (1946)

Seller (Humston) set the sales price for his property at $13,000 or any reasonable offer. Broker (Rattray) advised the seller that, as appraised by a competent appraiser, the fair market value of the property was $12,000; that the property should be listed at such price; and that a 5 percent commission would be paid to broker upon its sale.

In later correspondence, Rattray indicated that due to the property's location and high sales price, he was finding it difficult to negotiate with potential buyers, and that the price should be reduced to $10,000 cash. He suggested that Humston execute the price reduction during the exclusive listing period.

Broker produced a buyer (Kelly & Son) with whom he was associated, and forwarded to the seller a sixty-day option to purchase from Kelly & Son for $10,000. Humston informed the broker that $10,500 net was the least that he would accept. Subsequently, the seller compromised at a price of $10,250, after broker stated that $10,000 net was the very best price he could obtain.

Prior to the sale to Kelly & Son, Rattray had negotiated with a party by the name of Espey to purchase the property for $13,500. At no time did broker indicate to his principal that any other offers existed prior to opening of the Kelly & Son escrow.

The sale between Kelly & Son and Humston was consummated; escrow was opened; and the property was deeded over. Concurrent with this transaction, Rattray consummated a sale between Kelly & Son and Espey at the higher price of $13,500, which was handled in the same escrow.

At no time did Kelly and the original seller, Humston, communicate directly. All offers and correspondence between Kelly & Son and the seller were executed on Kelly & Son letterhead, with broker Rattray signing all documents.

Upon discovering the second sale, Humston filed a complaint with the Real Estate Commissioner to have Rattray's broker license revoked.

Rattray's broker license was revoked by the Commissioner under B&P Code §§10176(f) & 10177(f). Rattray asked Superior Court to halt revocation by writ of mandate, which was granted. Commissioner successfully appealed the writ, and Rattray's license was revoked.

Legal Principles. *Broker Rattray violated his fiduciary duties by making untrue and misleading statements so as to induce principal Humston to reduce his sales price. Specifically, broker advised that he was "unable to sell the property at the original listing price, and that $10,000 net was the best price obtainable," taking advantage of the lower price for his firm's own benefit.*

Broker Rattray failed to disclose a higher offer in existence prior to the sale of Humston's property to his associates, Kelly & Son. Broker must disclose not only that he is acting on his own account, but also all other facts which would have a bearing on the desirability of the transaction from the principal's viewpoint, such as the existence of a higher offer from Espey.

If an agent has an option to purchase, the law does not allow him to wait until someone makes an offer in excess of the agreed option purchase price, and then elect to purchase the property at the lesser price without informing the owner of the higher offer.

Existence of Offers Commissioner's Regulation 2785 (a)(2) prohibits representing to an owner of real property when seeking a listing that the licensee has obtained a bona fide written offer to purchase the property, unless at the time of the representation the licensee has possession of a bona fide written offer to purchase.

Example. A prospective purchaser enters the office of a real estate broker, inquiring about the availability of housing in a particular development. Broker contacts Mr. and Mrs. Lester, who own a residence in the same development, and tells them that he has an offer to purchase their house at a most favorable price, from a very qualified buyer. The broker induces the Lesters to list with him, even though he does not have a firm offer.

Commissions Negotiable Commissioner's Regulation 2785 (a)(3) prohibits stating or implying to an owner of real property during listing negotiations that the licensee is precluded by law, by regulation, or by the rules of any organization, other than the broker firm seeking the listing, from charging less than the commission or fee quoted to the owner by the licensee.

Printed Notice Required. Business and Professions Code §10147.5 provides that any printed or form listing agreement for the sale of real property consisting of four or fewer residential units must contain a notice in ten-point boldface type that the amount of the commission is not fixed by law and may be negotiable between seller and broker.

Broker Affiliation Commissioner's Regulation 2785 (a)(4) prohibits knowingly making substantial misrepresentations regarding the licensee's relationship with an individual broker, corporate broker, or franchised brokerage company or that entity's or person's responsibility for the licensee's activities.

Example. Broker advises a prospective seller to list with her firm, because she is a franchisee of a large national firm which advertises throughout the country. She indicates that the parent firm backs her guarantees and professional practices. This is not in fact the policy of the franchisor.

Closing Costs Commissioner's Regulation 2785 (a)(5) prohibits knowingly underestimating the probable closing costs in a communication to the prospective buyer or seller of real property in order to induce that person to make or to accept an offer to purchase the property.

Example. A broker avoids discussing the subject of closing costs with either the buyer or the seller on the theory that everyone knows that there will be closing costs in a real estate transaction, so it should not be necessary to disclose something that is well known and obvious. Further, the broker believes that neither a buyer nor a seller should make decisions based primarily on a minor consideration like closing costs, and in the context of the whole transaction, the broker considers closing costs relatively minor.

Deposits Commissioner's Regulation 2785 (a)(6) prohibits knowingly making a false or misleading representation to the seller of real property as to the form, amount, or treatment of a deposit toward the purchase of the property made by an offeror.

Example. An agent prepares a deposit receipt for the purchase of real property and acknowledges receipt of $1,000 from the buyer. The buyer does not have a checking account, but does have money on deposit in a savings account. The agent suggests that the buyer sign a demand promissory note for $1,000 but fails to inform the seller of the form of payment at the time the offer to purchase is presented.

Buyer's Qualifications Commissioner's Regulation 2785 (a)(7) prohibits knowingly making a false or misleading representation to a seller of real property, who has agreed to finance all or part of a purchase price by carrying back a loan, about a buyer's ability to repay the loan in accordance with its terms and conditions.

Example. A seller is often asked to take back a second trust deed in the sale of a residence primarily because the buyer is expected to have difficulty qualifying for a new first trust deed loan. In this case is the seller being asked to assume a greater risk in extending this credit? Is this greater risk a material fact to the seller? Does this greater risk place a greater responsibility on the real estate broker in qualifying the buyer? Should the broker simply take the buyer's word about his financial position, income, and credit record?

Unauthorized Changes Commissioner's Regulation 2785 (a)(8) prohibits making an addition to or modification of the terms of an instrument previously signed or initialed by a party to a transaction without the knowledge and consent of the party.

Example. If a licensee changes or modifies a document previously signed, this act may be in excess of his or her authority as agent, and might perpetrate a fraud upon the principal(s) concerned.

Misrepresenting Security Value Commissioner's Regulation 2785 (a)(9) prohibits making a representation as a principal or agent to a prospective purchaser of a promissory note secured by real property about the market value of the securing property without a reasonable basis for believing the truth and accuracy of the representation.

Example. The fair market value of a property which is made the security for a note secured by a trust deed or mortgage is a material fact to a prospective investor considering the purchase of such note. Misrepresentation of that value could violate §§10176(a) and 10177(j).

"Puffing" Commissioner's Regulation 2785 (a)(10) prohibits knowingly making a false or misleading representation or representing, without a reasonable basis for believing its truth, the nature or condition of the interior or exterior features of a property when soliciting an offer.

Example. Broker informs prospective buyer that the carpeting is in excellent condition, without having seen the interior of the residence or having been so instructed by the seller.

Misrepresenting Size and Boundaries Commissioner's Regulation 2785 (a)(11) prohibits knowingly making a false or misleading representation or representing, without a reasonable basis for believing its truth, the size of a parcel, square footage of improvements, or the location of the boundary lines of real property being offered for sale, lease, or exchange.

Example. Many listings placed with the Multiple Listing Services of Boards of Realtors® leave blank the space for disclosing the square footage of the dwelling and sometimes the spaces for disclosing the dimensions of the lot. If a licensee does not take measurements or otherwise obtain reliable figures, it is left to the buyer to see for himself the size of the building and the lot. If the broker makes no representations whatever about the square footage of a building, can that failure to disclose be interpreted as a "misleading representation"?

Concealing Use Restrictions Commissioner's Regulation 2785 (a)(12) prohibits knowingly making a false or misleading representation or representing to a prospective buyer or lessee of real property, without a reasonable basis to believe its truth, that the property can be used for certain purposes with the intent of inducing the prospective buyer or lessee to acquire an interest in the real property.

Case Study: People ex rel. Department of Transportation vs. Grocers Wholesale Co., 262 Cal. Rptr. 689 (1989) *In March 1984 buyer entered into a written contract to buy an undeveloped 81,000 square foot lot in San Francisco for $850,000. Buyer's intent was to build a mini-storage building. The lot was adjacent to a five-acre parcel owned by the State of California where Caltrans stored equipment. Before signing the offer to buy, buyer asked agent if Caltrans had any interest in the parcel, and was told no. This was untrue.*

The truth was that the salesperson had talked with Caltrans on several occasions and was aware that Caltrans had an interest in acquiring the property. During escrow, the title company wrote asking seller to acknowledge Caltrans' interest in acquiring the lot, and to hold the title company harmless from any claim arising from any condemnation action by the state. Seller did not comply. Accordingly, buyer refused to close escrow because of title problems, but remained willing and able to buy if title cleared.

The State filed eminent domain proceedings against seller's lot and deposited $850,000 "probable compensation" in 1985, and in 1986 took possession of the lot. Seller then sued buyer to quiet title to the lot, and buyer cross-sued seller and seller's broker and salesperson for fraud and negligent misrepresentation.

Prior to jury trial seller received the $850,000 deposited by the State, plus $80,000 from buyer, and buyer received from seller an "assignment of all rights and title" by quitclaim deed. Broker and salesperson received commissions.

At trial, the jury determined that fair market value of seller's lot was $1,241,258.50, that the State was liable to buyer for legal expenses, and that seller's broker and salesperson were liable to buyer for $1 million "lost profits" plus expenditures and punitive damages.

Legal Principles. Broker and salesperson were found jointly liable for fraud and negligent misrepresentation of facts about seller's property. The facts affected the property's value, usability, and desirability to the buyer, and had they been known the buyer would not have entered into the purchase agreement. This proved very costly to the licensees, but could have been more so, since trial evidence showed that buyer's "anticipated profits" were $2.5 million.

This case further illustrates the necessity for a broker to adequately supervise salespersons. California law imputes factual knowledge acquired by the salesperson to the broker. Thus brokers cannot escape personal liability for a salesperson's tortious conduct, performed within the scope of employment. A judgment for fraud in a civil action may result in license suspension or revocation.

Nondisclosure of Material Facts

Commissioner's Regulation 2785 (a)(13) prohibits when acting in the capacity of an agent in a transaction for the sale, lease, or exchange of real property, failing to disclose to a prospective purchaser or lessee facts known to the licensee materially affecting the value or desirability of the property, when the licensee has reason to believe that such facts are not known to nor readily observable by a prospective purchaser or lessee.

Case Study: *Vaill vs. Edmonds*, 6 Cal. Rptr. 2d 1; 4 Cal. App. 4th 247 (1991)

In April 1982 salesperson Vaill negotiated the sale of a home. Vaill resided on the same street, and was thus familiar with the neighborhood and the subject property.

Prior to opening of escrow, buyers inspected the property three or four times, talked with sellers who explained that the swimming pool was in the front yard because the back yard was on a "geologic fault," learned that neighbors two properties away had a "water problem" and a pump to prevent a landslide as had occurred in 1971, read a 1972 geological report on the property, and procured their own geological report that stated that the property dropped 175 feet down to the Pacific Coast Highway and was "locally eroded and exhibits signs of surficial instability."

With all the above knowledge, buyers opened escrow in March, 1983, and closed on May 3. They procured a policy of title insurance. It stated that the property was in a geological hazard area.

About two months after closing tiles began to crack inside the home, and about four months after, a fifteen-foot crevice opened up in the bluff and cracks appeared throughout the house. By January 1984 the City of Malibu condemned the property and ordered the owners to move out. Property value declined to zero.

Owners sued the real estate agents, sellers, geologists, the County of Los Angeles, and others for their losses, and filed a complaint about salesperson Vaill with the Department of Real Estate. An administrative law judge ruled that there was insufficient evidence of fraud, negligence, or incompetence to discipline the salesperson. Nevertheless, Real Estate Commissioner Edmonds *determined that Vaill had violated B&P Code Section 10177(g) through "negligence and incompetence." The Commissioner disciplined Vaill, revoking her license and issuing a restricted license.*

Vaill petitioned the Superior Court for a writ of mandamus (writ of review over Commissioner's action) to restore her license status. The court granted the writ and vacated the revocation. Commissioner Edmonds appealed. The Court of Appeal affirmed the Superior Court ruling. It ruled that Vaill had a duty to disclose to the buyer facts materially affecting the value or desirability of the property, and that she adequately did so by providing the 1972 report, pointing out the water problem at the nearby property, and encouraging buyers to obtain their own report, which they did. The court noted that the buyers were alerted to the property's problems but still decided to buy after almost a year of investigation.

Legal Principles. *The facts of this case differ from those in* Easton vs. Strassburger *(1984), which dealt with licensees' and sellers' failing to make full disclosure of material facts, and failing to suggest that buyers investigate causes of visible "red flags." In the Vaill case, the licensee and sellers were careful to point out and disclose what they knew about the property that would materially affect its value or desirability, and buyers on licensee's advice obtained their own geological report. Buyers thus made an informed decision. Subsequent problems were foreseeable, and they acquired property in full knowledge of their own risk.*

A comparison of this case and Easton *indicates that it is prudent for licensees and sellers to disclose all known negative factors, and in writing as well as orally advise buyers to conduct their own investigations through employment of qualified professionals.*

Failing to Present Offers
Commissioner's Regulation 2785 (a)(14) prohibits willfully failing, when acting as a listing agent, to present or cause to be presented to the owner of the property any written offer to purchase received prior to the closing of a sale, unless expressly instructed by the owner not to present such an offer, or unless the offer is patently frivolous.

Case Study: Nguyen vs. Scott, 253 Cal. Rptr. 800 (1988)
In 1976 two individuals, Nguyen and Truong, each bought an undivided half interest in an eighteen-unit apartment building in San Francisco. In 1986 Truong encumbered his half interest by obtaining a $285,000 loan from a private lender, Scott Inc., owned by real estate broker John L. Scott. The loan was secured by a second deed of trust and promissory note.

Later, Scott, Inc., sold the note to Barclay's Bank for the loan balance, and secured a service contract with the bank for servicing the loan, and received a 2.25 percent servicing fee.

Truong defaulted. The bank gave Scott power of attorney to pursue remedies against Truong. At the nonjudicial foreclosure sale of Truong's half interest in August 1986, Barclay's Bank, as highest bidder, purchased Truong's half interest for $320,530.95, and became undivided co-owner with Nguyen.

During the foreclosure proceedings and three-month reinstatement period, Nguyen negotiated with Truong to buy his interest, but was unable to do so. Broker Scott refused to delay foreclosure or sale or otherwise accommodate Nguyen. Following the sale, Nguyen tried to buy the bank's 50 percent interest *by negotiating with broker Scott who still represented the bank under the power of attorney. On September 9, 1986, Nguyen submitted a written offer to Scott's attorney to buy the bank's interest for $330,000, but the attorney gave a written rejection of the offer.*

Scott then made some efforts to sell the bank's 50 percent interest and posted a For Sale sign on the building. On September 22 Scott purchased the bank's interest for $325,000.

Nguyen filed suit against Scott alleging breach of duty of honest and fair dealing as a real estate broker, and seeking damages for failure to communicate his $330,000 offer to the bank. In the end, Court of Appeal ruled that Scott had breached his duty, and was legally obligated to convey the 50 percent undivided interest to Nguyen upon Nguyen's tender of the purchase price, and to pay Nguyen's costs of appeal.

Legal Principles. *The court explained in its ruling that the power of attorney granted by Barclay's Bank to broker Scott "was like a listing and imposed the statutory duties of a real estate broker upon Scott," as well as creating an agency relationship that obligated Scott to act in the bank's best interest in disposing of the property. Scott breached his duty of honesty and fair dealing by failing to convey a prospective purchaser's offer to the seller, and by secretly competing with the purchaser. The court found that "Scott should not be permitted to take advantage of his wrong by keeping the co-tenant's one-half interest that he acquired by wrongful conduct."*

While acting in the capacity of a listing agent, Scott changed his position from agent for the bank to a principal buying the property. In essence under the power of attorney Scott sold the property to himself, creating a built-in conflict of interest. In addition, he caused Nguyen's offer to be rejected and then purchased the bank's interest himself for $5,000 less than Nguyen's offer, clearly a breach of fiduciary duty to the principal.

Bias in Presenting Competing Offers

Commissioner's Regulation 2785 (a)(15) prohibits when acting as the listing agent, presenting competing written offers to purchase real property to the owner in such a manner as to induce the owner to accept the offer which will provide the greatest compensation to the listing broker without regard to the benefits, advantages, or disadvantages to the owner.

Case Study: Timmsen vs. Forest E. Olson, Inc. 6 Cal. App. 3d 860 (1979)

The Timmsens, in their sixties, owned a house in Van Nuys. They were inexperienced and unsophisticated in real estate matters. Mr. Timmsen went to a branch Olson office, and agreed to list his house. A licensed salesperson named Ramser prepared the Timmsens' listing agreement, including a commitment to "subordination" on the sale of their property. The meaning of this clause was not known to either the salesperson or the sellers.

Masters, a salesperson for Olson, learned of the listing and contacted a builder to advise him "since the terms would be so favorable to someone in the builder's position." Builder offered to buy it for $47,500, with the terms "purchase money encumbrance would be subordinated to a construction loan of not more than $300,000."

Instead of viewing the builder's proposition from the standpoint of their client, the two Olson salespeople (Ramser and Masters) immediately advised the Timmsens to accept the offer. Neither of the salespeople could answer the

Timmsens' questions concerning the subordination provision. For a sale involving subordination of this type, a reasonable price would have been at least $70,000, rather than the $49,500 final sales price.

When the Timmsens refused to sign the escrow documents, the builder sued for specific performance. This lawsuit was eventually settled for $7,500. Timmsen countersued Olson and its two salespeople for damages due to breach of fiduciary obligation to their principals. The trial court granted a nonsuit against the Timmsens.

A nonsuit is warranted when the judge concludes from all the facts presented that there will be no evidence of substance to support a judgment in favor of the plaintiff, but the Superior Court decision was reversed by the Appellate Court.

Legal Principles. *Based on the facts of the case, this judgment was reversed when the court concluded that the defendants failed to take into account the interests of and obligations owed to their principals, but acted solely for their own selfish interests and the interests of the purchaser; that as a result of this misconduct, the Timmsens suffered damages in attempting to avoid the sale.*

"Agents who violate their duty to use reasonable care, skill, and diligence are liable for any losses which their principals may sustain as the result of their negligence or breach of duty." The court found this to be the case because of the following facts: Timmsens were unsophisticated in real estate matters, while defendants were experienced salespeople and brokers. Defendants inserted a subordination provision in the listing, misadvising the Timmsens of its meaning. Defendants procured an offer that was financially unsound to the Timmsens' interests, and misrepresented to them that they were obligated to accept it. When the Timmsens refused to accept the offer, defendants obtained their consent to a counteroffer, which was also financially unsound to their interests.

In addition, defendants orally obtained the buyer's approval of the counteroffer, and signed the buyer's name to it, when they did not have the authority in writing to sign the buyer's name to the counteroffer. Thus the agreement was unenforceable, under the Statute of Frauds.

Not Explaining Contingencies Commissioner's Regulation 2785 (a)(16) prohibits failing to explain to the parties or prospective parties to a real estate transaction for whom the licensee is acting as an agent the meaning and probable significance of a contingency in an offer or contract that the licensee knows or reasonably believes may affect the closing date of the transaction, or the timing of the vacating of the property by the seller or its occupancy by the buyer.

Example. Where the seller has entered into an agreement to sell with a buyer, a frequent contingency is that the buyer be able to close the sale of an existing residence. Any statement by the agent to the seller, assuring the closing of escrow within the specified period, without first explaining to seller the significance of the contingency, would be a violation.

Nondisclosure of Agent's Interest (Seller's Agent) Commissioner's Regulation 2785 (a)(17) prohibits failing to disclose to the seller of real property, in a transaction in which the licensee is an agent for the seller, the nature and extent of any direct or indirect interest that the licensee expects to acquire as a result of the sale. The prospective purchase of the property by a person related to the licensee by blood or marriage, purchase by an entity in which the licensee has an ownership interest, or purchase by any other person with whom the licensee occupies a special relationship where there is a reasonable probability that the licensee could be indirectly acquiring an interest in the property shall be disclosed to the seller.

Case Study: Abell vs. Watson 155 Cal. App. 2d 158 (1957) *Abell was a licensed salesperson employed to sell Hubbard's residence. Hubbard wanted $17,500 net for his property. Abell arranged an escrow in which the purchaser was his sister or her nominee. Escrow closed and the deed conveyed the property to Abell's wife.*

Abell did not tell Hubbard that the purchaser was to be either his sister or his wife. Hubbard testified that it made no difference to him.

Abell was accused by the Department of Real Estate of fraud and dishonest dealing (Business and Professions Code §10176(i)) and after a hearing, his license was suspended for ninety days.

Abell petitioned the Superior Court for a writ of mandate; after a hearing, it was denied. Abell appealed, but the Superior Court decision was upheld by the Appellate Court.

Legal Principles. *These facts would not sustain a finding of fraud or dishonest dealing by Abell in the generally accepted meaning of these words. But the facts do sustain a finding of breach of fiduciary duty by Abell to his client, whether the client cared or not. The facts of this case come within the definition of fraud and dishonest dealing as these words are used in the Real Estate Law.*

To hold otherwise would be to approve a practice by which a real estate broker or salesperson could purchase a client's property without the seller's knowledge, through conveyance to a spouse or other relative of the agent. This is perceived as opening the door to all sorts of chicanery or double dealing, and would be contrary to the purpose and intent of the Real Estate Law.

Nondisclosure of Agent's Interest (Buyer's Agent) Commissioner's Regulation 2785 (a)(18) prohibits failing to disclose to the buyer of real property, in a transaction in which the licensee is an agent for the buyer, the nature and extent of a licensee's direct or indirect ownership interest in such real property. The direct or indirect ownership interest in the property by a person related to the licensee by blood or marriage, by an entity in which the licensee has an ownership interest, or by any other person with whom the licensee occupies a special relationship shall be disclosed to the buyer.

Example. A real estate broker acting as a buyer's agent owes the same fiduciary obligation to his principal, the buyer, that any other agent owes to his or her principal, such as a broker who has a listing on a property and is the agent of the owner. An agent is a person who represents another, called the principal, in dealings with third persons. If that agent also is the third person, an absolute conflict of interest is created. To whom shall the agent be faithful, himself or his client? Could a buyer's broker ever lawfully and ethically sell his own property to his own client?

Interest in Referrals Commissioner's Regulation 2785 (a)(19) prohibits failing to disclose to a principal for whom the licensee is acting as an agent any significant interest the licensee has in a particular entity when the licensee recommends the use of the services or products of such entity.

Example. Licensee directs the buyer to apply for a loan with a particular lender, whose loan officer is his broker's wife. She receives a commission for placement of the loans. Agent fails to disclose these facts to the borrower.

Kickbacks. Business and Professions Code §10177.4 sets out grounds for discipline of a real estate licensee who claims, demands, or receives a "kickback" for referral to any escrow agent, controlled escrow company, or underwritten title company.

Refunding Deposits Commissioner's Regulation 2785 (a)(20) prohibits the refunding by a licensee, when acting as an agent for seller, of all or part of an offeror's purchase money deposit in a real estate sales transaction after the seller has accepted the offer to purchase, unless the licensee has the express permission of the seller to make the refund.

Example. Both the Real Estate Law and the Commissioner's Regulations require that a licensee who accepts a deposit must do one of three things with the deposit prior to the end of the next business day, unless the licensee has specific instructions to the contrary. The broker may place the funds into the broker's trust account, or into a neutral escrow, or deliver the funds to the principal. When the broker accepts a deposit from a prospective buyer, the broker is accepting that deposit for, on behalf of, and in the name of the principal. It is as if the owner had accepted that deposit. What is the broker's position then if the prospective buyer demands the return of the deposit?

COMMISSIONER'S CODE OF PROFESSIONAL CONDUCT: UNLAWFUL CONDUCT IN LOAN TRANSACTIONS

(b) Unlawful Conduct When Soliciting, Negotiating or Arranging a Loan Secured by Real Property or the Sale of a Promissory Note Secured by Real Property. Licensees when performing acts within the meaning of subdivision (d) or (e) of §10131 of the Business and Professions Code shall not violate any of the applicable provisions of subdivision (a), or act in a manner which would subject the licensee to adverse action, penalty, or discipline under §§10176 and 10177 of the Business and Professions Code including, but not limited to, the following acts and omissions:

Misrepresenting Loan Availability Commissioner's Regulation 2785 (b)(1) prohibits knowingly misrepresenting to a prospective borrower of a loan to be secured by real property or to an assignor/endorser of a promissory note secured by real property that there is an existing lender willing to make the loan or that there is a purchaser for the note, for the purpose of inducing the borrower or assignor/endorser to utilize the services of the licensee.

Case Study: *Bell vs. Watson* 148 Cal. App. 2d 684 (1957) *The Morrises contacted Bell, a licensed real estate broker, to find a home for them. Because the Morrises had only a small downpayment, they sought to finance the purchase with a G.I. loan. Bell located a house for the Morrises and prepared a deposit receipt which stated that the offer was subject to suitable financing. At the time the transaction was ready to close, Bell informed the Morrises that G.I. financing could not be obtained. Bell recommended that the Morrises assume an existing first trust deed and a second trust deed which was* *due in full in six months. Bell stated that at the end of six months he could arrange G.I. financing because of the increased equity in the property. Six months after the Morrises purchased the house, Bell was unable to obtain G.I. financing and the Morrises were forced to sell the house to pay off the note secured by the second trust deed. Bell was accused by the Department of Real Estate of false and fraudulent misrepresentations and after a hearing, his license was revoked.*

Bell's petition to the Superior Court for writ of mandate was denied. On appeal of the Superior Court denial, the Court of Appeal upheld the Superior Court's determination that Bell had made a substantial misrepresentation, but reversed and remanded the case to the Real Estate Commissioner for a redetermination of the penalty to be assessed against Bell on the ground that the penalty of license revocation was excessive.

Legal Principles. *The above facts were sufficient to make a finding that Bell made a representation that he could obtain financing knowing that it was entirely problematic whether he could produce such financing. The positive promise was in that sense false and fraudulent.*

Misrepresenting Borrower's Qualifications

Commissioner's Regulation 2785 (b)(2) prohibits: (a) knowingly making a false or misleading representation to a prospective lender or purchaser of a loan secured directly or collaterally by real property about a borrower's ability to repay the loan in accordance with its terms and conditions.

(b) failing to disclose to a prospective lender or note purchaser information about the prospective borrower's identity, occupation, employment, income, and credit data as represented to the broker by the prospective borrower.

(c) failing to disclose information known to the broker relative to the ability of the borrower to meet his or her potential or existing contractual obligations under the note or contract including information known about the borrower's payment history on an existing note, whether the note is in default or the borrower in bankruptcy.

Case Study: U.S. vs. 403 1/2 Skyline Drive, La Habra Heights, California 79 Fed. Supp. 796 (1992)

In July 1986, borrower applied for a purchase money loan to buy a personal residence, from Great Western Bank, a federally insured lender. Borrower's loan application stated that he earned $8000 a month from a named employer, plus other monthly income from automobile sales. In trial, evidence revealed, among other things, that the named employer had not employed borrower during the years 1984 to 1986; employment and income statements were knowingly false and fraudulent, for the purpose of influencing the lender to grant the loan; in reliance and acting upon the borrower's financial statements, lender approved the loan to borrower, who purchased and occupied the subject dwelling.

When borrower defaulted on loan payments, the bank learned about the false financial statements and reported to the appropriate federal agencies. This was followed by U.S. Attorney action in federal court for seizure of the property pursuant to the Financial Institutions Reform, Recovery, and Enforcement Act (FIRREA), enacted in 1989 by Congress. Federal District Court, upheld on appeal, granted the seizure requested by the federal authorities, retroactively exercising their powers under FIRREA.

Legal Principles. *The facts of this case do not mention involvement of any real estate broker or salesperson. Nevertheless, this federal court ruling is a case of first impression in the western region of the United States, and of vital interest to any real estate licensee who assists buyers in any financing with a federally insured lender or with a federal loan program such as a G.I. loan, HUD low income loan, or FHA loan.*

FIRREA §936(a) provides for forfeiture to the United States of any real or personal property derived from proceeds traceable to violation of 18 U.S. Code §1014 which prohibits "knowingly making any false statement ... for the purpose of influencing in any way the action of ... any institution the accounts of which are insured by the Federal Deposit Insurance Corporation (FDIC) upon any application for a loan."

The present case is based upon an "in rem" action against the property rather than an "in personam" action against the borrower as an individual. In an in rem action (action against a thing), the government need only establish probable cause for forfeiture under FIRREA, similar to the evidence required to obtain a search warrant. The in rem judgment under FIRREA is designed to "ensure equitable reimbursement of the affected government agencies" where the borrower is not an "innocent borrower" under 21 U.S. Code §881(a)(6).

Practical Implications. *Real estate licensees are constantly engaged in helping buyers apply for loans. This case illustrates that there may be considerable exposure when a loan transaction involves a federally insured lender or federal loan program, because of the possibility of both in rem seizure and forfeiture under FIRREA, and in personam action for any civil or criminal acts of the principal or co-conspirators. The licensee should exercise extreme caution and supply an "Eliminating Written Disclaimer" asserting the licensee's lack of knowledge about the accuracy, truth, or validity of the borrower's loan application or any supporting materials.*

Underestimating Costs

Commissioner's Regulation 2785 (b)(3) prohibits knowingly underestimating the probable closing costs in a communication to a prospective borrower or lender of a loan to be secured by a lien on real property for the purpose of inducing the borrower or lender to enter into the loan transaction.

Case Study: *Realty Projects, Inc., vs. Smith* 32 Cal. App. 3d 204 (1973)

This case illustrates a variety of nondisclosures and self-dealing. Realty Projects and several of its employees were licensed mortgage loan brokers or salespersons. Through its employees, Realty negotiated and obtained loans from private individual lenders, for borrowers who employed Realty as their agent for this purpose. Realty was paid a commission for its services. Approximately 95 percent of the loans negotiated by Realty were loans in which the maximum compensation received was controlled by the ceilings specified in Business and Professions Code §10242. (Since 1991 the limits apply to first trust deed loans of less than $30,000 and to junior trust deed loans of less than $20,000.)

Due to a shrinking availability of funds, Realty commenced the practice of reducing the amounts of cash their lenders would have to provide, in situations where the loans exceeded the limits of Business and Professions Code §10242. Realty adopted a practice of occasionally taking its commission from the borrower in the form of a promissory note secured by a junior deed of trust.

Loan officers were told to obtain from customers the highest loan authorizations possible; in this way, Realty might receive the highest commissions. If employees negotiated an unregulated loan, they received additional compensation from Realty. Loan officers received no instructions whether they should advise prospective borrowers of the limits on loans, beyond which Realty's compensation was unlimited. Loan officers made no such disclosure to any prospective borrower.

The officer in charge of the day-to-day operations of Realty instructed the loan officers to include credit life and disability insurance in their loans whenever possible. His brother-in-law and sister were majority stockholders in the life insurance brokerage through which the credit insurance was sold. He was a minority shareholder.

The prime and controlling cause of the amount of each of the loans originated was the desire by Realty and its loan officers to place the amount of the loan above the statutory limits for regulated loans, so that borrowers could be charged higher commissions.

Each borrower interviewed indicated that he or she needed a loan within the limits of regulated loans, but authorized a loan in excess of the limits at the suggestion of the loan officers.

The Department of Real Estate found that this conduct violated various provisions within Business and Professions Code §§10176 and 10177. The discipline imposed by the Department of Real Estate ranged from suspensions to revocations. The suspensions and revocations ordered by the Commissioner were appealed, and affirmed by the courts.

Legal Principles. *Realty argued that the fiduciary duty did not apply, since such a duty cannot exist before the establishment of the agency relationship, and that this relationship does not come into existence until the loan authorization agreement has been executed by the borrower and by the loan officer.*

The court found the duty of fair and honest dealing by licensees, when acting in that capacity, extends to their dealings with prospective borrowers before the execution of any loan authorization agreement by the loan officer and the prospective borrower.

Loan brokers hold themselves out to prospective borrowers as loan experts, who will endeavor to obtain from lenders a loan adequate for the client's needs at the lowest practicable cost.

Since the amount of expenses and commissions will vary depending on whether the loan is limited by law, the knowing concealment from a prospective borrower of such a significant factor in the possible cost of a loan constitutes a substantial misrepresentation of the overall loan picture, as well as having the elements of fraud and deceit.

Misrepresenting Priority of a Lien Commissioner's Regulation 2785 (b)(4) prohibits, when soliciting a prospective lender to make a loan to be secured by real property, falsely representing or representing without a reasonable basis to believe its truth, the priority of the security, as a lien against the real property securing the loan, i.e., a first, second, or third deed of trust.

Case Study: *People vs. Slaton*, 271 Cal. Rptr. 61, 222 Cal. App. 3d 1041 (1990)

Broker Slaton made a practice of buying homes that had remained unsold for a long time, with anxious owners willing to take back an unrecorded trust deed. He did this not as a broker but as a principal dealing on his own account, although revealing to sellers that he was a licensed real estate broker.

After acquiring title to numerous properties in this way, broker submitted loan applications to institutional and other lenders for these properties, but each time failed to disclose existence of the unrecorded trust deed. He also submitted false rental agreements and financial statements for the properties, relied upon by the lenders.

After receiving loan funds, broker intentionally defaulted on both the new senior liens given the lenders and the junior liens given the sellers. Upon complaints by the lenders and sellers, the local district attorney seized from the lenders and sellers the false financial statements, loan applications, and unrecorded trust deeds and notes. Broker was convicted of criminal fraud and grand theft, and sentenced to six years and eight months in state prison.

Broker appealed on grounds that the documents were obtained from lenders without a warrant, breaching his right of privacy. Court of Appeal affirmed the conviction, quoting a Supreme Court ruling that "the Fourth Amendment does not prohibit the obtaining of information revealed to a third party and conveyed by him to government authorities, even if the information is revealed ... only for a limited purpose" such as a loan application.

Legal Principles. *The general public may not be aware of the significance of the priority of liens against real property, but real estate licensees are aware of that importance. The foreclosure of a prior lien "wipes out" the security of all junior liens. The holder of a junior lien should be in a position to cure any default on any prior liens in order to protect the security of the junior lien. The junior lienholder is thus in a much more precarious position than a senior lienholder. If there is no equity securing the junior lien, that lien is virtually unsecured. The risks involved in making a loan are material facts to a lender.*

California law provides that a real estate licensee found guilty of a crime involving moral turpitude may be subject to suspension or revocation of the real estate license. The broker in this case, though acting at the time only as a principal dealing on his own behalf, could lose his real estate license as well as serving a prison term.

"Free" Services

Commissioner's Regulation 2785 (b)(5) prohibits knowingly misrepresenting in any transaction that a specific service is free when the licensee knows or has a reasonable basis to know that it is covered by a fee to be charged as part of the transaction.

Case Study: *Bell vs. Watson* 148 Cal. App. 2d 684 (1957)

Bell, a licensed real estate broker, was employed by the Morrises to locate a home for them and subsequently to arrange a loan secured by a second trust deed to enable the Morrises to purchase the home. Bell failed to disclose that they were being charged a $500 bonus to the lender for the $26,150 loan. The note signed by the Morrises did not evidence the $500 payment. The closing statement showed as an additional item a $500 charge added to the purchase price identified as a commission to Bell.

Bell's petition to the Superior Court for writ of mandate was denied. On appeal of the Superior Court denial, the Court of Appeal upheld the Superior Court's determination that Bell had made a substantial misrepresentation, but reversed and remanded the case to the Real Estate Commissioner for a redetermination of the penalty to be assessed against Bell on the ground that the penalty of license revocation was excessive.

Legal Principles. *The above facts were sufficient to make a finding that Bell fraudulently concealed the fact that a $500 bonus was being charged as part of the transaction, as a bonus to the lender.*

False Information on Loan Payments Commissioner's Regulation 2785 (b)(6) prohibits knowingly making a false or misleading representation to a lender or assignee/endorsee of a lender of a loan secured directly or collaterally by a lien on real property about the amount and treatment of loan payments, including loan payoffs, and the failure to account to lender or assignee/endorsee of a lender as to the disposition of such payments.

Example. There are some private lenders who make real estate loans but do not like to service them. There are also investors who will buy existing real estate loan paper if the broker will service the loans for them. How important to such an investor are the details about what the broker is to do with payments?

Not Accounting for Advance Commissioner's Regulation 2785 (b)(7) prohibits, when acting as a licensee in a transaction for the purpose of obtaining a loan, and in receipt of an "advance fee" from the borrower for this purpose, the failure to account to the borrower for the disposition of the "advance fee."

Example. The Real Estate Commissioner's Regulations require an accounting of advance fees collected and their disbursements. In the case of an advance fee for the arrangement of a loan secured by real property or a business opportunity, the accounting must contain a list of the names and addresses of the persons to whom information pertaining to the principal's loan requirements were submitted and the dates of the submittals.

Security Property Value or Condition Commissioner's Regulation 2785 (b)(8) prohibits knowingly making a false or misleading representation or representing, without a reasonable basis for believing its truth, when soliciting a lender or negotiating a loan to be secured by a lien on real property, about the market value of the securing real property, the nature and/or condition of the interior or exterior features of the securing real property, its size or the square footage of any improvements on the property.

Example. A borrower applies to a real estate broker for a second trust deed loan of $100,000, assuring the broker that the building has a value of at least $200,000. The broker submits the loan application to a private lender and assures the lender that the building is indeed worth at least $200,000. Is the value of the building adequate to be the security for this second trust deed loan? The lender has no solid information.

SUGGESTIONS FOR PROFESSIONAL CONDUCT: SALE, LEASE, AND EXCHANGE TRANSACTIONS

The Real Estate Commissioner has issued suggestions for professional conduct in sale, lease and exchange transactions, and when negotiating or arranging loans secured by real property or sale of a promissory note secured by real property. The purpose of the suggestions is to encourage real estate licensees to maintain a high level of ethics and professionalism in their business practices when performing acts for which a real estate license is required. The suggestions are not intended as statements of duties imposed by law nor as grounds for disciplinary action by the Department of Real Estate, but as suggestions for elevating the professionalism of real estate licensees. They form a companion to the Code of Professional Conduct (§2785, Title 10, California Code of Regulations).

(a) Suggestions for Professional Conduct in Sale, Lease and Exchange Transactions.

Service Aspire to give a high level of competent, ethical, and quality service to buyers and sellers in real estate transactions.

> **Example: Ethical Dilemma**
>
> A long-time client of the broker, a woman for whom the broker has previously handled many transactions, has asked the broker to help dispose of a home in what has become a high-crime area. She tells the broker that she will "sacrifice" the property at a loss just to get rid of it. This broker also has a customer eager to buy a "starter home," a working couple with children whose incomes and downpayment have not qualified them to buy any property previously on the market in the area. Suddenly this distressed property can be available at a price and on terms these buyers can afford. The broker truly desires to give "a high level of competent, ethical, and quality service to buyers and sellers." If you were this broker, how would you proceed?

Communication Stay in close communication with clients or customers to ensure that questions are promptly answered and all significant events or problems in a transaction are conveyed in a timely manner.

Enforcement Cooperate with the California Department of Real Estate's enforcement of, and report to that Department evident violations of, Real Estate Law.

Advertising Use care in the preparation of any advertisement to present an accurate picture or message to the reader, viewer, or listener.

Offers Submit all written offers in a prompt and timely manner.

Knowledge Keep informed and current on factors affecting the real estate market in which the licensee operates as an agent.

Cooperation Make a full, open, and sincere effort to cooperate with other licensees, unless the principal has instructed the licensee to the contrary.

Arbitration Attempt to settle disputes with other licensees through mediation or arbitration.

Expertise Advertise or claim to be an expert in an area of specialization in real estate brokerage activity, e.g., appraisal, property management, industrial siting, mortgage loan, etc., only if the licensee has had special training, preparation, or experience.

Discrimination Prohibited Strive to provide equal opportunity for quality housing and a high level of service to all persons regardless of race, color, sex, religion, ancestry, physical handicap, marital status, or national origin.

Value Opinions Base opinions of value, whether for the purpose of advertising or promoting real estate brokerage business, upon documented objective data.

Codes of Ethics Make every attempt to comply with these Suggestions for Professional Conduct and the Code of Professional Conduct and the Code of Ethics of any organized real estate industry group of which the licensee is a member.

SUGGESTIONS FOR PROFESSIONAL CONDUCT: LOAN BROKERAGE

(b) Suggestions for Professional Conduct When Negotiating or Arranging Loans Secured by Real Property or Sale of a Promissory Note Secured by Real Property. In order to maintain a high level of ethics and professionalism in their business practices when performing acts within the meaning of subdivisions (d) and (e) of §10131 and §§10131.1 and 10131.2 of the Business and Professions Code, real estate licensees are encouraged to adhere to the following suggestions, in addition to any applicable provisions of subdivision (a), in conducting their business activities:

Service — Aspire to give a high level of competent, ethical, and quality service to borrowers and lenders in loan transactions secured by real estate.

> **Example: Ethical Dilemma**
>
> A mortgage broker has an investor who specializes in high-risk, high-interest loans, because he knows that foreclosures can be quite profitable. The investor insists only that the borrower have sufficient verifiable equity and no recent or prospective bankruptcy. Can the broker ethically match this lender with a prospective borrower with a very poor credit history who is seeking a second mortgage on his home for money to put into a "golden opportunity" business venture that is "just too good to be true"?

Communication — Stay in close communication with borrowers and lenders to ensure that reasonable questions are promptly answered and all significant events or problems in a loan transaction are conveyed in a timely manner.

Knowledge — Keep informed and current on factors affecting the real estate loan market in which the licensee acts as an agent.

Expertise — Advertise or claim to be an expert in an area of specialization in real estate mortgage loan transactions only if the licensee has had special training, preparation, or experience in such area.

Discrimination Prohibited — Strive to provide equal opportunity for quality mortgage loan services and a high level of service to all borrowers or lenders regardless of race, color, sex, religion, ancestry, physical handicap, marital status, or national origin.

Value Opinions — Base opinions of value in a loan transaction, whether for the purpose of advertising or promoting real estate mortgage loan brokerage business, on documented objective data.

Status Reports — Respond to reasonable inquiries of a principal as to the status or extent of efforts to negotiate the sale of an existing loan.

Net Proceeds — Respond to reasonable inquiries of a borrower regarding the net proceeds available from a loan arranged by the licensee.

Codes of Ethics — Make every attempt to comply with the standards of professional conduct and the code of ethics of any organized mortgage loan industry group of which the licensee is a member.

HIGHLIGHTS TO REMEMBER

ETHICS OF REAL ESTATE

Rules or standards governing the conduct of a profession

Regulated both by governments (Department of Real Estate) and by professional organizations (self-regulation)

Commissioner's Code revised 1990 as Code of Professional Conduct: defines unlawful acts and suggestions for professional conduct

Unlawful Conduct in Real Estate Transactions: Commissioner's Code of Professional Conduct, Sec. 2785(a)

(1) Misrepresenting market value to secure a listing or make a sale

(2) Misrepresenting existence of a written offer in order to secure a listing

(3) Stating or implying that commission amount is fixed (listing agreement form must contain printed statement that commission is negotiable)

(4) Misrepresenting licensee's relationship with an individual, corporate, or franchise broker

(5) Knowingly underestimating closing costs to influence seller or buyer

(6) Misleading seller about disposition or amount of offeror's deposit

(7) Misrepresenting buyer's qualifications to a seller who is carrying the loan

(8) Making unauthorized changes to a document previously signed by the parties

(9) Representing value of property securing a note, without adequate information

(10) Misrepresenting or making uninformed assertions about features of a property (puffing)

(11) Misrepresenting or making uninformed assertions about property size or boundaries

(12) Concealing or making uninformed assertions about use restrictions on a property

(13) Failing to disclose other material facts not obvious to the buyer or lessee

(14) Failing to present all offers up to closing, unless patently frivolous or expressly instructed not to by owner

(15) Presenting competing offers in a manner that induces owner to accept offer most advantageous to agent

(16) Failing to explain meaning of contingencies to the parties

(17) Seller's agent failing to disclose any direct or indirect interest in transaction

(18) Buyer's agent failing to disclose direct or indirect ownership interest in subject property

(19) Failing to disclose interest in entities whose services agent recommends

(20) Refunding offeror's deposit without express permission of seller

Unlawful Conduct in Loan Transactions: Commissioner's Code of Professional Conduct, Sec. 2785(b)

(1) Soliciting borrowers by misrepresenting availability of financing

(2) Misrepresenting borrower's qualifications to prospective lender or investor

(3) Knowingly underestimating closing costs to influence borrower or lender

(4) Misrepresenting priority of a loan (first, second, or third deed of trust)

(5) Representing a service as free when a fee is included in the transaction

(6) Misrepresenting to lender the amount or treatment of loan payments

(7) Not accounting to borrower for disposition of advance fees

(8) Misrepresenting or not substantiating value or condition of property securing a loan

Suggestions for Professional Conduct in Sale, Lease, and Exchange Transactions

High level of competent, ethical, quality service to buyers and sellers

Stay in close communication with clients

Cooperate with Department of Real Estate to support Real Estate Law

Be sure advertisements present accurate message

Submit written offers promptly

Keep informed on real estate market

Cooperate with other licensees unless prohibited by principal

Settle disputes with other licensees through mediation or arbitration

Claim special expertise only if one has special training or experience

Provide quality service without discrimination by race, sex, religion, handicap, etc.

Base opinions of value on documented objective data

Comply with Commissioner's and professional organizations' codes of ethics

Suggestions for Professional Conduct in Loan Transactions Secured By Real Property

High level of competent, ethical, quality service to borrowers and lenders

Stay in close communication with clients

Keep informed on real estate loan market

Claim special expertise only if one has special training or experience

Provide quality service without discrimination by race, sex, religion, handicap, etc.

Base opinions of value on documented objective data

Respond to principal's inquiries on status of sale of a loan

Respond to borrower's inquiries regarding net proceeds of a loan

Comply with Commissioner's and professional organizations' codes of ethics

Appendix

California Real Estate Law Disclosure Chart

SUBJECT	DISCLOSURE TRIGGER	DISCLOSURE REQUIREMENT (Brief Summary) FORM	C.A.R. INFORMATION SOURCE LAW CITATION
Death and/or AIDS	Sale, lease, or rental of <u>all</u> real property.	The transferor/agent has no liability for not disclosing the fact of any death which occurred more than 3 years prior to the date the transferee offers to buy, lease, or rent the property. Any death which has occurred within a 3-year period should be disclosed if deemed to be "material." Affliction with AIDS or death from AIDS, no matter when it occurred, need not be voluntarily disclosed. However, the transferor/agent must respond truthfully to any direct inquiry.	Q & A, "Disclosure of Aids and Death: The Legislative Solution," June 29, 1990. Cal. Civ. Code § 1710.2.
Earthquake Hazards - Homeowner's Guide	<u>Mandatory delivery</u>: Transfer of residential 1-4 real property of conventional light frame construction, built prior to January 1, 1960, if not exempt (same exemptions as for the Transfer Disclosure Statement). Additional exemption if the buyer agrees, in writing, to demolish the property within one year from date of transfer. <u>Voluntary delivery</u>: Transfer[2] of <u>any</u> real property.	<u>Mandatory delivery</u>: The licensee must give the transferor the booklet "The Homeowner's Guide to Earthquake Safety"[3] and the transferor must give this booklet to the transferee. Known structural deficiencies must be disclosed by the transferor to the transferee and the form in the booklet entitled "Residential Earthquake Hazards Report" may be used to make this disclosure. <u>Voluntary delivery</u>: If the Guide is delivered to the transferee, then the transferor or broker is not required to provide additional information concerning general earthquake hazards. Known earthquake hazards must be disclosed whether delivery is mandatory or voluntary.	Q & A, "Earthquake and Flood Hazard Disclosures," Jan. 13, 1993. Schwartz, <u>Earthquake Disclosure: Are You Prepared?</u>, Cal. Real Est., Nov. 1992, at 12. Cal. Bus. & Prof. Code § 10149, Cal. Gov't Code §§ 8897.1, 8897.2, 8897.5. Cal. Civ. Code § 2079.8.

Copyright © 1993 CALIFORNIA ASSOCIATION OF REALTORS® (C.A.R.) Legal Department. Permission is granted to reprint this material provided credit is given to the C.A.R. Legal Department.

California Real Estate Law Disclosure Chart

SUBJECT	DISCLOSURE TRIGGER	DISCLOSURE REQUIREMENT (Brief Summary) FORM	C.A.R. INFORMATION SOURCE LAW CITATION
Earthquake Hazards - Commercial Guide	<u>Mandatory delivery</u>: Sale, transfer, or exchange of <u>any</u> real property built of precast concrete or reinforced/unreinforced masonry with wood frame floors or roofs built before January 1, 1975, located within a county or city, if not exempt. Same exemptions as for Homeowner's Guide. In addition, any property built of unreinforced masonry with nonload bearing walls of steel or concrete frames is also exempt. <u>Voluntary delivery</u>: Transfer[4] of <u>any</u> real property.	<u>Mandatory delivery</u>: The transferor/transferor's agent must give the transferee a copy of "The Commercial Property Owner's Guide to Earthquake Safety."[5] <u>Voluntary delivery</u>: If the Guide is delivered to the transferee, then the transferor or broker is not required to provide additional information concerning general earthquake hazards. Known earthquake hazards must be disclosed whether delivery is mandatory or voluntary.	Q & A, "Earthquake and Flood Hazard Disclosures", Jan. 13, 1993. Schwartz, <u>Earthquake Disclosure: Are You Prepared?</u>, Cal. Real Est., Nov. 1992, at 12. Cal. Bus. & Prof. Code § 10147, Cal. Gov't Code §§ 8875.6, 8875.9, 8893.2, 8893.3. Cal. Civ. Code § 2079.9.
Flood Hazard Areas	Sale or lease of <u>all</u> improved real estate or mobilehomes located in flood hazard areas as indicated on maps published by the Federal Emergency Management Agency.[6]	The seller/lessor should disclose to buyer/lessee the fact that the property is located in such an area.[7] C.A.R. Forms DLF-14 and GFD-14 may be used.	Q & A, "Earthquake and Flood Hazard Disclosures", Jan. 13, 1993. Bogna, <u>Hazards to Real Property: Zone Disclosures</u>, 3 LEaDeR 3 (1991). 42 U.S.C. §§ 4001 et seq., § 4104a.
Home Energy Ratings	Transfer[8] or exchange of <u>all</u> real property or manufactured housing (including certain mobilehomes).	If a home energy ratings booklet to be developed by the State of California is delivered to the transferee, then a seller or broker is not required to provide additional information concerning the existence of a statewide home energy rating program. NEITHER THIS PROGRAM NOR THE BOOKLET IS AVAILABLE AT THIS TIME AND, MOST LIKELY, WON'T BE UNTIL 1995.	Cal. Civ. Code § 2079.10.

Environmental Issues & Obligations

California Real Estate Law Disclosure Chart

SUBJECT	DISCLOSURE TRIGGER	DISCLOSURE REQUIREMENT (Brief Summary) FORM	C.A.R. INFORMATION SOURCE LAW CITATION
Home Environmental Hazards	Transfer[9] or exchange of all real property or manufactured housing (including certain mobilehomes).	If a consumer information booklet[10] is delivered to the transferee, then a seller or broker is not required to provide additional information concerning common environmental hazards. However, known hazards on the property must be disclosed to the transferee.	Q & A, "Due Diligence and Disclosure of Environmental Hazards in Real Estate Transactions," Sept. 24, 1990. Q & A, "Information Resources for Environmental Hazards," Sept. 24, 1990. Freedman, Environmental Hazards: Issues Affecting Real Property, 5 LEaDeR 1 (1992). Cal. Civ. Code § 2079.7.
Lead-Based Paint - FHA/HUD Transaction	Sale of residential 1-4 real property built before 1978, including mobilehomes on a permanent foundation, which involve FHA loans or HUD-owned properties.	FHA Loans: A borrower must be given a notice entitled "Watch Out For Lead-Based Paint Poisoning!" which the borrower must sign (available from your local HUD office) before execution of the deposit receipt. If the notice is signed after the signing of the deposit receipt, the deposit receipt must be signed again by all parties. HUD Sales: Purchasers of HUD-owned properties must receive and sign the same notice mentioned above in addition to a lead-based paint addendum to the HUD Sales Contract (used in lieu of a deposit receipt for these transactions).	HUD Mortgagee Letters 92-24, 92-32. HUD Letter from Region IX, Chief Property Officer, Sept. 4, 1992.

Appendix **331**

California Real Estate Law Disclosure Chart

SUBJECT	DISCLOSURE TRIGGER	DISCLOSURE REQUIREMENT (Brief Summary) FORM	C.A.R. INFORMATION SOURCE LAW CITATION
Lead Hazard Pamphlet (effective in the future: 10/28/95)	Sale or lease of <u>all</u> residential property.	The seller/lessor must provide the buyer/lessee with a lead hazard information pamphlet and disclose the presence of any known lead-based paint. Additionally, the purchaser (not lessee) is permitted a 10-day period (unless the parties mutually agree upon a different time period) to conduct an inspection. The sales contract (i.e., deposit receipt) must contain a Lead Warning Statement and a statement signed by the buyer that the buyer has read the warning statement, has received the pamphlet, and has a 10-day opportunity to inspect before becoming obligated under the contract. The agent, on behalf of the seller/lessor, must ensure compliance with the requirements of this law. THIS LAW IS NOT YET IN EFFECT, AND THE PAMPHLET IS NOT YET AVAILABLE.	Residential Lead-Based Paint Hazard Reduction Act of 1992, Pub. L. No. 102-550, § 1018, U.S.C.S. Adv. (Law Co-op. Jan. 1993).
Mello-Roos District (effective in the future: 7/1/93)	Transfer[11] or exchange of residential 1-4 real property subject to a continuing lien securing the levy of special taxes pursuant to the Mello-Roos Community Facilities Act. Same exemptions as for the Transfer Disclosure Statement.	The transferor must make a good faith effort to obtain a disclosure notice concerning the special tax from each local agency which levies a special tax and deliver the notice(s) to the prospective transferee. The disclosure notice also provides a 3 or 5-day right of rescission to the transferee. There is no affirmative duty by an agent to discover a special tax or district not actually known to the agent.	Cal. Civ. Code § 1102.6b, Cal. Gov't Code § 53340.2.

California Real Estate Law Disclosure Chart

SUBJECT	DISCLOSURE TRIGGER	DISCLOSURE REQUIREMENT (Brief Summary) FORM	C.A.R. INFORMATION SOURCE LAW CITATION
Military Ordnance Location	Transfer[12] or exchange of residential 1-4 real property and lease of <u>any</u> residential dwelling unit when the transferor/lessor has actual knowledge that a former military ordnance location (military training grounds which may contain explosives) is within one mile of the property. Same exemptions as for the Transfer Disclosure Statement.	The transferor/lessor must disclose in writing to the transferee/lessee, that these former federal or state ordnance locations may contain potentially explosive munitions. The transferee has a 3 or 5-day right of rescission.	Bogna, <u>Hazards to Real Property: Zone Disclosures</u>, 3 LEaDeR 3 (1991). Cal. Civ. Code §§ 1102.15, 1940.7.
Seismic Hazard Zones	Sale of <u>all</u> real property which does contain or will eventually contain a structure for human habitation and which is located in a seismic hazard zone as indicated on maps created by the California Division of Mines and Geology. This law does not apply to any development or structure in existence prior to May 4, 1975. Other selected structures are also exempt from the law.[13]	The seller's <u>agent</u> or the seller without an agent must disclose to the buyer the fact that the property is in a seismic hazard zone if maps are available at the county assessor's, county recorder's, or county planning commission office. THESE MAPS ARE NOT CURRENTLY AVAILABLE. C.A.R. Forms DLF-14 and GFD-14 may be used.	Q & A, "Earthquake and Flood Hazard Disclosures", Jan. 13, 1993. Cal. Pub. Res. Code § 2690 <u>et seq.</u>

Appendix **333**

California Real Estate Law Disclosure Chart

SUBJECT	DISCLOSURE TRIGGER	DISCLOSURE REQUIREMENT (Brief Summary) FORM	C.A.R. INFORMATION SOURCE LAW CITATION
Smoke Detector Compliance	All existing dwelling units must have a smoke detector centrally located outside each sleeping area (bedroom or group of bedrooms). In addition, new construction (with a permit after August 14, 1992) must have a hard-wired smoke detector in each bedroom. Any additions, modifications, or repairs (after August 14, 1992) exceeding $1,000 for which a permit is required will also trigger the requirement of a smoke detector in each bedroom. (These may be battery operated.)	The seller of a <u>single family home</u> must provide the buyer with a written statement indicating that the property is in compliance with current California law. Same exemptions from compliance and disclosure as for the Transfer Disclosure Statement but only for single family homes and factory-built housing, not other types of dwellings. Transfers to or from any governmental entity, which are exempt under the TDS law, are <u>not</u> exempt from this law. LOCAL LAW MAY BE MORE RESTRICTIVE! Check with the local City or County Department of Building and Safety. C.A.R. Form SDC-11 may be used.	C.A.R. Memorandum, "Important Smoke Detector Update," Sept. 2, 1992. Cal. Health & Safety Code §§ 13113.7, 13113.8, 18029.6.
Special Studies Zones	Sale of <u>all</u> real property which does contain or will eventually contain a structure for human habitation and which is located in a special studies zone as indicated on maps created by the California Division of Mines and Geology.[14] This law does not apply to any development or structure in existence prior to May 4, 1975. Other selected structures are also exempt from the law.[15]	The seller's <u>agent</u> or the seller without an agent must disclose to the buyer the fact that the property is in a special studies zone, if maps are available at the county assessor's, county recorder's, or county planning commission office. C.A.R. Forms DLF-14 and GFD-14 may be used.	Q & A, "Earthquake and Flood Hazard Disclosures", Jan. 13, 1993. Cal. Pub. Res. Code §§ 2621 <u>et seq.</u>

334 *Environmental Issues & Obligations*

California Real Estate Law Disclosure Chart

SUBJECT	DISCLOSURE TRIGGER	DISCLOSURE REQUIREMENT (Brief Summary) / FORM	C.A.R. INFORMATION SOURCE / LAW CITATION
State Responsibility Areas (Fire Hazard Areas)	Sale of <u>any</u> real property located in a designated state responsibility area (generally a "wildland area") where the state not local or federal govt. has the primary financial responsibility for fire prevention. The California Department of Forestry provides maps to the county assessor of each affected county.[16]	The seller must disclose to the buyer the risk of fire, state-imposed additional duties such as maintaining fire breaks, and the fact that the state may not provide fire protection services. C.A.R. Form TDS-14 may be used.	Bogna, <u>Hazards to Real Property: Zone Disclosures</u>, 3 LEaDeR 3 (1991). Cal. Pub. Res. Code §§ 4125, 4136.
Subdivided Lands Law	Sale, leasing, or financing of new developments (condos, PUDs) or conversions consisting of 5 or more lots, parcels, or interests. However, a transfer of a single property to 5 or more unrelated people (unless exempt) may also trigger this law. There are exemptions too numerous to discuss in this chart.	The owner, subdivider, or agent, prior to the execution of the purchase contract or lease, must give the buyer/lessee a copy of the final public report (FPR), preliminary public report (PPR), or the conditional public report (CPR) issued by the DRE. No offers may be solicited until the DRE has issued one of these three reports. If the DRE has issued a CPR or PPR, then offers may be solicited, but close of escrow is contingent upon issuance of the FPR. Contracts entered into pursuant to a PPR may be rescinded by either party; contracts entered into pursuant to a CPR are contingent upon satisfaction of certain specified conditions.	Cal. Bus. & Prof. Code § 11018.1. <u>See generally</u>, Cal. Bus. & Prof. Code §§ 11000 <u>et seq.</u>; Cal. Code Regs., tit. 10, §§ 2790 <u>et seq.</u> Cal. Bus. & Prof. Code § 11018.12; Cal. Code Regs., tit. 10, § 2795.
Subdivision Map Act	Any division of real property into 2 or more lots or parcels for the purpose of sale, lease, or financing. There are exemptions too numerous to discuss in this chart.	The owner/subdivider must record either a tentative and final map, or a parcel map (depending on the type of subdivision). Escrow on the transfer cannot close until the appropriate map has been recorded.	Cal. Gov't Code §§ 66426, 66428. <u>See generally</u>, Cal. Gov't Code §§ 66410 <u>et seq.</u>

Appendix **335**

California Real Estate Law Disclosure Chart

ENDNOTES

1. This chart is current as of March 1, 1993 and all laws are currently effective unless otherwise noted. Although this chart summarizes disclosure requirements in the transfer of real property, agents should be aware that the seller/transferor, as well as the agent, is required to disclose all <u>known</u> information affecting the property which may be deemed "material." In addition, it is imperative to check local disclosure requirements. Local law may be more stringent than state law in certain areas or there may be additional disclosures required.

2. "Transfer" for purposes of this law means transfer by sale, lease with option to purchase, purchase option, ground lease coupled with improvements, or installment land sale contract.

3. This Guide is available from CAR and/or local Boards/Associations.

4. Same as number 2 above.

5. This Guide is available from CAR and/or local Boards/Associations.

6. The maps may be purchased from FEMA by calling (800) 358-9616.

7. Federal law actually imposes the duty on a federal lender to notify the purchaser/lessee, in writing, "or obtain satisfactory assurances that the seller or lessor has notified the purchaser or lessee," of special flood hazards in advance of the signing of the purchase agreement. In any event, this information <u>may</u> be deemed a material fact and, thus, should probably be disclosed by the seller/lessor.

8. Same as number 2 above.

9. Same as number 2 above.

10. The consumer information booklet entitled "Environmental Hazards, A Guide for Homeowners and Buyers" is available from C.A.R. and/or local Boards/Associations.

11. "Transfer" for the purposes of this law means transfer by sale, lease with option to purchase, purchase option, ground lease coupled with improvements, installment land sale contract, or transfer of a residential stock cooperative.

12. Same as number 11 above.

13. Although some developments or structures are exempt from this law, the fact that a property is located in a seismic hazard zone <u>may</u> be deemed a "material" fact and, thus, should probably be disclosed when the maps are available.

14. The maps may be purchased from BPS Reprographics by calling (415) 512-6550 with the names of the required maps. Special Publication 42 indicates the names of the maps of the Special Studies Zones. This publication is available from the California Division of Mines and Geology by calling (916) 445-5716.

15. Although some developments or structures are exempt from this law, the fact that a property is located in a special studies zone <u>may</u> be deemed a "material" fact and, thus, should probably be disclosed. However, structures damaged in the East Bay Fire of October 1991 which are located in the cities of Oakland and Berkeley may be exempted from this law. Cal. Pub. Res. Code § 2621.8.

16. Maps may also be obtained from the Teale Data Center, GIS Laboratory, P.O. Box 13436, Sacramento, CA 95813.

Index

Abatement contractors 163
Abell vs. Watson 318
Accessory housing units 61, 64
ADA (Americans with Disabilities Act) 20
Adjoining uses 169, 213-214, 241, 251
Advance fee 324
Affirmative duty 13, 243-244
Affordable housing 46, 49-69
Agency 243, 285-306
Agency Legislation Compliance Manual 291
Agricultural land 7, 28
AIDS 241
Air conditioning 91-92, 107, 129
Air quality 22, 44, 125, 162, 277
Air quality management district 45, 195
Alquist-Priolo Act 138, 150, 245
Alternative energy sources 106
Alternative Minimum Tax 270
American Society of Testing and Materials 177
Americans with Disabilities Act 20
Ammunition dump 252
AMT (Alternative Minimum Tax) 270
Anchor bolts 140, 143
Antiquities Act 1
Appliances 90, 105, 277-278 231
Appraisal 70, 71, 115, 187, 194
Appropriate inquiry (CERCLA) 189-190
AQMD (Air quality management district) 45, 195
ARARs (applicable, relevant and appropriate requirements) 231, 235
Archeology 16, 44, 186
Architectural styles 84, 86, 131-132
Asbestos 157-159, 181, 187, 193, 196, 206, 209, 219, 223, 233, 252
Asbestos Hazard Disclosure Act 251
ASPIS 169
Assessments 259
Atomic power 46
Automotive waste 171
Bell vs. Watson 319
Berkeley RECO 75
Biodiversity 125
Biological assessment 11, 14
Breach of contract 288, 293
Breach of duty 297
Bridge Housing Corporation 69
Buffer zone 169, 213, 251
Building code 25, 32, 34, 64, 68
Building materials 89, 166, 214, 227
Building permit 97, 259
Building records 196
Cal/OSHA 159
California Association of Realtors® 157, 258, 309
California Energy Commission 95

California Environmental Protection Agency 32
California Integrated Waste Management Board 171
California Registered Environmental Assessor 201
Caltrans 313
Cancer producing chemicals 29, 158, 165, 173, 210
Capital gain 266, 268
Carbon tax 274, 278
Care and skill 243
Carmel, California 42, 52
Caveat emptor 244, 294
CC&Rs 241, 262
Center for Disease Control 172
CEQA(California Environmental Quality Act) 25-27, 35-36, 43, 53, 61
CERCLA (Comprehensive Environmental Response, Compensation and Liability Act) 10, 177, 186-192, 203, 212, 219-223, 230, 236
CERCLIS 195, 202, 213
Certificate of Compliance 78, 98, 102-103
Chain of custody 225
Chain of title 190, 212
CHEERS (California Home Energy Efficiency Rating System) 110-113
Childhood Lead Poisoning Prevention Program 163
Chimneys 146, 154
CIWMB (California Integrated Waste Management Board) 171
Clay 126-127
Clean Air Act 6, 8, 19
Clean Water Act 6
Cleaning products 170
Cleanup 7, 10, 168, 191, 202, 230
Cleanup costs 177, 191, 219
Cleanup liens 189-190
Climate zones 96, 129, 131
Closing costs 312
Coal 277
Coastal zones 6, 18, 26, 61
Code of Professional Conduct 307
Commercial Property Owner's Guide to Earthquake Safety 135, 245
Common Interest Developments 251, 262
Community image 42, 45, 52, 55, 65, 235
Community Reinvestment Act 67
Community relations 225
Compaction 128
Compost 127
Comprehensive Environmental Response, Compensation and Liability Act (CERCLA) 10, 177, 189, 192, 203, 212
Computer simulation 98
Confidentiality 204, 303

Conflict of interest 181, 308, 316, 318
Conflict resolution 62
Congestion tolls 276-277
Construction 85, 87
Constructive fraud 297
Consultants 194
Consumer Product Safety Commission 159
Consumer protection 1, 95, 199, 244, 257, 294, 303
Contaminant migration 214, 224-229, 234
Contingency 317
Contingency plan 236
Contracts 244, 285-293, 303
Cooperating agent 291, 300
Corps of Engineers 65
Corrective actions 181-182, 196
Cortese list 169
Cost-benefit questions 22, 222
Costs 147-148, 159, 230-232, 245
Council on Environmental Quality 2, 5
CRA (community redevelopment agency) 45, 67
Cripple walls 138, 141
Critical habitat 11, 14, 188
Cultural resources management 36
Databases 9, 202, 206, 212-213, 227
Davis-Bacon Act 68
Death upon real property 241
Decontamination 172, 225-226, 236
Deed restrictions 262
Defensible space 249
Delivery requirements 253
Demography 71, 228
Department of Forestry 248
Department of Health Services 157, 168, 195, 252
Department of Housing and Urban Development (HUD) 18, 68, 71, 163
Department of Real Estate (DRE) 157, 244, 307
Depletion allowances 280
Deposit-return charges 280
Deposits 319
Depreciation 70, 269
Disasters 241
Disciplinary action 242, 286, 293-294, 307-308, 315, 323
Disclosure 72, 75, 115, 122, 135-136, 157, 199, 241-264, 285, 292, 295, 297, 303, 329-336
Discretionary projects 27
Discrimination 20, 50, 67-72, 325-326
Discriminatory lending practices 64
Divided agency 285, 286, 290
Division of Mines and Geology 149
Documentary research 179, 189-190, 199
Downzoning 41, 66
Drainage 44, 115-116, 118-120
Drinking water 172, 204

Index **337**

Drip irrigation 128
Drought-tolerant plants 124
Dual agency 286, 290-291, 296, 302
Due diligence 191-193
Dumps 8-9, 202
Duty to investigate 294
EAA (Environmental Assessment Association) 177, 200, 203
Earthquake 32, 34, 38, 85, 170, 245
Earthquake Hazard Disclosure 136–138
Earthquake insurance 247
Earthquake weaknesses 138
Easements 251, 262
Easton vs. Strassburger 253, 257, 295, 309, 315
EBMUD 121, 123-124
Economic issues 21
Economies of scale 50
EEM (energy efficient mortgage) 111, 113
EIR (environmental impact report) 27, 53-54, 56, 61
EIS (environmental impact statement) 5, 19, 27, 53-54
Electoral process 57, 59, 61, 65
Electric utilities 277
Electricity 106, 278
Emergency access 249
Emergency Planning and Community Right-to-Know Act 202
Emergency supplies 152
Eminent domain 45, 313
Emissions charges 273, 279
Employee or independent contractor 289
Endangered Species Act 10-13, 18, 63, 68, 186
Endangerment assessment 227
Energy 7-8, 26, 28
Energy audit 79, 98, 110-112
Energy conservation 75, 80, 82, 90, 92, 105, 107
Energy efficient mortgages 111, 113
Energy sources 106
Environmental Assessment Association (EAA) 177, 200, 203
Environmental charges 273-274
Environmental consultant 169, 178, 183-184, 190, 201, 204, 219
Environmental hazards 70, 186-187, 241
Environmental Hazards Management Procedures 177
Environmental Impact Report (EIR) 26-27, 43, 53-56, 61, 221
Environmental Impact Statement (EIS) 1, 4, 5, 19, 27, 53-54
Environmental impairment insurance 195
Environmental inspection 71, 177-218
Environmental License Plate Fund 26
Environmental medium 224, 227
Environmental Protection Agency (EPA) 5, 7, 63-65, 158, 162, 168, 202
Environmental risk analyst 194, 212, 222
Environmental risk policy 192
Environmental setting 212, 214, 215
EPA (Environmental Protection Agency) 7, 9, 65, 172-173, 180, 193, 195-196, 202, 221

Equal Dignities Rule 287
Equity loans 270
Escrow 296, 309
Estoppel 287-288
Euclid vs. Ambler 66
Evaporation 126
Exclusionary zoning 62
Exculpatory disclaimer language 243
Expanded Phase II 223–227
Expertise 178, 180, 201, 250, 258, 298, 325-326
Explosive 19
Farmland 7, 28
FDIC 177
Feasibility study 221, 232, 237
Federal action 4, 11
Federal Home Loan Bank 191
Federal Insurance Administration (FIA) 248
Federal National Mortgage Association (FNMA) 67, 70–71, 177–178, 193
Federal Register 180
Federally insured lender 321
FEMA (Federal Emergency Management Agency) 247
FHA Minimum Property Standards 25
Fiduciary 242, 288-298, 303, 311, 318, 322
Field work 232
FIFRA (Federal Insecticide, Fungicide and Rodenticide Act) 10
Fill 118, 128, 245
FINDS (Facility Index System) 202
Fire hazards 121-122, 153, 248
Fire-resistant plants 122-123
Fireplaces 91
FIRM (Flood Insurance Rate Map) 247
FIRPTA (Foreign Investment in Real Property Tax Act) 271
FIRREA (Financial Institutions Reform, Recovery, and Enforcement Act) 186, 320
Fish and Wildlife Service 188
Flood Hazard Boundary Map (FHBM) 247
Flood Insurance Rate Map (FIRM) 247
Flooding 38, 115-118
Floodplain 18
FNMA 67, 70-71, 177-178, 193
FOIA (Freedom of Information Act) 202, 213
FONSI (Finding of No Significant Effect) 5, 19
Foreclosure 177, 188, 191-192, 194, 222, 323
Forfeiture 321
Formaldehyde 160-161
Fossil fuel 277-278, 280
Foundation 138, 140-141, 143
Franchised brokerage 311
Fraud 312
Freedom of Information Act (FOIA) 202, 213
Gas station sites 193, 214, 219-222
Gasoline taxes 273
GDP (Gross domestic product) 274
General plan 39, 41, 53, 61, 149

Geologic hazards 28, 149, 314
Geologic report 43-44, 196, 215, 228, 245
Glossary of terms 173, 236
Government records 190, 202
Green fees 265, 272
Greenhouse effect 276-277
Ground shaking 149
Ground water 120, 149, 172, 181, 182, 187, 196, 214-215, 237
Growth controls 63, 66
Hardscape 130, 132
Hazardous materials 170, 174, 202, 249, 250
Hazardous Substances Cleanup Bond Act of 1984 169
Hazardous waste 7-9, 53, 59, 72, 168, 233
Hazardous waste sites 58, 169, 251
Hazards to renters 252
Heat gain/loss 97
Heating systems 90, 96-97
Historic resources 21, 28, 35, 44, 147, 186-187, 262
Historical records 179
History of property 241
Homesharing 64
Hotlines 159, 165-166, 171, 173
Household hazardous waste 170-171
Housing costs 46 Housing policy 29
HUD (Department of Housing and Urban Development) 18, 68, 71, 163
HVAC (heating, ventilation, and air conditioning) 96, 97
Hydrology 215, 237
Impact fees 279
In rem action 321
Incentives 58, 105
Inclusionary zoning 40, 67
Income taxes 273
Incremental costs 276
Incurable contamination 181
Independent contractor 289-290
Industrial properties 193, 219
Infrastructure 46, 63, 65-66, 68
Initial Phase II 220, 223
Initiatives 61
Innocent Landowner Defense (CERCLA) 10, 189, 192, 203, 212
Innocent misrepresentations 299
Inspect 136
Inspection 88, 92, 111, 118, 136, 158-159, 163, 179, 184, 195, 200, 243, 244, 250, 257
Insulation 78-79, 85, 88, 96, 105, 110, 158, 160, 209
Insurance 117, 148
Intercommunity planning 46
Interest deductions 269
Internal Revenue Code 265
Interviews 179, 196, 199, 211-214
Irrigation 124, 128
Jeopardy biological opinion 14
Judicial review 68
Kemp Report 49, 62-71
Kickback 319
Laboratory analysis 159, 163-164, 167, 172, 174, 180, 210, 220, 224, 232-233

338 *Environmental Issues & Obligations*

Land supply 64
Land uses 71
Land-value guarantees 58
Landfill 8, 50, 58, 168, 181, 219, 275
Landscaping 89, 92, 115-134
Landslides 117-118, 120, 149, 253
Lead 162-164, 206, 210, 331-332
Lead agency 5, 54
Leaking underground storage tanks 172, 203
Legal action 242
Legal description 204
Legal or tax advice 243
Legislation 61
Lenders 64, 178, 183
Liability 117, 177-178, 189, 191, 219, 242, 253, 288-290, 303
Liens 189-190, 203, 241
Lighting 78, 90
Limited partnership 268
Liquefaction 149
Listed species 11
Listing agreement 290-291, 296, 300
Litigation 59, 61, 182, 249, 308
Loan application 178, 192
Loan transactions (ethics) 319-326
Lobbying 60
Local autonomy 36, 52, 55, 65, 66
Local ordinances 34, 36, 39, 75, 245
Locational conflict issues 49-50
Low income housing credit 272
Low-flow plumbing 78-79, 92, 105
LULU (locally unwanted land use) 49, 52, 70, 72
LUST (leaking underground storage tanks) 172, 203
Mandatory measures (Title 24) 97-98, 104
Manufactured housing 64, 68
Maps 149-150, 247
Marginal excess burden 273
Market value 310, 312, 324
Master plans 46, 66
Material facts 72, 75, 115, 122, 241, 243, 250, 257, 294, 309, 314
MCLs (maximum contaminant levels) 164
Mediterranean climate 125
Microclimate 131
Mining 219, 280
Ministerial project 27
Misrepresentation 242, 308, 310, 323
Mitigation 4, 29, 51, 55, 58, 64, 167, 237
Model codes 68
Mortgage interest 269
Multiple Listing Service 291, 309
National Affordable Housing Act 68
National Association of Realtors® 307
National Contingency Plan (NCP) 230
National Environmental Policy Act (NEPA) 1-2, 4, 11, 18, 26-27, 53
National Flood Insurance Program (NFIP) 247
National Historic Preservation Act 15-18, 35-36
National parks 1
National Priority List (NPL) 195, 202, 231

National Register of Historic Places 15, 17, 35
Native plants 125
Natural hazard disclosures 245
NCP (National Contingency Plan) 230
Negligence 244, 253, 289, 298
Neighborhood analysis 70-72
NEPA (National Environmental Policy Act) 1-2, 4, 11, 18, 26-27, 53
New chemicals 250
NFIP (National Flood Insurance Program) 247
Nguyen vs. Scott 315
NIMBY (Not In My Back Yard) 49-69
NIMTOO 57, 66
No action alternative 56, 60, 221, 230
Noise 19
Non point-source pollution 6
Nondisclosure 253, 308-309, 314
Nonperforming loans 185, 188
Notifiers 9
Notorious sites 223
NPL (National Priority List) 195, 202, 231
Nuisance 51
Off-peak pricing 276-277
Offers 311-315
Office of Solid Waste 7
Office of Thrift Supervision (OTS) 177, 191
Open dumps 213
Open space 44
Operations and maintenance (O&M) 183-184, 233
Ordinary income 267
Orientation 129
OSHA (Occupational Safety and Health Administration) 32
Ostensible agency 287-288
OTS (Office of Thrift Supervision) 177, 191
Overriding considerations 29
Pacific Bell 152
Pacific Gas & Electric Co. 89, 105, 107, 129
Palm Desert zoning ordinance 42
Parcel maps 37
Passive activity 268
Passive solar design 89
Pay-by-the-bag 275
PCBs 182, 206, 211, 214, 225, 233
Penal institutions 50, 52, 58, 61, 72
Percolation 127
Performance standards 230
Permit process 43, 65
Pest control disclosures 242, 258
Pesticides 206, 219
PG&E 89, 105, 107
Phase I 177-179, 188-189, 195, 199-217
Phase I report format 203-210, 216
Phase II 179-180, 188, 196, 200, 209, 214-215, 219-220, 222
Phase II report format 228
Phase III 188, 196, 219, 221, 230
Phase III report format 234
Photographs 184-185, 189-190, 195, 199, 212

Pier-and-post foundations 142
Planned communities 42
Planning commission 38, 41
Plant selection 121-122
Point system (Title 24) 98, 101
Police power 40-41
Population 28
Portfolio activity 267
Power of attorney 287, 315
Power plants 50, 105
Preferred alternative 231
Prescriptive method (Title 24) 97-100
Primary energy 278
Principal residence 267
Priority of a lien 322
Private restrictions 41, 262
Product charges 279
Professional 243-244, 294-295, 307
Professional liability insurance 257
Professional organizations 177, 180, 203, 307
Property tax 35, 65, 148, 275
Property value 10, 50, 52, 56, 65-66, 70, 115, 187, 191
Proposition 13 66, 259
Proposition 65 29, 30
Public housing 163
Public opinion 42, 55-63
Public projects 50, 54
Public Resources Code 25
Puffery 308, 313
Quality control 180, 224-225, 229
Quality of life 49
Question of fact 291
R-value 88, 96
Radon 165-166, 182, 193, 196, 206, 210, 223, 233
Rattray vs. Scudder 310
RCRA (Resource Conservation and Recovery Act) 7-8, 19, 180, 186, 219, 222, 223
RCRA notifier list 9, 202, 213
Real Estate Commissioner 36, 38, 285-286, 308
Real Estate Law 285, 292, 295-296, 307
Real estate owned (REO) 187-188
Real Estate Transfer Disclosure Statement 75, 138, 157, 169, 243, 245, 248, 251-252, 254, 255-256, 259, 262
Realty Projects, Inc., vs. Smith 321
Reasonable care, skill, and diligence 243, 257, 293-295, 317
Reasonable person standard 298
Rebates 105
RECO (Residential Energy Conservation Ordinance) 75-78
Recommendations 215, 226
Recordation 38, 252
Recycling 3, 7, 171, 275, 280-281
Red flags 196, 199, 203, 250, 253
Redevelopment 45-46
Redlining 67
Reed vs. King 241
Referrals 319
Regional Water Quality Control Boards 168

Index **339**

Regulatory reform 68
Rehabilitation 16, 35, 64
Rehabilitation credit 272
Release or threatened release 190, 220-222
Remedial action 182-185, 188, 211, 219, 220-221, 229, 232, 234
Remedial alternatives 230
Remediation costs 233
Renewables 106
Rent control 64
Rental properties 268
REO (real estate owned) 187-188
Residential Energy Conservation Ordinance (RECO) 75-78
Resolution Trust Corporation (RTC) 177, 186, 200, 203, 216, 222, 224, 228, 234
Resource Conservation and Recovery Act (RCRA) 7-8, 19, 180, 186, 219, 222, 223
Respondeat superior 289
Retrofit ordinances 34, 90, 259
Riprap 118
Risk assessment 51, 229, 234
Risk management procedures 192
Rivers and Harbors Act 6
Rollover 267
Roofing 85, 121, 249
RTC (Resolution Trust Corporation) 177, 186-188, 200, 203, 216, 222, 224, 228, 234
Safe Drinking Water Acts 6, 18, 25, 29, 173
Safety equipment 226
Sampling 161, 215, 219-222, 224-225
SARA 10, 202, 213, 231
Scoping 5, 54-55
Screening 199, 230
Seasonal energy efficiency ratio (SEER) 9
Secret profit 293, 295, 308
Secretary of the Interior's Standards for Rehabilitation 16-17
Section 106 (NHPA) 15, 17, 36
Section 1031 (IRS Code) 272
SEER (Seasonal energy efficiency ratio) 92
Seismic disclosure laws 241, 245
Seismic Safety Commission 135
Selling agent 301
Senior exclusion 267
Shade 89, 105, 110
SHBC (State Historical Building Code) 34-35, 147
SHPO (State Historic Preservation Officer) 35
Significant effect 28, 54, 56
Single-room-occupancy (SRO) 64, 68, 69
Site inspection 179, 189-190, 199, 203, 214
Sitework 115, 117-120, 126
Siting 80
Skill and knowledge 295, 298
SLAPP (Strategic lawsuit against public participation) 59
Sludge 8
Smoke detectors 259-261

Soft story 144
Soil contaminants 181
Soil gas analysis 196
Soils 117, 126-128, 215, 228
Solar heat 91, 97
Solid waste charges 275
Solid Waste Disposal Act 8, 9, 19
Special resource values 186
Special Studies and Flood Hazard Disclosure 246, 116
Special Studies Zone 138, 150, 245
Special Studies Zone and Flood Hazard Disclosure 246, 330, 334
Specific plans 40
Spills 154
SRA (State Responsibility Area) 248
SRO (single-room-occupancy) 64, 68, 69
Standard of care 257
Starker case 272
State Historic Preservation Officer (SHPO) 35
State Historical Building Code 34-35, 147
State Responsibility Area (SRA) 248
State Superfund 202
Statement of limiting conditions 208
Statute of Frauds 285, 296, 317
Strategic lawsuit against public participation (SLAPP) 59
Strict liability 191
Structural defect 241
Style 84, 86, 131-132
Subagency 289, 291, 299
Subdivision controls 36-38, 262
Suggestions for Professional Conduct 324, 326
Sump 120
Sun 80-81, 84, 89, 129
Superfund 10, 32, 168, 177, 180, 193, 231
Superfund Amendment and Reauthorization Act 10, 202
Superlien states 183-184, 191
Supervision 290, 314
Tanks 172, 187, 196, 203-204, 210, 219, 223, 233
Tax credits 21, 272
Tax deferred exchanges 272
Tax incentives 15-16, 35
Tax Reform Act of 1986 (TRA 86) 15, 265-272
Tax shelters 268, 273
Technical studies 179
Termination of agency 288
Third parties 294-295
Threatened species 11
Timmsen vs. Forest E. Olson 316
Title 24 32, 82, 95-113
Title abstract 189, 199
Toll roads 276
Topographical information 43, 215
Torts 289, 299
Toxic Disclosures Act 250
Toxic Substance Control Act (TSCA) 10, 159
Toxic Substances Control Program 168, 171
Toxics 10, 19, 22, 238, 241, 244, 252

TRA '86 (Tax Reform Act of 1986) 265-272
Traffic 28, 44, 46, 72
Trees 121-122, 126
Trellises 126, 129
TSCA (Toxic Substance Control Act) 10, 159
TSCP (Toxic Substances Control Program) 168-169, 171
Tsunami 149-150
U-value 82, 97
U.S. Department of Agriculture (USDA) 215
U.S. Geological Survey (USGS) 215
U.S. Vs. 403 1/2 Skyline Drive 320
UFFI (urea formaldehyde foam insulation) 160-161, 206
Underground storage tanks 187, 196, 203-204, 219, 223
Undertaking 27
Underwriting 192, 194
Unlawful conduct 310
Unreinforced masonry 143, 145-146, 245
Urban-wildland interface 121-122, 249
Urea formaldehyde foam insulation (UFFI) 160-161, 206
USDA (U.S. Department of Agriculture) 215
Use restrictions 313
USEPA 158, 164-168
User fees 273, 275, 279
USGS (U.S. Geological Survey) 215
Utilities 46, 152
Utility costs 75, 111
UWIZ (Urban Wildland Interface Zones) 121-122, 249
Vaill vs. Edmonds 314
Variance 41
Vegetation control 121-122, 248
Ventilation 82
Visual inspection 209-211, 258, 295
Waste disposal 28, 193, 211, 214
Water 38, 53, 166
Water conservation 34, 78, 92, 122, 124
Water heater 138-139
Water Pollution Control Act 8, 18
Water quality 6, 28
Water supply 249
Water table 44
Wetlands 4, 7, 18, 186-188
Wild and Scenic Rivers Act 18
Wildland fire hazard areas 115
Windows 80, 82-83, 97, 146
World Resources Institute 265, 272
Xeriscapes 124-126
Zoning 39-42, 44, 52-53, 61, 63-64, 66, 241, 259